Populism and Contemporary Democracy in Europe

Josep Maria Castellà Andreu
Marco Antonio Simonelli
Editors

Populism and Contemporary Democracy in Europe

Old Problems and New Challenges

palgrave
macmillan

Editors
Josep Maria Castellà Andreu
University of Barcelona
Barcelona, Spain

Marco Antonio Simonelli
University of Barcelona
Barcelona, Spain

ISBN 978-3-030-92883-4 ISBN 978-3-030-92884-1 (eBook)
https://doi.org/10.1007/978-3-030-92884-1

This Palgrave Macmillan imprint is published by the registered company Springer Nature Switzerland AG.
The registered company address is: Gewerbestrasse 11, 6330 Cham, Switzerland

Foreword

What is populism? Like many "isms" (fascism, communism, Islamism...), especially when they are taken in the wrong way, we tend to point out easily what is unpleasant in order to denounce it as inadmissible, unacceptable.

This book, which brings together academics and other high-level specialists, will help make progress in defining the concept—which is difficult. Pierre Rosanvallon, in his book *Le siècle du populisme*, mentions three central elements of democracy as conceived by populists: it is direct, polarised and immediate. In my opinion, it is the third element, immediacy, which is the most decisive, and also the most worrying. Democracy can be polarised, but neither direct nor immediate: this is the British system. It can be direct, but neither polarised nor immediate: this is the Swiss system. These systems have their weaknesses and their slippages, but they have the merit of having established some of the oldest and most stable world democracies. A direct and polarised democracy instead would tend more towards the exclusion of the other. The most worrying thing, however, would be the shift to a so-called immediate democracy. The unthinking exercise of power.

What is done in Parliament? Talks, deliberations, and this is often what fuels anti-parliamentarianism. And yet, this is the essence of democracy. It is debate with arguments, not spontaneity, which is often a euphemism for thoughtlessness, incompetence and even manipulation. Firstly, with regard to voting on an issue. The Venice Commission therefore insists that referendums should be the outcome of a deliberative process involving parliament. This is the opposite of an immediate decision by the people. The citizens' assemblies that have appeared in some countries should be understood in the same sense. Their aim, far from being to let average citizens express themselves on a subject they do not know, is to involve them in public affairs and to enable them to debate these affairs.

Democracy does not have to be immediate either in terms of elections, including elections to an assembly. It is not enough to return to the slogan: "who loves me follows me!" This is why the Venice Commission, like other international organisations, does not (or no longer) judge an election on the basis of election day alone (including the count). On the contrary, the importance of equality of opportunity in the pre-election phase and of the free formation of the elector's will is regularly stressed. It cannot be achieved without debate, and in particular without access to the media. Hence, for example, the rules on speaking time on radio and television. But *what about* social networks? The question may sometimes arise as to whether they are deliberative spaces, and this is a question that would deserve further attention.

As for the populists' demand for direct democracy, the danger is above all the use of a so-called direct democracy of a plebiscitary nature, strengthening the power of the executive. Or to consider that the people decide on the truth, somewhat in the manner of Rousseau. Or rather the truth of the majority of the people, understood as a compact and homogeneous entity—capable of identifying the general truth. Direct democracy and referendums are an element, a complement to the representative and deliberative system, and are themselves the result of deliberation, even in states where they are commonly practised. According to the principle of the rule of law, the people can only express themselves within the framework of procedures defined by the legal order.

Finally, a word about polarised democracy. Democratic States are conceived with a majority and an opposition, and therefore with a certain degree of polarisation. What should be avoided here again is the logic of "us" and "them", of truth versus error, of friend and enemy *à la* Carl Schmitt. There is a majority and an opposition, not good and evil, and the opposition must be given rights as well as duties, as the Venice Commission pointed out.

In two words, democracy is not the dictatorship of the majority, but a system where everyone has a say, and where the exchange of ideas and opinions is essential. It is the opposite of a system where some hold the truth in the name of the people.

Gianni Buquicchio

President Emeritus
European Commission for Democracy through Law
Strasbourg, France

About This Book

When this edited volume was first conceived, in December 2019, the world was on the verge of entering the worst crisis in terms of human lives since the end of World War II. The pandemic, with its lockdowns and curfews, the social-distancing and the remote-working, had an impact on social and economic life that was simply unimaginable a couple of years ago. Also our publishing project, *si parva licet*, was significantly affected. It took us more than one year to organise the symposium, which constitutes the basis of this edited volume, and compelling reasons convinced us to broaden the scope of the project to cover the legal responses to the crisis, its consequences for democracy, and the opportunities it offered to populists.

The symposium, organised by the research group GEDECO (*Grupo de Estudios sobre Democracia y Constitucionalismo*) of the University of Barcelona, was finally celebrated online on 25 and 26 February 2021. Albeit not physically in Barcelona, the event gathered scholars from different parts of Europe to discuss the relationship between populism and constitutional democracy, and thanks to the partnership with the European Commission for Democracy through Law of the Council of Europe (best known as Venice Commission), it saw the interventions of its President, whom we shall thank for his foreword to this book, of the Secretary, and of some individual members; several of them also contributed to this volume.

The very idea of this book, its structure, and themes reflect almost three years of research work carried out in the context of the H2020 project 'DEMOS. Democratic Efficacy and Varieties of Populism in Europe'.[1] During this period, we had the opportunity to cooperate with the legal teams of the Centre for European and Comparative Legal Studies of the University of Copenhagen, the

[1] This research has received funding from the European Union's Horizon 2020 research and innovation programme under grant agreement No. 822590, DEMOS.

Institute of Legal Studies of the Budapest Center for Social Sciences, and the DIPEC of the University of Siena, coordinated respectively by Helle Krunke, Fruzsina Gárdos Orosz with Zoltán Szente, and Tania Groppi. Their participation in this book simply attests to our common effort in investigating populism and its remedies.

Besides, our participation, through the GEDECO, in a project funded by the Spanish Ministry of Science and Innovation[2] allowed a deeper investigation of themes common to the European project in the Spanish system, whose results are visible in this book.

Systematically, the book is divided into four parts, preceded by an introduction setting the background of the book and identifying the main points of frictions between populism and constitutional democracy (*Castellà and Simonelli*).

Part I provides the theoretical framework of the book, illustrating the reasons for the conflict between populism and constitutional democracy. As a starting point, the emergence of populism as an ideology that exploited the failures of representative democracy in answering societal and economic challenges is analysed (*Tudela Aranda*). Then, the fundamental tension between the populist ideology and constitutionalism is explained and revisited (*de Ghantuz Cubbe*). Lastly, the very idea of democracy according to populist parties is investigated through an analysis of the discourse of the French *Rassemblement National* (*Debras*).

Part II assesses the practical effects of populism on the institutions of constitutional democracy and the rule of law. Contributions in this part are mainly concerned with the impact of populism on the judiciary and constitutional courts, as these are the bodies that should enforce compliance with the rule of law in a democracy. The first two chapters offer a wide-ranging comparative overview of the effects of populism on European democracies, assessed from the standpoint of the Venice Commission opinions on judicial reforms (*Granata-Menghini*), and through an empirical analysis of normative data obtained with a comparative survey (*Gárdos-Orosz and Szente*). The other chapters of the part instead adopt a country-focused perspective: *Granat* takes the example of the Polish Constitutional Tribunal to illustrate the paradoxical role of a constitutional court in a populist-ruled state, and *González Campañá* shows the various forms through which populism is eroding constitutional democracy in Spain.

Part III adopts a European perspective, analysing the causes and effects of the populist malaise towards Bruxelles and the European Union reactions to the spread of illiberal values. Contributions in this part provide a critical analysis of the reasons why the EU actions have been largely ineffective against populism (*Pinelli*) and show what are the responsibilities of the EU institutions in the spread of populism in Europe (*Guerra*). The chapter by *Krunke, Tornøe* and *Wegener* instead

[2] Project 'Instrumentos Contramayoritarios en el Estado Constitucional' (PID2019-104414GB-C32).

turns the picture around and analyses the effects of populism on the EU legal order whilst the chapter by *Sáenz Pérez* contains an assessment of the European Court of Justice's role in upholding the rule of law in Europe via the dialogue with national judges.

Finally, Part IV contains a preliminary analysis of the impact of the COVID-19 pandemic on European democracies. The contributions of this part first investigate how constitutional democracy should be equipped to face future emergencies through an analysis of the position of the Venice Commission (*Castellà*) and how the emergency situation was managed at the state level, taking Spain as a case study (*Dueñas Castrillo*). Other contributions reflect upon the long-term effects of the pandemic: on populist politics (*Rubio Nuñez*) and on the institutional equilibrium of constitutional democracy (*Simonelli*). Finally, the chapter by *Groppi* tries to find the silver lining in the pandemic by pointing at the lessons that can be learnt from the pandemic to strengthen constitutional democracy.

Last but not least, we would like to thank all the persons working in the management team of DEMOS at the Centre for Social Sciences in Budapest for their support in the organisation of the symposium and in the publishing process.

Contents

List of Contributors

Josep Maria Castellà Andreu GEDECO Research Group, University of Barcelona, Barcelona, Spain

European Commission for Democracy through Law, Strasbourg, France

François Debras Department of Political Science, University of Liège, Liège, Belgium

Giovanni de Ghantuz Cubbe Institute of Political Science, TU Dresden, Dresden, Germany

Andrés Iván Dueñas Castrillo Department of Constitutional Law, University of Valladolid, Valladolid, Spain

Caroline Egestad Wegener DEMOS Research Group, University of Copenhagen, Copenhagen, Denmark

Fruzsina Gárdos-Orosz Institute for Legal Studies, Centre for Social Sciences, Budapest, Hungary

ELTE Law School, Budapest, Hungary

Núria González Campañá GEDECO Research Group, University of Barcelona, Barcelona, Spain

Miroslaw Granat Department of Constitutional Law, Cardinal Stanislaw Wyszyn′ski University, Warsaw, Poland

Simona Granata-Menghini European Commission for Democracy Through Law, Council of Europe, Strasbourg, France

Tania Groppi DIPEC Research Group, University of Siena, Siena, Italy

Giovanni Guerra DIPEC Research Group, University of Siena, Siena, Italy

Helle Krunke Centre for European and Comparative Legal Studies, University of Copenhagen, Copenhagen, Denmark

Cesare Pinelli Department of Legal and Economic Studies, University of Roma – La Sapienza, Rome, Italy

European Commission for Democracy through Law, Strasbourg, France

Rafael Rubio Nuñéz Department of Constitutional Law, Complutense University, Madrid, Spain

European Commission for Democracy through Law, Strasbourg, France

Cristina Sáenz Pérez School of Law, University of Leeds, Leeds, UK

Marco Antonio Simonelli University of Barcelona, Barcelona, Spain

Zoltán Szente Institute for Legal Studies, Centre for Social Sciences, Budapest, Hungary

National University of Public Service, Budapest, Hungary

William Alexander Tornøe DEMOS Research Group, University of Copenhagen, Copenhagen, Denmark

José Tudela Aranda Fundación Manuel Gimenez Abad, Zaragoza, Spain

University of Zaragoza, Zaragoza, Spain

List of Charts

Populism and Contemporary Democracy

Josep Maria Castellà Andreu
and Marco Antonio Simonelli

1 A Controversial Relationship?

The relationship between populism and contemporary constitutional democracy seems to escape any form of categorisation. The normative proposals of populists concerning how democracy should be reformed, which go under the name of populist constitutionalism,[1] do not compose

[1] Populist constitutionalism must be kept distinguished from constitutional populism, a doctrine originated in the 1990s in the United States and elaborated in the work of Akhil Reed Amer, who once stated 'I suppose if someone asked me, "What is your constitutional philosophy?" I might say that I am a constitutionalist, a textualist, and a populist'. The purpose of this doctrine was to correct the imbalance between the democratic and the aristocratic element of American democracy and advocated essentially for more instruments of democratic participation and less activism from the side of the US Supreme Court. To put it otherwise, constitutional populism does not seek to overstep the boundaries of constitutional democracy but to correct its current equilibrium, by offering a textual reading of the Constitution. See Reed Amar, *A Few Thoughts on Constitutionalism,* Textualism; Parker, *Here, the People Rule.*

J. M. Castellà Andreu (✉) • M. A. Simonelli
University of Barcelona, Barcelona, Spain
e-mail: castella@ub.edu

J. M. Castellà Andreu, M. A. Simonelli (eds.), *Populism and Contemporary Democracy in Europe*,
https://doi.org/10.1007/978-3-030-92884-1_1

a coherent alternative vision to liberal democracy.[2] Rather, they are piecemeal propositions constantly re-elaborated according to the changing social reality,[3] and characterised by an extreme simplification of the message (Tudela, in this book).

Amongst the elements shared by all populist narratives, the least common denominator seems to be the reaffirmation of the centrality of the sovereign will of the people that, in the populist discourse, is embodied not in the representative institutions, but in the populist party or leader itself. In force of this self-conferred democratic legitimacy, populists engage in a dichotomic dialectic of 'us and them', which allows them to affirm that any constraint on the will of the 'true people' imposed by the 'system' is an attack to popular sovereignty and democracy.[4]

In this way, the 'We, the People' of the US Constitution Preamble, enshrining the idea that the source of legitimacy of the whole legal order is to be found in the popular will, which by establishing the separation of powers and by delegating the government to representatives limits itself, is transformed by populists into 'We are the people'.[5] Simply with this small change of words, the message conveys a completely different meaning: populists pretend to speak in the name of every citizen.

According to Mudde, however, such a message is not entirely negative. Populism, in fact, may constitute 'an illiberal democratic response to undemocratic liberalism' (Mudde and Rovira 2013), and rather than an

[2] The political manifesto of this doctrine may be the famous speeches of Prime Minister Orbán delivered annually in Băile Tuşnad, in particular those of 2014 and 2019, where the Hungarian Prime Minister tried to frame 'illiberal democracy' as a legitimate alternative to liberal constitutional democracy. The text of the two speeches, translated into English, can be retrieved on the official website of the Hungarian government. Respectively at: https://2015-2019.kormany.hu/en/the-prime-minister/the-prime-minister-s-speeches/prime-minister-viktor-orban-s-speech-at-the-25th-balvanyos-summer-free-university-and-student-camp; https://2015-2019.kormany.hu/en/the-prime-minister/the-prime-minister-s-speeches/prime-minister-viktor-orban-s-speech-at-the-30th-balvanyos-summer-open-university-and-student-camp last accessed 30 September 2021.

[3] On the adaptability of the populist discourse, see *Debras*, in this book.

[4] Some authors outlined the main claims of a populist constitutional theory. These are namely: (1) the prevalence of the rule of men over the rule of law; (2) the unity and immediateness of the people will and (3) a strong accent on constitutional identity. See Corrias, *Populism in a Constitutional Key*, 6–26.

[5] This slogan was actually used by the German far-right political movement Pegida (*Patriotische Europäer gegen die Islamisierung des Abendlandes*) in the street rallies against German immigration policy in 2014 and 2015. See Mounk, *El pueblo contra la democracia*, 25.

attack on constitutional democracy, it would be a corrective to a deficit thereof. Constitutional democracy indeed presupposes an 'aspiration to a fair equilibrium' between, on the one hand, the democratic principle, reflected in the respective roles assigned to the parliament and the government in the decision-making process and, on the other hand, the rule of law, expressed by the subjection of the policymakers to the laws and the constitution, enforced mainly through the judicial review of legislation (Fioravanti 2011). In this light, this demand for more democratic legitimacy may actually constitute a legitimate effort to reaffirm the democratic principle *vis-à-vis* a perceived disempowerment of elected bodies provoked by the rise of unelected ones. Be that as it may, if we accept that the core element of populism is the claim to embody the sovereign popular will, we can evaluate the apparently ambiguous relationship between populism and constitutional democracy by looking at the concrete effects this claim has on the various components of constitutional democracy.

The questions to be answered are essentially two. First, how the pretence to embody the popular will affects the functioning of the ordinary mechanisms of representative democracy? And, second, how the affirmation of the primacy of the sovereign will of the people affects the rule of law and the role of the institutions that are deputed to check the majority's actions?

Without having the ambition of offering an all-embracing picture of these effects, the following pages will try to shed some light on the points of friction between populism and contemporary democracy, which will be the subject of a deeper analysis along the book, and show to what extent populism can be considered a healthy reaction to an existing imbalance in the democratic equilibrium.

2 Populism and Representative Democracy

Despite a generalised tendency to consider representative democracy incompatible with populism, Müller argues that without representative democracy there could not be populism (Müller 2014, 43). Populist parties indeed do not want to overcome representative democracy, their ambition is to be the first representative of the popular will and they participate in elections to achieve this goal. But, as we said, the question to be asked here is what consequence has the populist claim to embody the will of the people on the system of representation of constitutional democracy.

In the propositions of populist parties concerning the role of legislative assemblies, this claim is declined into two distinct forms. First, populists depict the parliaments as expensive and useless institutions protecting only the interests of the elite. Second, the only genuine form of democracy is, in the populist narrative, direct democracy, hence their tendency to advocate for an extensive use of referenda.

Concerning the former aspect, it may be worth remembering that populism tends to be strong in places with fragmented parliamentary systems: when the smooth functioning of parliaments has been hindered by an excessive fragmentation of political parties in the representative assembly, this constitutes the ideal breeding ground for populist phenomena to rise (Müller 2014). The populist solutions to the fragmentation and deadlocks of parliamentary systems are of two kinds. First, they propose the introduction of mechanisms to ensure the MPs' obedience to the party leader in order to foster internal party cohesion. In Italy, for instance, the 5 Star Movement supported by the League proposed the introduction of the most stringent form of control over MPs', the imperative mandate. However, as this would require amending Article 67 of the Italian Constitution, which explicitly prohibits imperative mandate, the 5 Star Movement adopted an internal rule against phenomena of 'floor crossing', providing the imposition of a pecuniary sanction of 100,000 Euros on the MP leaving the party.

On the other, they propose to reduce the size of parliaments, with the stated aim of reducing the cost of the institution. Always the 5 Star Movement managed to push through the parliament a constitutional reform which will reduce approximately one-third of the members of both chambers of the Italian Parliament (the Chamber of Deputies from 630 members to 400 and the Senate from 315 to 200 members).[6] A similar proposal is contained in the political programme of Marine Le Pen *Rassemblement National*, which aims at reducing the number of members of both the lower and upper house of the French parliament.[7]

[6] It is worth noting that, insofar, this represents the sole institutional reform proposed by the 5 Star Movement, that ultimately saw the light, after it was approved in a referendum held on the 20–21 of September 2021.

[7] Further, this proposal is accompanied by another which aims at introducing a majority bonus to the party who obtains at least the 30% of the popular vote in a newly designed proportional electoral system. Evidently, the combined effect of these proposals would be the injection of a further majoritarian element in the French democracy, to the detriment of parliamentarian component.

Another strategy pursued by populists to delegitimise parliaments is to curtail their functions. The events in Czechia are a good case in point. In 2013, Czech Republic's first directly elected president, Miloš Zeman, using the legitimacy deriving from its direct election proceeded to directly appoint his own government, completely bypassing the Czech parliament. This arrogation of the key power of government formation, that under the Czech constitution belongs to the parliament, made without any formal amendment to the Constitution, signals the idea of the parliament's subordination to the executive. Subsequently, in 2017, the winner of the parliamentary elections and current Prime Minister, Andrej Babiš, also pledged to abolish the upper chamber of the Parliament (Senate) and to reduce the number of MPs in the lower chamber from 200 to 101. Once again, the combined effect of these proposals results in a weakening of the parliament's role, which is deprived of its most significant check on the executive and reduced in size. Yet, unlike Orbán, Babiš does not have the required majority to push through the Parliament these constitutional amendments.

In Hungary, in fact, the powers of the National Assembly have been significantly curtailed by *Fidesz*'s reforms.[8] The Budget Council's veto right on approval of the annual budget law passed by the parliament is a good example in this regard. Although the Council, an organ supporting Parliament's legislative activities, may refuse to give consent only in specified cases (e.g. if the budget bill would allow state debt to exceed half of the GDP), in case the Budget Council denies its consent to the budget, the President of the Republic may dissolve the parliament and this constitutes an exceptional restriction of the Parliament's budgetary power. Evidently, in a parliamentary system, as Hungary formally still is, this constitutes a drastic curtailment of parliamentary prerogatives in a fundamental competence of the legislative assembly.[9]

To be fair, the problem of parliaments' marginalisation in constitutional democracy precedes the advent of populism in Europe. In order to give rapid answers to crises that have afflicted the European societies in the last two decades, executives became indeed primary norm-producer, reducing

[8] More in details on the reforms implemented by the Orbán's government concerning the role of parliament, see Szente, *How Populism Destroys Political Representation*, 1609–1618.

[9] Similar criticisms were revised in the first EU report on the rule of law situation in Hungary, the s.c. Tavares Report. See European Parliament ((2012/2130(INI)), *Report on the situation of fundamental rights: standards and practices in Hungary (pursuant to the European Parliament resolution of 16 February 2012.*

parliaments to mere validators of executive's actions (Curtin 2014). This shift of decision-making powers from the legislative to the executive opened up a legitimacy creep in constitutional democracy, that during the COVID-19 pandemic emerged in all its evidence.[10] Yet, populism, rather than fixing it, enlarges the creep by delegitimising the representative function of parliaments, portrayed as unnecessary and costly intermediary institutions, and introducing checks on parliamentary law-making powers.

As regards the populist preference for direct democracy, the last decade shows that one of the most visible consequences of the advent of populist politics in Europe has been a more extensive use of the referendum. The referenda celebrated in the UK on Brexit, in the Netherlands on the EU-Ukraine agreement, in Greece on the conditions imposed by the ESM for receiving financial assistance, in Hungary on the application of the migrant-quota, the referenda on same-sex marriage in Romania and Slovenia, and the illegal referendum on the independence of Catalonia, only to mention the most relevant, can indeed be all considered symptoms of populist rhetoric.

The Catalan illegal referendum that took place on 1 October 2017 well exemplifies the dangers inherent in the populist pretence to embody the popular will. The law declaring the referendum was approved by the Catalan parliament on 6 September 2017 along with the Law on legal transition and foundation of the Republic of Catalonia, containing a 'provisional constitution' of the Catalan Republic, which was approved the next day. Both bills were approved disregarding the rules disciplining the legislative process, in particular those concerning opposition's rights. More importantly, Article 3 of both laws self-attributed the two statutes supremacy over all conflicting norms, thereby including the Spanish Constitution and the Catalan Statute of Autonomy. The referendum law also stated that if the votes in favour of independence would be the majority, the result of the referendum would be binding with a simple majority, without requiring any participation or approval quorum. The Spanish Constitutional Tribunal declared the referendum unconstitutional on 17 October,[11] and the Law on legal transition null and void the following 8 November.[12] In the latter judgment, the Constitutional Tribunal stressed that the law was unconstitutional also according to the Statute of

[10] On this problem, see *Simonelli*, in this book.
[11] STC 114/2017, of 17 October 2017.
[12] STC 124/2017, of 8 November 2017.

Autonomy of Catalonia which requires a two-thirds majority in the Catalan parliament for any change to Catalonia's statute.

What the Catalan secessionist process demonstrates is that the pretence of populist parties to speak in the name of the people, depicted as a monolithic bloc even at a subnational level, refuses the checks inherent in constitutional democracy even and ultimately affects the rights of minorities which are not taken into account in the populist discourse.[13] As a matter of fact, the Catalan referendum of 2017, the government-sponsored referendum held in Hungary on the mandatory relocation of refugees,[14] and those, always sponsored by the government, on the ban of same-sex marriage in Romania and Slovakia,[15] all saw the participation of a minority part of the electorate—in all of them turnout was lower than 50%—thus demonstrating that the populist agenda is not always in line with the people's will.

The risk of marginalisation of minorities is particularly high in homogeneous societies, such as those of Central Eastern European states. Here, the exclusivist reference of populist parties to their people, in fact, results more often in a lowered protection of the rights of minorities and marginalised groups. The examples that can be offered in this regard are numerous: from the constitutionalisation of the prohibition of homelessness in Hungary to the challenges by Hungary and Slovakia of the EU Council Decision on the relocation of refugees among Member States, and the restrictive stance of all Central Eastern European states towards LGBTQ rights.

All in all, albeit populist parties do not seek to overcome representation as such—even populist governments, despite often being illiberal, remain tied to electoral legitimacy (Finchelstein 2017)—populism appears to reject the very foundation of representative democracy. Populist parties indeed pretend to be linked directly with the people, bypassing parliamentary intermediation. Also, claiming that the most genuine form of democracy is direct and participatory democracy,[16] populists advocate for referenda in the most important matters of the political agenda, for example, EU membership. The use of referenda ultimately betrays the populist

[13] More extensively on the Catalan secessionist process, see *González Campañá*, in this book.

[14] Ibid., 8.

[15] On these referenda, see Kuželewska, *Same-Sex Marriage – A Happy End Story?*.

[16] The use of instruments of participatory democracy is a typical feature of left-wing Latin American populism.

conception of representative democracy as the rule of the majority, where no space is reserved for the dialogue with minorities. In the populist discourse, democracy and representation go hand in hand until the limits and gridlocks inherent in representative democracy collide with the idea of democracy populist parties have.

3 Populism and Counter-Majoritarian Institutions: Constitutional Courts, Judicial Councils and Independent Authorities

3.1 Populism and Judges

In its quest for reinstating the legitimacy of the political system populism identifies various enemies. First and foremost, the organs deputed to safeguard and enforce the respect for the rule of law, that is, constitutional and ordinary judges.

What is particularly heinous for populists is the sophisticated version of the rule of law adopted in the European context, providing for strong constitutional courts checking the legality of the acts of the political branches.[17] The role of constitutional courts is substantially undisputed by populist parties in Western Europe—with the possible exception of Catalan independentists—in Central Eastern European States, conversely, constitutional judges have been frequently the target of attacks by populist governments.[18] During the transition to democracy of post-communist countries, a body entitled to perform judicial review of legislation was made a requirement under the 'Copenhagen criteria' and, generally speaking, all the constitutional jurisdictions of those States showed a somehow surprising readiness to overturn important statutes, often frustrating genuine attempts of reforms by incumbent governments (Schwartz 2000). Among these courts, the most active was the Hungarian Constitutional Court, that during the 1990s, acted as the guardian of the democratic transition. The Hungarian Constitutional Court was an example of judicial activism, especially with respect to the transposition of European standards concerning the rule of law, fundamental rights, and democracy

[17] Venice Commission, CDL-STD(1993)002-e, *Models of constitutional jurisdiction*—Science and technique of democracy, no. 2 (1993), 3.

[18] A comprehensive comparative account of these reforms is contained in *Granata-Menghini*, in this book.

in the country. Yet, in the end, the most powerful constitutional jurisdiction in Central Eastern Europe was the target of the most ferocious attack on its prerogatives and independence. By packing the constitutional courts with government-friendly judges and shrinking its jurisdiction and the rules of standing (Halmai 2019), the populist governments conveyed the message that the will of the ruling majority, being legitimated by the popular vote, cannot be subjected to the scrutiny of unelected bodies.

Nevertheless, it would be erroneous to identify a causal link between judicial activism in constitutional adjudication and a populist backlash against constitutional judges. The constitutional courts of Slovakia and Czechia, for instance, were able to reassert their position in the political system without abandoning an activist stance. Significantly, both courts embraced the doctrine of unconstitutional constitutional amendments:[19] the Czech court in 2009, and the Slovak one in 2016.[20] This doctrine, which represents the ultimate consequence of judicial activism, essentially empowers constitutional courts to strike down constitutional amendments and legislation for incompatibility with the higher principles of the constitution, sometimes identified by the judges themselves.[21] Even this 'extreme' form of judicial activism did not cost the two courts their independence. In the Slovak case, on the contrary, this judicial doctrine was adopted in the aftermath of a constitutional crisis, during which the President of the Republic refused to appoint three new judges to the Constitutional court, notwithstanding a ruling from the Constitutional Court that this constituted a violation of the Slovak Constitution.[22] After the 'surrender' of the President of the Republic, who finally appointed the three judges, and the election of a new liberal pro-European president, Zuzana Čaputová, it can be safely affirmed that, notwithstanding its judicial activism, the Czech Constitutional Court resisted the populist tide.

Also, the independence of ordinary judges has been put into question, especially in Central Eastern European countries, by populist parties challenging the validity of the European model of judicial independence.

[19] For a detailed illustration of this theory, see Roznai, *Unconstitutional Constitutional Amendments.*

[20] Judgement of Slovak Constitutional Court of 30 January 2019.

[21] In legal systems where the constitution contains an eternity clause, as it is case of Germany, the application of this doctrine is obviously less controversial.

[22] A complete illustration of this constitutional crisis can be found in the I-Connect Symposium on the case. The first episode of the saga is available at http://www.iconnectblog.com/2018/01/symposium-slovak-appointments-case-introduction/ last accessed 30 September 2021.

After the collapse of the Soviet Union, these countries, looking forward to joining the European Union, swiftly moved towards the European model of judicial independence, in which the key institution guaranteeing the independence of the judiciary is the judicial council.[23] In its version imposed on the Central European States as a requirement under the Copenhagen criteria, this model provides for a constitutionalisation of the judicial council, a majority of its members to be elected by the judges; and the transferral of all substantial decision-making powers concerning judges' career to the body. A certain degree of politicisation is admitted through the provision that parliament shall elect a minority of members, normally with a qualified majority.

In countries that had experienced 50 years of communist rule, characterised by a full dependency of the judiciary to political power, the adoption of these European standards resulted, as characterised by AG Bobek, in an 'extreme swing from zero judicial independence to 200%' (Bobek 2008). Both Hungary and Poland followed this model, and it has been argued that the granting of too extensive self-regulatory competences to a judiciary that just came out from an authoritarian regime, without any serious vetting procedure, may have indeed represented a major cause of the backlash against judicial independence in the two countries (Kosař, Baros and Dufek 2019, 445). Conversely, in Czechia, the only country which resisted the pressure coming from the Commission and the Council of Europe to institute a judicial council, the judiciary appears to have better safeguarded its independence, notwithstanding the rule of law record of the country in the last decade is far from being perfect.

Despite being the most common form of judicial self-government in Europe, also in Western Europe, the validity of this model has been challenged both by practice and by theory.

In practice, the major challenge came from Spain where, since 1985, it is the parliament that appoints the totality of the members of the judicial council.[24] Notwithstanding the recommendations coming from the Council of Europe to give the judges a say in the composition of the

[23] Albeit the requirement to have an independent judiciary was not explicitly mentioned in the 'Copenhagen criteria, during the accession talks leading to the 2004 enlargement the Commission required all candidate States to provide sufficient guarantees for judicial independence. See Kochenov, *Behind the Copenhagen Facade*, 20.

[24] Extensively on the Spanish judicial council, see Torres Perez, *Judicial Self-Government and Judicial Independence*.

judicial council,[25] the proposal advanced in October 2020 by Prime Minister Sánchez to modify the appointment system to the judicial council fully maintains a system in which the parliament appoints all the members. Further, as a response to the blockage of the renovation of the body by the opposition, it envisages a lowering of the majority required for the election of judicial council members[26] from three-fifths of the members of both chambers to absolute majority.[27] Thus, showing that intolerance to the gridlocks of representative democracy, and to judicial independence, is not exclusive to Central Eastern European populist parties.

Concerning the theory, already in 1983, Cappelletti criticised the European model for the 'risk of corporative insulation of the judiciary' (Cappelletti 1983, 61). Cappelletti addressed his criticism specifically to the Italian High Judicial Council, where he observed a situation of 'individual anarchy', consequence of a lax attitude of the body to exercise its control power over judges, and which led him to affirm that the Italian system 'might still be less fearful than one of dependency from the political power; it is not, however, necessarily less damaging' (Cappelletti 1983, 62). The problems that are currently afflicting the judiciary in Italy and Spain, attested by the worryingly bad performance of both countries in the EU Justice Scoreboard concerning the perceived level of judicial independence,[28] seem to have proved him right.

Probably then, the origin of the backlash against judicial independence is to be found in the blind acceptance of a model of judicial independence which was too unresponsive to political branches and societal needs. In any case, the solutions put forward by populists, court-packing, removal powers conferred on the ministry of justice and also the judicial council

[25] See GRECO Eval IV Rep (2013) 5E, Corruption prevention in respect of members of parliament, judges and prosecutors, adopted by on 6 December 2013. Recently the Greco repeated the necessity of a reform of the appointment system. See Greco RC4(2021)3, *Fourth Evaluation Round. Second Compliance Report.*

[26] Precisely, the proposal provides for the lowering of the majority of 12 of the 20 members of the Spanish judicial council, as for the other 8 Article 122(3) requires a three-fifth majority of the members of both the Congress of Deputies and the Senate.

[27] Strong critics against these proposals were raised both by judges and by opposition parties. Appointments to the Spanish Judicial Council are blocked since December 2018.

[28] According to the 2021 EU Justice Scoreboard, the perceived independence of the judiciary in the two countries is amongst the lowest in the EU, with more than 60% of the interviewed declaring to consider the level of judicial independence fairly or very bad. See 2021 EU Justice Scoreboard, 41. Available at: https://ec.europa.eu/info/sites/default/files/eu_justice_scoreboard_2021.pdf. last accessed 30 September 2021

fully elected by the parliament cannot be considered a legitimate attempt to strike a fair balance between judicial independence and the democratic accountability of the judiciary. In this regard, the institutional set-up of other judicial councils across Europe may offer useful examples of how to reconcile these two apparently contradictory concepts. In the French *Conseil Supérieure de la Magistrature*, for instance, 14 of the 22 judicial council's members are elected by judges amongst themselves, and the other 8 need to be persons from the outside the judiciary, that is, lay members. Yet, in the panels deciding on appointments, judges are in a minority and in the compositions deciding on disciplining sit an equal number of lay and judicial members. Leaving aside, for the moment, the question of the concrete arrangements put in place to achieve this fair balance, it can be concluded that even though a certain degree of politicisation of the judiciary is unavoidable and even desirable, the populist reforms aiming at placing the judiciary under the majority control blur the separation of powers, thus undermining the very foundation of the rule of law.

Similar conclusions can be drawn for populist reforms concerning constitutional courts. These reforms cannot be considered a proportionate reaction to an excessive judicial activism; they should be rather treated as symptoms of the populist malaise to accept any limit to the sovereign will of the people. The possibility of declaring a piece of legislation null and void for being in violation of the constitution is the ultimate consequence of the basic tenet of the rule of law: governors, including ruling majorities, are not above the law. The populist refusal of this fundamental principle renders hard to reconcile populism with the rule of law and its guardians.[29]

More generally, it is the very idea of a constitution capable of fixing the boundaries of the majority will that appears incompatible with populism in power. In fact, when populists obtain the necessary majority, like in Hungary, they transform the national constitution into an instrument of everyday politics, shielding their reforms from judicial review (Landau 2012, 189). Otherwise, they try to delegitimate the constitution and the compromise at its origin by proposing reforms seeking a total refashioning of the political system, like the 2018 proposal of constitutional reform by Greek Prime Minister Tsipras, or to capture the constitutional court to loosen down the constraint to its actions, like happened in Hungary and Poland.[30]

[29] Extensively on the point, see de *Ghantuz Cubbe*, in this book.

[30] This is the case of Poland. See *Granat*, in this book.

3.2 *Populism and Independent Authorities*

In contemporary constitutional democracy, the judiciary and the constitutional courts are not the only counter-majoritarian powers. Especially in new democracies, independent public bodies with the function of monitoring or directly exercising sensitive executive functions, like the organisation of elections, the regulation of media, and the oversight over the compliance with fundamental rights by public administrations, are becoming a common feature (Rose-Ackerman 2012, 676). These bodies, electoral commissions, media regulatory authorities, and ombudsmen shall be counted amongst counter-majoritarian powers, as long as they are not depending on the executive. Given their nature, populist governments end up colliding with them at some point, the capture of oversight authorities is in fact just another page of the populist playbook, the one about tightening the grip on power by rigging electoral competition.

As usual, Hungary and Poland are paradigmatic in this regard. In a nutshell, Orbán packed all the independent entities within the executive branch, including the Electoral Commission, the Budget Commission, the Media Board and the Ombudsman office, in most of the cases simply by removing incumbent members.[31] The negative effects of such a move are particularly visible in the case of the Electoral Commission, whose function is to ensure the fairness of all electoral consultations. The Orbán government proceeded to modify the composition and powers of the body in 2013; contextually, he also removed all the incumbent members.[32] The most worrying feature of the reform is the distinction between elected and delegated members. Whilst the latter are elected by the parliament with a two-thirds majority for a mandate of nine years, the delegated members, chosen by the opposition parties, took office just after the inauguration of the Parliament and their mandate ends when the government calls for a new election, meaning that they are not sitting in the Electoral Commission during the election process, when their presence is most needed.

The Polish PiS instead pursued a strategy focused on capturing the media system to prevent political pluralism. In December 2015, the PiS began its attack on the media independence and pluralism with a law disposing the premature termination of the mandate of all the members of

[31] For more details on the attack on the Hungarian independent authorities, see Carlino, *Ungheria: le autorità indipendenti e la 'democratic erosion'*.

[32] Act XXXVI of 2013 on Electoral Procedure.

the National Broadcasting Council, a body provided by the Polish Constitution for safeguarding the right to information and the public interest regarding radio broadcasting and television, and the temporary shift of its responsibilities to the treasury minister. In June 2016, the parliament then passed legislation creating a parallel National Media Council, which was attributed the power to appoint and dismiss the members of the governing bodies of the public media.[33] The body consists of five members, three appointed by the parliamentary majority and two by the President of the republic on the advice of opposition parties. Finally, in December 2017, the parliament passed a law terminating the mandates of the boards of all public-service broadcasters and gave each broadcaster a new board, whose members can be appointed and dismissed at any time by the Ministry of the Treasury.[34]

Such a dependency, in a context in which the National Media Council is already controlled by the parliamentary majority, threatens pluralism in the media sector, which according to the Venice Commission, is an essential element of a democratic society.[35]

As a last point, it is necessary to distinguish between independent authorities of a counter-majoritarian nature and authorities who lack such a character. Albeit it is hard to elaborate clear-cut categorisation amongst the vast array of independent authorities that can be found in European democracies, authorities with regulatory powers on highly technical and complex matters, like competition authorities or authorities for the regulation of financial markets, normally instituted within the executive, do not exercise any counter-majoritarian function and they are better defined as non-majoritarian institutions, in as much as they are excluded from the circuit of political representation. Originally a characteristic feature of the US system, these authorities became increasingly common also in Europe, where the EU pushed for a depoliticisation of the public sphere, to be realised by conferring regulatory powers to experts-composed bodies (De Somer 2017).

[33] Rule of Law Report 2020.

[34] More in details on the attack on freedom of expression by the Polish Government, see Fomina and Kucharczyk, *The Specter Haunting Europe*.

[35] CDL-AD(2005)017, *Opinion on the compatibility of the laws 'Gasparri' and 'Frattini' of Italy with the Council of Europe standards in the field of freedom of expression and pluralism of the media*, paras. 36 and 260, cited in CDL-PI(2020)008, *Compilation of Venice Commission opinions concerning freedom of expression and media*, 7.

The ensemble of these authorities is normally referred to as technocratic governance, defined as a system in which the legitimacy of decision-making is based on the rationale that, given the growing complexity of contemporary society, we should let the experts rule. In the last decades, the growth—both in number and competences—of regulatory agencies, has been uncontrolled, causing a marginalisation of the parliament's role.[36] Hence, in this regard, populism and technocratic governance are related phenomena as they both produce an imbalance in the separation of powers (Bickerton and Invernizzi Accetti 2017; Ackerman 2000). Yet, if technocratic governance relies on the assumption that complex decisions should be based on technical expertise, to the detriment of the democratic legitimacy of decision-making, populism essentially argues the opposite, the people always know what is best for them. A clash between technocratic institutions and populism is thus unavoidable. This clash happened, first and foremost, with the European Union, the epitome of technocratic governance.

4 Populism and the European Union

The exclusionary reference of the populists to their people cannot but affect the populist posture towards globalisation and transnational processes. In all populist narratives, international actors are indeed considered enemies of the people. From the left, the mistrust towards internationalism is motivated by a globalisation process that has left behind poorly qualified workers and fragile groups. From the right, the cosmopolitan and globalised society is presented as a menace for the cultural and ethnic identity of the national community. In this sense, a form of defensive nationalism can be considered a corollary of all forms of populism (De Marco 2020).

Needless to say, in Europe, populist anger has been directed mainly towards the EU.[37] Given its structural lack of direct democratic legitimacy and its strong reliance on technocratic governance, the EU makes an ideal enemy for populists, which depict it as an elite-driven project protecting

[36] Critics of technocratic governance point out that the delegation to regulatory authorities is actually a consequence of the political parties' failure to take decisions with long-term effects, as these may affect negatively their electoral performance, on which their permanence in power relies. See Pinelli, *The Populist challenge,* 12–13.

[37] In this book, *Guerra* explains why it is rightly so.

the interests of the international financial establishment.[38] More so after the 2010 sovereign debt crisis, when the EU unresponsiveness to its citizens contributed to the growth of anti-European sentiment, helped populist parties to generate scepticism towards the EU integration process itself and increase their electoral consensus.

This scepticism has been translated by populists into various forms. When at the opposition, populist parties challenge the very substance of the integration process. As a matter of fact, virtually every populist party in the EU, albeit for different reasons, has at some point called for a referendum on the EU membership, the last in order of time being the German right-wing populist party *Alternative für Deutschland*.[39] Alternatively, they propose Treaty revisions to take back the competences transferred to Bruxelles, above all on economic and monetary policy, but also concerning the European free movement space, that is, the pillars of the EU project. In any case, the elites are accused of having been incapable of opposing to, or for being complicit in, establishing EU's supranational technocracy (Martinelli 2018, 63).

When they are in power, or with concrete perspectives of reaching it, populists' attitude towards the EU becomes more ambiguous. They abandon the idea of completely dismantling the EU, whilst keeping the demand for their national sovereignty to be 'restored', obviously opposing any further attempt towards an 'ever closer union' (Bugaric 2019). Besides, they continue to blame the EU for threatening national identity by imposing from above values extraneous to the country's constitutional traditions and for the supposedly uncontrolled flux of immigrants entering the EU territory.

At the same time, however, populist governments have strong incentives to maintain a good relationship with the EU. According to the data made available by the European Commission, all Central Eastern European Member States are net beneficiaries of EU funds, with Hungary and Poland being the two biggest net beneficiaries of the EU.[40] Also, the pop-

[38] Arguably, national governments favoured this process, hiding behind the EU to justify failures and unpopular decisions. See, *Pinelli*, in this book.

[39] https://www.politico.eu/article/germanys-far-right-afd-alternative-for-germany-to-campaign-on-possible-eu-exit-alexander-gauland/ last accessed 30 September 2021.

[40] European Commission, *EU Budget 2018 Financial Report*, 75. Available at: https://ec.europa.eu/info/sites/default/files/about_the_european_commission/eu_budget/financial_report_web.pdf last accessed 30 September 2021. In 2018, the last year for which figures are available, the Hungarian government received from the EU five billions euros

ular support for the European Union in populist-ruled countries remains quite high: according to the 2021 Eurobarometer, 56% of Hungarian and 55% of Polish trust the EU, with an even greater percentage of citizens having an optimistic view about the future of the Union.[41] Once again showing how the populist portrait of society rarely corresponds to reality.

Leaving aside the question of what remedies the EU should deploy to counter democratic erosion in its Member States,[42] as long as exiting the EU remains an unattractive option for both local societies and executives, the EU contributes to prevent and limit democratic erosion in its Member States.

5 Preliminary Answers

At this point, it is time to try to answer the questions posed at the beginning.

Concerning the impact of populism on representative democracy, it can be affirmed that the real goal of populism is not to reinstate the democratic legitimacy of the constitutional system, but rather to realise a centralisation of powers in the hands of the executive, frequently controlled by a charismatic leader. This produces, as a consequence, a marginalisation of parliaments as fora for debating public policies with the involvement of the opposition, and which manifests itself in various forms, spacing from the abolition of the upper house, the reduction of the number of MPs, to the introduction of controls on individual MPs. Also, the claim ‘we are the people’, with its strong exclusionary character, is hardly compatible with the pluralistic nature of contemporary constitutional democracy as it often overlooks the real composition of the society and the respect for minorities.

more than what it contributed to the EU budget, and the Polish twelve billions, making Poland the biggest net beneficiaries of the EU budget. Just to give a term of comparison, such funding accounted respectively for 43% and 56% of all public investment in the two countries in 2018. These data have been excerpted from the European Semester Reports for the two countries. See SWD(2018) 215 final, *Country Report Hungary 2018*, 10; SWD(2018) 219 final, *Country Report Poland 2018*, 14. Respectively available at: https://ec.europa.eu/info/sites/default/files/2018-european-semester-country-report-hungary-en.pdf; https://ec.europa.eu/info/sites/default/files/2018-european-semester-country-report-poland-en_1.pdf last accessed 30 September 2021.

[41] European Commission, *Standard Eurobarometer 95 Spring 2021.Public opinion in the European Union*, 10. Available at https://europa.eu/eurobarometer/surveys/detail/2532 last accessed 30 September 2021.

[42] On this aspect, see *Krunke, Tornøe, Wegener*, in this book.

The populist attitude towards counter-majoritarian institutions is even more straightforward. Populism rejects any constraint on the popular will imposed by unelected institutions and seeks to replace the delicate system of checks and balances of constitutional democracy, with a system where the will of the elected must prevail in any case. This overbearing emphasis on the majority rule, as the almost unique method of decision-making, leads to the creation of monistic systems in which all power is detained by electorally legitimate bodies, free from any possible controls (Tarchi 2018, 913): an attitude that embraces also the opposition and minority groups in Parliament, which are deprived of meaningful oversight powers and excluded from the participation in the appointment of counter-majoritarian institutions.

Any justification for the claims of populist constitutionalism seems thus untenable. Whilst it can be agreed that theoretically populist constitutionalism aims to redress existing imbalances and flaws inherent in constitutional democracy, populist parties in power provide the wrong solutions to these problems (Ginsburg and Huq 2018, 68). More worryingly, they appear to act in bad faith, overstepping constitutional boundaries with the only aim to ensure their permanence in power. And, it is when they obtain the majority necessary to modify the constitution that populists become particularly dangerous, as they may cause constitutional democracy drifting towards authoritarianism.

Concerning the remedies, it may be true what David Landau affirms that the agenda to immunise constitutional democracy *vis-à-vis* the populist challenge is an almost impossible one (Landau 2012, 259). Yet, this should not lead to the conclusion that checks and balances of constitutional democracy are irrelevant, the opposite. The involvement of a plurality of institutional and political actors, in conjunction with qualified majorities, in the appointment process of constitutional tribunals and judicial councils appears to be a successful strategy to limit the most detrimental effects of a prolonged populist rule. Multilevel governance is also a solution. As illustrated by the Catalan secessionist process, the existence of various levels of governance is an effective barrier to the spread of the populist contagion. In this sense, notwithstanding all the criticisms directed to Bruxelles, the role of the EU in countering populism may have been much more decisive than what the many apparent failures of the EU actions suggest. All in all, the answer to the populist oversimplifications may well be more complex in the design of democratic institutions.

However, without civic engagement, a voiceful public opinion, and well-trained civil servants, even the best designed constitutional system is doomed to succumb to democratic erosion. After all, as Popper wrote '[i]nstitutions are like a fortress. They must be well designed and manned', and 'the functioning of even the best institutions will always depend to a considerable degree, on the persons involved' (Popper 2011, 120), in other words, on each of us.

In conclusion, populism is not a corrective to constitutional democracy, because once the flaw is identified it does not do anything to amend it; on the contrary, it rubs salt on the democratic wound, exacerbating and exploiting the weaknesses of the constitutional system. As long as democracy is in good health, it is capable to absorb the populist impact for a while. But at some point, it needs to answer back. In this regard, the pandemic may have been a useful shock.

Independently of the legal aspects of the crisis management,[43] national governments demonstrated substantial responsiveness to their citizens' concerns and needs, which seem to have put populism to sleep, as certified by the good electoral results of all traditional parties in national consultations across Europe. The suspension of the applicability of European budgetary rules and the launch of Next Generation EU, defined by Olaf Scholz as a 'Hamiltonian moment' for the EU, have allowed European governments to support their economies with an unprecedented amount of public investments and hopefully marked a turning point in the EU integration process.

Nonetheless, visible creeps remain in the institutional set-up of constitutional democracy, from executive dominance, and the consequent marginalisation of parliaments, to the blurred separation of powers between political branches and the judiciary. Those need to be fixed to prepare constitutional democracy for future challenges lying ahead.

Bibliography

Ackerman, John. "Understanding Independent Accountability Agencies." in *Comparative Administrative Law* edited by Susan Rose-Ackerman, Susan and Peter L. Lindseth, London: Edward Elgar, 2010, 688–700.

Ackerman, Bruce. "The New Separation of Powers." *Harvard Law Review* 113, no. 3 (2000): 633–729.

[43] For an overview of these issues, see *Castellà*, in this book.

Bickerton, Cristopher and Accetti Invernizzi, Carlo. "Populism and Technocracy," in *The Oxford Handbook of Populism* edited by Cristóbal Rovira Kaltwasser. Oxford: Oxford University Press, 2017.

Bobek, Michal. "The Fortress of Judicial Independence and the Mental Transitions of the Central European Judiciaries." *European Public Law* 14, no. 1 (2008): 99–123.

Bugarič, Bojan. "The Two Faces of Populism: Between Authoritarian and Democratic Populism." *German Law Journal* 20, no. 3 (2019): 390–400. https://doi.org/10.1017/glj.2019.20

Cappelletti, Mauro. " "Who Watches the Watchmen?" A Comparative Study on Judicial Responsibility." *The American Journal of Comparative Law* 31, no. 1 (1983): 1–62.

Corrias, Luigi. "Populism in a Constitutional Key: Constituent Power, Popular Sovereignty and Constitutional Identity." *European Constitutional Law Review* 12, no. 1 (2016): 6-26.

De Marco, Eugenio. "Sovranismo e populismo vs integrazione sovranazionale." *Federalismi*, no. 4 (2020): 1–8.

De Somer, Stéphanie. *Autonomous Public Bodies and the Law: A European Perspective.* Edward Elgar: London, 2017.

Fioravanti, Maurizio. *Constitución. De la Antigüedad a nuestros días.* Madrid: Trotta, 2011.

Finchelstein, Federico. *From Fascism to Populism in History.* Berkeley: University of California Press, 2017.

Fomina, Joanna and Kucharczyk, Jacek. "The Specter Haunting Europe: Populism and Protest in Poland." *Journal of Democracy* 27, no. 4 (2016): 58–68.

Ginsburg, Tom and Huq, Aziz Z. *How to save a constitutional democracy.* Chicago: Chicago University Press, 2018.

Kochenov, Dimitry. "Behind the Copenhagen Facade. The Meaning and Structure of the Copenhagen Political Criterion of Democracy and the Rule of Law." *European Integration Online Papers* 8, no. 10 (2004): 1–24.

Kosař, David, Jiří Baros and Pavel Dufek. "The Twin Challenges to Separation of Powers in Central Europe: Technocratic Governance and Populism." *European Constitutional Law Review* 15, no. 3 (2019): 427–461. https://doi.org/10.1017/S1574019619000336

Kużelewska, Elżbieta. "Same-Sex Marriage – A Happy End Story? The Effectiveness of Referendum on Same-Sex Marriage in Europe." *Białostockie Studia Prawnicze* 24, no. 1 (2019): 1–16. https://doi.org/10.15290/bsp.2019.24.01.01

Landau, David. "Abusive constitutionalism." *University of California Davis Law Review* 47, no. 1 (2012): 189–260.

Majone, Davide. "Europe's "Democratic Deficit": the Question of Standards." *European Law Journal* 4, no. 1 (1998): 5–28.

Martinelli, Alberto. "National Populism and the European Union." *Populism* 1, no. 1 (2018): 59–71.

Mounk, Yascha. *El pueblo contra la democracia*. Barcelona: Paidós, 2018.

Mudde, Cas and Rovira, Cristóbal. *Populism in Europe and the Americas. Threat or corrective for democracy?*. New York: Cambridge University Press, 2013.

Müller, Jan-Wermer. *¿Qué es el populismo?*. Madrid: Grano de Sal Ediciones, 2014.

Parker, Richard D. *Here, the People Rule: A Constitutional Populist Manifesto*, Cambridge: Harvard University Press, 1998.

Pinelli, Cesare. "The Populist Challenge to Constitutional Democracy." *European Constitutional Law Review* 7, no. 1 (2011), 5–16.

Popper, Karl. *The Open Society and Its Enemies*. London: Routledge, 2011 (1st version 1945).

Rose-Ackerman, Susan. "The Regulatory State" in *The Oxford Handbook of Comparative Constitutional Law*, edited by Michel Rosenfeld and András Sajó, 676. Oxford: Oxford University Press, 2012.

Roznai, Yaniv. *Unconstitutional Constitutional Amendments*. Oxford: Oxford University Press, 2018.

Schwartz, Hermann. *The Struggle for Constitutional Justice in Post-Communist Europe*. Chicago: The University of Chicago Press, 2000.

Tarchi, Rolando. "Democrazia e istituzioni di garanzia." *Rivista AIC*, no. 3 (2018): 894–995.

Torres Pérez, Aida. "Judicial Self-Government and Judicial Independence: the Political Capture of the General Council of the Judiciary in Spain." *German Law Journal* 19, no. 7 (2018): 1769–1800. DOI:https://doi.org/10.1017/S2071832200023233.

Zoltán, Szente. "How Populism Destroys Political Representation (Anti-) Parliamentary Reforms in Hungary after 2010." *DPCE Online*, no. 2 (2019): 1609–1618.

PART I

The Populist Ideology and Constitutional Democracy

From Populist Parties to Populist Politics. Populism as a Unifying Ideology

José Tudela Aranda

1 Explanation: The Ideology of Simplification

Analyses regarding the "health" of democracy and its relationship with constitutional law have proliferated in recent times. The information gleaned from these analyses is highly important, and it is necessary to understand this proliferation. There is virtual unanimity in the belief that this glut of analyses is the result of numerous symptoms which reflect a constant "erosion" of citizens' trust in the democratic system. Although this crisis is not equally acute in all countries, there exists a general feeling that practically all States are affected in one way or another. The capacity of Institutions to represent citizens is in question and, even more intensely, the confidence in their ability to solve problems has been seriously undermined (Dogan 2005, 14–16). These are two essential issues upon which there is consensus of opinion. Constitutional democracy has partially lost legitimacy and effectiveness for a significant number of citizens, whereas

J. T. Aranda (✉)
Deparment of Public Law, University of Zaragoza, Zaragoza, Spain
e-mail: jtudela@cortesaragon.es

J. M. Castellà Andreu, M. A. Simonelli (eds.), *Populism and Contemporary Democracy in Europe*,
https://doi.org/10.1007/978-3-030-92884-1_2

authoritarian political systems, at least convey a powerful perception of "efficiency". In addition, what has happened during the COVID-19 epidemic has augmented the loss of confidence in constitutional democracy.

Simultaneously, it is possible to make a different diagnosis of the health of democracy. Historically have there never been so many "apparently" democratic states (and never has the number of ostensibly authoritarian states been so small) and never has democracy had fewer declared enemies. Today, no one openly advocates putting an end to the basic rules of democracy. Contrary to what happened in the interwar period, in theory, nobody questions democracy. Democracy is understood to be the only viable and desirable political system. This means that, even today, democracy as an ideology retains its prestige to a large degree. It is an important asset for the necessary reconstruction of the political system. It requires the adoption of a concept of democracy free from the deviations that have proliferated in many States in recent years.

For years, studies have focused on the crisis of representative democracy.[1] A devaluation of the representative model caused, fundamentally, by two factors, has been the subject of these studies: on the one hand, the wrongdoing of political parties and, on the other, the shortage of participatory instruments. Political parties have distanced themselves from the citizens. They have not listened to them, and institutions such as Parliament have not debated the issues which are of interest to them. In addition, the proliferation of alleged corruption has discredited these institutions even further (Bustos Gisbert 2017, 35–39). On the other hand, participation via the right to vote is no longer enough in contemporary society. New channels of participation have had to be developed. The evolution of technologies allowing this development should be a "boost" to direct democracy (Cebrián 2012). In most cases, those who defended the development of these new means of democratic participation did so to strengthen representative democracy, but there were also those who defended this harking back to the old criticism: representative democracy is not really a true democracy.

The result of this evolution has been the strengthening of the democratic principle. "Participation" has become a sacred word, and the idea that nothing could stand in the way of the voice of the people has spread to certain political parties (Tudela, 2017, 136–144). This is the theoretical premise for the development of populist policies and of the so-called

[1] See, for instance, Dahrendorf, *Después de la democracia*.

illiberal democracies. Democracy has split in two: on the one hand, the democratic principle, and on the other, the conditions inherent to the Rule of Law, considered by some to be an obstacle to the development of "true" democracy; a model observed in states which are formally democratic. In this way, the optimistic view of the state of health of democracy is nuanced. Democracy is more widespread than ever, but a virus is spreading which distorts it even though "appearances" are kept up.

From an ideological point of view, the exaltation of the democratic principle is completed with the recovery of an old ideology: populism. Contemporary society, and its problems, is characterised by its complexity (Innerarity 2020, 56–60). It has never been so difficult to govern effectively or alleviate citizens' concerns. Leaders hesitate and often do not solve these problems satisfactorily. This is an environment conducive to the development of an ideology, which one might accuse of being an over-simplification. The complex is simple; different shades, hues and nuances no longer exist (everything is black or white); "the *baddies* are the others and the *goodies* are those who think like us"; everything for natives, nothing for foreigners—ideas which contradict all the premises which are the foundation of constitutional democracy. This democracy accepts and values complexity and pluralism and establishes procedures for decision-making so that everyone can feel integrated into the system.

In the following pages, an approach to this process is proposed based on the premise that is essential for understanding everything happening today and which often takes us by surprise: the intensity of social, economic, and cultural change which has taken place over the last 20 years as a consequence of a new technological era hardly admits comparison in historical terms; changes fundamentally characterised by the speed with which they are taking place—a "rhythm" that inevitably affects governance and political institutions which have not adapted to this new context. Adapting oneself to a new situation has always been difficult but, possibly, not enough effort is being made. This change has caused confusion, uncertainty, and fear in society and our governors do not convey confidence to the citizens. Along with this, the feeling that political systems are incapable of solving problems has spread. Be this true or not, citizens are overwhelmingly under the impression that their governments are largely ineffective or inept.

Next is to analyse how the convergence of this change with the emergence of populism has caused, in many cases, a notable "erosion" of institutions. In some cases, the weakness of the Rule of Law is evident. There exists a risk of a merely nominal democracy. Energy is in short supply to defend the importance of the institutions of the Rule of Law. Finally, the chapter briefly analyses the aforementioned ideology of simplification, defending the thesis that there is a risk that the seductive force of populist parties will end up contaminating all political players and groups.

These preliminary lines should end with two considerations: on the one hand, the need to consider the geography of the crisis being analysed; a crisis especially localised in the West—the legitimacy of political systems does not appear to be in question in the same way in eastern democracies. On the other hand, it is necessary to warn of the provisional nature of any conclusion. As we write, the COVID-19 epidemic is still a reality. When this comes to an end, many things will have changed. This is certainly an extraordinary event, but the aforementioned "rhythm" links this tragic situation to another of the characteristics of our time: "provisionality".

2 Essential Context: An Inefficient Democracy?

As indicated, any study on the health of contemporary democracy must be carried out bearing in mind the profound transformation of the context within which political systems operate. One only needs to remember what our lives were like 20 years ago to understand this depth of change, even in our private lives, or how political dynamics used to function. This chapter does not examine the causes or the most important features of this change, but only refers to some of their manifestations, especially those more closely related to the erosion of constitutional democracy and the rise of populist politics. Also, the chapter expounds on some of the circumstances characterising contemporary society and government, and which facilitate the development of populist discourse.

Efficiency has always been a condition for the proper functioning of a political system. Public powers must give a satisfactory solution to the citizens' problems (Vallespín and Bascuñán 2018). Power is also legitimised by its "functionality", and its ability to reduce the effects of uncertainty and alleviate the maladies of the population. Historically, it has been argued that democracy was not only the political model to embody and defend the most "precious" values but also the most appropriate for the development prosperity. Democracy has always been a necessary condition for economic and social development. However, in the last three decades, some authoritarian models have achieved indisputable success in this respect, to the extent that for some, an authoritarian model, like the one in place in China, can be legitimised on the strength of that success. But the appeal of some authoritarian formulae does not derive only from their relationship to economic development, it is also related to the widespread feeling that these models are more effective in solving the problems of contemporary society. Problems are reduced to a mixture of simplism and nationalism which allow the dissemination of an image of success in the face of the failure of traditional democratic states. Of course, in most cases, this is only a mirage of success; the real situation is usually very different from the image projected by the powers that be. But that does not matter, and the important thing is the message, the image. This formula has been triumphant.

However, true as these things might be, little time should be wasted trying to prove that this presumed "efficacy" is a fallacy; that the effectiveness of these states is inferior to that of our democracies. We should be aware that many citizens associate "virtue" with an improvement in their living conditions, and that they understand that these conditions are less favourable today than yesterday, and, above all, they believe that their children will have a more underprivileged life. Ideological legitimacy alone is not enough, it never has been, and surely today, more than ever, it is necessary to complement this with "functional" legitimacy. Politicians ought to be answerable to the citizens. Not only that, it is also necessary to know how to communicate success and avoid a state of mind which undervalues achievement and exaggerates mistakes. According to Carl Schmitt, the validity of institutions depends on the strength of principles and convictions. The paradox of contemporary democracy is that, at least for the moment, the majority still share the principles and convictions that sustain it. However, the crisis of democracy is real, and, underlying this, the generalised negative feeling towards its capacity to respond to the traditional and emerging needs of citizens; a circumstance conducive to the development of a populist discourse. In this context, it seems that democracy has been efficient in generating systems of values, but deficient in ensuring positive results. What should be clarified is whether, in a context of crisis, society prefers a "democracy of values" or another form of government capable of ensuring such positive results, even at the expense of sacrificing democracy itself.

In the analysis of the circumstances that lie at the origin of the transformation of contemporary politics, the word "complexity" stands out strongly, for two reasons: of course, as is often said, because one of the essential characteristics of contemporary populism is to "simplify" complex issues (Innerarity 2020). The biggest problems have a simple solution. If they are not resolved, then it is because there is no real will to do so. In this way, responsibility is completely shifted to governors whose sole wish is to remain in power. The face of these governors, so-called good politicians, that is, populist leaders, would easily solve these problems. In order to attain this, they state that they only need to come to power. To achieve this, the *message* is essential; communication has always been populism's main instrument. Populism has adapted to the transformation of the media better than anyone. The characteristics of the new media have facilitated populist messages. Both populism and the new media coincide in their "simplicity". Populism reduces complexity to an over-simplification incompatible with reality. The characteristics of the new media facilitate the success of their intentions.

However, complexity is also a protagonist for another reason: the complexity of the issues that governments have to resolve is real, possibly more complex than ever; they are technically complex and difficult to manage because there are many competing interests, and it is not possible to overlook any of these interests which are in permanent flux. A suitable solution for today may not be appropriate for tomorrow. If the populists come to power, no problem will exist: they will either solve the problem superficially or falsely or, as is more often the case, they will find an external *enemy* who prevents them from doing so. In this way, another of the characteristic features of populism appears: the creation of a kind of virtual reality; their capacity for this, ability to maintain it and to achieve their identification with reality is remarkable.

This simplification is also manifested in one of the essential characteristics of the populist political discourse: its reduction to the classic dialectic, "friend or foe" (Schmitt 1999, 62). In almost all cases, this is accompanied by the negation of their adversaries. There is only one true political option, because only one represents "the force of good". The consequences of this discourse are many, and none are positive for constitutional democracy. In few of the features of populism is its authoritarian background so clearly manifested. Pluralism and the essential rule that the other can also be "right" are denied. There is no plurality, no diversity. There is only one other who "denies me and who, consequently, is my enemy". Logically, nuances and the possibility of dialogue disappear, and with that, some of the essential characteristics of parliamentary democracy.

It is often said that a political system can only maintain a level of discontent at acceptable minimums so as not to affect the structure of the system

(Guillén 2019, 66). Populists know this and therefore seek to inflame discontent. Their ultimate goal is to build an alternative political system. To achieve this, as we have seen, they undermine trust with false arguments about complexity, but they also act in accordance with a system of values. Constitutional democracy responds to values that have been shared for decades. It should not be forgotten that democracy has only existed for a short time in the history of mankind. History has shown that any situation is subject to change. Populists know that this is true, and they also know that now is a time of change. Not only changes to our way of relating, communicating or accessing information, our values also change with time; this is unavoidable. We must not forget that the original ideas upon which constitutional democracy was based are changing rapidly (Muñoz Machado 2019, 15). One could argue that this is not the case, and that the values of justice, freedom, equality or representation are still valid. Possibly so, but their meaning must be adapted to this very different social atmosphere. If we do not do this, then the populists will take full advantage. They will denounce these values as false and will create dangerous alternatives. This danger is very real. The future of constitutional democracy does not only depend on finding an institutional model which knows how to respond to old and new problems, we also need to review our system of values to be able to disseminate these values effectively within a changing society.

Many other objective circumstances can be mentioned which are harmful to the proper functioning of constitutional democracy and favour populist discourse, but it is not possible to analyse them here. It is essential to refer to some of the circumstances we call "subjective", as they are directly related to the behaviour of our leaders. Two circumstances need to be pointed out: on the one hand, the wrongdoing of many of the contemporary parties and governments; on the other, the problems resulting from our way of choosing our leaders in this contemporary society.

Many of us agree that populism is not the best choice. Not only that, populist political forces pose a threat to the proper development of constitutional democracy, but this diagnosis must be completed by trying to understand the reasons why populism is so worrying today (Vallespín and Bascuñán 2018). Change, confusion and uncertainty will always facilitate a climate for populism. Along with this, some characteristics of this new social model are exploited by populism with great skill, but there are other factors. One could even affirm that everything has been easier for populist parties because of the mistakes and malpractices of traditional parties. Two stand out from the rest: on the one hand, an inability to understand what is happening in society, and, on the other, a reiteration of bad practices. Words like "distance", and "disaffection", are already common in political analysis (Bustos Gisbert 2017, 64–69). Citizens consider that politicians are not devoted to the problems which affect them. Their only interests are their own: guaranteeing power for themselves, forgetting about the living conditions of the citizens. Of course, in some cases, this is true, in many it is not, but this does not matter. It is enough that a negative public opinion has become widespread.

Along with the above, and facilitating that perception, would be the proliferation of irregular or criminal practices within political parties. The wrongdoing of governors and politicians is inevitable. A democratic system must develop all possible instruments to avoid bad practice as much as possible, but the complete prevention of it is impossible. It always has been. Today, there are circumstances that have modified the control on public life. This change has come about from a triple perspective: on the one hand, and the most important of these, a greater facility to know about and judge public policy. Even the private life of public figures is controlled. On the other, the ineffective functioning of many instruments of control, which will be discussed later, and finally, in some countries, an upsurge in malpractice.

Logically, populism takes advantage of these circumstances. In some cases, these will be essential for its rise. The slogan, "They do not represent us", coined in Spain in 2014, is a good example of this (Torreblanca 2015). It is important to bear this in mind. It is not enough to denounce the inherent risks of populist parties and populist politics in general. We need to fully understand the causes which have brought about this political tendency. To resolve some of these problems is not easy, but others have an objectively simpler solution. We must make an appeal that traditional political forces regain virtue.

Finally, another central question needs to be addressed: the selection of leaders (Blanco Valdés 2016, 28). At times, it seems to be forgotten that one of the essential functions of democracy is the selection of our governors, who are supposed to establish political criteria in order to steer politics, but also to deal with the everyday problems of the citizens. Many share the following diagnosis: the problems which public power must deal with are more complex than ever. And also, there exists a shared idea that the capacity of our leaders is waning. Repeatedly, it is said that the quality of our "ruling class" has declined markedly. It is not a question of a politician's academic training. The absence of leadership and the virtues which allow a governor to deal with complicated situations are lamented. In short, a loss of legitimacy is generalised which is a serious problem for democracy. An analysis of this phenomenon goes beyond the scope of this chapter, but it is possible to allude to an important fact, directly related to it: politics' loss of prestige and attractiveness. Both people with more training and skills and those most interested in the common good prefer to operate within the private sector; the public sector, especially within the political sphere, but also in administration, is no longer attractive. When the difficulties are greater and more skill is required, problems worsen. To this, one could add an excessive appeal of politics to younger politicians who lack essential experience in governmental positions.

The weakness of the ruling class is an essential cause of the rise of populism. Faced with leaders who are unable to hide their limitations, populist political groups introduce candidates to the public who boast about their virtues and attributes, again, with the aid of marketing campaigns which ignore their defects, and contribute, once again, to the creation of a virtual or even false reality. Even more worrying is that history has shown us that if the populists come to power, they will become highly resistant to political "wear and tear", even though poor management reveals their limitations.

3 A Crisis of Democracy: Institutional Deterioration

What has been analysed so far is fundamentally related to the deterioration of institutions. The overall functioning of the system is deteriorating, especially its institutions. Again, a distinction must be made between a deterioration unrelated to the direct action of populism and that which is directly caused by it. This institutional deterioration began *before* the emergence of populist parties and could be blamed on factors which have nothing to do with them. One could assert that one of the reasons for the current relevance of this deterioration is precisely that it was already in place. Populist political groups take advantage of this and attempt to aggravate things further. For populism to develop and thrive, it needs institutions to be weak. Populism only develops comfortably in a context of institutional weakness. The reason for this is clear: in a democratic system, the organisation of institutions has two basic functions in relation to power—on the one hand, its limitation and control, and on the other, to make the exercise of power "predictable". Democracy is, by definition, a political system which rationalises power. It is essential that citizens know what the limits to the unfolding of power are. Therefore, it is impossible to extricate democracy from the Rule of Law (Tudela 2016, 479–481).

As we are aware, populism seeks to exercise absolute power. Populist leaders assume the complete representation of all the people and that people cannot be opposed to limits or controls. In this way, populism is radically distanced from constitutional democracy. A permanent evolution towards a greater rationalisation of power forms part of the history of this political model: the history of a struggle against arbitrary power. A power subject to the Rule of Law, subject to controls which condition it and which is limited, and respectful towards established norms—a necessary requirement of any "quality" democracy. Populist parties not only distance themselves from these ideas, but also seek to render them ineffective until they actually disappear from public life. They do this with a simple discourse which seeks, above all, to communicate efficiently. What has happened in recent years shows that this strategy is successful. Not only are these political parties growing in number and influence, but, beyond that, as will be seen, they contaminate the entire political arena, so, one could say that today, populism is a way of going about things which have come to characterise most political parties. This has come about due to weak leaders and the half-hearted convictions of traditional parties. Of course, another salient factor is a favourable technological context. But the fundamental key to their success is a political erosion of institutions which has characterised many political systems, even before the emergence of populist parties.

It is not possible to analyse all the manifestations of this erosion here, not even to give a rough overview, the scope of this chapter is limited to describing two features which are particularly relevant for understanding the changes transforming many political systems and, in general, the way politics is understood. On the one hand, it is essential to make a brief reference to the deterioration of classic intermediaries. Political parties and the mass media have suffered, and are suffering, the impact of a technological model that has radically changed the traditional scenario; on the other, the weakness of many of the classic institutions of the Rule of Law. That weakness is reflected both in specific damage to institutions and in a cultural change which eliminates some of the values which sustain constitutional democracy and whose being in force is essential for the proper functioning of the system.

The weakness of traditional parties is a widespread trait in Western democracies. Traditionally, disaffection has had one of the most reliable indicators of this phenomenon, manifested as a low turn-out at elections. This continues to be the case, but, in recent years, the relevant circumstance as regards the position of political parties within the system as a whole is the instability of classic parties and a sudden facility for the emergence of parties, social movements that end up drastically transforming the party system (Bustos Gisbert 2017). Modern democracy is built upon the existence of diverse political parties and is hardly imaginable otherwise (Kelsen 1934; Garcia Pelayo 1986). Society changes and it is inevitable that parties will also do so; this is even necessary. Parties must adapt their functioning to new social dynamics, but they should do this whilst preserving the need for deliberative democracy and therefore avoiding the most negative aspects of this new society, such as extreme polarisation and the aforementioned oversimplification of political discourse. Until now, traditional parties have not managed to respond effectively to this, allowing populism to occupy important areas and become a fundamental player in this new political arena.

If political parties have been one of the traditional vectors of the contemporary political system, then the other side of the coin is used to correspond to public opinion. In the middle, freedom of speech and the right to access information were the fulcrum to that balance, and *primus inter pares* among the other rights and freedoms, precisely because of their direct relationship to the forming of free public opinion and, consequently, to a proper development of democracy (Villaverde 2018). Again, it is clear that it is impossible to describe the world in the same terms as ten years ago. The shaping of public opinion has radically changed in recent years. The technological revolution has had a great impact on how we communicate and gain access to information (Sartori 2002). Our sources of information have multiplied; the traditional media have witnessed how their importance and presence have greatly diminished. In conclusion, a social sphere, apparently without rules, regulations or control, has emerged which, in a very short time, has become an indispensable reference to political dynamics. It is a crucial fact that more than a *symptom*, it is a *cause*: one of the fundamental causes of the objective transformation of the political system. The changes in communication and in the protagonists of today are closely linked to the successful development of populism, but although this is not the main cause of this success, it is an important factor for understanding it. The simplification and radicalisation of messages are characteristic of communication within networks. And not only this, nowadays anyone can become a "communicator". There is no quality control. The demands of a newsroom committed to the prestige and history of a particular publication or means of communication have disappeared. Only the "impact" of what is placed on the new networks matters. Somehow, the information itself has disappeared. Only the act of communicating is relevant. This benefits populism in two ways: on the one hand, it causes social changes which make a part of society more receptive to that kind of discourse, and on the other, it favours the development and permeation of populist messages. Today, these features of political communication are ideal for the pervasion of populist ideas.

The debilitation of the Rule of Law is possibly the most relevant issue for the future of our political systems. In these pages, only two points are highlighted: firstly, the progressive weakening of the systems of control affecting democracy. Constitutional democracy consists of power being answerable to the citizens (Aragón 1987, 34–36). Constitutional democracy is the result of the balance between the principle of legality and the democratic principle. Legality is an expression of the power of the people. Once formulated, that power is subject to the Law, and laws can change, but always in accordance with following the appropriate procedures. There can be no contradiction between democracy and legality because the latter is an expression of democracy itself. From this premise, a broad system of controls exists to guarantee that public power abides by the law unconditionally.

The functioning of this model has never been perfect anywhere, and there have always been times when procedures have been respected more in some places and less in others. Over the last few years, with differences depending on the countries in question, there has been a negative trend. Two contributory factors are particularly important: on the one hand, the strength acquired by the democratic principle, in some cases, has come to be considered a supreme value. The presumed *will* of the people should be limitless. On the other, the wrongdoing of parties and leaders who, seeking to cover up their bad (or even outright illegal) practices, have debilitated the systems of control. The consequence of this is that the Rule of Law has been worn away from a double perspective. It has lost its legitimacy in favour of an erroneous understanding of the democratic principle as well as losing functionality and effectiveness. Naturally, this situation is fertile ground for a populism that bases a good part of its ideological discourse on an understanding of the democratic principle without limits while failing to respect the Rule of Law.

On the other hand, in the contemporary debate about democracy, attention must be drawn to the weakness of the Law. This is a central issue which does not usually receive too much attention. Among the topics related to this issue, first of all one should mention that the Law has weakened as an instrument of the expression of the will of the majority, and therefore as the maximum expression of democracy; along with this, secondly, the Law's ineffectiveness as a regulatory instrument, with the consequent delegitimisation of the entire system; thirdly, the disempowerment of public institutions which, without effective Law, are deprived of their main instrument of government and fourthly, the incidence of this weakness in the drawing up, formulation and effectiveness of fundamental rights. Finally, inevitably, one must refer to the impact which the new distribution of power has upon the legal system, both territorially and economically. This scenario is particularly conducive to the rise of different populisms which, on the one hand, are comfortable in *anomie* and, on the other, take advantage of the negative consequences which this situation inflicts upon the political system.

For these and other reasons, the institutional system built around the Rule of Law has been weakened. Logically, the situation is not the same in all countries, but this debilitation is sufficiently generalised to make it possible to affirm that it is a general trait of contemporary political systems; a characteristic directly linked to populisms which thrive on the confusion, fear and impotence that this erosion of classic institutional systems can bring about which exacerbate the growth and consolidation of populism. For this reason, populisms will take advantage of the damage caused by the malpractice and mistakes of others, and they will do their best to undermine the democratic system even further. If the populists come to power, then their objective will be to destroy the system, merely keeping up whichever appearances they deem necessary to legitimise themselves.

4 Consequence: The Emergence of Populism

In recent years, the emergence of political parties and groups generically described as "populists" has been of particular interest to political scientists, since these groups all share the classic features of such movements: charismatic leaders, a direct appeal to the population, the oversimplification and facile nature of their discourse, an understanding of politics within the framework of the "friend or foe"/"the populace or the elite" dialectic (Vallespín and Bascuñán 2018). Historically, there were, have been and are political parties which identify themselves with conservative or reactionary positions, and others with, supposedly, "progressive" ideas. Whichever the case may be, studying their "supposed" ideology has not always been the best way to understand them. To understand them properly, it is better to study the traits derived from their condition as populists. The phenomenon of the rise of populism was first observed with curiosity, but later analysed with concern. Populist leaders and movements have triumphed in such high places as the Presidency of the United States and Brazil or, as witnessed in the UK, the gaining of a large enough majority to allow the United Kingdom to leave the European Union, while in other places, the populists' political relevance was no longer simply anecdotic, as in the cases of separatist nationalism in Catalonia, the *Front National* in France, or the *Movimento 5 Stelle* in Italy. These are just a few examples. The breadth of these parties is much greater, and obliges us to study this phenomenon from another perspective. This chapter argues that it is more accurate to speak of contemporary politics as *populist* politics than to try and evaluate the "insertion" of populist movements within traditional democracies.

The sheer geographical extension of this phenomenon, and the fact that the triumph of these parties should not be considered as anything extraordinary, would be sufficient to allow the defence of the above thesis (Vallespín and Bascuñán 2018), but it is decisive that "traditional" political groups have become contaminated by many of the features which characterise populism and, in fact, even adopt populist politics themselves. Of course, there are differences between different countries and even among the political groups of the very same country. But the different characteristics of populism are sufficiently widespread to at least affirm that populism has profoundly polluted the whole political arena.

At this point, it is necessary to identify what are the most salient traits of populism. In particular, the exaltation of "the new" as opposed to the "old" politics, of the establishment: the idea of politics as a communicative spectacle, the reduction of public debate to a simplification incompatible with reality, the search for a radical polarisation which might eliminate political consensus. Logically, there are other important features, and we will refer to some of these, but, those mentioned are the most easily identifiable, even within parties which, in theory, align themselves with a more orthodox vision of politics.

This exaltation of "the new" is a common feature with diverse manifestations. On the one hand, the "new" distances itself from current political reality. There is no relationship between "old" and "new" politicians because they are completely different. Explicitly, populism wishes to offer a completely different model, breaking with an anachronistic and inefficient model. Along with this, these populist politicians will bring along with them new attitudes, new ways of going about political life and the use of new instruments and tools. To a large extent, one of these instruments will be communication and a different use of the opportunities which communication and information technologies offer to politics. But, similarly, the "new" will signify an almost complete rejection of current habits and rules, of culture and of traditional politics.

Coupled with the above, one can observe the consolidation of the understanding of politics as a spectacle; this is a natural consequence of the changes which have occurred in information and political communication. The new instruments of communication promote a vision of politics where "appearance" and "image" dominate up to a point where "content" is irrelevant. Contemporary politics cannot be understood if one does not pay careful attention to the changes in communication techniques. Just as when television erupted onto the scene, these changes, by themselves, allow us to speak of a "new" political era. The politics of spectacle is fertile terrain for the simple and striking messages of populism. Inevitably, this way of understanding politics favours the growth of these types of parties, but the most important thing is that no political group will be able to stop playing this game. Not only has the way of putting these populist messages across changed, but also the behaviour of political protagonists has radically transformed and homogenised, making it difficult to distinguish the "new" (populist) politicians and those from the more traditional school.

Along with these features, populism has caused a generalisation of the aforementioned policy of simplification. Complexity and nuance have been lost to the benefit of reductionist messages intended to capture the attention of an audience accustomed to "tweeting". Radical simplification is now part of the contemporary politician's manual. This manual is drafted by their image and communication consultants, and their criteria are clear. The political consumer neither has the time nor is he/she accustomed to long and reasoned arguments. One has to condense the message to the maximum degree. In this way, politics ends up creating a false world where it operates as if reality did not exist. Just when everything is more complex, when nuances are more important than ever, politics has dispensed with them, because what at first was mere communication, today has seeped into all aspects of political activity, and, once again, it is no longer possible to distinguish between populists and traditional politicians.

All of the above inevitably leads to the radicalisation of political discourse. A radicalism which rejects all that came before; the primacy of spectacle or the extreme simplification of discourse is hardly compatible with moderation and dialogue—on the contrary, confrontation is necessary. Extremism is a condition of a politics devoid of nuance and incapable of complex reasoning and, above all, this is a condition for effective communication; understanding that communication is the only important thing, the very essence of politics is sacrificed: dialogue, moderation, agreement. Colloquially speaking, confrontation "sells" more; it is more attractive than calm dialogue and potential agreements. For this reason, compromise is no longer regarded as a prime objective of political action. Once again, this trait can be observed in all political groups; after all, they all perform in the same play upon the same stage.

These are not the only features of populism to become generalised to the point of saying that we ought to start talking in terms of the *predominance* of populist politics. In first place, mention should be made also of the undervaluation of institutional demands. Although it is true that there are notable differences between different political parties, it is possible to affirm that a "lax" attitude has become generalised regarding what are known as the "formal" demands of the Rule of Law. Either an appeal for efficiency or the will of the people are arguments which are repeated to facilitate the non-compliance to such demands. Secondly, it is worth remembering a generalisation of procedures for the selection of leaders which facilitate *hyper-leadership*. Paradoxically, an appeal for internal democracy as a criterion for the selection of leaders builds strong leaderships that even undermine the dynamics of the very organisation itself. The party or movement identifies with the leader to such an extent that it is difficult to imagine that party without him/her.

Finally, one could make reference to the ideological strength of nationalism. This is a transversal characteristic of populist movements. Of course, the most salient expression of this is the proliferation of nationalist parties. But, the way nationalism increasingly contaminates traditional political parties can also be observed. This is only natural. Populism and nationalism are very closely related. They share many common characteristics:

over-simplicity, politics as a spectacle and, above all, the search for an "enemy" as a significant strategy. If populism grows, then it is inevitable that strictly nationalist groups will also grow, and those who are not nationalist will allow themselves to be influenced by this ideology.

All parties, and politics in general, have always been somewhat populist, to the extreme of it being possible to identify a certain degree of populism which is compatible with the orthodoxy of constitutional democracy. Politics has always had certain populist traits, but today things are different; isolated populist behaviour has been replaced by a general understanding of politics which one could call *populist*. There are parties which are essentially nothing more than populist, but what makes today's politics unique is that there are hardly any parties where a populist vision and strategy does not predominate. The parties evolve towards strong movements and leaderships which the citizens can relate to directly. Political parties turn politics into a battle between "*goodies* and *baddies*" and, in general, politics is reduced to the way it is communicated, to the extent that it is possible to say one thing today and quite the opposite tomorrow. If mistakes are made, then politicians are "unrepentant"—real content did not matter yesterday or today, only the "good-timing" of the message. This era of populism is consolidating itself as a time devoid of politics (Innerarity 2015, 215–217). It could be said that traditional politics has disappeared and a new political model is emerging.

Bibliography

Aragón Reyes, Manuel. "El control como elemento inseparable del concepto de Constitución." *Revista Española de derecho Constitucional, no. 19*(1987): 15–52.

Blanco Valdés, R. "Profesionalización de los partidos, selección inversa de sus élites y desafección política." In *La reforma del Estado de partidos*. Edited by Carlos Garrido Lopez and Eva Sáenz Royo, 19–38. Madrid: Marcial Pons, 2016.

Bustos Gisbert, Rafael. *Calidad democrática. Reflexiones constitucionales desde la teoría, la realidad y el deseo*. Madrid: Marcial Pons, 2017.

Cebrián Zazurca, Enrique, *Deliberación en Internet*, Zaragoza: Fundación Manuel Giménez Abad, 2012.

Dogan, Mattei, ed. *Political mistrust and the Discrediting of politicians*. Leiden: Brill Nijhoff, 2005.

García Pelayo, Manuel. *El estado de partidos*. Madrid: Alianza, 1986.

Guillén López, Enrique. *Repensando la forma de gobierno. Constitucionalismo, democracia y parlamentarismo en contextos posnacionales*. Madrid: Marcial Pons, Ediciones Jurídicas y Sociales, 2019.

Innerarity, Daniel. *La política en tiempos de indignación*. Barcelona: Galaxia Gutemberg, 2015.
Innerarity, Daniel. *Una teoría de la democracia compleja*. Barcelona: Galaxia Gutemberg, 2020.
Kelsen, Hans. *Esencia y valor de la democracia*. Madrid: Labor, 1934.
Muñoz Machado, Santiago. *Prólogo a La sociedad menos injusta*. Madrid: Iustel, 2019.
Schmitt, Carl. *El concepto de los político*. Madrid: Alianza Editorial, 1999.
Sartori, Giovanni. *Homo videns: la sociedad teledirigida*. Madrid: Taurus, 2002.
Torreblanca, Ignacio. *Asaltar los cielos. Podemos o la política después de la crisis*. Madrid: Debate, 2015.
Tudela Aranda, José. "El derecho a decidir y el principio democrático." *Teoría y Realidad Constitucional, no.37*, (2016): 477–498.
Tudela Aranda, José. "La democracia contemporánea. Mitos, velos y (presuntas) realidades." *Revista Española de Derecho Constitucional* 111, (2017): 25–152.
Vallespín, Fernando and Bascuñán, Máriam. *Populismos*. Madrid: Alianza Editorial, 2018.
Villaverde Menéndez, Ignacio. "Comentario al artículo 20 de la Constitución." In *Comentarios a la Constitución española*. Edited by Miguel Rodríguez-Piñero and Maria Elisa Casas Baamonde, 581–625. Madrid: Ministerio de Justicia-Fundación Wolters-Kluwer, 2018.

Populisms, Constitutions, Constitutional Courts, and Constitutional Democracy

Giovanni de Ghantuz Cubbe

1 Introduction

In the present day, populist parties and movements are becoming increasingly stronger (Hawkins et al. 2019; Heinisch et al. 2017; Mudde 2004). As many scholars have already emphasised, they share important common features. They understand 'the people' as a homogeneous entity, foster a dualistic vision of society (the people against the corrupted elite), and, in the case of right-wing populism, hold nationalist and nativist stances and tend towards authoritarianism (Hawkins et al. 2019; Mudde 2017). Because of their similarities, they are usually seen as 'members' of the same party-family or movement-family (de Ghantuz Cubbe 2021), and populism is often interpreted as a homogeneous phenomenon or even as a kind of 'spectre' or 'shadow' crossing modern democracy (Arditi 2019; Ionescu and Geller 1969). This interpretation has always offered and still offers a fundamental contribution to the research on populism, but at the same

G. de Ghantuz Cubbe (✉)
Institute of Political Science, TU Dresden, Dresden, Germany
e-mail: giovanni.de_ghantuz_cubbe@tu-dresden.de

J. M. Castellà Andreu, M. A. Simonelli (eds.), *Populism and Contemporary Democracy in Europe*,
https://doi.org/10.1007/978-3-030-92884-1_3

time, brought many scholars to play down the importance of the 'varieties of populism' (Blokker 2019; Gidron and Bonikowski 2013; Tushnet 2019) as well as that of the different contexts within populists act (Heinisch and Mazzoleni 2017). Indeed, stressing the common features of populism risks not adequately taking into consideration its various forms.[1] As an example: if one affirms that the contraposition between the 'elite' and 'the people' is a central attribute of populism, this does not help us to understand concretely what 'elite' means in the ideology of a certain populist party, nor what this party means when it refers to 'the people'. In this sense, as Reinhard Heinisch and Oscar Mazzoleni write,

> 'the people' may refer to 'us in general', to 'natives' but not all nationals or citizens, to 'the people of the heartland' but not of the metropolis, to so-called 'genuine citizens', or to the 'common folk', to 'hardworking tax payers' or to certain kinds of voters alluded to in political campaigns. (Heinisch and Mazzoleni 2017, 108)

This problem—that is to say, the insufficiency of the focus on central, general attributes and the secondary focus on specific, contextual features—affects not only the analysis of populism itself but also that of the relation between populism and constitutionalism (Bugaric 2019, 390.). For a long time, the literature has been stressing the existence of a fundamental tension between the former and the latter (Arato 2017; Mudde 2013; Urbinati 2014). According to Nadia Urbinati, for example, populists seek to "implement an agenda whose main and recognisable character is hostility to liberalism and the principles of constitutional democracy, from minority rights, division of power, and a pluriparty system" (Urbinati 2014, 129). Now, even accepting this interpretation and the centrality of the idea of 'a fundamental tension', one cannot disregard that too often the *specific forms* of this tension have been placed in the background (de Ghantuz Cubbe 2021) and that the research on "the interrelation between populism and constitutionalism still lacks a more systematic and comparative analysis" (Blokker 2019, 332.). In other words: without a differentiated analysis, the idea of a fundamental tension between populism and constitutionalism risks being analytically incomplete, because it does not

[1] For example, Isaiah Berlin (1968) famously affirmed "that a single formula to cover all populism everywhere will not be very helpful".

help us to specify what the concrete modalities of this tension look like and precisely what effects they produce.

Some scholars have tried to solve this problem by categorising the different forms which constitutionalism may take under the influence of authoritarian and/or populist actors—for example, authoritarian, abusive, and populist constitutionalism (Blokker 2020; Ginsburg et al. 2013; Halmai 2019; Landau 2013). However, the challenge of finding a systematic approach for the description of the concrete interplay, frictions, and conflicts between populism and constitutionalism remains open.

This chapter aims to revisit the analytical contraposition between populism and constitutionalism, holding to the idea of a fundamental tension but suggesting a differentiated methodology to investigate its specific forms. The approach is interdisciplinary, strongly connected to research on populism by political scientists, to institutional studies, and to constitutional theory. The first section discusses the merits and the limits of the analytical dichotomisation of populism/constitutionalism and argues for the introduction of a differentiated approach. The second section investigates the relation between populisms and constitutions, whilst the third analyses the different forms of interaction between populisms and constitutional courts. Finally, in the conclusions the differentiated methodology is combined with the idea of an axis between 'populism vs. anti-populism', which may also be useful for the analysis of possible future scenarios for constitutional democracy.

2 Populism and Constitutionalism

The concept of populism brings us back to that of people's sovereignty. Populism considers the people as the only legitimate holder of sovereignty and, therefore, aims at accentuating and radicalising the majority principle and puts the system of representation under strong pressure (Vorländer 2011, 2019). In this sense, it promotes a direct relationship between the people and the populist leader (Turato 2018)—the latter incarnating the will of the former—and condemns every institution, party, politician, or intellectual who interposes in this relationship. Such characteristics—it is almost superfluous to mention it—do not fit with constitutionalism, at least in its liberal form. Constitutionalism, indeed, can exist only through its system of checks and balances (which populism rejects and/or strongly wants to alter), through the limitation of people's sovereignty, the protection of minorities, and the system of representation (de Ghantuz Cubbe

2021; Mudde 2013; Tarchi 2019). Hence, a general conclusion is undeniable: a fundamental tension exists between populism and (liberal) constitutionalism. This conclusion has three fundamental merits:

- It identifies the central core of populism and the central core of (liberal) constitutionalism.
- It underlines that populism, in order to affirm itself, may modify, change, exploit (Blokker 2020; Mudde 2013), or, in radical cases, even overturn (liberal) constitutionalism.
- Consequently, it implies that (liberal) constitutionalism should defend itself from populist attacks.

That being said, the analytical dichotomisation between populism and constitutionalism is limited. Jan-Werner Müller states very clearly that the relationship between populism and constitutionalism "is far more complicated than clichéd invocations of Rousseau and the general will, or simple schemas that put populism on the side of democracy and constitutionalism on the side of liberalism, would suggest" (Müller 2017) Similarly, Paul Blokker affirms that "the relationship between constitutionalism and populism is [...] more complex than a straightforward dichotomic view would allow for" (Blokker 2020, 115). We can identify two central reasons for this.

Firstly, there is not just one populism. On the contrary, populism is a complex phenomenon with various manifestations, which are tightly connected to the social context in which populists act (Sztompka 2016). This is why in recent years some literature has progressively branched away from an 'essentialist' interpretation of populism (Heinisch and Mazzoleni 2017), increasingly referencing *populisms* (in plural), *varieties of populism*, or directly *populist parties* (Blokker 2019; Tushnet 2019). By 'pluralising' populism, we obtain important advantages; on the theoretical level, talking about *populisms* makes it easier to take into account important differentiations such as those between left- and right-populism (Backes 2020; de Ghantuz Cubbe 2020a; Manow 2018; Rosanvallon 2011), inclusionary and exclusionary populism (Mudde and Rovira Kaltwasser 2011), or populism of the government and populism of the opposition (Akkerman 2017; Fournier 2018; Turato 2018). On the empirical level, it permits us to differentiate between the various populist forces and not to confuse the impact of, for example, Donald Trump on USA constitutionalism and his attacks against the Supreme Court with the populist rhetoric of a leader like Luigi Di Maio in Italy (Five-Star-Movement) (Biorcio and Natale 2018; de Ghantuz Cubbe 2020a), whose agenda and impact regarding Italian constitutionalism and the Italian Constitutional Court are definitely marginal. In conclusion: "not all populists approach constitutionalism in the same way" (Rovira Kaltwasser 2013, 1).

Secondly, there is also not just one constitutionalism that populists may have an impact on. On the contrary, constitutionalism presents itself differently according to different historical, social, cultural, and political contexts (Mongardini 2011, 245), and even if its fundamental characteristics are shared by all modern (western) democracies, we cannot avoid the fact that different constitutionalisms (Viola 2009), different 'paths' of constitutionalism (Grimm 1991; Preuß 1994; Rehberg 2008, 58; Vorländer 2004), and/or different 'constitutional cultures' exist (Wyrzykowski 2001), on which is unlikely that populisms will always have the same effect. Moreover, each constitution—the central pillar of each form of constitutionalism—has its own specificity or 'typus': "every constitution contains the experience and the culture of a people as well as the ideal elements [and goals] expressed from [a certain] society" (Mongardini 2011, 245). Furthermore, as Hans Vorländer affirms: "Constitutions are always embedded in cultural and historical contexts; therefore, they are implanted in a political culture, from which the rank, position, and regulatory content of the constitution emerge" (Vorländer 2004).

Hence, the necessity of a differentiated approach. However, a central question arises: *how do we combine the idea of a fundamental tension between populism and constitutionalism and the necessity to consider all its different forms and empirical manifestations?* In order to find an answer, one may refer to the idea of populist constitutionalism. As Paul Blokker writes:

> While it seems true that a general skepticism towards liberal constitutionalism and the rule of law can be found among many populists, it equally appears correct to sustain that populists are increasingly engaging with constitutionalism as a discourse and practice of power [...] Populists, in particular once in power, engage with the constitution in a variety of ways, not least in order to safeguard and perpetuate their political power in the name of a 'pure' people. (Blokker 2020, 115)

In this context,

(a) "it appears that populist constitutional projects cannot be entirely reduced to a mere dismantling of constitutional democracy, but also include forms of constitution-making, for better or worse" (Blokker 2020). This is the reason that Blokker affirms—as we already mentioned above—that a simple dichotomic view does not allow for the complex relationship between constitutionalism and populism.
(b) However—and this is a central point—he also admits that the "populist-constitutional mindset potentially leads to a wider erosion of liberal-constitutional ideals" (Blokker 2020).

To some, this may look like a contradiction. However, it is not. On the contrary, it connects differentiation and general perspective: on the one side (a), Blokker (and all the literature about populist constitutionalism), by adjectivising constitutionalism as 'populist' and taking into account the various 'populist constitution-making experiences', challenges the dichotomisation of populism and constitutionalism (not least, through a differentiated, comparative approach). On the other side (b), he focuses on the long-term consequences of such experiences and on the fundamental distance between populism and liberal constitutionalism. By doing so, he 'regains' the afore-challenged dichotomisation by applying it as an *analytical background* and/or as an *analytical instrument for possible scenarios.*

Hence, we can draw an important conclusion: the analytical dichotomisation between populism and constitutionalism can and should be combined, as Blokker shows, with a differentiated approach and—on the other side of the coin—the differentiated approach can and should occur *within the framework* of the fundamental tension. There is no reason to separate these two perspectives. On the contrary, one fulfils the other. While the differentiation specifies the dichotomisation, the latter allows the subsumption of the differences in a general perspective.

3 Populisms and Constitutions

An important step to fostering a differentiated analysis consists of 'decomposing' constitutionalism and focusing on its pillars. Let us begin with constitutions. The relation between populisms and constitutions is a complex one. Populist forces act in a variety of ways and effect different consequences on constitutions. Moreover, constitutions have varied characteristics, parts, functions, and resistance capacity against populist attacks. In this context, affirming, for example, that a certain populist party affects, attacks, or instrumentalises a constitution means virtually nothing, if one does not specify what the attack consists of and what aspects of the constitution are under attack. Hence, it is necessary to distinguish some levels of analysis to categorise the different forms of populist impact on constitutions.

(1) It is helpful to refer to the classical division between formal and material constitutions (Mortati 1958; Mortati 1998). While the first term refers to the constitution as a written document and namely to its textuality, the second one indicates the extra-textual dimension, that is to say, the link between the constitution itself and the social and political order, the evolving constitutional interpretation, and the fundamental role of the political institutions themselves.[2] Between the formal and the material constitution there is (or there should be) a permanent connection (Mortati 1958; Pinelli 2010), which, however, can be weakened or—in radical cases—even broken off.[3] Now, all this is fundamental for the analysis of the impact populist forces may have on constitutions. Indeed, populists can *(a)* affect the formal constitution; *(b)* affect the material constitution; and

Chart 1 Populist strategies to impact constitutions

Impact levels	*Strategy*
Formal level	– Textual changes through constitutional reform
Material level	– Material changes following from textual changes – Alteration of constitutional practices, customs, and conventions
Interconnection between formal and material level	– Alteration through formal or material changes – Political delegitimisation of the judicial and political institutions

[2] As Julian Arato (2012) writes: "The constitutional text, as important as it may be, is only part of the overall constitution, along with other important legal norms, interpretations, settled practices, and constitutional customs or conventions that are developed during the life of the constitution through a variety of formal and informal means".

[3] One simple example of a distancing between formal and material constitutions is desuetude: "Some norms in the document may fall into desuetude, while others are expanded by legislative, executive, and judicial bodies to mean all sorts of things – often totally unanticipated by the text and sometimes at cross-purposes with other aspects of the document". Arato (2012, 636).

(c) affect the connection between formal and material constitution (see Chart 1).

In the first case (*a*), populist actors plead directly for the change of a specific part, section, or article of the constitution; that is to say, they will act directly within the textual dimension. Should the populist attempt be successful, a constitutional reform will follow. In the second case (*b*), populists consider the idea of interfering with the material structures, institutions, and conventions that surround the constitution. As opposed to the first case, a constitutional reform here is not essential for populists.[4] Finally, in the third case (*c*), populists may attempt to directly change the relationship between formal and material constitutions. Even if a change in this sense may be implicit both in case *a* and *b*, it is still necessary to separate this third situation analytically. Let us imagine, for example, the political campaign of an opposition populist party attacking the interpretation of the constitution from a constitutional court, or affirming that all political and judicial institutions of the 'elite' are traitors of the constitution. This party being in the opposition and not having any power to produce constitutional changes, its campaign would not have any effect either on the formal or on the material constitution, but may *politically* affect their relationship by weakening the connection between the constitutional text and its application/interpretation by the political and judicial institutions. In this sense, while the first two levels always affect the juridical dimension, the third one may, in contrast, not involve it.

(2) Constitutions have different kinds of 'elasticity' (Lanchester 2011; Amato 2016). According to Lanchester, the 'vitality' of a constitutional text lies on the one hand in the way it is 'felt' by the political institutions—which, we can say, might be more or less attached to it—and on the other hand, on its own capacity to correspond to the needs and goals of the society it was written for (Lanchester, 41–42). In simple words, we may affirm that the concept of elasticity refers to the capacity of a constitutional text to support forms of 'stress' on these two levels (e.g. forms of detachment from the political class or too rapid social change provoking a tension between formal and material constitution). It is important to underline that elasticity has limits. Should the constitutional stress be too strong, a breaking point will be reached. According to Lanchester, the Italian situation offers a good example of this. After the crisis of 1993/94

[4] That is to say, material changes (*b*) *can* occur due to textual changes deriving from a constitutional reform (*a*), but they may also exist without variations in the constitutional text.

(de Ghantuz Cubbe 2020b), as all the parties that founded the Italian Constitution disappeared and the consequent 'infinite transition' of the political system destabilised the whole constitutional regime, the Constitution suffered a severe blow:

> [… In Italy,] the end of the transition has never come and [there is the risk] that this situation will overturn the original constitutional system with a new form and with substantial new content. There are, indeed, increasingly clear phenomena of constitutional enervation, which create the fear of a breaking point. (Lanchester 2011, 5)

Moreover:

> I support the thesis that the new political forces at the basis of the political-constitutional system that originated from the […] crisis of 1993–94 […] do not seem to recognize themselves unconditionally in the […Constitution] of 1948, as on the contrary the […previous] ones […] that existed until 1994 did. I affirm also that this situation weakened the capacity of the constitutional text to be the basis of the implementation of the legal order. (Lanchester 2011, 39–40)[5]

The concept of constitutional elasticity and that of constitutional stress are fundamental to consider when we deal with populism. This is very clear in a comparative perspective. If one compares, for example (as Lanchester does), the Italian situation with the American one, he or she will notice that while in Italy the Constitution almost reached its breaking point because of the crisis of 1993/1994, in the United States, not even the existence of *three* different regimes (Deferential and Republican, from the colonial period to the 1820s; Party and Democratic, from the 1830s to the 1930s; and Populist and Bureaucratic, from the 1930s to the present; Keller 2007) could alter the fundamental consensus of the political forces around the American Constitution (Lanchester 2011, 52–53) or provoke high levels of constitutional stress. In the same way, the Italian situation is completely different from the German one. In Germany, the strong attachment of the political class and the German citizens to the *Grundgesetz* and the enormous trust in the *Bundesverfassungsgericht*, as well as the general stability of the political system, permit a very low level of 'stress' for the German Constitution. Now, it is clear that eventual

[5] Both passages were translated by the author.

populist attacks against the weakened Italian constitution may have very different consequences than in the United States and in Germany. It follows that the analysis of the ways populisms affect constitutions cannot disregard a (comparative) analysis of constitutional elasticity.

(3) Finally, constitutions have different functions that populist forces may affect. According to Vorländer (2009), the first function of the constitution is the constitutive one (*konstituierende Funktion*), which consists of the foundation of the political order and its fundamental values and norms (Febbrajo 2008). The second one is the legitimising function (*legitimierende Funktion*), by which the constitution, through its presence, permanently lends legitimacy to the established order and connects it back to the moment of its foundation (Febbrajo 2008). The third function is the limitative one (*limitative Funktion*), which provides boundaries to the political power by dividing it and, by doing so, grants the balance of all constitutional institutions. The fourth function—the identity-endowing and integrative one (*indentitätsstiftende und integrative Funktion*) (Rehberg 2008, 62)—allows the citizens to strongly identify with the constitutional values through the celebration of the constitution and the remembrance of the foundation act. In this context, populists may affect one or more constitutional functions. For example, they can deny the *legitimacy* of an existing constitutional regime and argue for the foundation of a new one, as Viktor Orbán did in 2011 in Hungary by abolishing the then-existent constitution and substituting it with another one (Halmai 2018; Tóth 2012; Gomez and Leunig 2021). Moreover, they can attack the separation of power (limitative function) in order to radicalise the majoritarian principle or try to overturn the identity-endowing and integrative function of the constitution with the goal of establishing their own 'constitutional culture'.

In conclusion, it can be argued that the combination of these three levels of analysis presents three central advantages. First, it makes it easier to specify the different consequences that populists may have on constitutions. Second, it allows for viewing populism as a force acting *from within* the constitutional world and having available constitutional tools to reach its aims (this is the case, for example, in populist governments, which have constitutional and legal instruments to initiate constitutional reform). Third, in case of a populist attack on the constitution, it makes it easier to observe the different resistance capacities of the various constitutions and to elaborate targeted strategies of constitutional defence.

4 Populisms and Constitutional Courts

Populisms and constitutional courts are not good friends. Usually, populists see constitutional courts as a part of the 'corrupted elite' that limits the people's sovereignty. As Andrew Arato emphasises:

> By identifying the genuine people's will with his or its own, the populist leader or group inevitably sees the intervention of courts as linked to the secret work of an oligarchical enemy [...]. Once the will is incarnated, there is no reason to move to higher levels of legitimacy and to alternative procedures to test whether it is a genuine democratic will. (Arato 2017)

Moreover, populists claim a centralisation of political power for themselves, in order to foster the radicalisation of the majoritarian principle—even at the cost of minorities. Constitutional courts, which grant the division of power, protect democracy from the abuse of the majoritarian principle, and defend minorities, contrast with populism (de Ghantuz Cubbe 2021). However, a detailed analysis is worth delving into in order to understand the complex interaction between populists and constitutional courts.

Let us focus on the institutional authority of constitutional courts and elaborate a systematic approach for the analysis of populisms' impact on it. Constitutional courts have a particular form of authority (Brodocz 2006; Lembcke 2007); through their decisions, they can bind all other institutions to their interpretation of the constitution. In this way, they are the highest interpreters and protectors of the *Leitideen*, the goals, the values, and the norms that are contained in the constitution (Vorländer 2006). This authority, however, is not unchangeable (Brodocz 2006) and not immune from attacks. As with every form of authority, it needs to be recognised: differently from power, authority cannot exist without people who freely submit themselves to it (Arendt 1994; Lembcke 2007). Hence, it is necessary to analyse the modalities in which the courts' authority is recognised (or rejected). Following the German constitutionalist André Brodocz, we can differentiate three levels: the symbolic, the structural, and the practical (Brodocz 2006).

The first level refers to the symbolic legitimisation of the court as guardian of the constitution. The stronger the connection between the court and the constitution is perceived to be, and the more stabilised in public opinion and under the political forces the court's role as interpreter of the fundamental values and norms of the society, the higher its authority on the symbolic level (de Ghantuz Cubbe 2021). The second level refers to the structural and/or organisational dimension of the court, that is to say, its position in the judiciary system, its organisation, the extension of its competences, and the length of the offices of the judges. The higher its position in the judiciary system, the more solid its organisation and the more extended its competences, the more central and rooted is its role in the constitutional regime in which it is embedded. The third level concerns the decisions of the courts and their effects on other authorities and on public opinion (Brodocz 2006); simply put, the higher the public consensus regarding the decisions of the court, the more the latter can claim authority in practice.[6]

Even if these three levels are kept analytically separated, in reality they can strongly influence each other. For example, the structural level is fundamental for symbolic recognition (a court with restricted competences, for instance, has de facto fewer opportunities to act and to let its symbolic authority as guardian of the constitution grow) and the symbolic and structural levels strongly influence the practical one (it goes without saying that the decisions of a highly recognised court with a strong position in the judiciary system will be more difficult to challenge and attack than those of a court with weak symbolical authority and a marginal position in the judiciary system).

Now, if we also apply this categorisation of the courts' authority levels to the relationship between populist actors and the courts, we can systemise the possible ways the former can affect the latter. In this context, populists can act on the symbolic, the structural, and/or the practical level.

(1) On the symbolic level, populists can try to weaken the relationship between the court and the constitution and to delegitimise the general role of the court as guardian of the constitution. Italy is an example of this. In 2008, the Berlusconi government passed a law (the so-called Lodo Alfano) that suspended ongoing criminal proceedings against people who hold high state offices. This benefitted not least Silvio Berlusconi himself. In 2009, the Italian Corte

[6] For example, Nick Friedman (2019, 5) writes that "courts can, and sometimes successfully do, bolster their institutional strength [...] by enhancing the public's perception of their legitimacy through decisions that track the public's prevailing political mood over time". Friedman.

Costituzionale classified the Lodo Alfano as unconstitutional, which meant that the trials against Berlusconi were immediately resumed. Unsurprisingly, the latter then staged himself as the victim of a politicised judiciary that modified or overturned laws to his and his government's disadvantage. For several months, the Italian prime minister questioned the entire role of the constitutional court as guardian of the constitution: the Italian Constitutional Court was not an 'impartial guarantee organ', but a political 'fighting body of the left', which therefore could not fulfil its fundamental function (La Repubblica 2009). In a similar way, the German populist party Alternative for Germany (AfD) tried to delegitimise the entire role of the German *Bundesverfassungsgericht*. The party used a 2016 ruling of the court, in which the latter argued against a generalised headscarf ban, to accuse the court of not respecting the values of German culture and society and promoting the 'Islamization of Germany' (AfD-Landatsgsfraktion Baden-Württemberg 2016).

(2) On the structural level, populists may interfere with the structure and/or organisation of the court through constitutional reform, reduce its competences, or influence the nomination of judges. There are examples of this in Hungary and Poland. Under the right-wing populist Government of Viktor Orbán, a new constitution was adopted in Hungary in 2011 and flanked by various reforms restricting the constitutional court. This increased the influence of Orbán's Fidesz party on the appointment of constitutional judges and limited the scope of the constitutional review. In Poland in 2015, the PiS Government (Law and Justice) began a process of weakening judicial power by substituting independent judges of the Constitutional Tribunal with party loyalists. It is important here to notice the difference between the Italian populist strategy and the Hungarian and Polish ones. In the latter instances, both populist governments focused on the structural weakening of the constitutional court rather than on a symbolic delegitimisation strategy à la Berlusconi. Unlike in his case, they did not aim to delegitimise the constitutional court through a direct symbolic attack. Instead, they were concerned with getting the courts under control.

(3) On the practical level, populism deals directly with single decisions of the courts. Single decisions represent the simplest and fastest

occasions for populists to criticise a court. Through these decisions, namely, they may easily find a concrete pretext, a 'motive' to attack. This is the case of the aforementioned examples of Berlusconi in 2008 and the AfD in 2016, which both initiated their attacks starting with single decisions of the courts. These two examples indicate, moreover, to what degree the different levels of the populist attacks on the courts' authority can influence each other and result in multiple consequences. Both Berlusconi and the AfD, indeed, not only criticised the decisions themselves (practical level) but also used them to 'shift' their attacks on the whole role of the courts (symbolic level). For conciseness, Chart 2 shows the impact that a populist attack on one level may have on the others.

I tried to show that given the complexity of the populist strategies and of their consequences, it may be very reductive to assimilate them without differentiation under the same umbrella. Methodologically, the subdivision between the three levels of the courts' authority and the respective populist strategies can contribute to increasing the analytical differentiation and facilitate empirical and comparative research.

5 From Differentiation to Generalisation: Populism vs. Anti-populism?

The preceding chapters focused on the importance of a differentiated approach and tried to suggest a methodological scheme for the analysis of the relationship between populisms and constitutionalism, constitutions, and constitutional courts. At this point is thus necessary to combine such an approach with a general, more abstract perspective. As we have seen by referring to Blokker (Sect. 2), the general contraposition of populism/

Chart 2 Populist attacks against constitutional courts and their consequences

Populist attack	*Populist attack extended to other levels*	*Multiple consequences for the authority of the courts*
Symbolic	Structural and/or practical	Symbolic level And/or Structural level And/or Practical level
Structural	Symbolic and/or practical	
Practical	Symbolic and/or structural	

constitutionalism is very useful as an analytical background and/or as an analytical tool for the description of possible scenarios of constitutional democracy and its institutions. However, scholars have also underlined the importance of other perspectives, which can be particularly helpful. The theorisation of an axis between populism and anti-populism plays a central role.

Referring, among other things, to the role and the future of judicial supremacy in the United States, Richard D. Parker (1994) and later Larry D. Kramer (2004) observe the existence of a dichotomy between populism and anti-populism, which is interpreted by Parker as a 'matter of sensibility'.[7] While the populist sensibility believes in majority rule and understands "constitutional law as [simply] a set of tools enabling the expression of political will of ordinary people", the anti-populist sensibility "is wary of the release of political energy of ordinary people, and understands constitutional law as a set of mechanisms reining in the passions of the ruling majority" (González-Jácome 2017). The role of constitutional review, and in general of judicial supremacy, is strictly connected here to anti-populist sensibility: "Seeing democratic politics as scary and threatening, [... supporters of judicial supremacy] find it obvious that someone must be found to restrain its mercurial impulses, someone less susceptible to the demagoguery and shortsightedness that afflict the hoi polloi" (Kramer 2004, 1003).

Now, even if the topic Parker and Kramer deal with is very specific—especially for Kramer, who strongly focuses on the contraposition between judicial supremacy and popular constitutionalism in the history of the United States—their division of populism/anti-populism also brilliantly explains the current fundamental tension between populism, constitutions, and constitutional courts, and in addition can be analytically applied to constitutional democracy in general. Indeed, it is possible to hypothesise that in the coming decades, constitutional democracy will be stuck between the populist and anti-populist sensibility. A central question is whether and/or when one of the two 'poles' of the axis might prevail over the other. On the one hand, it is difficult at the present time to think about a predominance of the populist view; as Neil Walker affirms, "populism is [still] inherently fragile and unstable" (Walker 2018, 16). On the

[7] It should be underlined, however, that both authors do not always clearly distinguish between the terms 'popular' and 'populist', while 'populism' is used very broadly as a synonym for all instances that stand for the enforcement of popular democracy.

other hand, experiences like those in Hungary or Poland reveal to what degree populists have power in altering constitutionalism, constitutions, and constitutional courts. There is, therefore, no answer to this question. However, what we can do is observe the tension between the two poles of the axis and elaborate, when necessary, targeted strategies of constitutional defence. The idea of an axis of populism/anti-populism has the merit of being extremely flexible and adapting effectively to differentiated and comparative approaches. However, the studies addressing this topic are still limited in an important respect. The relation between populism/anti-populism has been investigated mostly under a discursive perspective (Stavrakakis 2014; Stavrakakis et al. 2018) and from a political science view (Moffitt 2018; Ostiguy 2009; Zanotti 2019), but has attracted less interest in legal science. Moreover, its concrete institutional and legal consequences have not been the object of systematic investigations. It is crucial, therefore, to focus more on an interdisciplinary approach.

6 Conclusion

Populist parties are increasingly common among governing forces and among the strongest opposition parties in modern Western democracies. They interact more and more with constitutionalism and its institutions—primarily constitutions and constitutional courts. In view of their increased importance and—in many cases—their danger to constitutional democracies (Blokker et al. 2019), it seems necessary to take a more detailed look at the specifics of this interaction. It is necessary to observe populism from the inside of constitutionalism and to adapt our analytical strategy to its changeable nature. The combination of differentiated levels of analysis presents important advantages in this context. It makes it easier to specify the impact that populists have on constitutional democracy, to bring context back into focus, and to boost comparative research. Moreover, the differentiated approach towards populisms, constitutions, and constitutional courts fosters a stronger connection between political science and legal science, at the same time requiring a deep analysis of political dynamics and their effects on the juridical order.

Bibliography

AfD-Landtagsfraktion Baden-Württemberg. "Die Islamisierung schreitet voran: Verfassungsrichter erlauben Kopftuch in Kitas." AfD-fraktion-bw.de, 2016. https://afd-fraktionbw.de/aktuelles/148/Die+Islamisierung+schreitet+voran%3A+Verfassungsrichter+erlauben+Kopftuch+in+Kitas.

Akkerman, Tjitske. "Populist Parties in Power and Their Impact on Liberal Democracies in Western Europe." In *Political Populism: a Handbook*, edited by Reinhard Heinisch, Christina Holtz-Bacha, Oscar Mazzoleni, 169–180. Baden-Baden: Nomos, 2017.

Amato, Giuliano. "L'elasticità delle costituzioni rigide". *Nomos*, 1 (2016): 1–6.

Arato, Andrew. "Populism and the Courts". *Verfassungsblog*, April 25, 2017, https://verfassungsblog.de/populism-and-the-courts/.

Arato, Julian. "Constitutionality and Constitutionalism Beyond the State: Two Perspectives on the Material Constitution of the United Nations." *International Journal of Constitutional Law* 10, no. 3 (2012): 627–659.

Arditi, Benjamin. "Il populismo come spettro della democrazia. Una risposta a Margaret Canovan." In *Anatomia del populismo*, edited by Marco Tarchi, 159–170. Frattamaggiore: Diana Edizioni, 2019.

Arendt, Hannah. *Zwischen Vergangenheit und Zukunft: Übungen im politischen Denken I.* München: Piper, 1994.

Backes, Uwe. "Einführung." *Totalitarismus und Demokratie*, 17, no. 1 (2020): 3–6.

Berlin, Isaiah. To Define Populism. The Isaiah Berlin Virtual Library 6, 1968. http://berlin.wolf.ox.ac.uk/lists/bibliography/bib111bLSE.pdf.

Biorcio, Roberto and Paolo Natale. *Il Movimento 5 Stelle: dalla protesta al governo.* Udine: Mimesis, 2018.

Blokker, Paul. "Populist Constitutionalism." In *Routledge Handbook of Global Populism*, edited by Carlos de la Torre, 113–128. London: Routledge, 2020.

Blokker, Paul. "Varieties of populist constitutionalism: The transnational dimension." *German Law Journal* 20, no. 3 (Special Issue) (2019): 332–350.

Blokker, Paul, Bojan Bugaric and Gábor Halmai. "Introduction: Populist constitutionalism: Varieties, complexities, and contradictions." *German Law Journal*, 20 no. 3 (Special Issue) (2019): 291–295.

Brodocz, André. "Die souveränen Deuter. Symbolische Voraussetzungen—instrumentelle Rahmenbedingungen—praktische Auswirkungen." In *Die Deutungsmacht der Verfassungsgerichtsbarkeit*, edited by Hans Vorländer, 95–120. Wiesbaden: Verlag für Sozialwissenschaft, 2006.

Bugaric, Bojan. "The two faces of populism: Between authoritarian and democratic populism." *German Law Journal* 20 (2019): 390–400.

de Ghantuz Cubbe, Giovanni. "Lega und Fünf-Sterne-Bewegung: Rechts- und Linkspopulismus?" *Totalitarismus und Demokratie* 17, no. 1 (2020): 45–66.

de Ghantuz Cubbe, Giovanni. "Kontinuität statt Zäsur: Die Entwicklung von Parteien und Parteiensystem in Italien nach den Parlamentswahlen von 2013 und 2018." *Zeitschrift für Parlamentsfragen* 51, no. 4 (2020b): 909–926.

de Ghantuz Cubbe, Giovanni. "Populistische Parteien und Verfassungsgerichte. Zu den Spezifika eines grundlegenden Spannungsverhältnisses." *Recht und Politik*, Beiheft 5 (2021): 110–119.

Febbrajo, Alberto. "Costituzione e cultura giuridica." In *Il senso delle Costituzioni*, edited by Carlo Mongardini, 141–168. Rome: Bulzoni, 2008.

Fournier, Théo. "From Rhetoric to Action—a Constitutional Analysis of Populism." *EUI Working Paper LAW*, no. 08 (2018).

Friedman, Nick. "The Impact of Populism on Courts: Institutional Legitimacy and the Popular Will." The Foundation for Law, Justice and Society, 2019. https://www.fljs.org/sites/www.fljs.org/files/publications/The%20Impact%20of%20Populism%20on%20Courts.pdf.

Gidron, Noam and Bart Bonikowski. "Varieties of Populism: Literature Review and Research Agenda." *Weatherhead Working Paper Series*, no. 13-0004. (2013)

Ginsburg, Tom, Zachary Elkins and James Melton. "The Content of Authoritarian Constitutions." In *Constitutions in Authoritarian Regimes*, edited by Tom Ginsburg and Alberto Simpser, 141–164. Cambridge: Cambridge University Press, 2013.

Gomez, Gabriel and Sven Leunig. "Fidesz, Liberale Demokratie und das Grundgesetz in Ungarn". In *Zeitschrift für Politikwissenschaft*, 2021. https://doi.org/10.1007/s41358-021-00297-w

González-Jácome, Jorge, "From Abusive Constitutionalism to a Multilayered Understanding of Constitutionalism: Lessons from Latin America." *International Journal of Constitutional Law* 15, no. 2 (2017): 447–468.

Grimm, Dieter. *Die Zukunft der Verfassung*. Frankfurt am Main: Suhrkamp, 1991.

Halmai, Gábor. "Illiberal Constitutionalism? The Hungarian Constitution in a European Perspective." In *Verfassungskrisen in der Europäischen Union*, edited by Stefan Kadelbach, 85–104. Baden-Baden: Nomos, 2018.

Halmai, Gábor. "Populism, authoritarianism and constitutionalism." *German Law Journal* 20 (2019): 296–313.

Hawkins, Kirk A., Ryan E. Carlin, Levente Littvay and Cristóbal Rovira Kaltwasser, ed. *The Ideational Approach to Populism. Concept, Theory, and Analysis*. London: Routledge, 2019.

Heinisch, Reinhard, Christina Holtz-Bacha and Oscar Mazzoleni, ed. *Political Populism: a Handbook*. Baden-Baden: Nomos, 2017.

Heinisch, Reinhard and Oscar Mazzoleni. "Analysing and Explaining Populism: Bringing Frame, Actor and Context back in." In *Political Populism: a Handbook*, edited by Reinhard Heinisch and Christina Holtz-Bacha and Oscar Mazzoleni, 105–122. Baden-Baden: Nomos, 2017.

Ionescu, Ghita, and Ernest Gellner. *Populism: Its Meaning and National Characteristics*. New York: Macmillan, 1969.

Keller, Morton. *America's Three Regimes: A New Political History*. Oxford: Oxford University Press, 2007.
Kramer, Larry D. "Popular Constitutionalism" *California Law Review* 92, no. 4 (2004): 959–1012.
La Repubblica. "Il premier attacca la Consulta. "Sono stanco delle ipocrisie"." Repubblica.it, 2009. https://www.repubblica.it/politica/2009/12/10/news/il_premier_attacca_la_consulta_sono_stanco_delle_ipocrisie-1822153/.
Lanchester, Fulco. *La Costituzione fra elasticità e rottura*. Milano: Giuffrè, 2011.
Landau, David. "Abusive Constitutionalism." *UC Davis Law Review* 47 (2013): 189–260.
Lembcke, Oliver W. *Hüter der Verfassung. Eine institutionentheoretische Studie zur Autorität des Bundesverfassungsgerichts*. Tübingen: Mohr Siebeck, 2007.
Manow, Philip. *Die politische Ökonomie des Populismus*. Berlin: Suhrkamp, 2018.
Moffitt, Benjamin. "The Populism/Anti-Populism Divide in Western Europe." *Democratic Theory* 5, no. 2 (2018): 1–16.
Mongardini, Carlo. *Pensare la politica: per una analisi critica della politica contemporanea*. Rome: Bulzoni, 2011.
Mortati, Costantino. *Istituzioni di diritto pubblico*. Padova: CEDAM, 1958.
Mortati, Costantino. *La Costituzione in senso materiale*. Milan: Giuffrè, 1998.
Mudde, Cas and Cristóbal Rovira Kaltwasser. "Voices of the Peoples: Populism in Europe and Latin America Compared." *Kellog Institute Working Paper*, no. 378 (2011).
Mudde, Cas. "The populist zeitgeist." *Government and Opposition* 39, no. 4 (2004): 542–563.
Mudde, Cas. *Are Populists Friends or Foes of Constitutionalism?*. The Foundation for Law, Justice and Society, 2013. https://www.fljs.org/sites/www.fljs.org/files/publications/Mudde_0.pdf.
Mudde, Cas. *The Populist Radical Right: A Reader*. London: New York: Routledge, Taylor & Francis Group, 2017.
Müller, Jan-Werner. "Populist Constitutions—A Contradiction in Terms?." Verfassungsblog, April 23, 2017. https://verfassungsblog.de/populist-constitutions-a-contradiction-in-terms/.
Ostiguy, Pierre. The High and the Low in Politics: A Two-Dimensional Political Space for Comparative Analysis and Electoral Studies. *Committee on Concepts and Methods Working Paper Series*, 35, 2009.
Parker, Richard D. "Here, the People Rule. A Constitutional Populist Manifesto." *Valparaiso University Law Review* 27, no. 3 (1994): 531–584.
Pinelli, Cesare. *Costituzione formale-costituzione materiale*. Dizionario di Storia Treccani, 2010. https://www.treccani.it/enciclopedia/costituzione-formale-costituzione-materiale_(Dizionario-di-Storia)/.
Preuß, Ulrich K. *Zum Begriff der Verfassung. Die Ordnung des Politischen*. Frankfurt am Main: Fischer-Taschenbuch Verlag, 1994.

Rehberg, Karl-Siegbert. "La costituzione come "simbolo di testo". Osservazioni teoriche nella prospettiva dell'analisi istituzionale." In *Il senso delle Costituzioni*, edited by Carlo Mongardini, 53–66. Rome: Bulzoni, 2008.

Rosanvallon, Pierre. "Penser le populisme" (Leçon inagurale au Collège de France, Paris, July 18, 2011).

Rovira Kaltwasser, Cristóbal. *Populism vs. Constitutionalism? Comparative Perspectives on Contemporary Western Europe, Latin America, and the United States.* The Foundation for Law, Justice and Society, 2013. https://ora.ox.ac.uk/objects/uuid:0b3a92d0-401b-4af8-a4bd-89afb98e7454/download_file?file_format=pdfandsafe_filename=Kaltwasser.pdf.

Stavrakakis, Yannis. "The Return of "the People": Populism and Anti-Populism in the Shadow of the European Crisis." *Constellations* 21, no. 4 (2014): 505–517.

Stavrakakis, Yannis, Giorgos Katsambekis, Alexandros Kioupkiolis, Nikos Nikisianis and Thomas Siomos. "Populism, anti-populism and crisis." Contemporary Political Theory 17, no. 3 (2018): 4–27

Sztompka, Piotr. "The "Demand Side" of Populism: The Case of Poland." In *Populism on the Rise: Democracies Under Challenge?*, edited by Alberto Marinelli, 73–92. Milan: ISPI, 2016.

Tarchi, Marco. "Che cos'è il populismo." In *Anatomia del populismo*, edited by Marco Tarchi, 17–34. Frattamaggiore: Diana Edizioni, 2019.

Tóth, Gábor Attila. *Constitution for a Disunited Nation. On Hungary's 2011 Fundamental Law.* Budapest: Central European University Press, 2012.

Turato, Fabio. *Capipopolo: leader e leadership del populismo europeo.* Roma: Castelvecchi, 2018.

Tushnet, Mark. "Varieties of Populism." *German Law Journal* 20, no. 3 (Special Issue) (2019): 382–389.

Urbinati, Nadia. *Democracy Disfigured.* Harvard: Harvard University Press, 2014.

Viola, Francesco. "Costituzione e costituzionalismi." *Iustitia* 62, no. 2 (2009): 247–255.

Vorländer, Hans. "Die drei Entwicklungswege des Konstitutionalismus in Europa." In *Die Europäische Union als Verfassungsordnung*, edited by Institut für Europäische Verfassungswissenschaften, 21–42. Berlin: Berliner Wissenschafts-Verlag, 2004.

Vorländer, Hans. "Deutungsmacht—Die Macht der Verfassungsgerichtsbarkeit." In *Die Deutungsmacht der Verfassungsgerichtsbarkeit*, edited by Hans Vorländer, 9–36. Wiesbaden: Verlag für Sozialwissenschaft, 2006.

Vorländer, Hans. *Die Verfassung: Idee und Geschichte.* Munich: Beck, 2009.

Vorländer, Hans. "The Good, the Bad, and the Ugly. Über das Verhältnis von Populismus und Demokratie—Eine Skizze." *Totalitarismus und Demokratie* 8, no. 2 (2011): 187–194.

Vorländer, Hans. "Populismus und die repräsentative Demokratie." In *Die Grammatik der Demokratie. Das Staatsverständnis von Peter Graf Kielmansegg*, edited by Ahmet Cavuldak, 227–246. Baden-Baden: Nomos, 2019.

Walker, Neil. "Populism and Constitutional Tension." *University of Edinburgh, School of Law Research Paper Series*, no. 18 (2018).

Wyrzykowski, Miroslaw. *Constitutional Cultures*. Warsaw: Institute of Public Affairs, 2001.

Zanotti, Lisa. Populist polarisation in Italian politics, 1994–2016: an assessment from a Latin American analytical perspective. PhD thesis, Universiteit Leiden, 2019. https://scholarlypublications.universiteitleiden.nl/access/item%3A2980440/view.

The Sirens' Song. When Right-Wing Populism Deals with "Democracy". The Case of the Rassemblement National in France

François Debras

1 Introduction

Historically, the literature has defined the "far right" and "right-wing populism" (hereafter RWP) as political organisations that oppose to democracy. Depending on the author considered, this opposition is institutional (RWP wants to overthrow democratic institutions) or value-driven (RWP, through the ideologies it adopts, would be incompatible with a democratic society). However, as the literature also points out, if we question the political field, RWP in its discursive dimension presents itself as the defender of democracy. Thus, in France, the *Rassemblement National*

F. Debras (✉)
Department of Political Science, University of Liège, Liège, Belgium
e-mail: francois.debras@uliege.be

J. M. Castellà Andreu, M. A. Simonelli (eds.), *Populism and Contemporary Democracy in Europe*,
https://doi.org/10.1007/978-3-030-92884-1_4

(RN) aims to "recover",[1] "restore",[2] "recapture"[3] or "protect"[4] the French democracy. In this way, the RN underlines that democracy is a fundamental principle of the French Republic. Through this rhetoric, the literature argues that this is essentially a symbolic discourse rooted in a strategy of "normalisation" of the party to make it respectable in the eyes of the voters.

I aim to further revise this assumption by asking the question: in the discourse of the RN, is "democracy" only a symbolic term, a strategic argument or—and this is our working hypothesis—is the word "democracy" also ideologically loaded? In other words, it be argued that "democracy", in populist discourse, corresponds to a symbolic argument as well as a very specific ideological corpus?

To answer this question, it is necessary to focus on the relationship between RWP and the concept of democracy as studied in the literature. Second, the approach and methodology that were selected to address this issue are presented. Third, the term "democracy" in RN speeches is examined by carrying out a lexicometric analysis before combining it with a critical discourse analysis (hereafter CDA) from a more qualitative perspective. Then this chapter deals with different functions of the term "democracy" in the RN's discourse while highlighting some of the tensions in its rhetoric. Finally, this chapter concludes by answering the following question: in the RN's discourse, is "democracy" a rhetorical argument, or does it also carry ideological values?

2 RWP and Democracy

According to Cas Mudde, the study of the far right, and also RWP, refers to a potentially normative field where personal conceptions of politics and scientific analyses are likely to collide. Thus, some researchers define RWP as the antithesis of their own political and democratic positions. However, despite this introductory reservation, one can note, within the literature, a form of consensus on the opposition between RWP and democracy (Mudde 1996).

[1] Le Pen, *La Grèce*.

[2] Murer, *La Commission Européenne*.

[3] Le Pen, *Marine Le Pen en Meeting à Metz*.

[4] Aliot, *Question n°19-00087*.

Uwe Backes defines the far right and RWP as "all political movements that aggressively oppose the most important values, institutions and operating rules of democracy" (Backes 2004, 458). In the same vein, Elisabeth Carter considers that questioning the "anti-democratic" nature of a party can call into question its categorisation as RWP (Carter 2005). More recently, Kevin Passmore pointed out that extremism, by its very "nature", is different from the "democratic spirit" (Passmore 2016). By means of a discourse analysis approach, Ruth Wodak reveals that the RN mobilises fundamentally "anti-democratic" values: racism, inequality, anti-immigration (Wodak 2013). According to Anton Shekhovtsov, this French party relies on an "anti-democratic" agenda by promoting a national preference and an ethnic vision of liberalism (Shekhovtsov 2013).

Without questioning the above elements, Jean-Yves Camus and Nicolas Lebourg argue that, in recent years, RWP has acted within the framework of representative democracy by respecting the electoral result as well as the functioning of institutions (Camus and Lebourg 2015). Much more than that, today, RWP parties employ the term "democracy" in their rhetoric. Various authors have then questioned the use of this term in the RWP's discourse. According to René Monzat, RWP presents itself as democratic in the eyes of the electorate, in that it denounces other parties or institutions that are not or insufficiently democratic (Monzat 2014). So, as Pierre-André Taguieff writes, RWP is no longer opposed to democracy. On the contrary, it aims to defend or protect democracy against immigration and Islam. Today, RWP thus comes to present themselves as the "saviours" of democracy that would be flouted by "Eurocracy" or the "traditional political system" (Taguieff 2012). These analyses are shared with Shaun Bowler, David Denemark, Todd Donovan and Duncan McDonnel, who consider that these parties "present themselves as the 'real' defenders of democracy, concerned to restore popular sovereignty, which they consider threatened by a series of elites and 'others' dangerous" (Bowler et al. 2017).

For all these previously mentioned authors, the discourse is changing—it normalises itself by moving away from its most extreme components—but the underlying ideology remains undemocratic. RWP parties would still make statements related to immigration, national identity and inequality between individuals. Thus, if RWP adopts a "democratic discourse", it does so for tactical reasons (Wieviorka 2013; Kallis 2013; Gauthier 2015; Pupovac 2015; Halikiopoulou 2018). It is a strategy of "normalisation" that aims to win votes during elections (Mondon 2014; Guillet and

Afiouni 2016). The term "democracy" would be used as a symbolic word. It would be relied upon to criticise actors (traditional parties, European Union, Islam, etc.) but would not refer to any specific political project given that RWP would be opposed to it by its nature.

Looking at Marine le Pen's statements, Cécile Alduy and Stéphane Wahnich claim that the RN president adapts the party's speech by using "sweet and republican words", such as the term "democracy". Marine Le Pen uses this term more frequently than her father, Jean-Marie Le Pen, did in the past (2% against 0.9%). This is a normalisation whose objective would be to move away from the traditional discourse of the French RWP. Nevertheless, in Cécilé Alduy and Stéphane Wahnich's opinion, this "evolution" is not a "revolution". In the RN's speech—for Jean-Marie Le Pen as well as for Marine Le Pen—democracy is not "an absolute value but has more a practical representation". In this way, the authors conclude that the term "democracy" is purely "cosmetic" (Alduy and Wahnich 2015, 51).

As has already been argued, in the context of this chapter, this observation will be questioned through a study of the ideological value of the term "democracy" in the discourse of RWP, more specifically, in the current RN rhetoric.

3 Approach and Methodology

According to Christian Le Bart, each political party have an ideology characterised by a discourse that evokes actors, enemies, memory and values (Le Bart 2003). Accordingly, discourse analysis is a central element of the study of politics. In the context of this chapter, this method is adopted and "Discourse" is here defined as the addition of a text and its context structured by an enunciation system (Van Dijk 2001; Maingueneau 2016). By applying CDA, we concur with Stefan Titscher and Johannes Angermüller—among others—who takes the view that discourse must be studied as a tool or as a mode of access to intentions, strategies or ideologies (Titscher 2000; Angermüller 2007). Thus, discourse is in this chapter also considered as a "social practice" (Fairclough and Wodak 1997; Krzyzanowski 2010). Also, it is worth stressing that, whilst CDA encompasses multiple approaches, currents, and fields of study, they all consist of the systematic and explicit analysis of the various structures and strategies of different levels of a text in its context (Van Dijk 2001). For these reasons, CDA seems relevant to the research question on the use of the term "democracy" in the discourse of RWP.

The present case study has to meet a number of criteria. First, the party studied has to be unanimously regarded as a member of RWP. It must also share a desire to influence the political system not only through its participation in elections but also through its presence inside institutions. In addition to these considerations, two other remarks have to be made: one practical, that is related to the knowledge of the language necessary to study a discourse; the other theoretical, namely concerning the relevance of the selected case. In this light, the choice of the RN as a case study is fully justified, as the RN is a political party historically categorised as "far right" or as "RWP" (Wieviorka 2013; Gauthier 2015; Jamin 2016). Besides, it should be noted that, since the nomination of Marine Le Pen to the presidency in 2011, the party has begun a "normalisation" process of its rhetoric by removing any reference to anti-Semitism and early twentieth-century authoritarian regimes and by integrating ideas of secularism, state of law, gender equality and democracy (Pelinka 2013). From an electoral point of view, the increase in its election results, as well as its presence in the institutions, led Pelinka to consider that, within the RWP, there would be no equivalent of the RN (Pelinka 2013).

For this research, all the discourses of the RN available on its websites between 1 January 2015 and 31 December 2018 have been analysed. This choice seems pertinent for various reasons. First, according to Cas Mudde, a party's discourses have the advantage of being publicly validated (Mudde 2000). In addition, these sources, unlike newspaper articles, are targeted at a community of individuals who share a sense of belonging to the same world of meanings and values. In view of the gap that may exist between communication and political action, it has been necessary to diversify the speakers and media and to extend the period of time considered. Speeches change according to the audience and the period of time. Varying types, audiences, and time periods make it possible to have a broader vision of the party's ideology and to identify the differences that may appear (Pauwels 2011).

Regarding the origin of the sources, Fabienne Greffet underlines that the Internet is no longer a simple tool for disseminating information but a central platform for mobilisation, activation, and promotion. In her view, party websites are "essential media outlets" (Greffet 2011). Dominique Cardon affirms that the websites of political parties constitute "central authorities" in the distribution of their camp's links (Cardon et al. 2011). As for the RN, Alexandre Dézé explains that the party website is the central medium for its communication, where each event is commented upon, each representative presented and each action explained (Deze 2011).

Finally, it is worth specifying that this is a two-step analysis. First, a lexicometric approach studies a document based on a word count. It "searches" what the document contains while proposing a "total" and "objective" mode of exploitation of the data (Mucchielli 2006). The research seeks to identify all the documents in which the term "democracy" occurs and to classify them according to two variables: the type of discourse and the time period. Second, CDA aims to contextualise these documents. It examines how a specific rhetoric is used and in which particular contexts. According to Constanza Ihnen and John Richardson, "language is a social practice which, like all practices, is dialectically linked to the contexts of its use" (Ihnen and Richardson 2013, 234). CDA is related to the research question on the term "democracy" within the discourse of RWP since, according to its theorists, any discourse is part of an ideology, the latter can be identified and analysed through the context of the enunciation of the discourse, the genre, the speaker, the public, the themes broached and its objectives (Fowler and Kress 1979; Titscher 2000; Wodak and Meyer 2001). For the present research, some of the discourses of the RN that contain the term "democracy" are presented and assessed according to the "functions" given to the term "democracy". In addition, some of the tensions that may exist in the party's rhetoric are also highlighted in order to gain a more accurate understanding of how its members use the term "democracy".

4 The Case of the "*RN*"

4.1 Lexicometric Approach

Out of the 3460 documents published on the RN website (between 1 January 2015 and 31 December 2018), the lemma "democracy" appears 681 times in 350 documents.[5]

[5] "a-démocratique" (1), "anti-démocrate" (1), "anti-démocratique" (46), "démocrate" (20), "démocratie" (378), "démocratique" (216), "démocratiquement" (11), "démocratisation" (2), "démocratiser" (2), "non-démocratique" (3) and "post-démocratique" (1). In addition, the term is used in 34 quotations, 11 names (the "Democratic Party" in the USA, the "Slovenian Democratic Party", the "Swedish Democratic Party", the "Democratic Republic of the Congo" and the "Democratic Republic of Vietnam") and one place name ("*le Palais de la Démocratie*").

The number of occurrences of the lemma "democracy" varies according to two parameters: the type of speech and the time period. This lemma is proportionally more often used in types initially intended for a wider audience, that is to say, press conferences and speeches have a much higher ratio than any other type of documents (announcement, press release, intervention, etc.).[6]

	Occurrences of the lemma	*Number of documents with the lemma*	*Total documents of this type*	*Ratio*
144 commitments	/	/	3	/
Announcement	17	3	36	0.08
Press release	415	260	2622	0.10
Press conference	18	3	7	**0.43**
Speech	129	26	42	**0.62**
Headline of an elected	/	/	4	/
Intervention	31	17	425	0.04
Open letter	1	1	1	1
Not classified	/	/	3	/
Photo	/	/	90	/
Reportage	1	1	1	1
Tribune	69	39	226	0.17

Occurrences also vary according to the time period. The lemma appears proportionally more often during election periods. This is the case for April 2017 (presidential election campaign) and December 2015 (regional election campaign).

	J	*F*	*M*	*A*	*M*	*J*	*J*	*A*	*S*	*O*	*N*	*D*	
Ratio	0.02	0.14	0.15	0.12	0.12	0.18	0.18	0.06	0.06	0.12	0.08	0.13	2018
Total of documents during the month	63	65	65	84	83	95	50	33	83	75	87	54	
Number of documents with the lemma	1	9	10	10	10	10	9	2	5	9	7	7	

(*continued*)

[6] These documents are categorised by the RN on its website.

(continued)

	J	*F*	*M*	*A*	*M*	*J*	*J*	*A*	*S*	*O*	*N*	*D*	
Ratio	0.08	0.12	0.16	**0.19**	0.10	0.13	0.03	0.15	0.08	0.08	0.10	0.05	2017
Total of documents during the month	53	51	61	28	30	39	28	13	50	78	83	37	
Number of documents with the lemma	4	6	10	5	3	5	1	2	4	6	8	2	
Ratio	0.13	0.12	0.09	0.12	0.12	0.14	0.16	0.05	0.14	0.11	0.04	0.04	2016
Total of documents during the month	87	112	114	125	94	91	44	39	74	74	51	44	
Number of documents with the lemma	11	13	10	15	11	13	7	2	10	8	2	2	
Ratio	0.05	0.09	0.11	0.07	0.11	0.08	0.11	0.04	0.14	0.09	0.05	**0.21**	2015
Total of documents during the month	90	103	110	91	93	108	98	47	96	124	106	57	
Number of documents with the lemma	5	9	12	6	10	9	11	2	13	11	5	12	

These first quantitative data allow me to affirm that the lemma "democracy" is more often employed in types of discourse initially intended for large audiences and during electoral campaigns. Teun Pauwels' consideration on the variations in discourse according to audiences and periods (2011) is here empirically confirmed (Pauwels 2011). As the literature claims, it could therefore be argued that the term "democracy" has a symbolic charge, that it is used in specific places and at specific times in order to catch the voter's attention. However, on the basis of the present approach, this statement would be meaningless if we did not question the semantic environment and the situational context in which the discourse is held. To study the lemma "democracy" in the rhetoric of the RN by using CDA allows to understand the use of the term and find out whether it is a rhetorical argument or ideologically structured or even both.

4.2 CDA

The above lexicometric analysis highlights that the term "democracy" is more often used during election campaigns and in political speeches.

During the 2017 French presidential election campaign, for instance, Marine Le Pen attacked other politicians in a speech. She considers them as "anti-democratic" (*example 1*):

> François Bayrou, Jean-Christophe Lagarde, … These experts in electoral negotiations, these guardians of the temple of old politics, of tricks, of apparatus arrangements, who ask to pay for their support. Be lucid about the role of these old men: they are here to arrange the distribution of posts; they pay themselves in legislative constituencies […] That is the reality! That is the political scam we do not want anymore. Where is the government project? Where is the sincerity of political commitment? Where are these people's values? […] The system, in reality, does everything to try to survive. Have no doubt, they use all means, even illegal, immoral, anti-democratic, anti-republican. But against the Left of money, against the Right of money, against this greedy system, we are campaigning for the French people.[7]

Marine Le Pen denounces a "system" and politicians who have no project or value, who only want to "survive" and enrich themselves by using different methods considered as "anti-democratic", "anti-republican" or "illegal". As such, the *Front Républicain* is more than once judged to be an "anti-democratic" practice.[8] The attack is both general since it concerns the "system" and personal when it refers to François Bayrou and Jean-Christophe Lagarde. The expressions "that is the reality" and "no doubt" show that this "system" lies to the French. In her dichotomous speech, Marine Le Pen stands out herself from the other parties by working for the people. By protesting against the "system", Marine Le Pen campaigns "for the French people". The RN slogan during the campaign was "In the name of the people". The RN, unlike other political parties, is said to have a programme, to act according to values and wishes for

[7] Le Pen, *Discours de Marine Le Pen à Châteauroux.*

[8] Bay, *Elections départementales.*

renewal, and this in the name of the people, in the name of the Republic, in the name of democracy. The speech is built around the presentation of two points of view, one demonised, the other incensed.

This same rhetoric can be found in another criticism from Marine Le Pen, this time against the director of *La Voix du Nord*, a media organisation (*example 2*):

> You thought it appropriate to devote two full pages of your newspaper, announced in front page, twice to calling for a vote against me in the regional elections. You do so without even giving me the floor, which already has a long way to go in terms of your professional ethics and the particular conception of democracy that seems to animate you.[9]

Marine Le Pen indirectly reminds us of the need for a press organisation to remain neutral. Hence, by not giving the president of the RN the opportunity to express herself and respond to her opponents, *La Voix du Nord* does not respect democracy. Marine Le Pen thus delivers an attack on the newspaper director's personal ethics as well as her biased and partisan conception of democracy. Again, the attack is of two kinds, both private and political. In general, criticism about the media and journalists is recurrent in the RN's discourse. It mainly concerns the lack of neutrality and the failure of pluralism by removing the RN from debates.[10] In this manner, the RN presents itself as a victim, as politicians who are not given the right to express themselves, who are refused a chance to express their views.

Examples 1 and 2 show that, in the RN's discourse, "democracy" is used as a rhetorical argument. In the party's use of "democracy", it is a discursive tool to denounce what is not at all or not sufficiently democratic in the nature or actions of political opponents. The word "democracy" is therefore a discursive argument. One can find this "democracy argument" deployed against other actors such as, for example, left-wing movements—described as "violent", "anti-patriotic", "anti-democratic"[11]—but also, in a recurrent way, against the European Union—characterised as "tyrannical", "totalitarian", "anti-democratic"[12]—or the European

[9] Le Pen, *Nous demandons un débat*.

[10] Collard, *Proposition de Loi*; Jacobelli, *Sous-Représentation du RN*.

[11] De Saint Just, *Marianne de Fontenay*.

[12] Le Pen, *Discours de Marine Le Pen à l'Université d'Oxford*; Le Pen, *Discours de Marine Le Pen à Châteauroux*; Le Pen, *Réunion Publique de Marine Le Pen à Mirande*.

Commissioners—depicted as "unknown", "ignorant", "subject to banks", "disconnected".[13] For these actors, the RN rhetoric is constructed in the same way. The "democracy argument" aims mainly to point the finger at political opponents, to criticise their programmes and practices and, finally, to highlight the differences between them and the RN. The procedure is also symbolic and normative in that it makes it possible to draw a line between the "good" and the "bad", the "right" and the "wrong".

The "democracy argument" isn't just a tool that is used to attack opponents. The "democracy argument" is also used to defend the party. To illustrate this, let us quote a statement made by Marine Le Pen in July 2018. At that time, the RN had to deal with the seizing of part of its public endowment ordered by two judges in the "parliamentary assistants case"—party members were suspected of having hired, with European funds, assistants who worked for the party without working on European issues. Marine Le Pen declared: (example 3)

> This is an issue that concerns all citizens because it involves democracy. It also concerns all parties. If confirmed, this decision would set a formidable precedent for public life because sooner or later there will be judges to continue to twist the law and challenge legal funding of other political movements. There is no worse dictatorship than those of judges. They have, by the powers vested in them, the possibility of ruining you, imprisoning you, and, in the event of error, unjustly and often irreparably tarnishing your reputation […] We are not asking for preferential treatment but at least the treatment of any litigant.[14]

Throughout the speech entitled "Democracy Alert", the "democracy argument" underlies all of Marine Le Pen's remarks. The president denounces a political act and a questionable interpretation of the law. During his speech, Marine Le Pen refers to a "death penalty" for the RN and a "stake" in democracy. According to the president of the RN, judges would not respect the separation of powers, would misuse the law for political purposes and would attack an opposition party. The statements are alarmist: "alert", "dictatorship", "ruin", "irreparable" and so on. Faced with this situation, the party launched a website—*alerte-democratie.fr*—to receive donations from militants and all French people who are

[13] Le Pen, *Discours de Marine Le Pen au Meeting de Bordeaux*; Le Pen, *Meeting de Marine Le Pen à Ajaccio*.

[14] Le Pen, *Alert Démocratie*.

"committed to democratic freedoms".[15] This example shows the dichotomy between democracy, which would be everyone's business, on the one hand, and the dictatorship of judges who would seize judicial power for political purposes, on the other. Marine Le Pen severely criticises this power of judges who "unfairly" and "irreparably" damage a person's reputation. The discourse personalises the attack, plays on a form of victimisation and inclusion of the audience: "us" and "you". The trial against the RN becomes a personalised political attack on Marine Le Pen. She also presented it as an attack on her electorate and, even more generally, on the French people as a whole.

This example perfectly illustrates an "image repair strategy" (Benoit 2015; Amossy 2018; Sadoun-Kerber 2018). According to these authors, when a political personality is attacked at a political level, he has several response strategies. The main ones are denial, dilution or reduction of responsibilities; reduction of offense; corrective action and mortification or mea culpa. The "parliamentary assistants case" is an attack on the "image" of the RN. Marine Le Pen therefore tries to react to it. To do so, she uses a strategy that can be called "reducing the offence" by challenging the legitimacy of the accuser. The judges and the government would not be reliable given their lack of neutrality, misinterpretation of the law and violation of proportionality. The "judges' government" attacks an opposition party but also, according to Marine Le Pen, "democracy". She thus pursues a second discursive strategy by using the term "democracy" as a transcendental argument.

Thus we can indirectly, via examples 1, 2 and 3, observe a symbolic and an emotional function of the term "democracy" in Marine Le Pen's speech. This element is clearly illustrated in the following quotation (example 4):

> The question is, at the same time, simple and cruel: will our children live in a free, independent, democratic country? Will they still be able to refer to our value system? Will they have the same way of life as we and our parents did before us?[16]

[15] Le Pen, Marine. "Alert Démocratie: Marine Le Pen conference de presse". *Rassemblement National,* July 9, 2018c, https://rassemblementnational.fr/conferences-de-presse/alerte-democratie/).

[16] Le Pen, *Assises Présidentielles de Lyon.*

The vision is backward-looking. It presents an endangered societal continuity. It should also be highlighted here the use of an inclusive "our" and the questioning of the future of "children". These elements concerning a deteriorating future and an inclusion of auditors play on the emotions filed (Charaudeau 2008). The RN's discourse takes stock of a French society in crisis: immigration, identity, education, labour and security.[17] Marine Le Pen points out the leaders: the European Union, the government and the other political parties that have promoted globalisation, Europeanisation, the rise of communitarianism and economic deregulation space. After describing this situation, she presents herself as the actor of change and sets out its programme to rectify the situation.[18]

On the basis of these first four examples, a parallel can be drawn between the literature questioning the term "democracy" in RWP and RN discourses. The term is essentially used as an argument, as a symbolic and emotional term, as a rhetorical device to attack or defend the party against political opponents (parties, institutions, presses, judges). At this stage, the term "democracy" is not leant on according to specific values. If one now leaves the context of the elections, if one broadens the scope by emphasising tensions in the discourse, one can notice that the term "democracy" may also reflect a particular vision of the world, a particular ideological agenda. To illustrate this, two quotations are particularly helpful: one concerning Brexit (example 5) and another relating to the Catalan referendum (example 6).

> The FN would like to start by congratulating Ms. May on the consistency of her position and her determination to respect the sovereign decision of the British people. Faced with multiple national and European pressure, the British Prime Minister is giving search a great lesson of democracy to all those tempted to move, once again, beyond the popular will.[19] While the sense of independence is clearly in the minority in Catalonia and democratic political forces that respect the Constitution of the Spanish State and its unity are opposed to these separatist and extremist tendencies, we would like to know the Commission's position, knowing that the Spanish State is a sovereign nation.[20]

[17] Bay, *Initiative Citoyenne*.
[18] Le Pen, *Réunion Publique de Marine Le Pen à Monswiller*.
[19] Rassemblement National, *Brexit*.
[20] Aliot, *Question Ecrite*.

Through examples 5 and 6, it can be argued that the RN does not propose any definition of the concept "democracy" or that "democracy" is multiple and variable according to events. These elements confirm the use of the term "democracy" in a purely cosmetic manner. The RN shows itself in favour of popular sovereignty and referendum (example 5) and against extremism, separatism and referendum (example 6). However, this analysis only takes democracy into account as an argument. If democracy is now studied as an ideologically loaded signifier, if we question it not with regard to the referendum but with regard to nationalist ideology, the two above quotations are no longer contradictory.

Indeed, following the RN, the concept of democracy is linked to the nation-state. A referendum is therefore legitimate when it does not call into question this nation-state and when it is organised against the European Union. Using RN's rhetoric, when a referendum aims to restore national sovereignty, it is considered as "democratic". On the other hand, if a referendum undermines the State, then it is considered as "anti-democratic". In the case of Catalonia, according to the RN, the referendum is opposed to the sovereignty of the Spanish state and is therefore "anti-democratic". It is consequently not so much the referendum that seems important but a State's national sovereignty. "Democracy" is then for the RN an ideological term that legitimises and justifies a nationalist position. With these examples, it can also be argued that the referendum is not necessarily a guarantee of democracy from the RN's standpoint.

Examples 5 and 6 illustrate that nationalist and sovereignst thinking is prominent in the rhetoric of the RN and guides its representation of democracy. In this sense, Marine Le Pen has already explicitly used the phrase "national democracy".[21] Conversely, democracy is thought within a national framework and justifies the need for France to "recover",[22] "restore"[23] but also "protect"[24] national sovereignty. The two elements are intimately linked and are articulated in a discourse that aims to rediscover national borders in order to fight against immigration, Europeanisation and globalisation.[25] Other quotations show this position (example 7 and example 8):

[21] Le Pen, *Marine Le Pen Répond.*
[22] Le Pen, *La Grèce.*
[23] Murer, *La Commission Européenne.*
[24] Aliot, *Question n°19--00087.*
[25] Le Pen, *Discours de Marine Le Pen à Kintzheim.*

> Democracy exists only within the national framework. Brussels does not have to impose a biased view of criminal law on nations, let alone support citizens or illegal immigrants who violate our laws. These new attempts at destabilization remind us of the urgent need to break with a model that denies the freedom and sovereignty of our nations.[26] It is first and foremost necessary to restore national sovereignty, the first condition of the Nation's democratic life.[27]

Any entity superior to the nation-state is regarded here as "anti-democratic". In this sense, the European Union is one of the main enemies of "French democracy". Unlike this "union", the RN therefore favours the elaboration of a Europe "based on the principle of freely consented cooperation, respectful of sovereignty and the inalienable right of nations to self-determination".[28] In the RN's discourse, concepts such as sovereignty, independence, national specificity and the right of peoples to self-determination are all inseparable from democracy. Democracy can therefore only apply if it is French people who vote for French representatives and the latter act in the name of France's interests. As various representatives of the RN assert, questioning the nation-state is tantamount to questioning democracy.

These examples, in addition to a nationalist ideology, also express a desire for "direct democracy". Even if the phrase is barely mentioned in the party's speeches—five times in the whole corpus—one finds several calls and allusions to a return to popular sovereignty. Politicians would be "corrupt", "illegitimate", "acting in the name of private interests",[29] whereas, as Marine Le Pen advanced, "if we are in a democracy, it is up to the sovereign people to decide"[30] as "people are always right".[31]

The notion of democracy is thus intimately linked to the term "people" and to matters of general interest and popular sovereignty. However, it is interesting to note that, in its speeches, the RN is opposed to the implementation of participatory democracy experiments including, among others, the participatory budget. The RN saw it as a "rattle given to the

[26] Bay, *Initiative Citoyenne.*

[27] Rassemblement National, *Réaction de Marine Le Pen.*

[28] Rassemblement National, *La Commission Européenne.*

[29] Martin, *Parlement Européen*; Le Pen, *Discours de Marine Le Pen à Nantes.*

[30] Le Pen, *Réunion Publique de Marine Le Pen à Monswiller.*

[31] Le Pen, *Discours de Marine Le Pen à Châteauroux; Le Pen, Réunion Publique de Marine Le Pen à Mirande.*

people",[32] "a pseudo-democratic masquerade designed to satisfy a few bohos with a budget that would have been welcome elsewhere".[33] On the other hand, the question of the referendum is dealt with several times (example 9):

> I will create a popular initiative referendum, which works so well in Switzerland, Italy and other countries. This means that the referendum will no longer be on the initiative of the president of the Republic alone, but also of the French people, if 500,000 citizens manage to collect signatures on a bill or a proposal to withdraw a law. Adult democracy is a democracy that trusts the people, because it knows that they are wise.[34]

In this example, one also finds the appeal to the people, trust in the people and the notion of popular sovereignty in relation to the issue of democracy. The aim of the referendum is to underline and affirm the decision-making power of French citizens and to mobilise them not only in electoral periods. The people would then be the central subject of democracy. The RN goes further however and also adds an identity component. In this sense, "democracy" and "identity" are two terms that are also linked within the same ideological dimension (*example 10*):

Our struggle is that of our identity and therefore that of our sovereignty. A country that loses its wealth is weakening. A country that burdens itself with taxes is getting poorer. A country that sees its identity erased is threatened because it no longer knows where it comes from, who it is. But a country that breaks with both its sovereignty and its identity is lost. However, as you can see every day, France is experiencing an amputation of its sovereignty and our people are losing their identity [....] We no longer wish to be deprived of our democratic power![35]

The appeal to the people and to democracy is therefore issued not only in a protest mode—against the European Union—but also in an identity mode—France would be characterised by a language, a custom, a tradition and so on. The identity people establish a border between an inner "we" and an outer "they". The French people as viewed by the RN are thus defined by an identity: "France is first and foremost the French people,

[32] De Saint Just, *Budget Participatif.*

[33] Rassemblement National, *Anne Hidalgo.*

[34] Le Pen, *Conférence pour Ethique.*

[35] Le Pen, *Réunion Publique de Marine Le Pen à Mirande.*

our people. The French people is you and it is us".[36] In the discourse of the RN, this French identity distinguishes the French people from a group of foreigners to the nation. Thus, if in the discourse of the RN, there is not any explicit opposition between the notion of democracy and that of immigration, one can nevertheless attest to a strong distinction between the French people and migrants and between French traditions and multiculturalism—defined as "gangrene".[37] (or the "breeding ground for terrorism".[38] This ideology, which usually takes the form of political proposals in favour of national preference, aims to redefine public action and the management of socio-economic resources in terms of national solidarity—designated as "national chauvinism" or "nativism" (Kitschelt 1995; Ivaldi 1999; Hainsworth 2000; Neyrat 2014). Some rights and services are reserved only for nationals, that is, those who hold French nationality.

All these examples illustrate that the term "democracy" is not used in RN rhetoric in a neutral manner. It has a specific content. It crystallises an ideology while also being structured by this same nationalist, populist and identity-based ideology. It can therefore be affirmed that the term "democracy" has an ideological function too.

5 Conclusions

The RWP parties use the term "democracy" in their speeches. According to the literature, this is a process of normalisation initiated by these parties to make themselves respectable in the eyes of the voters. "Democracy" is essentially used as a "cosmetic" term. Nevertheless, our working hypothesis was that the term is not empty of meaning, is not just an argument, but that it is also ideologically loaded. To demonstrate this, a two-step process has been followed: first a lexicometric analysis and then a CDA.

The lexicometric analysis allowed us to affirm that the term "democracy" is, quantitatively, more often employed during electoral periods and in texts intended for large audiences. It is therefore campaign speeches and press conferences that show the highest ratio as regards the use of the term. Subsequently, the CDA questioned the context in which this term is

[36] Le Pen, *Discours de Marine Le Pen aux Estivales de Fréjus.*

[37] Le Pen, Marine. "Discours de Marine le Pen à Paris". *Rassemblement National,* December 15, 2015a, https://rassemblementnational.fr/discours/discours-de-marine-le-pen-a-paris-10-decembre-2015/.

[38] Martin, *Parlement Européen.*

used and permitted to uncover different functions of the term "democracy". The rhetorical function constitutes an argument of attack or defence. The term is used to identify political opponents and criticise their programmes or actions. The term is moreover used to protect the party by relying upon an argument that delegitimises the opponent. The term "democracy" also has an emotional function that allows to script and dramatise a discourse by referring to the notions of "crisis", "degradation" but also to "restore a glorified and lost past". Finally, by questioning tensions within the party's rhetoric, an ideological function identified too. As well democracy is not just a rhetorical or symbolic argument. It also crystallises an ideology. Nationalism, populism, identity are all elements that revolve around the term "democracy". Finally, it should be noted that these functions are not independent of each other, in the discourse they are linked to each other and the same use of the term "democracy" can thus refer to several functions.

The ideological function of the term allows me to argue that there is a need to encourage reflection on democracy in addition to its links with the RN and, more generally, the RWP. Indeed, to return to my initial considerations, these parties are today employing the term "democracy" in their rhetoric. Some of these parties have a long-term presence on the political scene and sometimes sit on the executive. To judge their use of the word "democracy" to be merely cosmetic is to dismiss part of the analysis. In politics, words are not empty, where, if they are emptied through contrary use, they are nevertheless ideologically loaded by the actors who use them. One must then understand their meanings. If these parties bow to the electoral game and the institutions of their democratic states, they have a particular vision of democracy and, through that word, they convey a nationalist, populist and identity-based ideology. The term "Identity democracy" or "national democracy" is not necessarily an oxymoron but rather a matter for debate to be grasped.

Bibliography

Alduy, Cécile, and Wahnich, Stéphane. *Marine Le Pen Prise aux Mots. Décryptage du Nouveau Discours Frontiste*. Paris: Le Seuil, 2015.

Amossy, Ruth. "Analyser la Réparation d'Image dans le Discours Electoral: Bilan et Perspectives." *Langage et société*, no. 164 (2018): 9–23.

Angermüller, Johannes. "L'Analyse du Discours en Europe." In *Analyse du Discours et Sciences Humaines et Sociales,* edited by Bonnafous Simone, Temmar Malika, 9–23. Paris: Editions Ophrys, 2007.

Backes, Uwe. "Les Multiples Facettes d'une Catégorie d'Analyse." In *Extrême Droite et National-Populisme en Europe de l'Ouest,* edited by Blaise Pierre, Moreau Patrick, 445–465. Bruxelles: Centre de recherche et d'information socio-politiques, 2004.

Benoit, William. *Accounts, Excuses and Apologies; Image Repair Theory and Research.* Albany: Suny Press, 2015.

Bowler, Shaun, David Denemark, Todd Donovan, Duncan McDonnell. "Right-Wing Populist Party Supporters: Dissatisfied but not Direct Democrats". *European Journal of Political Research,* no. 56 (2017): 70–91.

Camus, Jean-Yves, and Lebourg, Nicolas. *Les Droites Extrêmes en Europe.* Paris: Seuil, 2015.

Cardon, Dominique, Guilhem Fouetillou, Clémence Lerondeau, Christophe Prieur. "Esquisse de Géographie de la Blogosphère Politique (2007–2009)." In *Continuerlalutte.com; les Partis Politiques sur le Web,* edited by Greffet Fabienne, 73–94. Paris: Presses de la fondation nationale des sciences politiques, 2011.

Carter, Elisabeth. *The Extreme Right in Western Europe; Success or Failure.* Manchester: Manchester University Press, 2005.

Charaudeau, Patrick. "Pathos et Discours Politique." In *Emotions et Discours; l'Usage des Passions dans la Langue,* edited by Rinn Michael, 49–58. Rennes: Presses Universitaires de Rennes, 2008.

Deze, Alexandre. "Un Parti 'Virtuel' ? Le Front National au Prisme de son Site Internet." In *Continuerlalutte.com; les Partis Politiques sur le Web,* edited by Greffet Fabienne, 139–152. Paris: Presses de la fondation nationale des sciences politiques, 2011.

Fairclough, Norman, and Wodak, Ruth. "Critical Discourse Analysis." I*n Discourse as a Social Interaction*, edited by Van Dijk Teun, 258–284. New York: Sage Publications, 1997.

Fowler, Roger, and Kress, Gunther. *Language and Control.* London: Routledge and Kegan Paul, 1979.

Gauthier, Elisabeth. *Droites Populistes en Europe; les Raisons d'un Succès.* Vulaines sur Seine: Editions du croquant, 2015.

Greffet, Fabienne. *Continuerlalutte.com; les Partis Politiques sur le Web.* Paris: Presses de la fondation nationale des sciences politiques, 2011.

Guillet, Nicolas, and Afiouni, Nada. *Les Tentatives de Banalisation de l'Extrême Droite en Europe.* Bruxelles: Editions de l'Université de Bruxelles, 2016.

Hainsworth, Paul. *The Politics of the Extreme Right (from the Margins to the Mainstream).* London: Pinter Publishers, 2000.

Halikiopoulou, Daphne. "The Far Right Challenge. Comment on 'The Rise of Post-Truth Populism in Pluralist Liberal Democracies: Challenges for Health Policy." *International Journal of Health Policy and Management,* no. 7 (2018): 195–198.

Ihnen, Constanza, and Richardson, John. "On Combining Pragma-Dialectics with Critical Discourse Analysis." In *Keeping in Touch with Pragma-Dialectics*, edited by Fetris Eveline, Garssen Bart, Henkemens Francisca, 231–244. Amsterdam: John Benjamins Publishing Company, 2013.

Ivaldi, Gilles. "L'Extrême Droite ou la Crise des Systèmes de Partis." *Revue internationale de politique compare*, no. 6 (1999): 201–246.

Jamin, Jérôme. *L'Extrême Droite en Europe*. Bruxelles: Bruylant, 2016.

Kallis, Aristotle. "Far-Right 'Contagion' or a Failing 'Mainstream'? How Dangerous Ideas Cross Borders and Blur Boundaries." *Democracy and Security*, no. 9 (2013): 33–54.

Kitschelt, Herbert. *The Radical Right in Western Europe, a Comparative Analysis*. Ann Arbor: University of Michigan Press, 1995.

Krzyzanowski, Michal. *The Discursive Construction of European Identities; A Multi-Level Approach to Discourse and Identity in the Transforming European Union*. New York: Peter Lang, 2010.

Le Bart, Christian. "L'Analyse du Discours Politique: de la Théorie des Champs à la Sociologie de la Grandeur." *Mots, les langages du politique*, no. 72 (2003): 97–110.

Maingueneau, Dominique. "Enonciation et Analyse du Discours." *Corela, Cognition, Représentation, Langage*, no. 19 (2016): 1–11.

Mondon, Aurelien. "The Front National in the Twenty-First Century: From Pariah to Republican Democratic Contender?" *Modern and Contemporary France*, no. 22 (2014): 301–320.

Monzat, René. "Qu'est-ce qui ne Tourne pas Rond?" *Revue Lignes*, no. 45 (2014): 119–129.

Mucchielli, Roger. *L'Analyse de Contenu des Documents et des Communications*. Montrouge: Editions ESF, 2006.

Mudde, Cas. "The War of Words; Defining the Extreme Right Party Family." *West European Politics*, no. 19 (1996): 225–248.

Mudde, Cas. *The Ideology of the Extreme Right*. Manchester: Manchester University Press, 2000.

Neyrat, Frédéric. "Une Hégémonie d'Extrême Droite; Etude sur le Syndrome Identitaire Français." *Revue Lignes*, no. 45 (2014): 19–31.

Passmore, Kevin. "Les Tentatives de Banalisation de l'Extrême Droite dans l'Histoire et dans l'Historiographie Française." In *Les Tentatives de Banalisation de l'Extrême Droite en Europe*, edited by Guillet, Nicolas, and Afiouni, Nada, 19–38. Bruxelles: Editions de l'Université de Bruxelles, 2016.

Pauwels, Teun. "Measuring Populism: a Quantitative Text Analysis of Party Literature in Belgium." *Journal of elections, public opinion and parties*, no. 21 (2011): 97–119.

Pelinka, Anton. "Right-Wing Populism: Concept and Typology." In *Right-Wing Populism in Europe: Politics and Discourse*, edited by Wodak Ruth et al., 3–22. London: Bloomsbury Academic, 2013.

Pupovac, David. *The Radical Right in Policy Space: a Comparative Analysis of Radical Right Parties in Eastern and Western Europe*. Ph.D. Dissertation, Budapest: CEU, 2015.

Sadoun-Kerber, Keren. "Gestion et Réparation d'Image : Emmanuel Macron dans l'Emission Politique." *Langage et société*, no. 164 (2018): 75–95.

Shekhovtsov, Anton. "From Para-Militarism to Radical Right-Wing Populism: The Rise of the Ukrainian Far-Right Party Svoboda." In *Right-Wing Populism in Europe: Politics and Discourse*, ed. by Wodak, Ruth, 249–263. London: Bloomsbury Academic, 2013.

Taguieff, Pierre-André. *Le Nouveau National-Populisme*. Paris: CNRS Editions, 2012.

Titscher, Stefan. *Methods of Text and Discourse Analysis*. New York: Sage Publications, 2000.

Van Dijk, Teun. "Critical Discourse Analysis." In *The Handbook of Discourse Analysis*, edited by Schiffrin, Deborah, 349–371. Malden-Oxford: Blackwell Publishers, 2001.

Wieviorka, Michel. *Le Front National; entre Extrémisme, Populisme et Démocratie*. Paris: Maison des Sciences de l'Homme, 2013.

Wodak, Ruth, and Meyer, Michael. *Methods of Critical Discourse Analysis*. New York: Sage Publications, 2001.

Wodak, Ruth. *Right-Wing Populism in Europe: Politics and Discourse*. London: Bloomsbury Academic, 2013.

Primary Sources

Aliot, Louis. "Question Ecrite de Louis Aliot, Député Français au Parlement Européen". *Rassemblement National*, January 13, 2016, https://rassemblementnational.fr/interventions/question-ecrite-de-louis-aliot-depute-francais-au-parlement-europeen/.

Aliot, Louis. "Question n°19-00087 de Louis Aliot, Député, à Monsieur Le Premier Ministre". *Rassemblement National*, May 10, 2018, https://rassemblementnational.fr/communiques/question-n-19-00087-de-louis-aliot-depute-a-monsieur-le-premier-ministre/.

Bay, Nicolas. "Elections Départementales: l'Implantation Locale, la Clé des Succès de Demain !". *Rassemblement National*, March 27, 2015, https://rassemblementnational.fr/tribunes-libres/elections-departementales-limplantation-locale-la-cle-des-succes-de-demain/.

Collard, Gilbert. "Proposition de Loi Visant à Etendre la Transparence de la Vie Publique aux Patrons des Entreprises de Presse". *Rassemblement National*, March 4, 2016, https://rassemblementnational.fr/interventions/proposition-de-loi-visant-a-etendre-la-transparence-de-la-vie-publique-aux-patrons-des-entreprises-de-presse/.

De Saint Just, Wallerand. "Budget Participatif, Parodie de Démocratie". *Rassemblement National,* October 5, 2016, https://rassemblementnational.fr/communiques/budget-participatif-parodie-de-democratie/.

De Saint Just, Wallerand. "Marianne de Fontenay : la Violence, Seul Argument de l'Extrême Gauche". *Rassemblement National,* October 6, 2015, https://rassemblementnational.fr/communiques/marianne-de-fontenay-la-violence-seule-argument-de-lextreme-gauche/.

Jacobelli, Laurent. "Sous-Représentation du RN dans les Médias : le CSA Doit Réagir". *Rassemblement National,* October 12, 2018, https://rassemblementnational.fr/communiques/sous-representation-du-rn-dans-les-medias-le-csa-doit-reagir/.

Le Pen, Marine. "Discours de Marine le Pen à Paris". *Rassemblement National,* December 15, 2015a, https://rassemblementnational.fr/discours/discours-de-marine-le-pen-a-paris-10-decembre-2015/.

Le Pen, Marine. "Discours de Marine Le Pen à l'Université d'Oxford". *Rassemblement National,* February 6, 2015b, https://rassemblementnational.fr/discours/discours-de-marine-le-pen-a-luniversite-doxford/.

Le Pen, Marine. "Nous Demandons un Débat à Monsieur Pierre; Lettre Ouverte de Marine Le Pen au Directeur Général du Groupe 'La Voix du Nord'". *Rassemblement National,* December 1, 2015c, https://rassemblementnational.fr/tribunes-libres/lettre-ouverte-de-marine-le-pen-au-directeur-general-du-groupe-la-voix-du-nord/.

Le Pen, Marine. "Assises Présidentielles de Lyon : Discours de Marine Le Pen". *Rassemblement National,* February 5, 2017a, https://rassemblementnational.fr/videos/assises-presidentielles-de-lyon-discours-de-marine-le-pen/.

Le Pen, Marine. "Discours de Marine Le Pen à Nantes". *Rassemblement National,* February 27, 2017b, https://rassemblementnational.fr/videos/discours-de-marine-le-pen-a-nantes-26022017/.

Le Pen, Marine. "Conférence pour Ethique". *Rassemblement National,* March 9, 2017c, https://rassemblementnational.fr/conferences-de-presse/alerte-democratie/.

Le Pen, Marine. "Marine Le Pen en Meeting à Metz". *Rassemblement National,* March 9, 2017d, https://rassemblementnational.fr/videos/marine-le-pen-en-meeting-a-metz/.

Le Pen, Marine. "Discours de Marine Le Pen à Châteauroux". *Rassemblement National,* March 11, 2017e, https://rassemblementnational.fr/videos/discours-de-marine-le-pen-a-chateauroux/.

Le Pen, Marine. "Discours de Marine Le Pen au Meeting de Bordeaux". *Rassemblement National,* April 2, 2017f, https://rassemblementnational.fr/videos/discours-de-marine-le-pen-au-meeting-a-bordeaux/.

Le Pen, Marine. "Réunion Publique de Marine Le Pen à Monswiller en Alsace". *Rassemblement National,* April 6, 2017g, https://rassemblementnational.fr/videos/reunion-publique-de-marine-le-pen-a-monswiller-en-alsace/.

Le Pen, Marine. "Meeting de Marine Le Pen à Ajaccio". *Rassemblement National,* April 9, 2017h, https://rassemblementnational.fr/tribunes-libres/la-lettre-de-marine-14-avril-2017/.

Le Pen, Marine. "Discours de Marine Le Pen à Kintzheim". *Rassemblement National,* February 27, 2018a, https://rassemblementnational.fr/discours/discours-de-marine-le-pen-a-kintzheim/.

Le Pen, Marine. "Discours de Marine Le Pen aux Estivales de Fréjus". *Rassemblement National,* June 26, 2018b, https://rassemblementnational.fr/videos/discours-de-rentree-de-marine-le-pen-a-frejus/.

Le Pen, Marine. "Alert Démocratie: Marine Le Pen conference de presse". *Rassemblement National,* July 9, 2018c, https://rassemblementnational.fr/conferences-de-presse/alerte-democratie/.

Martin, Dominique. "Parlement Européen : le Système UMPS Tombe les Masques". *Rassemblement National,* April 5, 2016, https://rassemblementnational.fr/communiques/parlement-europeen-le-systeme-umps-tombe-les-masques/.

Murer, Philippe. "La Commission Européenne Veut Imposer plus de Réformes Structurelles aux Français". *Rassemblement National,* March 9, 2016, https://rassemblementnational.fr/communiques/la-commission-europeenne-veut-imposer-plus-de-reformes-structurelles-aux-francais/.

Racheline, David. "Un Climat Antidémocratique Grave et Inquiétant se Lève à l'Approche de l'Election Présidentielle". *Rassemblement National,* February 26, 2017, https://rassemblementnational.fr/communiques/un-climat-antidemocratique-grave-et-inquietant-se-leve-a-lapproche-de-lelection-presidentielle/.

Rassemblement National. "Anne Hidalgo, Vous n'Avez pas Honte ?". *Rassemblement National,* January 14, 2015, https://rassemblementnational.fr/communiques/anne-hidalgo-vous-navez-pas-honte/.

Rassemblement National. "Brexit: le Divorce Doit se Faire à l'Amiable". *Rassemblement National,* March 30, 2017, https://rassemblementnational.fr/communiques/brexit-le-divorce-doit-se-faire-a-lamiable/.

PART II

Populism in Practice. Its Impact on the Rule of Law

Populism and Constitutional Courts: A Perspective from the Venice Commission

Simona Granata-Menghini

1 Introduction

The Venice Commission (European Commission for Democracy through Law) is the Council of Europe's independent expert body on constitutional law. It is a so-called enlarged agreement, its membership comprising all the 47 member states of the Council of Europe plus 15 non-European countries.[1] Since its establishment in May 1990, the Commission has

[1] Algeria, Brazil, Canada, Chile, Costa Rica, Israel, Kazakhstan, Republic of Korea, Kosovo, Kyrgyzstan, Mexico, Morocco, Peru, Tunisia and the United States of America. Belarus is an associate member. There are four observers: Argentina, the Holy See, Japan and Uruguay;

The views expressed are personal and do not necessarily represent those of the Venice Commission.

S. Granata-Menghini (✉)
Human Rights and Rule of Law (DG-I)—European Commission for Democracy Through Law, Council of Europe, Strasbourg, France
e-mail: Simona.GRANATA-MENGHINI@coe.int

J. M. Castellà Andreu, M. A. Simonelli (eds.), *Populism and Contemporary Democracy in Europe*,
https://doi.org/10.1007/978-3-030-92884-1_5

provided over 1000 country-specific analysis of constitutional and legal texts, already adopted or in preparation, and has provided ensuing recommendations to the relevant countries on how to redress possible problems and shortcomings, based on international and, specifically, European standards, comparative material, previous experience of comparable member states and its own "wisdom".

The Commission is a technical, non-political body. Its statute prevents it from taking up country-specific issues on its own initiative: country-specific opinions may be provided only upon request either of the authorities of the country concerned, or of the Council of Europe bodies, or of organisations or bodies having a special status of co-operation with the Commission (e.g. the European Union and OSCE). This limitation shields the Commission from having to make choices which would inevitably be seen as political, if only because its limited means would not enable it to analyse all comparable issues in all its 62 member states.

The Commission is an advisory body, whose recommendations are non-binding; they are however routinely used in monitoring procedures of political bodies such as the Parliamentary Assembly of the Council of Europe or the European Parliament, and relied upon—and also stimulated—by the European Commission in accession and stabilisation processes and, more recently, in rule of law conditionality processes. The International Monetary Fund and the World Bank also increasingly rely on the Commission's advice (Granata-menghini and Kuijer 2020). Recently, the Financial Action Task Force has also looked into the Commission's work in its own assessment to study the unintended consequences of the FATF Standards' intersection with due process and procedural rights issues.[2] Together with the independent, professional and competent nature of the Commission's advice, this explains the high rate of compliance with the Commission's recommendations.[3]

Owing also to the channels through which it may be activated, notably the Parliamentary Assembly of the Council of Europe and, albeit indirectly, the European Commission, the work of the Venice Commission

the European Union, South Africa and the Palestinian National Authority have a special co-operation status. https://www.venice.coe.int/ last accessed 30 September 2021.

[2] This concerns in particular the report of the Venice Commission on the foreign funding of associations: http://www.fatf-gafi.org/publications/fatfgeneral/documents/outcomes-fatf-plenary-june-2021.html last accessed 30 September 2021.

[3] https://www.venice.coe.int/WebForms/followup/default.aspx?lang=EN last accessed 30 September 2021.

often goes to the very heart of the most controversial issues in Europe. Its opinions are made public and invariably find a large echo in the national press, in the national debates, and also in international circles. The Commission's opinions very rarely go unnoticed, including in those even more rare cases in which the authorities decided to ignore them. This explains why the decision of whether or not to request an opinion of the Commission is a very delicate one for any government: a critical assessment may haunt that government, but the risk that such request be made by one of the international channels of activation of the Commission may lead to even greater difficulties.

Typically, the Commission starts assessing pending reforms in one country, then similar reforms in other countries, and further, noticing tendencies and recurrent problems, it may move to analysing such phenomena in general, trying if need be to identify general principles that it finds should be applicable to them. The Commission has done so, for example, as concerns the independence of the judiciary[4] and of the prosecution service,[5] or referendums,[6] where it has elaborated reports and guidelines based on the numerous country-specific opinions it had elaborated.

2 Populism and Constitutional Courts

The Venice Commission has not (yet) analysed populism as a phenomenon, nor defined any government as populistic in any of its opinions so far. It has however analysed constitutional and legal reforms in several countries which are governed by populist governments.

Populists are against constitutionalism in a thick sense of the term, referring not merely to the written document called constitution but to a body of legal and political principles that meaningfully constrain governmental power and protect civil liberties. However, populists are not

[4] CDL-AD(2007)028-e, Judicial Appointments, Report adopted by the Venice Commission at its 70th Plenary Session (Venice, 16–17 March 2007); CDL-AD(2010)004-e, Report on the Independence of the Judicial System Part I: The Independence of Judges, Adopted by the Venice Commission at its 82nd Plenary Session (Venice, 12–13 March 2010).

[5] CDL-AD(2010)040-e, Report on European Standards as regards the Independence of the Judicial System: Part II—the Prosecution Service, Adopted by the Venice Commission at its 85th plenary session (Venice, 17–18 December 2010).

[6] CDL-AD(2020)031, Revised guidelines on the holding of referendums, Approved by the Council of Democratic Elections at its 69th online meeting (7 October 2020), Adopted by the Venice Commission at its 124th online Plenary Session (8–9 October 2020).

necessarily against constitutionalism defined in a thin sense of the term: in the sense of governance that accords in a formal or technical sense with written rules of a constitution, including rules about what institutions there are, how they are constituted and how they should function.[7]

Populists therefore do not necessarily reject constitutional frameworks, even though it could be expected that they would refuse any constitutional constraints. Populist leaders have wanted to write their own constitutions, setting out their own rules and principles. And because populist governments see and present themselves as the only legitimate representatives of the whole people, they see themselves as the only legitimate constituent power: populist constitutions are written without consultation of the opposition or of civil society (Werner Müller 2016). The Venice Commission has criticised this non-inclusive constitution-making process in Hungary[8] and in the election to the Constituent Assembly of Venezuela,

[7] Friedman, The impact of Populism on Courts: Institutional Legitimacy and the Popular Will, The Foundation for Law, Justice and Society, 2019, https://www.fljs.org/sites/default/files/migrated/publications/The%20I last accessed 30 September 2021.

[8] In its Opinion on three legal questions arising in the process of drafting the New Constitution of Hungary, the Commission recalled that "transparency, openness and inclusiveness, adequate timeframe and conditions allowing pluralism of views and proper debate of controversial issues, are key requirements of a democratic Constitution-making process": Opinion on CDL-AD(2011)001-e, Opinion on three legal questions arising in the process of drafting the New Constitution of Hungary, Adopted by the Venice Commission at its 86th Plenary Session (Venice, 25–26 March 2011); see also Opinion on the new constitution of Hungary, CDL-AD(2011)016-e, Opinion on the new Constitution of Hungary, Adopted by the Venice Commission at its 87th Plenary Session (Venice, 17–18 June 2011).

In its opinion on Venezuela, the Commission concluded: "The Venice Commission wishes to stress that in the case of the election of a new National Constituent Assembly, the need for consensus must be especially emphasized. As the Venice Commission has previously stated, this procedure is one of the most sensitive issues of any constitution. It is also a highly political issue that can only be determined in light of the history of the country and its political and legal culture. For this reason, the adoption of a new and good Constitution should be based on the widest consensus possible within the society and a wide and substantive debate involving the various political forces, non-government organizations and citizens associations, the academia and the media is an important prerequisite for adopting a sustainable text, acceptable for the whole of the society and in line with democratic standards. For this to happen, states' positive obligations to ensure unhindered exercise of freedom of peaceful assembly, freedom of expression, as well as a fair, adequate and extensive broadcasting of the arguments by the media are equally relevant. The shortcomings of the procedure and of the electoral rules for the election of the National Constituent Assembly of Venezuela are such as to undermine the credibility of the attempt to prepare a new constitution". CDL-

for example. According to the Commission, a transparent, accountable, inclusive, and democratic process of enacting (constitutions and) laws is a constitutive element of the rule of law.[9]

Courts are an easy target for populists, on account of the counter-majoritarian dilemma that judges are unelected, and so suffer from a democratic deficit; that these unelected judges often have the power to invalidate the statutes of a democratically elected legislature; and third, that courts give certain groups an unequal opportunity to influence the political process.[10] Populist leaders have therefore tended to interfere with the independence of the judiciary as a constraint on government power through a variety of measures, ranging from making negative public remarks to amending constitutions or packing courts with loyalists.

Constitutional courts are the guardians of the Constitution, and their role is to ensure the supremacy of the Constitution. This role is essential for the separation of powers in a democratic state and is especially important in times of strong parliamentary majorities. The Venice Commission has strongly encouraged the setting up of constitutional courts and has consistently supported their independence and effective functioning (Dürr 2020, 215).

Populist constitutionalism has weakened the role of constitutional courts in several European countries. In Turkey, Hungary, and Poland, populist regimes have not abolished constitutional courts; they have instead preserved them, modifying their jurisdiction to fit the leader's designs and packing them with party loyalists. These changes have enabled them to work within a formal constitutional framework.

This makes sense from the populist perspective. Courts and constitutions are politically and symbolically powerful. It is better for populists to have courts work with them than against them. As long as the courts are

AD(2017)024-e, Venezuela, Opinion on the legal issues raised by Decree 2878 of 23 May 2017 of the President of the Republic on calling elections to a national constituent Assembly, Endorsed by the Venice Commission at its 112th Plenary Session (Venice, 6–7 October 2017).

[9] Venice Commission's Rule of Law Checklist, Benchmark A, Legality, 5. Law-making procedures: CDL-AD(2016)007rev, Rule of Law Checklist, Adopted by the Venice Commission at its 106th Plenary Session (Venice, 11–12 March 2016), Endorsed by the Ministers' Deputies at the 1263rd Meeting (6–7 September 2016), Endorsed by the Congress of Local and Regional Authorities of the Council of Europe at its 31st Session (19–21 October 2016), Endorsed by the Parliamentary Assembly of the Council of Europe at its 4th part Session (11 October 2017).

[10] Friedman, footnote 10 above.

working with them, they will have diminished incentives to interfere with them. Occasionally, however, populists attempt at overtly unconstitutional moves in order to subdue counter-majoritarian institutions.

3 Measures Affecting the Work of the Constitutional Courts

The Venice Commission has assessed numerous measures which were designed to interfere or have resulted in an interference with the work of constitutional courts—either constitutionally or unconstitutionally, including, but not exclusively, by populist governments (Dürr 2019).

It should be underlined that some constitutional courts have not been exempted from justified criticism. It is an unintended—but arguably inevitable—consequence of the institution-building work of international organisations (and of the Venice Commission) having urged to bestow constitutional protection, and *in primis* inamovability, on constitutional court judges, that in some cases such guaranteed tenure has created permeability to corruption and political influence, which are difficult to combat without having recourse to exceptional measures. The Venice Commission, however, has insisted that effective solutions need to be found within the framework of the constitution and the principle of the rule of law.

The following is a non-exhaustive analysis of measures taken in respect of Constitutional Courts. In most cases, several of these measures were taken in a cumulative manner.

(a) *Early dismissal of the judges of the Constitutional Court*

Early dismissal of constitutional judges is a recurrent temptation, especially, but not exclusively, when a major political change if not a "revolution" has taken place in a country.

In Armenia, the constitutional amendments in 2015 had brought inter alia a shift from the life-time tenure of constitutional justices to a fixed-term mandate; after the so-called velvet revolution in 2019, the authorities after an unsuccessful attempt to offer early retirement to those constitutional judges, whose mandate was still until retirement (see below), introduced constitutional amendments terminating the mandate of the Chairperson and the life-appointed judges. The stated purpose of the amendments was to ensure the constitutionality of the composition of the Constitutional Court and to remedy the lack of confidence by both the public and other branches of power in the current formation of the Constitutional Court. The Commission stressed the importance placed on security of tenure of judges for safeguarding the independence of the judiciary, including the Constitutional Court, but recognised the legitimacy of the authorities wish to ensure that the composition of the Constitutional Court reflects within a reasonable time-frame the provisions of the current Constitution, which guarantee high standards concerning the independence of the Court and their concern to ensure equal status among the constitutional judges. Under these exceptional circumstances, the Commission was prepared to accept a transitional period allowing for a gradual change in the composition of the Court in order to avoid any abrupt and immediate change endangering the independence of this institution.[11] The authorities however did not follow the recommendations of the Commission and proceeded with the immediate dismissal of the six judges and with the revocation of the function of President of the Court. They subsequently appointed the new judges.

In Ukraine, in the autumn of 2020, following the adoption of a controversial decision that invalidated large parts of the anti-corruption legislation in force, President Zelenskyy presented a draft law in Parliament which would declare null and void the Court's decision, ensure the continuity of the annulled provisions of the Criminal Code and the Law on the Prevention of Corruption, terminate the powers of the judges of the Constitutional Court and ensure the selection and appointment of new judges of the Court. The Venice Commission argued that the decision of the Constitutional Court was final and binding, and it was an obligation under the rule of law for the authorities to abide by it. The Venice Commission nevertheless identified several important weaknesses in the reasoning followed by the Constitutional Court in its decision and indicated how they could be addressed and corrected, relying on international

[11] CDL-AD(2019)024-e, Armenia, Joint Opinion of the Venice Commission and the Directorate of Human Rights (DHR) of the Directorate General of Human Rights and Rule of Law (DGI), on the amendments to the Judicial Code and some other Laws, Adopted by the Venice Commission at its 120th Plenary Session (Venice, 11–12 October 2021); CDL-AD(2020)016-e, Armenia, Opinion on three legal questions in the context of draft constitutional amendments concerning the mandate of the judges of the Constitutional Court, Adopted by the Venice Commission on 19 June 2020 by a written procedure replacing the 123rd Plenary Session.

standards and by invoking inter alia the international obligations of Ukraine to fight against corruption.[12] The Commission in parallel recommended necessary improvements in the legislation on the Constitutional Court.[13] The Verkhovna Rada followed the recommendations of the Commission and on 15 December 2020 adopted legislation which, implementing at least formally the decision of the Constitutional Court, re-established the anti-corruption system.[14] President Zelenskyy further annulled the decree of appointment of two constitutional court judges who had been appointed by President Yanoukovich. While these two judges filed an appeal with the Supreme Court, which after a first decision in their favour is pending before the Plenary, President Zelenskyy is taking steps to nominate two judges to replace these two.[15]

In Moldova,[16] on 23 April 2021 the parliament refused to abide by a decision of the Constitutional Court, which had validated the decision of

[12] CDL-AD(2020)038-e, Ukraine, Urgent Joint Opinion of the Venice Commission and the Directorate General of Human Rights and Rule of Law (DGI) of the Council of Europe on the Legislative Situation regarding anti-corruption mechanisms, following Decision N° 13-R/2020 of the Constitutional Court of Ukraine, issued pursuant to Article 14a of the Venice Commission's Rules of Procedure on 9 December 2020, Endorsed by the Venice Commission on 11 December 2020 at its 125th online Plenary Session (11–12 December 2020).

[13] CDL-AD(2020)039-e, Ukraine, Urgent opinion on the Reform of the Constitutional Court, issued pursuant to Article 14a of the Venice Commission's Rules of Procedure on 9 December 2020, Endorsed by the Venice Commission on 11 December 2020 at its 125th online Plenary Session (11–12 December 2020); CDL-AD(2021)006-e, Ukraine, Opinion on the draft law on Constitutional Procedure (draft law no. 4533) and alternative draft law on the procedure for consideration of cases and execution of judgements of the Constitutional Court (draft law no. 4533-1), Adopted by the Venice Commission at its 126th Plenary Session (online, 19–20 March 2021).

[14] Law of Ukraine "On Amendments to the Law of Ukraine 'On Corruption Prevention' to Restore the Institutional Mechanism of Corruption prevention", no. 4470, https://www.rada.gov.ua/en/news/News/News%202/200882.html last accessed 30 September 2021.

[15] See Presidential Decree No. 365/2021 of 17 August 2021.

[16] A very serious constitutional crisis took place in Moldova in 2019 due to the rogue conduct of the Constitutional Court which, through a series of judgments issued in breach of the Court's procedure and not in line with its case-law, ruled that parliament was to be dissolved. The Venice Commission issued an opinion on such constitutional situation (CDL-AD(2019)012, Opinion on the constitutional situation with particular reference to the possibility of dissolving parliament, Adopted by the Venice Commission at its 119th Plenary Session (Venice, 21–22 June 2019)). It recalled that "an essential role of the Constitutional Court is to maintain equal distance from all branches of power and to act as an impartial arbiter in case of collision between them. One of the aims of any Constitution is

the newly elected President Maia Sandu to dissolve parliament; parliament issued a vote of non-confidence in three judges of the Constitutional Court and revoked the appointment of the President of the Court. The Venice Commission President issued a public statement recalling that disregarding a decision of a Constitutional Court is equivalent to disregarding the Constitution and the Constituent Power, which attributed the competence to ensure the supremacy of the Constitution to the Constitutional Court. Parliament and the executive power must respect the role of the Constitutional Court as the "gatekeeper of the Constitution", even when they are dissatisfied with a decision or are of the view that the Court made a mistake. He added that "a decision of the Constitutional Court that dissatisfies the legislative or executive powers does not amount to an abuse of power or an arbitrary decision. Nor does voting in favour of an unpopular decision of the Court amount to a violation of the oath taken by the Constitutional Judges. Such oath is not taken to the benefit of the political majority of the day. It is an oath to support the Constitution, regardless of whether this entails disappointing such majority".[17] On 27 April, the Constitutional Court declared unconstitutional the Parliament's decisions of 23 April 2021. President Sandu dissolved parliament, and early elections were subsequently held. The Constitutional Court has remained in place.

(b) *Removal of judges through early retirement*

to maintain the constitutional order and one of the main functions of any Constitutional Court is, by upholding the principles of the Law, to keep the constitutional system functioning. This function of arbitration presupposes by definition the use of economy as well as equity, and requires respect for the solutions reached by democratically legitimate institutions. A constitutional court, like any other state institution and court, on the one hand deserves institutional respect but, on the other hand, must respect its own procedures when they provide for adversarial proceedings which guarantee the principle of equality of the parties". The Commission quite exceptionally revisited the decisions and reasoning of the Constitutional Court and pointed to a different conclusion. It also warned that should the Constitutional Court fail to "decide within the parameters of their legal authority and responsibility", the robustness of State Institutions in the country in line with the Constitution would be seriously undermined and the democratic functioning of state institutions would be irreparably compromised. The Constitutional Court subsequently revoked its own decisions and the judges resigned.

[17] https://www.venice.coe.int/webforms/events/default.aspx?id=3137 last accessed 30 September 2021.

In Armenia, in an attempt to remove the constitutional judges who still enjoyed life tenure under the old constitution and were closely associated with the previous ruling majority, Prime Minister Nikol Pashinyan offered them a very advantageous early retirement scheme. The authorities openly argued that they wanted to offer these judges, whom they associated with the "old regime", a "dignified exit", which was justified in the prevailing revolutionary context, and by the public distrust in the current composition of the Constitutional Court. The Venice Commission defended the security of tenure of constitutional court judges as an essential guarantee of their independence, designed to shield them from influence from the political majority of the day. The Commission reiterated that it would be unacceptable if each new government could replace sitting judges with newly elected ones of their choice. The Commission found that as a matter of principle, where the early retirement scheme remains truly voluntary, i.e. it excludes any undue (political or personal) pressure on the judges concerned, or when it is not designed to influence the outcome of pending cases, there are no standards that would lead to opposing such a scheme, even though considerations of possible hampering of the effective functioning of the court could become relevant in case of early retirement of several judges at the same time.[18] None of the judges of the Constitutional Court of Armenia accepted this proposal. This led to the more radical measures indicated above.

(c) *Increase or decrease in the number of constitutional court judges, packing with party loyalists, amendment of rules on the appointment and dismissal of the constitutional judges*

Court-packing is a typical measure which is taken when the ruling majority may appoint constitutional judges without the participation of the opposition. When there are no vacancies or it is not possible to create vacancies through early retirement, pressure or other measures, constitutional majorities have at times amended the constitution in order to

[18] CDL-AD(2019)024, Joint opinion of the Venice Commission and the Directorate of Human Rights (DHR) of the Directorate General of Human Rights and Rule of Law (DGI) of the Council of Europe on the amendments to the judicial code and some other laws, Adopted by the Venice Commission at its 120th Plenary Session (Venice, 11–12 October 2019).

increase the number of constitutional judges and/or to amend the rules on the appointment of the judges in favour of the majority.

In Hungary, in 2010 the rules on appointment of constitutional judges were amended; under the new rules, they are nominated by a nominating committee consisting of members of the parliamentary groups of the parties represented in parliament; and the number of members per parliamentary group on the nominating committee shall be proportionate to the parliamentary group's size in relation to the total number of Members of Parliament. In 2011, the number of Constitutional Court judges was increased to 15 from 11, and due to that change, 5 new judges were nominated and elected by the governing party. In 2012, the mandate was increased from 9 to 12 years. In December 2013, the upper age limit in place for Constitutional Court judges (then of 70 years) was decreased, without any negotiations with the opposition.

In Poland, a transitional provision of the Act on the Constitutional Court of June 2015 allowed the governing majority, the Civic Party Platform, to elect, with simple majority, five new judges of the Constitutional Court, despite the fact that only three judicial offices were vacated. Consequently, two of the five judges were chosen to replace judges whose term would end during the next term of the Sejm. The parliamentary elections of October 2015 were won by the Law and Justice Party, which immediately after the elections passed the Act of November 2015, amending the Act of June 2015 on the Constitutional Tribunal. The reform aimed to repeal the election of all five judges by the Sejm of the previous term and to appoint new judges, which was done on 2 December 2015 ("the December judges").[19] The latter were sworn in in December 2016 by the Acting President of the Court, after a year during which the Court only had 12 out of 15 judges. By a judgment of 3 December, the Constitutional Court ruled that the transitional provision having allowed the Civic Platform to elect two judges whose mandate had not yet expired was unconstitutional, but that the election of three judges to replace those whose tenures expired during the previous Sejm's term did not violate the Constitution. The Commission found that a proposed solution providing that all judges of the Tribunal be replaced, even if it was adopted by a constitutional majority in Parliament, would be in flagrant violation of European and international standards. It called on both

[19] https://www.fljs.org/constitutional-court-poland-battle-judicial-independence last accessed 30 September 2021.

"majority and opposition to do their utmost to find a solution" in the issue of the appointments of the "October judges" and the "December judges", based on the obligation to respect and fully implement the judgments of the Constitutional Tribunal.[20]

In Turkey, the new constitution empowered the President, who had already the power to appoint some of the judges of the Constitutional Court, to appoint 4 out of 13 members of the Council of Judges and Prosecutors, in addition to the Minister of Justice who presides the CJP. The Venice Commission stressed that these changes regarding the manner of appointment of the members of the CJP would have repercussions on the Constitutional Court. The CJP is responsible for the elections of the members of the Court of Cassation and the Council of State. Both courts are entitled to choose two members of the Constitutional Court by sending three nominees for each position to the President, who makes the appointments. The influence of the Executive over the Constitutional Court would therefore be increased.[21]

In the Russian Federation, the constitutional amendments adopted in 2020 reduced the number of judges of the Constitutional Court from 19 to 11, including the Chairman of the Court and his/her deputy. However, Article 3 (7) of the Amending Law provided that the judges of the Constitutional Court who are in office on the day of entry into force of the Amending Law would continue to exercise their powers and no new judges would be appointed until a number of 11 is reached (the current number of judges was 12).[22] Further, the amendments gave the President the power to propose to the Federation Council the termination of the mandate of the President, the Vice-president, and the judges of the Constitutional Court of the Russian Federation "in the event of them committing a violation tarnishing the honour and dignity of judge, as well

[20] CDL-AD(2016)026, Opinion on the Act on the Constitutional Tribunal, Adopted by the Venice Commission at its 108th Plenary Session (Venice, 14–15 October 2016).

[21] CDL-AD(2017)005, Opinion on the amendments to the Constitution adopted by the Grand National Assembly on 21 January 2017 and to be submitted to a National referendum on 16 April 2017. Adopted by the Venice Commission at its 110th Plenary Session (Venice, 10–11 March 2017), § 121. A formal amendment in Article 146 of the Constitution also reduced the number of justices from 17 to 15 following the abolition of the High Military Court of Appeals and the High Military Administrative Court.

[22] CDL-AD(2021)005, Interim opinion on Constitutional Amendments and the procedure for their adoption, Adopted by the Venice Commission at its 126th Plenary Session (online, 19–20 March 2021), § 158–171.

as in other situations established by federal constitutional law demonstrating impossibility for a judge to continue discharging of its powers". The Venice Commission found that the "committal of a violation tarnishing honour and dignity of judge" was a very vague ground for dismissal which placed the constitutional judges in a position of uncertainty which might have a chilling effect on the independence of the judicial power.[23] Further, shifting the initiative for the termination of powers of the constitutional judges from the Court itself to the President of the State constituted a severe interference with the independence of judges.[24]

(d) *Harassment of judges*

In September 2015, the Commission learned that the judges of the Constitutional Court of Georgia and their families were being harassed, through manifestations and pickets held in front of their homes, the President issued a public statement, in which he reminded that the judgments of a constitutional court are final and binding, and in a state which respects the rule of law, they are executed. The public can express critical views on these judgments, but only "in a respectful and legal manner".[25]

In Poland, following the legislative amendments of 2016, a new President of the Constitutional Tribunal was elected on the basis of a questionable procedure; the new President delegated her powers to another judge, who had been elected on a legal basis that had been found unconstitutional by the Tribunal; the Vice-President of the Tribunal, who was not among the loyalists, was sent on a vacation he had not asked for, and the election of three sitting judges was challenged seven years after their election. The President of the Commission reacted with a public statement on 16 January 2017, in which he qualified these measures as "practical steps ... taken with the apparent aim to ensure that the Tribunal act in accordance with the will of the current political majority" and expressed concern that the Tribunal was being put in the impossibility to exercise its "crucial role to ensure respect for human rights, the rule of law

[23] Ibidem, § 158.
[24] Ibidem, § 166.
[25] https://www.venice.coe.int/webforms/events/default.aspx?id=2104 last accessed 30 September 2021.

and democratic principles in Poland", which the Constitution assigned to it.[26]

(e) *Changes in the jurisdiction of the Constitutional Court*[27]

In Hungary, as a result of a constitutional amendment in November 2010, a serious limitation of the competences of the Constitutional Court was introduced.[28] According to this amendment, as long as the state debt exceeded half of the Gross Domestic Product the Constitutional Court may assess the constitutionality of Acts related to the central budget, central taxes, stamp duties and contributions, custom duties and central requirements related to local taxes exclusively in connection with the rights to life and human dignity, the protection of personal data, the freedom of thought, conscience and religion or with rights related to the Hungarian citizenship.[29] The Commission recalled that "a sufficiently large scale of competences is essential to ensure that the court oversees the constitutionality of the most important principles and settings of the society, including all constitutionally guaranteed fundamental rights. Therefore, restricting the Court's competence in such a way that it would review certain state Acts only with regard to a limited part of the Constitution runs counter to the obvious aim of the constitutional legislature in the Hungarian parliament "to enhance the protection of fundamental rights in Hungary"".[30]

[26] https://www.venice.coe.int/webforms/events/default.aspx?id=2352&lang=en last accessed 30 September 2021.

[27] In Armenia, a constitutional amendment limiting the scope of a general ex ante review of constitutional amendments by the Constitutional Court and reverting to a control of conformity with non-amendable provisions of the Constitution and imposing a two-week time-limit for such review were considered unproblematic by the Venice Commission: CDL-AD(2020)016, Opinion on three legal questions in the context of draft constitutional amendments concerning the mandate of the judges of the Constitutional Court, Adopted by the Venice Commission on 19 June 2020 by a written procedure replacing the 123rd Plenary Session, §§ 60–70.

[28] This limitation was included also in the new Fundamental Law of 2013, which replaced the 2011 Constitution, while the applicability condition of being in excess of 50 percent of the GDP was removed.

[29] CDL-AD(2011)001, Opinion on three legal questions arising in the process of drafting the new constitution of Hungary, Adopted by the Venice Commission at its 86th Plenary Session (Venice, 25–26 March 2011), § 9.

[30] CDL-AD(2011)016, Opinion on the new Constitution of Hungary, Adopted by the Venice Commission at its 87th Plenary Session (Venice, 17–18 June 2011), § 99.

In Turkey, the Constitutional Court under the new constitution of 2017 lost the possibility of controlling, as it did before, laws empowering the Council of Ministers to issue decrees having force of law. The President under the amendments will not need an empowering law. While the amendments define limits to the Presidential legislative activity with a formal prevalence of laws over decrees, the Constitutional Court has not been given the express power to decide over the conflicts which will inevitably arise in this respect.[31]

(f) *Constitutionalisation of unconstitutional norms*

In Hungary, a series of provisions[32] of the Fourth Amendment to the Fundamental Law, adopted in March 2013, entrenched in the Constitution matters which had previously been found unconstitutional by the Constitutional Court, thus preventing the Court from declaring them unconstitutional. The Commission, while recognising that in itself the possibility of constitutional amendments is an important counterweight to a constitutional court's power over legislation in a constitutional democracy, as well as an important element in the delicate system of checks and balances which defines a constitutional democracy, found that "this approach can only be justified in particular cases, based on thorough preparatory work, wide public debate and large political consensus—as in general is necessary for constitutional amendments".[33] The Commission therefore expressed grave concern, including because it observed that

[31] CDL-AD(2017)005, Opinion on the amendments to the Constitution adopted by the Grand National Assembly on 21 January 2017 and to be submitted to a national referendum on 16 April 2017, Adopted by the Venice Commission at its 110th Plenary Session (Venice, 10–11 March 2017), § 122.

[32] Article L.1 of the Fundamental Law relates to decision 43/2012 (family ties); Article VII of the Fundamental Law—decision 1/2013 (recognition of churches); Article IX.3 of the Fundamental Law—decision 1/2013 (limitation of media access for political parties); Article IX.5 of the Fundamental Law—decisions 30/1992, decision 18/2004, 95/2008 (freedom of speech); Article X.3 of the Fundamental Law—decision 69/2009 (autonomy of universities);Article XI.3 of the Fundamental Law—decision 32/2012 (student grants); Article XXII.3 of the Fundamental Law—decision 38/2012 (homeless): see CDL-AD(2013)012, footnote 58.

[33] CDL-AD(2013)012, Opinion on the fourth amendment to the fundamental law of Hungary, Adopted by the Venice Commission at its 95th Plenary Session (Venice, 14–15 June 2013).

shielding ordinary law from constitutional review had become a systemic pattern in Hungary.

(g) *Removal of possibility to refer to previous case-law*

The Fourth Amendment of Hungary further prevented the Constitutional Court from referring to its earlier case-law. The authorities justified this provision with the concern that the previous case-law could result in the perpetuation of the old constitution. The Commission, however, found that there were no grounds for this concern, and the Hungarian Constitutional Court which was not legally bound by its former case-law could have further developed arguments and principles or have them replaced by new ones, if necessary, depending on the contents of the new Fundamental Law.[34]

(h) *Refusal to publish judgments*

In Poland, in the middle of the struggle between the Court and the ruling party, Prime Minister Beata Szydło did not recognise the judgment of 8 March 2016, whereby the Court had annulled the Act of December 2015 introducing severe limitations to the functioning of the Court and refused to publish it. The Commission found that the refusal to publish judgment "would not only be contrary to the rule of law, such an unprecedented move would further deepen the constitutional crisis [...]. Not only the Polish Constitution but also European and international standards require that the judgments of a Constitutional Court be respected. The publication of the judgment and its respect by the authorities are a precondition for finding a way out of this constitutional crisis".[35]

(i) *Changes in the procedure before the Constitutional Court*[36]

[34] CDL-AD(2013)012, §§ 88–99.

[35] CDL-AD(2016)001-e, Opinion on amendments to the Act of 25 June 2015 on the Constitutional Tribunal of Poland, Adopted by the Venice Commission at its 106th Plenary Session (Venice, 11–12 March 2016), § 143. The matter of the publication of the judgements of the Constitutional Court continued to be the object of modifications and criticism.

[36] In Ukraine, after the Constitutional Court issued in 2020 a judgement practically annihilating the anti-corruption system, several stakeholders and representatives of NGOs argued that the quorum for taking decisions ought to have been raised from 14 to 16 judges, as it was preferable to prevent the court from taking any decision, compared to the risk of having

In some cases, legislative changes made it more difficult for constitutional courts to exercise their jurisdiction.[37]

In Hungary, the Fourth Amendment imposed on the Constitutional Court a 30-day time-limit to review the constitutionality applications from ordinary judges. The Venice Commission recalled that while concern for speedy constitutional proceedings was understandable, this should not be done in a way that renders ineffective constitutional review as an essential element of checks and balances.[38] This time-limit was subsequently extended to 90 days by the Fifth Amendment.

In Poland, on 15 December 2015 the Law and Justice Party presented more amendments to the Act on the Constitutional Court, which proposed an increase in the minimum number of judges necessary to constitute a full bench; a requirement of two-thirds majority to deliver a judgment; a requirement to consider the cases in the sequence in which they were filed (without any exceptions); a provision allowing the removal of a judge from office "in particularly serious cases" by the Sejm, through a resolution upon a motion of the General Assembly of Judges of the Constitutional Court; a provision allowing disciplinary proceedings to be initiated against a judge of the Court upon a motion filed by the Minister of Justice or the President of Poland. The Commission concluded that these measures, especially in their combined effect, would slow down the work of the Constitutional Tribunal and render it ineffective, and reminded that "Crippling the Tribunal's effectiveness will undermine all three basic

to deal with bad decisions. Bills were introduced in parliament to this effect. CDL-AD(2020)039, Urgent Opinion on the reform of the Constitutional Court, Issued pursuant to Article 14a of the Venice Commission's Rules of Procedure, Endorsed by the Venice Commission on 11 December 2020 at its 125th online Plenary Session, § 12.

[37] Non-appointment of judges may also be used to prevent the Court from functioning, and the Venice Commission has consistently recommended to provide for an anti-deadlock mechanism in order to avoid the paralysis in the Constitutional Court's activity in case of the constitutionally empowered authority's failure to appoint a judge: see, for example, in Ukraine: CDL-AD(2006)016-e, Opinion on possible Constitutional and Legislative Improvements to ensure the uninterrupted functioning of the Constitutional Court of Ukraine, Adopted by the Venice Commission at its 67th Plenary Session (Venice, 9–10 June 2006), §§ 12 ff.; for Georgia: CDL-AD(2016)017, Opinion on the Amendments to the organic law on the Constitutional Court and to the law on constitutional legal proceedings, Endorsed by the Venice Commission at its 107th Plenary Session (Venice, 10–11 June 2016), § 20.

[38] CDL-AD(2013)012, Opinion on the fourth amendment to the fundamental law of Hungary, Adopted by the Venice Commission at its 95th Plenary Session (Venice, 14–15 June 2013), § 117.

principles of the Council of Europe: democracy—because of an absence of a central part of checks and balances; human rights—because the access of individuals to the Constitutional Tribunal could be slowed down to a level resulting in the denial of justice; and the rule of law—because the Constitutional Tribunal would become ineffective".[39]

(j) *Refusal to execute the judgments of the Constitutional Court*

Several of the other measures listed in this chapter (e.g. the refusal to publish a judgment) amount to refusals to execute the judgments of the constitutional court, when they do not aim at preventing undesired judgments.

In Turkey, the refusal was most explicit. After issuing a pilot judgment setting out the principles to be applied by the courts when dealing with cases originated by the attempted coup of 2016, the Constitutional Court ruled that the detention of two journalists, Messrs. Alpay and Altan, was unconstitutional. The government issued very critical statements, and the courts refused to release the two journalists.

4 Conclusions

Constitutional courts have proved to be a fundamental safeguard of constitutionalism in modern European states. They contribute towards the smooth functioning of the state institutions by clarifying and completing the mechanisms set out in the constitution and defend the latter against attempts to alter the institutional balance, including by playing a deterrent role. They also protect individual human rights, especially in countries where full individual complaint is admitted.

[39] CDL-AD 2016 01, § 138. Another amendment to the Act on the Constitutional Court of July 2016 introduced further changes, including an exception to the obligation for the court to decide the cases in the sequence in which they were filed (decision of the Court's president); an obligation to postpone a full bench hearing in the event of the absence of the Prosecutor General; a requirement of a motion of the president of the Constitutional Court to the prime minister in order to publish a Constitutional Court judgement. Some of these changes were subsequently mitigated, but the cumulative effect of these measures remained: CDL-AD(2016)026, Opinion on the act on the Constitutional Tribunal, Adopted by the Venice Commission at its 108th Plenary Session (Venice, 14–15 October 2016), §§ 121–124.

Difficulties in the functioning of constitutional courts have been caused or exploited, notably but not exclusively by populist regimes, to enjoy a free hand in the realisation of their winner-take-all programmes.

Constitutional courts are vulnerable to attacks, as more in general the judiciary is. Courts rely on the goodwill of the other two branches and ultimately on the will of the electorate to ensure compliance with their orders.[40] The executive and the legislature dispose, as the analysis above has shown, of a wide array of tools—in primis legislative and even constitutional amendments—to correct or bypass judicial decisions, in an attempt to subdue constitutional courts. Mere threats to do so may have a chilling effect on constitutional courts, which might not necessarily be willing or able to fight against the threats of populism, and might end up accommodating to rising political trends in order not to be attacked.

The main tool at the disposal of a Constitutional Court is that it declares the legislative amendments unconstitutional, as has happened, for example, in Poland, but such findings are unlikely to affect the strong determination of the governments which have initiated them.

The Venice Commission has done its utmost to protect constitutional courts, as institutions, not in a specific composition, from attacks and measures designed to undermine them.

Since 2015, the Commission's President has issued several public statements in support of constitutional courts,[41] or urging the setting up of a court.[42]

[40] N. Friedman the impact of populism on courts, op. cit. In his dissent in Baker v. Carr (369 U.S. 186 [1962]), Supreme Court Justice Felix Frankfurter identified the dependence of the US Supreme Court (or any US court, for that matter) on its legitimacy among the mass public: "The Court's authority—possessed of neither the purse nor the sword—ultimately rests upon sustained public confidence in its moral sanction" (369 U.S. 186, 267).

[41] As regards Georgia: https://www.venice.coe.int/webforms/events/default.aspx?id=2104 last accessed 30 September 2021. As regards Poland, Turkey and Georgia: https://www.venice.coe.int/webforms/events/default.aspx?id=2193 last accessed 30 September 2021.; as regards Poland: https://www.venice.coe.int/webforms/events/default.aspx?id=2352 last accessed 30 September 2021.; As regards the Republic of Moldova: https://www.venice.coe.int/webforms/events/default.aspx?id=2104 last accessed 30 September 2021. and https://www.venice.coe.int/webforms/events/default.aspx?id=3137 last accessed 30 September 2021.; as regards Armenia: https://www.venice.coe.int/webforms/events/default.aspx?id=2892&lang=en last accessed 30 September 2021.

[42] In Tunisia: https://www.venice.coe.int/webforms/events/default.aspx?id=2104 last accessed 30 September 2021. The President of Tunisia, after concentrating powers in his hands under emergency legislation in summer 2021—emergency legilsation which ought to have been validated by the not-yet established Constitutional Court—questioned the need

The Commission has also supported their institutional role at times in difficult circumstances through amicus curiae briefs. The role of these briefs is often major: not only do they steer the courts in the right direction or keep them on the right track: they may also provide necessary support to a court which faces attacks or criticism and needs to take brave decisions.[43]

The Venice Commission has also assessed several of the measures taken against constitutional courts. The impact of the Commission's opinions has however been limited, on account amongst others of the lack of interest for multilateralism and also specifically for their lack of interest in foreign advice. As has been observed, "the rise of illiberal democracies represents an entirely new challenge for independent and international bodies such as the Venice Commission. Populist governments not only tend to abolish independent courts and counter-majoritarian authorities within the country. They also nourish among the people a politics of fear against foreigners, and a correspondent suspicion for whichever suggestion coming from international technical bodies". Several populist regimes have also been recalcitrant to follow the requests of the institutions of the European Union, which instead normally disposes of very powerful leverage often resulting in the Venice Commission's recommendations being largely followed.[44]

A recurrent and rather powerful argument which is invoked in order to interfere with the work of the constitutional courts is that the judges are corrupt. This argument has generally a very broad support in the society and among the international community: the crucial importance of ensuring that the courts are exempted from corruption is evident. It is clear that the guarantees of irremovability of constitutional judges, which are in principle an essential guarantee of independence for the whole court, may become a recipe for impunity, when they are bestowed upon individuals who do not abide by the high standards of honesty and respect for the public good which should guide constitutional judges. It therefore becomes necessary, and even urgent, in several countries to revise the

for Tunisia to even set up a constitutional court: https://www.businessnews.com.tn/kais-saied--avions-nous-vraiment-besoin-dune-cour-constitutionnelle-,520,115729,3 last accessed 24 January 2022.

[43] Since 2004, the Commission has issued more than 40 amicus curiae briefs.

[44] Pinelli, Parliaments, Constitutional Transitions and the Venice Commission, https://www.venice.coe.int/files/articles/Pinelli_Parliaments_Constitutional_Transitions_Venice_Commission.pdf.

mechanisms of accountability of the judges, through clear rules on conflict of interest, through requirements of asset declarations, through improved disciplinary proceedings. Restoring trust in the constitutional courts should reduce the chances of popular support for the attacks of the Executive on them. Conversely, faulty or insufficient guarantees and rules on the appointment and dismissal of judges and on the functioning of the constitutional courts may result in increased politicisation and temptations to take over the courts.

The Venice Commission will continue to support constitutional courts but stands ready to carry out this reflection.

Bibliography

Dürr, Schnutz R. "Constitutional Justice—A key mission of the Venice Commission." In *Venice Commission, 30 Year Quest for Democracy through Law, 1990–2020*, edited by Simona Granata-Menghini and Ziya Caga Tanyar, 215-232. Lund: Juristförlaget i Lund, 2020.

Dürr, Schnutz R. "Constitutional Courts: an endangered species?" in *Les Cours constitutionnelles, garantie de la qualité démocratique des sociétés?*, edited by Dominique Rousseau, 111–136. Issy les Molineaux: LGDJ, 2019.

Granata-Menghini, Simona and Kuijer, Martin, "Advisory or de facto binding? Follow up to Venice Commission's opinions: between reality and perception." In *Venice Commission, 30 Years of Quest for Democracy through Law, 1990–2020*, edited by Simona Granata-Menghini and Ziya Caga Tanyar, 281–293. Lund: Juristförlaget i Lund, 2020.

Werner Müller, Jan. *Qu'est-ce que le populisme?*. Paris: Gallimard, 2016.

Constitutional Effects of Populism in EU Member States, 2010–2020

Zoltán Szente and Fruzsina Gárdos-Orosz

1 Introduction

According to conventional wisdom, populism is one of the most characteristic political trends in contemporary Europe, posing a significant challenge to the traditional values and institutions of constitutional democracies. It is generally thought that one of the distinguishing features of modern populism is its "constitutional project", that is, the ambitions of populists to pursue constitutional changes to achieve their goals when

This research has received funding from the European Union's Horizon 2020 research and innovation programme under grant agreement No. 822590, DEMOS. The research was also supported by 29245 programme on Populism in the policy and law making funded by the National Research Development and Innovation Office. We owe special thanks to Emese Szilágyi and Domonkos Polonyi for their contribution to the research project.

Z. Szente (✉) • F. Gárdos-Orosz
Institute for Legal Studies, Centre for Social Sciences, Budapest, Hungary
e-mail: Szente.Zoltan@tk.mta.hu; orosz.fruzsina@tk.hu

J. M. Castellà Andreu, M. A. Simonelli (eds.), *Populism and Contemporary Democracy in Europe*,
https://doi.org/10.1007/978-3-030-92884-1_6

they come to power (Blokker 2019a). Although the contemporary decline or backsliding of liberal democracies is defined in various ways, such as "constitutional breakdown" (Sadurski 2019), "stealth authoritarianism" (Varol 2015), or "democratic recession" (Diamond 2015, 142), and the political systems that have emerged as a result of these tendencies are often referred to as "hybrid regimes" (Bogaards 2009), "illiberal" or "non-liberal democracies" (Drinóczi and Bień-Kacała 2019; Walker 1997), competitive (Levitsky and Way 2010) or electoral (Schedler 2013) authoritarianism, "autocratic legalism" (Scheppele 2018), "counter-constitutionalism" (Blokker 2019b), or "abusive constitutionalism" (Landau 2013, 213), perhaps the most sophisticated and elaborated explanation for these changes is the theory of populist constitutionalism.

In this study, we explore how the characteristics of populism have been transformed into constitutional law in the EU Member States or, in other words, which attributes have been institutionalised in these countries, and to what extent. In doing so, we wanted to know whether there are more general European trends, that is, if we assume that populism is a political movement that is widespread in many countries of the continent, whether it generates similar constitutional changes in different countries. Ultimately, we were looking for an answer to the theoretical question of whether, on the basis of the actual constitutional development of the past period, it is possible to identify populist constitutionalism as a specific form of modern European constitutionalism.

While much of the literature on populist constitutionalism has focused on the concept of this phenomenon, there has been little empirically based analysis of the characteristics of populist constitutionalism from a comparative perspective. Rather, the decline of constitutional democracy and the rule of law have been examined in only a few countries, most notably Poland and Hungary, and these developments have been described as manifestations of populist constitutionalism. In our study, we attempt to fill this gap to some degree by empirically examining the extent to which the criteria of populist constitutionalism has characterised constitutional changes in EU Member States over the past decade.

For this purpose, we designed a questionnaire focusing on the characteristics of populist constitutionalism identified in the literature. The questionnaire has been edited and discussed among the members of the law team of the DEMOS project, notably the experts of the University of Barcelona, the Centre for Social Science of the Hungarian Academy of Sciences, the University of Copenhagen and the University of Siena. This questionnaire was a tool for collecting data and information about the legal repercussions of populist politics or ambitions in the EU Member States. We are aware that it contains quite general and abstract questions, some of which cannot be interpreted in some countries at all, while in other countries, a whole study or book would be needed to reply to them. It is also to be noted that our goal here was not to describe in depth the constitutional development of the EU Member States; however, the respondents were requested to answer all the questions (apart from the fact-finding ones) in relation to populism or populist trends in their own countries. We asked the national experts[1] to give us as much precise data as they could, indicating, for instance, the legislative acts and judicial decisions to which they refer.

The questionnaire concentrated on both the changes in constitutional values and the institutional transformations of the last decade in the EU Member States. The questions were based on the presumption that populist governments make efforts to consolidate their own power and to weaken the institutional guarantees of constitutional democracy. We asked respondents to list the constitutional changes that have taken place in the last ten years in each country, specifying the date and content of constitutional amendments, as well as the failed attempts at constitutional changes. The data collection extended to the form and content of constitutional identity and "unconstitutional constitutional amendment" in the

[1] The following experts contributed to the research by preparing the country reports: Prof. Konrad Lachmayer, Sigmund Freud University, Vienna (Austria), Prof. Marc Verdussen, UC Louvain (Belgium), Prof. Djordje Gardasevic, University of Zagreb (Croatia), Dr Vlastimil Havlík, Masaryk University, Brno (Czech Republic), Prof. Helle Krunke and Dr Sune Klinge, University of Copenhagen (Denmark), Prof. Bertrand Mathieu, University of Panthéon-Sorbonne Paris I (France), Mr Vadim Poleshchuk, Legal Information Centre for Human Rights (Estonia), Prof. Lando Kirchmair, University of Munich (Germany), Prof. Dimitri Sotiropoulos, University of Athens (Greece), Prof. Zoltán Szente and Dr Fruzsina Gárdos-Orosz, Institute for Legal Studies, Budapest (Hungary), Eoin Carolan, University College, Dublin (Ireland), Dr Marco Antonio Simonelli, University of Barcelona (Italy), Inese Freimane, Riga Graduate School of Law (Latvia), Prof. Jurgita Pauzaité-Kulvinskiené, Law Institute of Lithuania, Vilnius, (Lithuania), Prof. Miroslaw Granat, Cardinal Stefan Wyszynski University, Warsaw (Poland), Dr Teresa Violante, Max Planck Institute for Comparative Public Law and International Law, Heidelberg (Portugal), Prof. Simina Tanasescu, Bucharest University (Romania), Mr Simon Drugda, PhD Candidate, University of Copenhagen (Slovakia), Prof. Jose Maria Castellà Andreu, University of Barcelona (Spain), Prof. Henrik Wanander, Ms. Lovisa Häckner Posse, Ms. Lisa Kerker, Dr Vilhelm Persson, Lund University (Sweden), Prof. Merris Amos, Queen Mary University London (United Kingdom), Samo Barduczky, University of Ljubljana (Slovenia), Mr George Coucounis, advocate (Cyprus).

domestic constitutional discourse and law. Other questions covered the major institutional and procedural changes in the legislature, the changes in electoral laws and the development in governmental decision-making. The changes in the rules governing the legal status, procedural rules and the scope of responsibility of the politically neutral or control institutions such as the constitutional court, the judiciary, the audit commission, the ombudsman and similar public authorities were also explored. A further group of questions focused on the relationship or balance between the branches of public power with special attention to how the role of the various power institutions has changed in the recent years. The questionnaire included some questions on the legal forms of direct democracy and citizens' participation, the constitutional-legal changes in recent years affecting the autonomy of non-governmental organizations (churches, higher education, civil organisations), and whether the legal status of political parties has changed in the last ten years. We have further assessed the relationship between European/international law and domestic law, if there have been any conflicts between the two legal systems.

We also posed questions about populism's impact on law, legal concepts and the juridical process. We presumed that even in countries where populist parties have not come to power, populist challenges have had an impact on various legal proceedings, including administrative and judicial procedures. The other major issue here was, therefore, to investigate which constitutional guarantees have been effective in resisting or repealing populist challenges or, alternatively, which constitutional institutions/policies/procedures have been successfully used in the EU Member States to strengthen liberal constitutionalism. Thus, in this section of the questionnaire, we focused on the practice of constitutional bodies not in general terms, but in relation to populist politics or tendencies. We asked if the jurisprudence of the constitutional court (or any other high court having constitutional review power) has changed, and if any changes have occurred in administrative procedures. We asked respondents which procedures have proved to be most successful in hindering or, conversely, promoting the development of populism.

Constitutional changes were originally examined between 2010 and 2018, but due to the delay caused by the COVID-19 pandemic and some important recent changes, we sought to extend the period of analysis to 2020, where this was possible. It is important to bear in mind, however, that constitutional frameworks are constantly changing in contemporary Europe, partly due to the pandemic and the spread of populism, so it is almost impossible to get a completely accurate snapshot of changes in constitutional regimes. Nevertheless, we believe that an overview of the most important constitutional changes over the last ten years or so provides an opportunity to identify broader trends and developments, and to assess the impact of populism on the constitutional polities. Given that the United Kingdom was still a member of the European Union when our research began, the data collection and analysis was extended to this country, which may be all the more justified as modern European populism is often associated with Brexit, the referendum initiative that resulted in Britain leaving the EU.

The whole of the research was carried out under the Democratic Efficacy and the Varieties of Populism in Europe (DEMOS) project. This research programme aims at obtaining a better understanding of populism, addressing the contemporary populist challenge through the lens of democratic efficacy.[2] Basically, our analysis was grounded on this data collection: 23 national experts have completed the questionnaires themselves, and in 5 cases (Malta, Luxembourg, the Netherlands, Finland and Bulgaria), the scholars of the DEMOS group completed the questionnaire based on desk research and asked national experts to verify, complete or comment on the data that they found.[3]

Below, we will first review the conceptual attempts at defining populist constitutionalism and its criteria, and then we will consider the limitations of the applied research methodology and the scope of our findings. In the next section, we examine whether there are trends in actual constitutional change that can be linked to the supposed phenomenon of populist constitutionalism. Then we explore how and in what context the individual characteristics emerge in the constitutional development of various countries. Finally, our conclusions will be presented, trying to provide an answer to the original research question, namely whether the theory and analytical tools of populist constitutionalism can be empirically supported, that is, whether populist constitutionalism provides an adequate theoretical framework for explaining and understanding real constitutional changes across Europe.

[2] "DEMOS H2020—The Project".

[3] Martin Belov for Bulgaria, Katalin Cseres for the Netherlands, Janne Salminen from Finland, Málta arranged by Helle Krunke and Luxembourg arranged by Jose Maria Castellà Andreu.

2 Concepts and Methods. Concept and Conceptual Criteria of Populist Constitutionalism

However, in order to assess or test the explanatory power of the theory of populist constitutionalism, it is necessary to define what this concept means, all the more so because, like populism itself, it is a contested notion.

Like populism, which is an essentially contested concept, populist constitutionalism does not have a widely shared definition. Instead, a variety of conceptualisations is known (Szente 2021). Thus, constitutional populism can be characterised by populist governments, which have implemented populist-oriented constitutional reforms (Anselmi 2018).

Populist constitutionalism is defined by some scholars through its relationship to democracy, emphasising that "it is a theory of constitutions and constitutional practices that emphasizes their populist character and recommends that they develop along a populist trajectory" (Doyle 2019, 164). According to its characteristics, populist constitutionalism can also be understood as a coherent political theory (Doyle 2019, 165). In this view, populist regimes are not fighting for an improved liberal constitutionalism, but for an alternative one based on direct legitimacy through the people (Landau 2018, 541). Just as liberal constitutionalism is in fact an aspirational idea, so illiberal constitutionalism can also be a normative concept, albeit in the opposite direction (Tushnet 2017). Populism has a sui generis constitutionalism, a counterpart of liberal constitutionalism, and "constitutional populism" is characteristic of government-run, institutionalized populism that pursues populist constitutional reforms, such as in Venezuela, Bolivia or Hungary (Anselmi 2018, 87).

However, the concept of populist constitutionalism is most often defined by its most important characteristics, or, more exactly a specific combination of them. The identification of conceptual elements is essential for an in-depth analysis, so that they can be compared with actual constitutional changes, and the prevalence and validity of populist constitutionalism can be verified, at least to some extent, empirically, rather than as a matter of subjective judgement. This purpose was served by the method we have chosen to distinguish between the primary and secondary criteria of populist constitutionalism. This distinction of conceptual elements was based on their acceptance in the academic literature; we considered those criteria as "primary" aspects that are included in most definitions, that is, those around which there is a significant professional consensus, while others are "secondary" features that are attributed to populist constitutionalism by some academics but do not have a general recognition in scholarship. Many of these criteria are also closely related to and overlap each other, but it is worth separating them for analysis and clarity.

In our research methodology, the primary criteria include:

- the preference of popular sovereignty and the promotion of direct democracy;
- the claim to authentic representation and, together with this, anti-pluralism;
- an extreme approach of majoritarianism;
- the strong leader and the personification of power.

As in the classical definition of populism, it is "a thin-centered ideology that considers society to be ultimately separated into two homogeneous and antagonistic camps, 'the pure people' versus the 'corrupt elite', and which argues that politics should be an expression of the *volonté générale* (general will) of the people" (Mudde and Kaltwasser 2017, 5). Populists postulate that the public interest, or the popular will, is unified and ascertainable (Müller 2016, 26; Corrias 2016, 11), and both the political and constitutional systems must represent it as accurately as possible (Scholtes 2019, 354). According to the populist concept of popular sovereignty, the majority formed in elections is the sole source of democratic legitimacy (Mueller 2019, 1033), and direct democracy should be preferred to representative democracy: "Populism, for its part, refuses the model of representation, by proposing a return to a direct approach to democracy which would give the people the opportunity to influence and change the constitution without passing through parliamentary representatives" (Fabbrizi 2020, 438). The emphasis of popular sovereignty may be closely linked to the anti-institutionalism that characterises populism in general, questioning the legitimacy of representative institutions. If it is true, then this attitude could generate constitutional changes when populists are in government.

The emphasis on the supremacy of the popular will in the populist conception is associated with a kind of anti-pluralism and the need for authentic representation. There is also a broad consensus among scholars that populists are against pluralism, considering themselves the only exclusive representatives of the real interests of the people (Mudde 2004, 543;

Müller 2016, 3, 2017, 593; Bugaric and Kuhelj 2018, 26). Although the authentic representation of the popular will by populist parties and politicians is a moral claim (Müller 2016, 39), its accomplishment requires institutional changes, which is why it can be included among the primary criteria of populist constitutionalism. This ambition is often associated with a strong anti-elitism, stemming from the opposition between the ruling elites and ordinary people, and aims to ensure that political decision-making puts the public interest first, rather than the special interests of the elites.

Populist constitutionalism can be characterized by an extreme conception of majoritarianism which is based on a specific approach to democracy, which regards electoral empowerment as an expression of the will of the people and, on that basis, rejects the constitutional restriction of power (Landau 2018, 533; Mudde 2004, 561; Mueller 2019, 1035; Scheppele 2018, 562; Urbinati 2018, 113). This idea may justify weakening non-elected controlling institutions, rejecting any veto of majority decisions based on legal or constitutional considerations, and ultimately contrasting the majority principle with the rule of law (Fournier 2019, 366.).

Charismatic and strong leadership and the personification of power are also very common among the basic characteristics of populism in academic literature (Bugaric and Kuhelj 2018, 27; Drinóczi and Bień-Kacała 2019, 1159; Landau 2018, 33; Pappas 2019, 71–72; Kaltwasser 2018, 68). Constitutional law self-evidently can be an effective tool for centralising power, either by strengthening the executive or by neutralizing counter-balancing institutions or removing re-election barriers.

In addition to this, we have identified as secondary criteria:

promotion of constitutional identity;
abusive legal borrowing;
the use of means provided by crisis management;
restriction of certain fundamental rights together with the intolerance of or discrimination against certain minorities;
anti-globalism and nativism and
clientelism and state capture.

In addition to the principle of popular sovereignty, populists also like to refer to constitutional identity (Corrias 2016, 9) as an expression of the self-identity of a united people and its separation from other nations. In fact, they can associate with this concept any values they like, which can be contrasted with the universal principles and requirements favoured by international organisations. The background motivation can be to symbolically strengthen the political unity of the people (or their supporters) and, through this, to legitimize populist governance (Thornhill 2020, 2; Walker 2019, 522).

The legitimacy of populist governance is also served by the practice of concealing the arbitrary exercise of power by institutions and procedures borrowed from consolidated democracies. Indeed, the so-called abusive legal borrowing is the arbitrary adoption and application of certain otherwise well-admitted techniques or legal solutions out of context, as long as they serve populist purposes.

Some scholars also specify *crisis management* as a source of legitimacy for populism because an external threat gives populists the opportunity to legally break free from the limits of power (Levitsky and Ziblatt 2018, 93), and as experience shows, people are more permissive towards restrictions when their security is threatened, and are more inclined to expect protection from political hardliners.

The government of populists is often referred to as illiberal rule, both because the authoritarian exercise of power is often accompanied by restrictions on certain fundamental rights, especially political liberties, and because it often discriminates against certain minorities (migrants, LGBTQ groups, religious sects) claiming that they do not belong to the people or endanger national culture and identity.

Populists are often characterised by nativism and anti-globalism, as these movements and politicians often claim that international organisations represent "foreign" interests and thus threaten the culture and identity of the national community. They are therefore usually distrustful of international organisations that represent supranational interests and values, like the European Union, international human rights organisations or the European courts.

Similarly, we evaluated clientelism and state capture as secondary criteria, because these phenomena are also often associated with populism. According to some authors, systematic clientelism (Müller 2016, 597; Pappas 2019) and the "colonisation" of the state, that is, the "capture" of key institutions (filling them with politically loyal people), are characteristics of populism (Pappas 2019, 73; Landau 2013, 200).

In our opinion, even if some of its elements are controversial, this set of criteria taken from the academic literature on populist constitutionalism is capable of making theoretical assumptions and findings about populist constitutionalism assessable and controllable. Even if it is not possible to determine exactly which combination of these criteria is needed to achieve a weak version of constitutional populism, it is only possible to rationally establish the existence of a new kind of constitutionalism if at least the majority of the primary criteria are present together in a constitutional system.

Before examining the nature and directions of constitutional change in terms of the characteristics attributed to populist constitutionalism, we must be aware of the circumstances that limit the scope of validity of our analysis.

Perhaps the most important of these is to emphasise that individual indicators cannot in themselves be interpreted as populist characteristics. The use of direct democratic procedures, for example, can improve democracy through the effective involvement of the citizens and can only be seen as a tool for populist political ends in a specific context. Similarly, strong leadership is not a characteristic of populist politicians alone; in constitutional democracies, there are also leaders who exert a decisive influence on political decisions. Then, democracies are often grouped according to their majoritarian or consensual character, and extreme interpretations of the majoritarian principle or the weakening of neutral, controlling institutions are typical of authoritarian regimes in general, not (only) of populism. Or, constitutional identity is recognised in EU law and in the constitutional systems of several EU Member States, while crisis management can also be imposed in constitutional democracies in emergencies, and so on. We have, therefore, at each stage tried to take into account the context in which some of the criteria of populist constitutionalism have emerged in different countries. It was not possible to assess as a populist trait, for example, if certain solutions, which are also characteristic of populist politics, were applied by mainstream political parties as part of a reform process that had been started earlier, without other elements of the populist toolbox being applied. However, even if the primary criteria may only together constitute populist constitutionalist regimes, then it would be an exaggeration to require that all criteria must be met in order to recognize the existence of populist constitutionalism.

It is also important to note that, since the theory of populist constitutionalism claims that populism can develop a particular variety of constitutionalism which has distinguishable characteristics from other developments, our analysis covered only the formal constitutional changes occurring in the last decade. This is important because, when we scrutinised the data, we often found that certain characteristics only appeared as elements of political communication, without any practical consequences, and our research was focused specifically on the phenomenon of constitutional, rather than political populism.

Moreover, we found that the characteristics of populist constitutionalism should not be examined in a quantitative way, because there can be huge differences in the significance of individual attributes: while the Brexit referendum, for example, has caused constitutional conflicts over several years in Britain, and will probably have long-term effects on the British public law system, the nine so-called national consultations held informally in Hungary have had no constitutional or political impact, although in both countries these events have taken place under the buzzword of "direct democracy". Therefore, even if we have been able to identify some characteristics of constitutional populism in a country, we have tried to assess its legal impact.

Likewise, it is difficult to assess cases where primary or secondary populist characteristics have been attempted but failed (e.g. in the case of referendums or constitutional amendments in support of populist ambitions). On the one hand, it may be possible to detect certain populist aspirations in this way, but the institutional and legal changes necessary for constitutional populism to prevail have not been made, and, on the other hand, the rejection of such initiations may be an indication of the failure of populist constitutionalism.

3 Assessing Populist Constitutionalism in the Constitutional Development of the EU Member States

When looking for the major trends of populist constitutionalism in Europe, we wanted to know the extent or frequency of the possible constitutional effects of populism reflected in the constitutional development of EU countries. Are there similar constitutional changes at least in those countries where populist parties have been part of the government in recent years, or which are usually considered to be the states most affected by populism? As a matter of fact, if one of the main features of modern populism is indeed its constitutional ambitions, it is reasonable to expect that it will at least seek to impose the primary features of its preferred constitutionalism.

The analysis of constitutional changes over the last ten years shows that some form of rights restrictions has been the most common of the above-identified criteria. However, these have been of different types and degrees, and the reasons for the restrictions have varied widely. Certain limitations were introduced because of the migrant crisis or the threat of terrorism under governments dominated by traditional social democratic or conservative parties.

Interestingly, many rights restrictions have been related to the regulatory environment of NGOs, although one might think that the aim of the discussion on populism in the positive sense is to enhance civil participation in public matters. The legal conditions of the activity of non-governmental organisations have been tightened in several EU Member States. Although in some countries, such as in Luxembourg, support for human rights organisations has been increased in recent years, in the Netherlands significant debates erupted when certain civil organisations that had acted against the "public good" were banned. Austria introduced a ban on foreign financial support for Islamic organisations, while Bulgaria, similarly to Hungary, introduced special transparency rules that made the life of NGOs more expensive and difficult. In Latvia, the requirement to list the traditional religious associations (churches), which has not happened before, was surprising, since its purpose was not clear to the public. The Ministry of Justice mentioned purposes such as the recognition of the special relationship between the traditional churches and the state, but the concrete goals remained unclear, according to the national rapporteur. Although in Latvia we also experienced wide constitutional debates about the autonomy of higher education, because the Rector of one of the universities was appointed arbitrarily, in the overall assessment we would say that in Latvia, for example, counteractions were much more significant than the attempts to restrict rights (BNN 2019). In many cases restrictive rules proceeded very slowly in the legislative process because of the strong deliberation mechanisms and opposition. Apart from this significant worry about the conditions of civil society, some other populism-related concerns have been raised in human rights matters in relation to terrorism and migration. In Austria, the Kurz government in the fight against terrorism introduced an act on extensive surveillance, and the Constitutional Court annulled it as unconstitutional and against international law and ECHR provisions (EDRi 2019). On the other hand, in Lithuania, although there are no specific state-related problems mentioned regarding the operation of civil society, the national rapporteur interestingly noted that there is no strong independent mass media, which is so crucial in democratic society. Radio and the television are largely commercialised, and the daily and private papers have been replaced mostly by commercial on-line sites and weekly periodicals. What can be classified as public national broadcasting is often accused of being politically biased.

Nevertheless, it is noteworthy that in Hungary and Poland since the beginning of populist government (2010 and 2015), there have been the kind of restrictions on rights that have not occurred in other countries. These have included both fundamental political rights, such as freedom of expression and right to association, and personal liberties. In both countries, for example, the government has captured the public media and turned them into a tool of political propaganda, and has also used market instruments to bring about significant changes in the media market. In Hungary in particular, the activities of NGOs have been restricted, stigmatising human rights organisations that receive financial support from abroad. In this country new legislation in 2021 imposed discrimination against LMBTQ groups, while in Poland the right to abortion has been severely restricted.[4]

Restrictions on certain political rights were also increased in Spain in connection with the imposition of criminal sanctions for expressing political disapproval by burning a picture of the Spanish royals,[5] and the criminal procedures and convictions of the leaders of the Catalan separatist movement.[6] However, while the first case started in 2007, before the new wave of populism, the second case was more about condemnations of Catalan separatism, which is considered populist in many respects (Callejón 2018).

Both during the world financial crisis and the COVID-19 pandemic, many restrictions of fundamental rights have taken place. The cuts in state salaries and pensions, in Greece, Italy, Spain and Portugal, were debated before the constitutional courts, but have not yet been significantly linked to the populist debate. In Italy, the financial crisis and the support requested and finally received from the EU has held back populist aspirations in some fundamental rights matters. The COVID-19 related cases with regard to rights restrictions were not closely connected with the discussion on populism. Rights restrictions were quite similar in all states,

[4] K 1/20 Judgment of the Constitutional Tribunal.

[5] ECtHR *Stern Taulats and Roura Capellera v. Spain*, 13 March 2018.

[6] Sentencia 177/2015 of the Constitutional Court.

and the measures taken, although not independent in nature, were independent in effect from populist aspirations. In the first period of COVID-19 in Spring 2020, for example, Sweden decided not to apply such severe restrictions on rights as other EU states and in the third term, in spring 2021, Hungary was quite restrained in its lockdown measures.

A comparative analysis of constitutional changes shows that in the last decade there have been reforms in several countries that have affected the status of independent and countervailing institutions. It seems that extreme majoritarianism and its corollaries, the strengthening of executive power and weakening of institutional checks and balances are very characteristic of those countries that are usually considered to be model states of populist governance, notably Poland, Hungary and Romania. Constitutional courts, and the central administration systems of courts, in particular, have been major targets of political restructuring. Yet, even if not to the same extent, there are examples of similar institutional reforms in non-populist countries. In Sweden, for example, the constitutional reform of 2011 introduced a clearer separation of the judiciary and the administrative authorities, and a new method of appointing judges in order to promote transparency and strengthen judicial independence (Zamboni 2019). Similarly, a significant development of judicial independence took place in the United Kingdom when the Supreme Court was established in 2009, taking over the role of supreme judicial authority from the House of Lords.

However, such institutional changes have not taken place in several countries where populists have also been in government (e.g. Austria, Italy and the Czech Republic).

There are also some examples of conflicts between national and European law, questioning the supremacy of EU law over national constitutions in general, or simply opposing certain EU policies on specific issues. The first can be illustrated by the Lisbon judgement of the German Federal Constitutional Court. It should be noted that, in this respect, the two features of populist constitutionalism are in many cases closely intertwined, in so far as constitutional identity is set against the principle of the supremacy of EU law. However, this is not only the case for populist governments' claims, as in Hungary or Poland, but also for Germany, where there is a strong history of this sort of legal conflict, which can hardly be linked to any populist politics. Similarly to the German case, the decision of the French Constitutional Council related to the EU-Canada agreement is a good example illustrating the protection of constitutional identity against the EU. In this case, the *Conseil Constitutionnel* declared that the decisions that belong to the exclusive competence of the EU can be examined by the Council if such decisions interfere with the constitutional identity of France.[7] In Italy, the Constitutional Court openly defied a judgement of the European Court of Justice very recently. The concept of constitutional identity has been also employed by the *Corte Costituzionale* in its last preliminary reference to the ECJ, albeit with a more conciliatory tone (Catalano 2019). In conclusion, constitutional identity is a concept that is being used by the Italian Constitutional Court to resist the primacy of EU law, in a form of constitutional patriotism, oriented towards a higher degree of the protection of individual rights.

These decisions—also discussed as part of the wave which emphasizes constitutional identity—are present all over Europe, but their strength and anti-EU nature differ depending on their context.

There are several examples of Euroscepticism limited to a single issue, as well. In Austria, although in overall terms the Constitutional Court pushes the European and international agenda, the "Gold-plating" argument appeared when the Kurz government used this concept to argue that EU law should be implemented in a minimum way, without giving the national parliament the possibility to add further content. The introduction of border control in relation to Slovenia and the withdrawal of certain family benefits from non-Austrian EU citizens were both qualified as anti-EU legal actions. In Greece, however, while the populist parties have a rather pro-EU political stance, non-populist, outsider political parties (Golden Dawn and the Communist Party of Greece) advocated an even more aggressive stance towards the country's creditors, effectively renouncing all debt obligations and cutting ties with the EU. In addition to this, in recent years in Italy, there have been several conflicts between Italian domestic law and both the ECHR and EU systems, especially at a judicial level. The national expert calls attention to the fact that the two populist parties, the Five-Star Movement and the Northern League, had very different stances before and after getting to power. A good example is their attitude towards the Euro. Before 2018, both parties were pushing for a referendum on an Italian exit from the Euro area. Confronted with the legal obstacles, both parties dropped the proposal when in government. Both the Northern League and the Five-Star Movement are also clamouring for reform of the TSCG (Coordination and Governance in the

[7] Décis. 2017-749 DC, Conseil Constitutionnel.

Economic and Monetary Union) in order to abrogate the provision obliging Member States to have a balanced budget, notwithstanding this obligation is now contained in the Italian Constitution in Article 81.

We can therefore conclude that, although conflicts between national law and EU law involving the Member States' need to respect their constitutional identity have been relatively frequent in recent times, these phenomena are not only found in countries with populist governments, and are often not linked to other criteria of populist constitutionalism.

As another example of a special kind of Euroscepticism, or even nativism, the more and more restrictive immigration policies observed in many countries can be highlighted. Nevertheless, although this has emerged in its toughest form in the Central European countries where populism is strong, there have also been many restrictions in traditionally hosting countries with strong multicultural traditions, such as Germany or Sweden. However, the opposition to migration is not unanimous, even among populist parties, and legal restrictions on immigration are not unique to populist governments. Although, for example, the so-called Visegrad countries (the Czech Republic, Hungary, Poland and Slovakia) are more or less on the same platform in this respect, in Lithuania the populist parties have not even proposed or supported any policy measures which would be inconsistent with European measures relating to refugees and migrants status. Or, while the Northern League and the Five-Star Movement in Italy were asking for a reform of the Dublin Regulation of the EU, tightening immigration policy, the Greek Syriza/Anel coalition government did not react negatively to EU migration policy and did not adopt anti-immigration legislation.

We also examined the patterns, that is, combinations, of the alleged characteristics of populist constitutionalism in each country, as it is assumed that if populism is characterised by a particular constitutional conception, then similar types of constitutional change will occur where populism is a significant political force. Our analysis of country studies, however, shows the opposite

Overall, it is difficult to discover any trend towards an emergence of the criteria of populist constitutionalism in European constitutional change over the past decade. A comparative analysis of the recent constitutional developments in the EU Member States shows that there are no defining patterns in the criteria of populist constitutionalism; if one or more of its indicators can be identified in each country, they occur in varying combinations.

It is also worth noting that even though there are many similarities between the constitutional ambitions of populist government and parties, if they have proved unsuccessful and have not led to real constitutional change, then at best we can speak of similar aspirations, not constitutional populism. If the attempts to attack the liberal concept of constitutional democracy have finally failed, this shows the limits of populism, or the capability of the existing constitutional system to resist populist challenges. The examples confirm our thesis that formal constitutional changes are very rare in Europe. An incomplete attempt to amend the constitution took place in 2018 in Greece under the populist coalition government of the radical left party Syriza and the nationalist right-wing Anel (Independent Greeks) party on the expansion of instances in which referenda are called. Other failed proposals for amendments include the decoupling of the election (by parliament) of the President of the Republic from the dissolution of parliament and early elections, the introduction of proportional representation in parliamentary and local elections, the introduction of mechanisms of popular legislative initiatives, among others. But we could mention Italy as well, where a significant populist reform also failed to change the constitution substantively by first of all changing the representation of the people in the parliament to a more centralized and less regionalised system. In Italy, conversely to the typical attribute of populist constitutionalism favouring direct democracy, one element on which both the Five-Star Movement and the Northern League have based their electoral campaigns is the very functioning of the existing form of representation, that is, parliamentary democracy. Between 2013 and 2018, the Five-Star Movement was claiming that the government was lacking legitimacy because it was "unelected". Similarly, Matteo Salvini claimed that, after the formation of the second Conte government, voters were deprived of their right to vote and the government was not legitimate.

No clear conclusions can be drawn even when examining the reflection in constitutional law of the individual features of populist constitutionalism in the various countries. In fact, constitutional changes typical of populist constitutionalism have occurred with very different frequency in Europe in the past decade. In addition, each characteristic can be found in very different contexts, while certain hallmarks of populism do not appear at all in formal constitutional law.

For example, although the decisive influence of a strong, charismatic leader is considered by most authors to be one of the main characteristics of populism, this is hardly reflected in constitutional law, even in countries where a populist politician has a truly prominent influence, like Viktor Orbán in Hungary, or Kaczinsky in Poland. It seems to be a feature of political, rather than any kind of constitutional, populism. Here it is worth noting that in our experience there is a significant difference between the constitutional and the political approach: many political initiatives classified as populist are not institutionalised or do not even aim at legal changes in the first place. Likewise, although to provide better, and mostly direct, representation for the people in order to enhance democracy is one of the most prominent claims of populists, it is hardly reflected in actual legal changes. Although it could be said that it is easy to organise better means of direct participation, as we can see in Finland, which introduced a new form of direct participation, in reality there has not been much change to facilitate direct democracy. In Hungary, for example, which might be a model country of nationalist populism, the procedural rules of the national referendum have been tightened, as the constitutional requirement of its validity was raised by the 2011 Constitution from 25% to 50% of voters. In addition, the National Election Commission, packed by the populist government, has rejected all referendum initiatives since 2010, with the only exception being when the government itself initiated a national referendum.

What is more, the characteristics identified as features of populist constitutionalism are almost as prevalent in countries with non-populist governments as in populist ones. For instance, the aforementioned constitutional identity as such cannot be attributed to populist politics; at most, it can be argued that populists use it for their own purposes. It is common in several countries to invoke it against the extension of EU competences, but this in itself is independent of populist aspirations (it can be limited to a single issue, or it can express non-populist Euroscepticism, too).

The situation is similar for non-political control institutions. While populist state capture often begins by removing the independence of constitutional courts, like in Hungary and Poland, where these bodies were packed soon after the populists came to power, controversial institutional reforms have taken place in a number of other countries, as well. In particular, thorough reforms of the central administration of judiciary took place in some Member States. However, whereas in Hungary and Poland the forced retirement of some judges, and the removal or replacement of certain judicial leaders were clearly aimed at undermining judicial independence, the constitutional reform of 2011 in Sweden, by introducing a clearer separation of the judiciary and the administrative authorities or a new procedure for appointing judges, served to increase the integrity and transparency of courts. Moreover, in Greece, the non-populist government appointed many judges and prosecutors, which became a subject of a public debate regarding the undue packing of institutions. Interestingly, during the populist government, an anti-corruption office was established (Law 4022/2011), and some measures strengthened the organisation system of public administration and justice.

In sum, the restriction of the independence of the countervailing institutions is the most typical feature that can be detected in some countries with populist governments (Hungary, Poland, Romania), but it is not specific for certain countries where populists take part in the government coalition (such as in Austria, Italy and the Czech Republic). In addition, controversial changes have also occurred in countries with non-populist governments.

Notably, in many countries no clearly populist characteristics can be detected in the recent formal constitutional changes at all, as is the case in Germany, Ireland, Luxembourg, Portugal and Sweden. Indeed, the very recent constitutional development under review tends to show that some countries have been very effective in resisting not only populism but also anti-democratic tendencies in general: Spain, Cyprus, Estonia, Latvia and Croatia can be classified in this group of countries. However, even this efficiency of constitutional systems can be explained in different ways: in certain cases, there is convincing evidence of the effective operation of a militant democracy, as in Germany, where the Constitutional Court has remained unaffected by recent global challenges and has maintained its stable jurisprudence. The situation was different in Croatia, where the national ambition and efforts to join the EU has overridden the populist tendencies that were undoubtedly present. There is no doubt that accusations or suspicions of populism are also regularly raised in these countries with regard to certain political aspirations or even constitutional ambitions, but these have not yet had any constitutional consequences.

Several of the features of populist constitutionalism which have been studied can be found in the UK, Bulgaria and Poland, but also, for example, in Denmark.

From a formal point of view, the Hungarian constitutional system shows the most characteristics of populist constitutionalism, but even there it is lacking several of its fundamental features (e.g. the preference for popular sovereignty and direct democracy, or the legal recognition of a strong leader).

4 Conclusions

If we examine the presumptions of the theory of populist constitutionalism in the light of recent constitutional changes in Europe, empirical evidence suggests that the postulates of this theory have only modestly influenced the real constitutional development of EU Member States over the last decade. As a matter of fact, no strong correlation was found between the prevalence of the criteria of populist constitutionalism and the constitutional development of countries with populist governments or strong populist parties.

Contrary to the mainstream academic literature, populist constitutionalism, understood as a set of specific formal-legal characteristics, has not had a significant influence on the constitutional development of EU Member States. These characteristics are virtually undetectable in about half of the countries surveyed. Although certain features, the combination or co-existence of which is often considered to be a characteristic of populist constitutionalism, can be identified in several countries, they are hardly indicative of populism in themselves. Certain indicators may be democratic in character, a logical consequence of previous reforms, or may be on the agenda of non-populist governments too. But even in the countries considered to be the most populist, there is no definite pattern of these characteristics, and many of the features held to be fundamental do not prevail. Political populism, if it exists, has only a very modest impact on constitutional arrangements: it is more likely to result in policy changes within a more or less unchanged institutional-constitutional framework. The historical-institutional context of the constitutional systems is arguably more likely to have a greater influence on constitutional reforms than any kind of conception or ideology of populist constitutionalism.

In some senses, empirical evidence from our research does not support the theory of populist constitutionalism: the characteristics that some of the literature identifies as defining this concept have not systematically emerged in the course of constitutional changes in Europe in the past years.

Nonetheless, there are warning signs: in several countries, there have been attempts to strengthen the central government's influence on the judiciary, to restrict certain fundamental rights, and a new wave of Euroscepticism has emerged, with the invocation of national constitutional identity and the renewed question of supremacy between national constitutions and EU law. In addition, and most worryingly, nationalist populism in some EU Member States, most notably in Hungary and

Poland, has partially dismantled the system of the rule of law, which could set an example for other governments. The decline of constitutional democracy is unfortunately a real danger—even if it is not threatened by a specific, populist form of constitutionalism, but simply by authoritarian politicians and governments.

References

Anselmi, Manuel. *Populism. An Introduction*. Abingdon: Routledge, 2018.

Blokker, Paul. "Populism as a Constitutional Project." *International Journal of Constitutional Law* 17, no. 2 (2019a): 536–553.

Blokker, Paul. "Populist Counter-Constitutionalism, Conservatism, and Legal Fundamentalism." *European Constitutional Law Review* 15, no. 3 (2019b): 519–543.

BNN, "Administrative Court Decides to Overturn Non-approval of Muižnieks as LU Rector." *BNN-News*, October 1, 2019, https://bnn-news.com/administrative-court-decides-to-overturn-non-approval-of-muiznieks-as-lu-rector-205782.

Bogaards, Matthijs. "How to Classify Hybrid Regimes? Defective Democracy and Electoral Authoritarianism." *Democratization* 26, no. 2 (2009): 399–423.

Bugaric, Bojan and Alenka Kuhelj. "Varieties of Populism in Europe: Is the Rule of Law in Danger?" *Hague Journal on the Rule of Law* 10, no. 3 (2018): 21–33.

Callejón, Francisco Ballaguer. "Constitutional Courts Under Pressure—New Challenges to Constitutional Adjudication: The Case of Spain." In *New Challenges to Constitutional Adjudication in Europe: A Comparative Perspective*, edited by Zoltán Szente and Fruzsina Gárdos-Orosz. Abingdon: Routledge, 2018.

Catalano, Stefano. "Rinvio pregiudiziale nei casi di doppia pregiudizialità. Osservazioni a margine dell'opportuna scelta compiuta con l'ordinanza n. 117 del 2019 della Corte costituzionale." *Osservatorio costituzionale* 4 (2019): 1–10.

Corrias, Luigi. "Populism in a Constitutional Key: Constituent Power, Popular Sovereignty and Constitutional Identity." *European Constitutional Law Review* 12, no. 1 (2016): 6–26.

Doyle, Oran. "Populist Constitutionalism and Constituent Power." *German Law Journal* 20, no. 2 (2019): 161–180.

DEMOS H2020—The Project. Accessed September 22, 2021. https://demos-h2020.eu/en/about-demos.

Diamond, Larry. "Facing up to the Democratic Recession." *Journal of Democracy* 26, no. 1 (2015): 141–155.

Drinóczi, Tímea, and Agnieszka Bień-Kacała. "Illiberal Constitutionalism: The Case of Hungary and Poland." *German Law Journal* 20, no. 8 (2019): 1140–1166.

EDRi, "Austrian Government Hacking Law is Unconstitutional." *EDRi*, December 18, 2019, https://edri.org/our-work/austrian-government-hacking-law-is-unconstitutional/.

Fabbrizi, Valerio. "Constitutional Democracy in the Age of Populisms: A Commentary to Mark Tushnet's Populist Constitutional Law." *Res Publica* 26, no. 3 (2020): 433–449.

Fournier, Théo. "From Rhetoric to Action, a Constitutional Analysis of Populism." *German Law Journal* 20, no. 3 (2019): 362–381.

Kaltwasser, Cristóbal Rovira. "How to Define Populism? Reflections on a Contested Concept and its (Mis)use in the Social Sciences." In *Populism and the Crisis of Democracy. Volume 1: Concepts and Theory*, edited by Gregor Fitzi, Jürgen Mackert, Bryan S. Turner, 62–78. Abingdon: Routledge, 2018.

Landau, David. "Abusive Constitutionalism." *UC Davis Law Review* 47 (2013): 189–260.

Landau, David. "Populist Constitutions." *The University of Chicago Law Review* 85 (2018): 521–543.

Levitsky, Steven and Daniel Ziblatt. *How Democracies Die*. New York, NY: Crown Publishing, 2018.

Levitsky, Steven and Lucan A. Way. *Competitive Authoritarianism: Hybrid Regimes After the Cold War*. Cambridge: CUP, 2010.

Mudde, Cas and Rovira Kaltwasser. *Populism: A Very Short Introduction*. Oxford: OUP, 2017.

Mudde, Cas. "The Populist Zeitgeist." *Government and Opposition* 39, no. 4 (2004): 541–563.

Mueller, Axel. "The Meaning of 'Populism'." *Philosophy and Social Criticism* 45 (2019): 1025–1057.

Müller, Jan-Werner. "Populism and Constitutionalism." In *The Oxford Handbook of Populism*, edited by Cristóbal Rovira Kaltwasser, Paul Taggart, Paulina Espejo Ochoa, Pierre Ostiguy, 590–606. Oxford: OUP, 2017.

Müller, Jan-Werner. *What Is Populism?* Philadelphia, PA: University of Pennsylvania Press, 2016.

Pappas, Takis. "Populists in Power." *Journal of Democracy* 30, no. 2 (2019): 70–84.

Sadurski, Wojciech. *Poland's Constitutional Breakdown*. Oxford: OUP, 2019.

Schedler, Andreas. *The Politics of Uncertainty Sustaining and Subverting Electoral Authoritarianism*. Oxford: OUP, 2013.

Scheppele, Kim Lane. "Autocratic Legalism." *The University of Chicago Law Review* 85 (2018): 545–583.

Scholtes, Julian. "The Complacency of Legality: Constitutionalist Vulnerabilities to Populist Constituent Power." *German Law Journal* 20, no. 3 (2019): 351–361.

Szente, Zoltán. "Populism and Populist Constitutionalism." In *Populist Challenges to Constitutional Interpretation in Europe and Beyond*, edited by Fruzsina Gárdos-Orosz and Zoltán Szente, 4–29. Abingdon: Routledge, 2021.

Thornhill, Chris. "Constitutionalism and Populism: National Political Integration and Global Legal Integration." *International Theory* 12, no. 1 (2020): 1–32.

Tushnet, Mark. "The Possibility of Illiberal Constitutionalism?" *Florida Law Review* 69 (2017): 1367–1384.

Urbinati, Nadia. "Political Theory of Populism." *Annual Review of Political Science* 22 (2018): 111–127.

Varol, Ozan O. "Stealth Authoritarianism." *Iowa Law Review* 100 (2015): 1673–1742.

Walker, Graham. "The Idea of Non-Liberal Constitutionalism." In *Ethnicity and Group Rights*, edited by Ian Shapiro and Will Kymlicka, 154–184. New York, NY: New York University Press, 1997.

Walker, Neil. "Populism and Constitutional Tension." *International Journal of Constitutional Law* 17, no. 2 (2019): 515–535.

Zamboni, Mauro. "The Positioning of the Supreme Courts in Sweden—A Democratic Oddity?" *European Constitutional Law Review* 15, no. 4 (2019): 668–690.

On the Experiences of a Constitutional Court in an Illiberal Democracy. Incapacitated but Necessary

Miroslaw Granat

1 Takeover of the Constitutional Tribunal

Several stages can be distinguished in the degradation of the Constitutional Tribunal's position. The first one took place between November 2015 and November 2016, and we will refer to it as the takeover of the Constitutional Tribunal by the government. This stage is well described in the literature (Bugarič and Ginsburg 2016; Garlicki 2002; Koncewicz 2016; Koncewicz et al. 2017; Kustra 2015; Safjan 2011; Sadurski 2014; Sadurski 2018), so let me recall only certain key problems from this period.

This chapter has been written as part of the research programme NCN 2018/31/B/HS5/02667 "Konstytucyjność prawa bez sądu konstytucyjnego."

M. Granat (✉)
Department of Constitutional Law, Cardinal Stanislaw Wyszyński University, Warsaw, Poland
e-mail: m.granat@uksw.edu.pl

J. M. Castellà Andreu, M. A. Simonelli (eds.), *Populism and Contemporary Democracy in Europe*,
https://doi.org/10.1007/978-3-030-92884-1_7

One manifestation of the government's assault on the Constitutional Tribunal was the introduction of the so-called understudy judges. The Constitutional Tribunal is composed of 15 judges. They are elected individually by the absolute majority of votes in the Sejm for a term of office of nine years (Article 194 par. 1). Individual election means that a separate vote is held on each candidate (no joint election is possible). Second, each judge holds an individual term of office for a strictly defined period of time. The judges are selected "from amongst persons distinguished by their knowledge of the law" (Article 194 par. 1) who hold qualifications required for the office of a judge of the Supreme Court or for the office of a judge of the Supreme Administrative Court (Article 3 of the Act of November 30, 2016, on the Status of the Judges of the Constitutional Tribunal).

In 2015, at the turn of the seventh (2011–2015) and the eighth (2015–2019) terms of the Sejm, a conflict broke out over filling the vacant seats in the Tribunal, which appeared after three judges (elected back in 2006) had completed their terms of office. The outgoing Sejm of the seventh term added a new provision (Article 137a) to the then binding Act on the Constitutional Tribunal of 2015, which made it possible to elect five judges, including three judges for seats which were vacated in October 2015 and two judges 'in advance' (i.e. for seats which would be vacated in the future). The elections took place on October 8, 2015. The judges elected 'in advance' were to hold seats in the Constitutional Tribunal, which would be vacated in November and December 2015, after the expiry of seventh term of the Sejm. The assessment of electing judges 'in advance' must be unambiguous. It is a scandalous situation which should never take place in a state ruled by law. However, the effects of this scandal were averted thanks to the Tribunal's judgement of December 3, 2015 (K 34/15). The Tribunal 'liquidated' the two seats filled in advance, ruling that Article 137 of the Act on the Constitutional Tribunal was unconstitutional. At the same time, the Tribunal did not examine the Sejm's resolutions on the election of particular persons for judicial posts, which was the right approach (the Sejm's resolutions may not be subject to constitutional review). The awareness of how devastating it is even to attempt to elect judges 'in advance' was present among lawyers, and perhaps also among politicians. In 1997, the newly adopted Constitution of Poland (of April 2, 1997) increased the number of constitutional judges from 12 to 15. The left-wing majority in the Sejm refrained from attempts to fill three new seats several months in advance. Of course, it must be emphasised that it is unacceptable both to elect judges 'in advance' and to elect judges for seats already filled.

The newly elected judges take an oath before the President of the Republic. The significance of this act was precisely explained in the judgements of the Tribunal in 2015 and 2016.[1] The President is obliged to immediately take the oath from a judge elected by the Sejm. He has no discretion to decide whether or not to take the oath. The role of the President in the procedure of electing judges is subordinated to the effect which results from exercising the power to elect judges by the Sejm. Adopting a different view, that is, the President has discretion to take the oath from a judge or not, would make the President another body, in addition to the Sejm, which co-decides on the staffing of the Tribunal, which is not the case.

The President, however, did not take the oath from any of the five judges elected on October 8, 2015.

The newly elected Sejm of the eighth term (2015–2019) stated that the resolutions on the election of judges adopted by the Sejm of the seventh term had no legal force. As a result, the Sejm elected another five judges. The President took the oath from them. The judges, however, did not start work in the Constitutional Tribunal immediately. The President of the Constitutional Tribunal refused to allow them to adjudicate. They took up judicial posts gradually. Two judges started to adjudicate in January 2016. They were elected for seats vacated by 'old' judges (in November 2015). On the other hand, the remaining judges started to adjudicate as late as in January 2017. At that time, the term of office of the President of the Constitutional Tribunal, Prof. Andrzej Rzepliński, expired. Prof. Rzepliński consistently defended the independence of the Constitutional Tribunal.

In fact, the issue of the legality of the election of judges to the Tribunal has not been resolved to date.

The Provincial Administrative Court in Warsaw, in the judgement of June 20, 2018,[2] stated that the election of three judges of the Constitutional Tribunal by the Sejm on October 8, 2015, had been

[1] On the importance of the oath of a judge of the Constitutional Tribunal, see the judgements of the Constitutional Tribunal of December 3, 2015 (K 34/15), and of December 9, 2015 (K 35/15).

[2] Cf. V SA/Wa 459/18, LEX no. 2530153.

valid. A candidate acquires the status of a judge of the Tribunal once he or she has obtained the required majority of votes in the Sejm. According to the Provincial Administrative Court, the resolution of the Sejm on the election of a judge of the Constitutional Tribunal is final and cannot be overridden. As a result, the Sejm may not revoke its decision, annul it, declare it null and void or confirm it *ex post*. The court in question also rightly emphasised that the power of the Sejm to elect a judge can be exercised only when there is a vacant judicial post which requires staffing. Therefore, since the Sejm of the seventh term had already validly filled three seats in the election held on October 8, 2015, the Sejm of the eighth term could not validly elect other judges for seats already taken. This practice can be compared, for example, to selling tickets for already occupied seats.

It should also be emphasised that the Constitutional Tribunal 'defended itself' against being staffed by invalidly elected judges. This was manifested, for example, in the aforementioned full-bench judgements of the Constitutional Tribunal (K 34/15 of December 3, 2015, and K 35/15 of December 9, 2015). In particular, in the first of these judgements, the Constitutional Tribunal stated that the provision authorising the election of judges was constitutional to the extent in which it concerned the election of three judges for seats vacated in November 2015. However, to the extent in which it concerned judges whose term of office expired in December 2015, the provision was unconstitutional.

In 2021, the situation related to staffing of the Constitutional Tribunal is that three judges of the Constitutional Tribunal validly elected on October 8, 2015 (by the Sejm of the seventh term), have not been sworn in by the President. The President still refuses to take the oath from them. On the other hand, the judges elected on December 2, 2015 (by the Sejm of the eighth term), including three judges elected for already filled seats, have been sworn in by the President. The latter judges are called 'understudy judges'. Since these judges adjudicate, doubts arise as to whether the judgements issued by them or with their participation are legal. For example, the Ombudsman has raised such doubts on a number of occasions. In some cases, he withdraws his applications from the Tribunal if the panel of judges includes 'understudies'. The presence of 'understudy judges' in the Tribunal negatively affects the perception of the position of this court. It also paralyses the Tribunal's ability to adjudicate.

The conflict over the election of judges is extremely serious. However, despite the gravity of the conflict, in my opinion, there was an even more important factor, namely the Prime Minister's refusal to publish the Tribunal's judgements of 2016 in the *Journal of Laws*. The judgements in question were not in line with the government's views. Therefore, the government claimed that they had been issued by the Constitutional Tribunal in violation of the procedure. The government stated that these judgements were issued "over coffee and cookies". This situation demonstrated that it was the Council of Ministers (as an executive body) that assessed the activity of the Constitutional Tribunal. Thus, the recognition of the Tribunal as a judicial body depended on the government's discretion. It requires no justification that such an attitude of the government to judgements issued by the court leads to the destruction of the rule of law in Poland.

Apart from making personal changes in the composition of the Tribunal, the Sejm elected in 2015 adopted a series of laws on the Tribunal, referred to by the government as "remedy laws". These were the Acts of November 19, 2015, of December 22, 2015, and of July 22, 2016. Sometimes, three more laws on the Constitutional Tribunal of November and December 2016 are included in this category. They constitute the current legal basis for the functioning of the Tribunal.

A notable example in this regard was one of the so-called remedy laws on the Constitutional Tribunal (of December 22, 2015) adopted by the Sejm of the eighth term (2015–2019). By means of this law, the parliamentary majority aimed to paralyse the activity of the Constitutional Tribunal. It limited the Tribunal's activity in that it required all cases to be examined in full bench in the order in which they were submitted. The law also introduced a number of other extraordinary solutions affecting the work of the Tribunal and the status of its judges.

The Sejm attempted to make it impossible for the Tribunal to examine the constitutionality of this law. First and foremost, it decided on its immediate entry into force (by intentionally removing *vacatio legis*). The Sejm assumed that the Tribunal, when examining this law, would have to adjudicate on its basis and therefore would not be able to rule on its unconstitutionality. In such a situation, the Tribunal would be forced to rule on its constitutionality. As a consequence, the law would not be subject to the principle of constitutionalism, as it would be impossible to verify its constitutionality. Adopting the position of the Sejm by the Constitutional

Tribunal would result in a sort of incapacitation of the Constitution by means of a statute. The Tribunal solved this dilemma by directly adopting the provisions of the Constitution and selected provisions of the Act on the Constitutional Tribunal of 2015 as the basis for adjudication in the judgement of March 9, 2016 (K 47/15). The Tribunal ruled that the remedy law under review was unconstitutional in its entirety. The judgement indicated that the principle of constitutionalism means not only the formal existence of a constitution. First and foremost, it means the necessity to adhere to it as the supreme law.

It should be emphasised that calling acts which were supposed to block the Tribunal's activity "remedy laws" was deeply misleading. This is because the Tribunal was 'bombarded' by the government with these new laws. These acts shifted the Constitutional Tribunal from the position of an independent court—which it enjoyed under the Constitution and which it had developed over the previous 30 years—towards a body dependent on the influence of the executive. As a result, these laws systemically changed the position of the Tribunal in the tripartite system of government.

It must be added that the changes in law were accompanied by a propaganda campaign against the constitutional judges as well as judges in general. They were accused of corporatism and laziness, among others. They were referred to as 'bastards' or 'individuals' in robes.

Despite the Tribunal's struggle to maintain its position of an independent court (which was manifested, e.g. in the judgement of March 9, 2016), the government 'took over' the court in late 2016. It did so using both illegal means ('understudy judges') and legal means, that is enacting the aforementioned "remedy laws". Many provisions were constitutionally questionable, but their review was no longer possible. In the opinion of the Venice Commission, all these solutions paralysed the functioning of the Tribunal as an independent court.[3]

The second stage covers the period from the beginning of 2017 to April 2020, and we will refer to it as the stage of the Tribunal's loss of authority.

[3] See: Venice Commission opinions CDL-AD(2016)001, Opinion on Amendments to the Act of June 25, 2015, on the Constitutional Tribunal, Adopted by the Venice Commission at its 106th Plenary Session (Venice, 11–12 March 2016); and CDL-AD(2016), Opinion on the Act on the Constitutional Tribunal, Adopted by the Venice Commission at its 108th Plenary Session (Venice, 14–15 October 2016).

2 Loss of Authority

This section deals with the functioning of the Constitutional Tribunal in the years 2020–2021.

In this period, a large number of cases have been brought before the Constitutional Tribunal by state bodies (e.g. by the Public Prosecutor General, who also holds the office of the Minister of Justice). They are settled in accordance with the government's wishes. An analysis of judgements issued in the period 2017–2020 shows that the Tribunal confirms the constitutionality of the laws adopted by the ruling majority. The judgements were in line with the expectations of the applicants (state bodies). According to M. Szafnicka (judge of the Tribunal in the years 2011–2020), the function of the Tribunal is to rubber-stamp government actions, especially in the context of minority protests and criticism from European institutions. In recent years, however, the Tribunal has not acted as a defender of the parliamentary minority. Therefore, it can be said that the Constitutional Tribunal is the guardian of the law enacted by the ruling majority. Such a role of a constitutional court departs from the standard approach to the position of such an institution (Szafnicka 2020, 44).

Let me point out that state bodies (e.g. the Sejm, the government) may independently issue and change legal provisions in accordance with the Constitution. However, they submit applications to the Constitutional Tribunal, shifting the burden of responsibility towards this body. A good example is the judgement on abortion issued by the Constitutional Tribunal on October 22, 2020.

The Tribunal delivers most of its judgements in closed sessions. The number of public (open) hearings is small. This is inconsistent with the Act of November 30, 2016, on the Organisation of the Constitutional Tribunal and the Mode of Proceedings Before the Constitutional Tribunal. Examining a case at a sitting in camera is admissible only in three situations enumerated in Article 92. In general, these are situations in which the case examined is not complex. The Tribunal very rarely issues judgements in full bench (15 judges). According to the Act on the Organisation of the Constitutional Tribunal and the Mode of Proceedings Before the Constitutional Tribunal, the full bench includes at least 11 judges (until 2016 it was at least 13 judges). Moreover, the practice of shaping the full bench is important. According to M. Szafnicka, a retired judge of the Constitutional Tribunal, the Public Prosecutor General played an active role in shaping the full bench by submitting applications for excluding judges elected by the previous ruling majority. This possibility was used only in certain cases, which confirms the motives behind such applications. Obviously, in some cases (e.g. U 1/17), the Public Prosecutor General's applications for excluding 'old judges' were approved. As a result of such activities, the Constitutional Tribunal 'in full bench' ruled on the constitutionality of the 2016 amendments to the Act on Assemblies.

In practice, cases are usually examined by small panels (five judges). Thus, the government does not have to control all judges: with 'their own' president and a group of trusted judges, the case law can be controlled by appointing smaller panels.

The Constitutional Tribunal adjudicates in full bench only when it is obligatory, that is when it is explicitly required by law (e.g. in disputes over authority).

Currently, there are 13 judges elected after 2015 (including the so-called understudy judges) in the 15-member bench of the Constitutional Tribunal. Essentially, such a situation should solve the problem of the full bench. However, it is surprising that this is not always the case. For example, the constitutional review of the so-called Deubekization Act of 2017 has been prominent recently. The law reduces the pensions of secret service officers and police officers who worked at least one day in such institutions. It does not matter if such persons were verified after 1989 and worked in free Poland.[4] According to the government, the aim of the law is to restore justice and punish the perpetrators of the totalitarian system. These regulations were referred to the Constitutional Tribunal in February 2018 by the Ombudsman. The law has been in force for over three years, but the Constitutional Tribunal has not been able to issue a judgement in this case yet. The case was dropped from the docket many times. A common opinion is that the government 'is not sure' what judgement the Tribunal may issue.[5] In the meantime, common courts (e.g. the District Court in Częstochowa) and the Supreme Court commented on the unconstitutionality of specific provisions of this act. Currently, the complaint against this law has been accepted for consideration by the European Court of Human Rights. In their complaint to the ECtHR, the applicants

[4] It is reported that the law reduced pensions and disability pensions of around 40,000 people, including 8000 widows and children of former officers.

[5] Kostrzewski, *Miliardowe odszkodowania za dezubekizację. Rząd do maja ma złożyć wyjaśnienia do Strasburga* [Billion compensation for deubekization. The government to submit explanations to Strasbourg by May], Gazeta Wyborcza, 26.03.2021

invoked Article 6 of the Convention, which states that "everyone is entitled to a fair and public hearing within a reasonable time" (emphasis mine).

An analysis of the adjudicating panels in important (systemic) cases shows that the principle of assigning judges to cases in alphabetical order is not observed. According to M. Szafnicka, the list of duties of individual judges shows that the principle of assigning judges in alphabetical order set out in the Act on the Organisation of the Constitutional Tribunal and the Mode of Proceedings Before the Constitutional Tribunal is not observed. In the years 2017–2019, the judges elected by the Sejm of the eighth term had much more work than the 'old judges'. 'New judges' were assigned to adjudicating in complex cases of systemic importance immediately after being elected. The statistics in this regard are clear.[6]

Moreover, it happens that the Constitutional Tribunal is unable to resolve some cases. Such cases are postponed indefinitely. A first example is the already mentioned case concerning the so-called Deubekization Act. Another example in this regard is the application filed by a group of Law and Justice MPs to examine the constitutionality of Article 3 par. 6 of the Act on the Ombudsman of 1987. The application concerns the extent to which the current Ombudsman (with a five-year term of office) may perform his duties until the Sejm elects a new person for this position. The applicants claim that this provision is inconsistent with Article 2 of the Constitution (the principle of a democratic state ruled by law) and with Article 209 par. 1 of the Constitution (it specifies the Ombudsman's term of office). They believe that the Ombudsman (whose term of office expired on October 8, 2020) is performing his duties illegally. His mandate may therefore be questioned. At the same time, however, all attempts to elect a new Ombudsman in the parliament have failed due to the candidates' failure to obtain the required majority in the Senate. Returning to the situation in the Constitutional Tribunal, it should be emphasised that the hearing in this case has already been scheduled nine times. However, all these hearings were cancelled at the last minute.

A consequence of such functioning of the Constitutional Tribunal is its loss of credibility. The Tribunal has lost its authority among lawyers but also among citizens. There was a significant decrease in the number of cases brought before the Constitutional Tribunal in each mode of review. For example, before 2016, the Tribunal issued over 60 judgements a year (including complex cases), while in 2020 the Tribunal issued 19 judgements. An objective measure of the Tribunal's loss of credibility among

[6] Cf. M. Szafnicka, op. cit., p. 43.

Table 1 Number of questions of law submitted to the Constitutional Tribunal

Year	*Number of questions*
2014	80
2015	135
2016	21
2017	21
2018	15
2019	16
2020	12

ordinary court judges may be the number of questions of law referred by courts. Due to their complexity and importance, questions of law were a highly valued mode of initiating constitutional review. However, after 2016, their number has dropped dramatically, as shown in the Table 1.

The above-mentioned facts on the activities of the Polish Constitutional Tribunal lead to the conclusion that the politicians who came into power in 2015 were by no means interested in creating a 'new model' of the functioning of the Tribunal. Therefore, they did not intend, for example, to eliminate the shortcomings in the functioning of this court (e.g. by shortening the time of case examination) or to protect human rights more effectively (e.g. by introducing the so-called broad model of constitutional complaint). The programme documents of the Law and Justice party assume a very weak position of the Constitutional Tribunal. The position of the Tribunal was shaped in this way in practice.

3 The Constitutional Tribunal in the Hands of the Government

The third stage of the Tribunal's degradation began in April 2020. The court in the current composition, as well as the ruling majority, has abandoned a certain game of appearances resulting from the existence of the Constitutional Tribunal. The Tribunal does not even preserve the specific decorum that is appropriate for the mechanism of division and balance of powers. The connection between the Tribunal and the government came into sight. This stage can be illustrated with the decisions on the so-called disputes over authority (Sect. 3.1) and the judgement on abortion (Sect. 3.2).

3.1 *The Disputes over Authority*

The Constitutional Tribunal examined the so-called disputes over authority between central state bodies. Unusual judgements were issued in these cases, which were criticised by lawyers, but pleased the government. They demonstrate playing with the constitutional category of disputes over authority (Article 189 of the Constitution). The judgements concerning these pseudo-disputes are used by the government in order to challenge resolutions of the Supreme Court and in fact are directed against the Court of Justice of the EU. As it is noted in the doctrine, the decision of the Constitutional Tribunal of April 21, 2020, in the part concerning the judgement of the Court of Justice of the EU of November 19, 2019, constituted "a withdrawal of adherence to EU law" (Biernat 2020, 827).

Playing with the category of "disputes over authority" by the government and the Constitutional Tribunal can be illustrated with the judgements of April 20, 2020, and April 21, 2020. The starting point for these rulings was the judgement of the Court of Justice of the EU of November 19, 2019.[7] It was issued in response to several prejudicial questions submitted by the Polish Supreme Court. The essential legal problem concerned the assessment—in the context of EU law—of the procedure for appointing judges in Poland in relation to the requirement that judges be independent. In the judgement, the Court of Justice specified the conditions resulting from EU law which should be fulfilled for the Disciplinary Chamber of the Supreme Court established in Poland in 2018 to be considered a 'court' as understood in EU law. Another issue was whether the National Council of the Judiciary, which participates in appointing judges, could be recognised as a body independent of the legislative and executive powers (Biernat 2020, 827.). The Court of Justice left it to the Supreme Court itself to make the final decisions in this respect. The Supreme Court, following the guidelines from the judgement of the CJEU, stated that the Disciplinary Chamber of the Supreme Court did not meet the requirements for a 'court' in the light of EU and Polish law. Likewise, the National Council of the Judiciary, in the current state of law, does not guarantee a fair procedure for presenting candidates for judges to the President of Poland (Biernat 2020, 819).

[7] Joint cases C-585/18, C-624/18 and C-625/18 against the National Council of the Judiciary and the Supreme Court.

The most important statement of the Supreme Court in the cases concerning the Disciplinary Chamber and the National Council of the Judiciary was the resolution of January 23, 2020, adopted by the three joined Chambers of the Supreme Court (the Civil Chamber, the Criminal Chamber and the Labour Law and Social Security Chamber). In the resolution, the Supreme Court held that the Disciplinary Chamber is not a court as understood in EU law, and therefore is not a court as understood in national law. In other words, it is a faulty body. The Supreme Court stated that the Chamber is "an organizational structure which is not a court". Next, on April 4, 2020, the CJEU itself (in another case) issued interim measures ordering the immediate suspension of the application of the provisions on the Disciplinary Chamber. Unfortunately, the Polish government implemented this decision only partially.

Second, with regard to the National Council of the Judiciary, the Supreme Court stated that this body was not staffed in the manner required by the provisions of the Constitution. As a result, the Council could not exercise its constitutional powers. This fact should be taken into account by the President of the Republic in taking decisions on the appointment of judges.

The Supreme Court's resolution of January 23, 2020, differentiated the effects of a faulty appointment to the position of a judge, depending on the type of court. Thus, the Supreme Court judges appointed on the basis of a defective procedure should not perform judicial activities. On the other hand, judges of common courts appointed on the basis of a defective procedure should refrain from adjudicating until it is determined whether the defect in the appointment process constitutes—in particular cases—a breach of the standard of judicial independence.[8]

After the Supreme Court issued the resolution, the ruling party decided to 'counteract' its effects. As a result, the Prime Minister referred the resolution to the Constitutional Tribunal to examine its compliance with the Constitution and with the Treaty on European Union. On the other hand, the Marshal of the Sejm submitted an application to the Constitutional Tribunal to resolve a dispute over authority between the Sejm and the Supreme Court and a dispute over authority between the President of the Republic and the Supreme Court.

[8] Ibid.

Having examined both applications, the Constitutional Tribunal issued a judgement of April 20, 2020, and a decision of April 21, 2021. Scholars argued that both cases should not have been accepted by the Constitutional Tribunal for substantive resolution (the proceedings should have been discontinued). They point out that "these judgements crossed another border" in the activity of the Polish Constitutional Tribunal after 2016. Like in a lens, we can observe here "a decline in the prestige of the Constitutional Tribunal, deliberate reduction of the importance of the judiciary, including the Supreme Court, questioning the role of the EU and the case law of the CJEU" (Biernat 2020, 820). This is a manifestation of the degradation of Poland's position in the European Union. It is characteristic that the statements of reasons to both judgements were published with a very long delay (over a year). It is noted in the literature that the judges-rapporteurs were probably not able to prepare the draft statements, because of the contradictions that must arise in the reasoning.

In the judgement of April 20, 2020 (U 2/20),[9] the Constitutional Tribunal acted as a court of 'higher instance' than the Supreme Court. This is obviously not the case, as the courts in question are completely different judicial bodies. The Constitutional Tribunal held that the Supreme Court's resolution is "a legal provision" issued by a central state body. Despite the evident lack of legitimacy, the Tribunal interfered with the sphere of judicial activity of the Supreme Court. Thus, the Tribunal acted not only outside the scope of its powers, but also in breach of the constitutional principle of the independence of courts in performing their judicial function. In turn, the "anti-European edge" of the judgement can be seen in an attempt to block the implementation of the judgement of the CJEU (of November 19, 2019) by the Supreme Court and other Polish courts. However, all courts are bound by the interpretation of the law carried out by the CJEU. Such actions of the Constitutional Tribunal go beyond the limits of its constitutional legitimacy.[10] It is evident that the Constitutional Tribunal has no power to review the constitutionality of the Supreme Court resolutions or other acts of law application issued by courts. Without going into further analysis of the judgement of April 20, 2020, it can be summed up with the opinion of the Team of Legal Experts

[9] Cf. OTK ZU 2020, series A, item 61.

[10] This is a reference to the dissenting opinion of the judge of the Constitutional Tribunal, P. Pszczółkowski, submitted to the judgement under discussion. Cf. OTK ZU 2020, series A, item 61.

of the Stefan Batory Foundation: "this is another judgement of the Constitutional Tribunal, the quality of which is an offense to Polish constitutionalism".[11]

The decision of the Constitutional Tribunal of April 21, 2020 (Kpt 1/20), is even more important.[12] The case concerned alleged disputes over authority between the Supreme Court and the Sejm, and between the Supreme Court and the President of the Republic. According to the Constitutional Tribunal, the source of these disputes was the resolution of the Supreme Court of January 23, 2019. The Tribunal ruled that the Supreme Court did not have the power to issue this resolution, because it had a legislative character, and thus changed the state of the current law. In particular, the Supreme Court was held to interfere with the President's exercise of the power to appoint judges. An analysis of the Constitutional Tribunal's decision is difficult due to the fact that it is chaotic and contains numerous repetitions. The Tribunal critically examined the views of the Supreme Court, which were actually missing in the resolution of January 23, 2019, or which were presented by the Constitutional Tribunal in a distorted form.[13] Let me emphasise, however, the most important shortcomings of the Constitutional Tribunal's ruling: (a) the case under discussion did not concern any disputes over authority, because the powers of particular bodies did not overlap; (b) the Tribunal's position towards EU law is a copy of the government's position in this respect adopted in public and in proceedings before EU bodies; (c) the Constitutional Tribunal stated that EU law does not take precedence over the provisions of the Polish Constitution; (d) the Constitutional Tribunal refused to recognise the binding force and effectiveness in Poland of the judgement of the CJEU issued in response to the prejudicial questions submitted by the Polish Supreme Court; (e) the decision of the Constitutional Tribunal, in the part concerning the judgement of the CJEU and its effects on the domestic legal order, is in fact a withdrawal of adherence to EU law (Biernat 2020).

[11] Cf. the position of the Team of Experts of the Stefan Batory Foundation on the decision of the Constitutional Tribunal of April 20, 2020 (U 2/20), Warsaw, April 24, 2020. https://www.batory.org.pl/oswiadczenie/stanowisko-zespolu-ekspertow-prawnych-w-sprawie-rozstrzygniecia-trybunalu-konstytucyjnego-dotyczacego-aborcji/ (accessed: March 29, 2021).

[12] Cf. OTK ZU 2020, series A, item 60.

[13] Cf. S. Biernat, op. cit., p. 823.

3.2 The Constitutional Tribunal Judgement on Abortion

Second, let me focus on the judgement of the Constitutional Tribunal of October 22, 2020, on abortion.[14]

In the judgement of the Constitutional Tribunal of October 22, 2020, on the provisions of the abortion law of 1993, one of the three legal grounds for abortion (referred to as eugenic premise) was declared inconsistent with Article 38 of the Constitution (in conjunction with Articles 30 and 31 par. 3). As a result, the abortion law, which was already considered to be strict, was further tightened.

It is not my goal to discuss the Polish abortion law in detail. Let me only highlight the basic arguments raised against the judgement in question. The following points were noted: first, the Tribunal failed to take into account the need to protect the inherent and inalienable dignity of women. Thus, the Tribunal failed to properly balance the values associated with the conflicting regulations. There is no doubt, however, that such values were both on the side of the mother and the foetus. Second, removing the eugenic premise leads to a violation of the prohibition of cruel treatment and torture, the right to protection of private life and the right to health protection. Third, the judgement of the Constitutional Tribunal reduced the standards of human rights protection under the UN Convention against Torture and Other Cruel, Inhuman or Degrading Treatment or Punishment of December 10, 1984, and the UN International Covenant on Civil and Political Rights of December 16, 1966, and the Convention for the Protection of Human Rights and Fundamental Freedoms of the Council of Europe of November 4, 1950.[15]

The judgement triggered massive protests not seen in Poland for many years. As a result, it turned out to be very troublesome for the government. The Prime Minister has a constitutional duty to publish each judgement immediately (Article 190 par. 2). The judgement was published in late January 2020 (more than three months after it was issued).

For three months, the government position seemed to be to pretend that the judgement "simply did not exist". The Council of Ministers in

[14] File no. K 1/20.

[15] Cf. https://www.batory.org.pl/oswiadczenie/stanowisko-zespolu-ekspertow-prawnych-w-sprawie-rozstrzygniecia-trybunalu-konstytucyjnego-dotyczacego-aborcji/ (accessed: March 29, 2021).

the "statement" of December 1, 2020, referred to the "state of higher necessity" and made the publication of the judgement conditional upon the statement of reasons (in fact, on its acceptance of the statement of reasons).

In practice, for three months there was a kind of "legal vacuum": the judgement had been delivered, but it wasn't there. According to press reports, some clinics refused to perform abortions on eugenic grounds despite the fact that the judgement had not been published, while others performed such abortions. Now that the judgement has been published, abortion on eugenic grounds cannot be carried out.

The government undermined the position of the Constitutional Tribunal in an official document (it made the publication of the judgement conditional upon the statement of reasons). This situation didn't raise any objections from the Constitutional Tribunal. It seemed as if the Tribunal itself assumed that the judgement in question hadn't been delivered. This is why the title of the Chapter mentions that the Polish Constitutional Tribunal is "incapacitated" or, more precisely, is "self-incapacitated".

The position expressed by the Council of Ministers in the "statement" of December 1, 2020, is based on a completely different balance of powers than the one enshrined in the 1997 Constitution. The statement assumes that the executive is superior to the judiciary, and what is more, the former can influence the latter. Such a relationship between the executive and the judiciary, and vice versa, makes delivering judgements by the Constitutional Tribunal pointless.

4 Conclusions

Illiberal constitutionalism remains strong in Poland. It shifts the boundaries in constitutional law, which only a few years ago, even with the same ruling party, seemed "impossible to shift". The point is that the finality of the Constitutional Tribunal judgements was instrumentalised (Article 190 par. 2 of the Constitution). In practice, non-final final judgements appeared. With regard to the abortion judgement, the government undermined the finality of the Constitutional Tribunal's judgements in such a way that it delayed the publication of a troublesome judgement. On the other hand, with regard to the judgements concerning pseudo-disputes over authority, the government publishes these judgements and emphasises that they are final. It invokes their finality in disputes with the European Union regarding the rule of law in Poland (e.g. with regard to the method of appointing judges).

To sum up, the government approves of the key judgements of the Constitutional Tribunal depending on its assessment of the political situation. A judgement which is not in accordance with the government policy is deprived of its final character. If a judgement is consistent with the government policy, the government strongly emphasises its finality. The government therefore has discretion as to the finality of judgements. This is inconsistent with the Constitution and with our ideas of what a constitutional court is. By the way, this practice is somewhat reminiscent of the position of the Tribunal in the late 1980s, that is, the period when Poland was a "real socialist" state, when the judgements of the Tribunal were not final. This is a sign of the "regress" of constitutionalism that occurred in Poland. Perhaps, populist politicians do not destroy democratic institutions completely, but exploit them in a specific way.

The paradox of the position of the Constitutional Tribunal in an illiberal democracy in Poland is that despite the degradation of the position of this court, it is still a necessary institution. In some situations, it is an institution that is necessary for the government to achieve its goals. The position of the constitutional court can be constantly relativised according to political needs. Therefore, it is not enough to talk about the degradation of the position of this court—as is the case in the doctrine. An example of case law in pseudo-disputes over authority shows that the Tribunal can be a valuable tool in the hands of populist politicians.

To some degree, however, ordinary courts are taking over the function of constitutional review. Despite government objections to such activity of ordinary courts, a seed of constitutional review exercised by courts has been sown. There are judgements in this respect which are of great importance for human rights.[16] In this context, delivering a judgement by the Constitutional Tribunal becomes less important (e.g. no one is waiting for the ruling of the Constitutional Tribunal on the so-called deubekisation), because cases are settled by ordinary courts. It is possible that, thanks to decisions of brave judges, the system will move towards decentralised review.

[16] See, for example, a series of judgements of the District Court in Częstochowa concerning the so-called deubekisation. Cf. the judgement of September 20, 2019, no. IV U 826/19.

At this point, it is necessary to go back to the starting point of this chapter, that is, the influence of the degradation of the Constitutional Tribunal on the shape of constitutionalism in Poland. The fact is that after 2016 the Tribunal functions in a system which can be described as illiberal constitutionalism, a system in which the basic law is no longer the supreme law. Since the constitution ceased to play the role of the final arbiter in legal disputes, the Constitutional Tribunal lost its significance. Even though it may be too much to define such a situation as illiberal constitutionalism, it shares with illiberal constitutionalism some aspects and features.

The illiberal nature of illiberal constitutionalism results from how it perceives the individual and his/her position in the state. In the liberal order, an individual is autonomous and somewhat 'separated' from the nation, while in the illiberal order an individual is united with the nation; a human being is not only an individual but an individual immersed in the nation and in its dignity.

A different nature of illiberalism can be seen against the fact that in liberal constitutionalism, human dignity, freedom and equality are superior to the written constitution itself. This is expressed in Article 30 of the Constitution of Poland, but the provision has lost its significance. In my opinion, it was manifested in the failure to fully use this norm in the judgement on abortion of October 22, 2020. As has already been indicated, human dignity is a value which is present on both sides of the conflict over the eugenic premise for abortion.

Finally, a feature of illiberal constitutionalism is a kind of dynamic that 'dissolves' the institutions and checks of the democratic system. The final stage of illiberal constitutionalism is undermining democracy as a system 'in which power can be lost'. This is why illiberal constitutionalism has a built-in aggression mechanism, without which it would make no sense. As a result, one of its characteristics is 'taking over' institutions 'which make it difficult to govern properly'. An example of such an institution is the constitutional court. The phenomenon under discussion is even more starkly visible in Hungary, where, according to Chronowski and Halmai, "*all* [italics added] other internal checks and balances are dismantled".[17]

[17] Chronowski and Halmai, *Human Dignity for Good Hungarians Only. The Constitutional Court's Decision on the Criminalization of Homelessness*, https://verfassungsblog.de/human-dignity-for-good-hungarians-only/ (accessed: March 29, 2021).

Having the information monopoly, the government is able to direct hostility towards any social group, and the EU institutions have proved unable to enforce the values referred to in Article 2 of the Treaty on European Union.

In discussions about illiberal constitutionalism, the problem is often downplayed as not dangerous because it passes quickly or it is said that this kind of constitutionalism 'should not exist'. Nonetheless, it exists and should not be treated lightly, with the use of an oxymoron—as a false friend or as wooden iron. Such an approach detracts from the dangers posed by illiberal constitutionalism. It appears then as a kind of a minor rash or only a temporary ailment of the system. However, this is not the case. It is a symptom of a dangerous disease of the democratic system.

Bibliography

Bugarič, Bojan and Ginsburg, Tom. "The Assault on Postcommunist Courts." *Journal of Democracy* 27, (2016): 69–82.

Biernat, Stanislaw. *Trybunał Konstytucyjny wypowiada posłuszeństwo prawu Unii Europejskiej* [The Constitutional Tribunal withdraws adherence to EU law]. In *Wokół kryzysu praworządności, demokracji i praw człowieka. Księga Jubileuszowa Profesora Mirosława Wyrzykowskiego* [Around the crisis of the rule of law, democracy and human rights. Jubilee Book of Professor Mirosław Wyrzykowski]. Warsaw, 2020.

Garlicki, Lech. "The experience of the Polish Constitutional Court." in *Constitutional Justice, East and West: Democratic Legitimacy and Constitutional Courts in Post-Communist Europe in a Comparative Perspective*, Sadurski, edited by Wojciech Sadurski, 265–282. The Hague: Kluwer International, 2002.

Koncewicz, Tomasz Tadeusz. "Of institutions, democracy, constitutional self-defence and the rule of law: The judgments of the Polish Constitutional Tribunal in Cases K 34/15, K 35/15 and beyond." *Common Market Law Review* 53, (2016):1753–1792.

Koncewicz, Tomasz Tadeusz, et al., *Poland* in Albert, Richard; Landau, David; Faraguna, Pietro and Drugda, Šimon. *The I·CONnect-Clough Center 2016 Global Review of Constitutional Law.* Clough Center for the Study of Constitutional Democracy, 2017.

Kustra, Aleksandra. "Reading the Tea Leaves: The Polish Constitutional Tribunal and the Preliminary Ruling Procedure." *German Law Journal* 16, (2015):1543–1568.

Sadurski, Wojciech. *Rights Before Courts. A Study of Constitutional Courts in Postcommunist States of Central and Eastern Europe*. Dordrecht: Springer, 2014.
Sadurski, Wojciech. "Solange, chapter 3: Constitutional Courts in Central Europe—Democracy—Europe." *European Law Journal* 14, no. 1 (2018): 1–35.
Safjan, Marek. "Poland: The Constitutional Court as a Positive Legislator." In *Constitutional Courts as Positive Legislators: A Comparative Law Study*, edited by Allan Brewer-Carias, 701–718. Cambridge: Cambridge University Press, 2011.
Szafnicka, Małgorzata. *Trybunał Konstytucyjny a rebours* [The Constitutional Tribunal a rebours], Państwo i Prawo, no. 5, (2020): 44.

Constitutional Erosion in Spain: From the Catalan Pro-Independence Crisis to the (Intended) Judiciary Reforms

Núria González Campañá

1 Introduction

In the last decade of the twentieth century, with the collapse of the Soviet Union and the fall of the Berlin Wall, liberal democracy seemed to have triumphed everywhere. However, despite the number of democracies began to grow, the liberal elements within many democracies have been declining. Zakaria was one of the first to warn that although "democracy is flourishing, constitutional liberalism is not" (Zakaria 1997, 23). So, the idea of democracy understood primarily as the will of the people is still globally ascendant, but liberal democracy is losing track. And Europe is the place where liberal democracy has declined most precipitously in recent years (Wind 2020, 3).

N. González Campañá (✉)
University of Barcelona, Barcelona, Spain
e-mail: nuria.gonzalez@ub.edu

J. M. Castellà Andreu, M. A. Simonelli (eds.), *Populism and Contemporary Democracy in Europe*,
https://doi.org/10.1007/978-3-030-92884-1_8

In a liberal (or constitutional) democracy, democracy is not only about voting or about the wishes of the majority. This approach to democracy advances a "shallow conception, whereby democracy becomes simply a majoritarian principle prevailing over any other consideration" (Closa 2016, 249). This resembles the populist conception of democracy, which argues that politics should mainly be an expression of the general will of the people (Mudde 2004, 543). Constitutional democracy amounts to much more than a mere aggregation of the preferences of the majority. As Closa argues

> By relegating rule of law (legality), "democracy as majoritarianism" breaks the axiological balance that characterizes democratic constitutionalism: the synthesis between the rule of majority and the Rule of Law. (Closa 2020, 52)

In effect, democracy means people deciding, but doing so according to rules that can only be changed following the amendment procedure foreseen in the very same rules, guaranteeing transparency, checks and balances, pluralism, fundamental rights and particularly rights of minorities. Viewed correctly, Rule of Law is not in conflict with democracy. In fact, the Rule of Law has been described by the European Commission as the "backbone of any modern constitutional democracy".[1]

But in certain populist narratives, the concept of democratic legitimacy takes prevalence over the principle of legality and the popular will is conceived as the main and only source of power. People's voice should have no limits, no restraints. Populism is inherently hostile to the idea and institutions of liberal or constitutional democracy. In fact, populism is one form of what Fareed Zakaria popularised as "illiberal democracy", but which could also be called democratic extremism (Mudde 2004, 561).

Democracies might fail in the hands of armed people, but they might also die slowly in the hands of elected (and populist) politicians: when independent judges look like enemies of the people or pluralism is seen as a risk, rather than a strength, a gradual erosion of democracy takes place, what has been labelled by Ginsburg and Huq as "democratic erosion": a process of incremental, but ultimately still substantial, decay in constitutional democracy (Ginsburg and Huq 2018).

[1] European Commission COM(2014) 158 final, *A new EU Framework to strengthen the Rule of Law*.

Spain, although still regarded as a full democracy by a variety of international index[2], is not alien to this phenomenon of populist narratives and constitutional erosion. As it will be shown, in the last years Spain has experienced some setbacks as for the quality of our constitutional democracy because of populist approaches. Some erosions have taken place at the national level, but others (in our view, the most relevant ones) have occurred at a subnational or regional level: for example, the Catalan secessionist bid led by the Catalan autonomous government.

The second section of this chapter provides an overview of the Catalan case highlighting the constitutional erosion that occurred in the last decade. The third part analyses how the Spanish central government has also undermined liberal democracy by promoting (although not completing) certain reforms in the judicial system. A short conclusion will wrap up the main ideas of this chapter.

2 The Catalan Crisis

In order to properly explore the populist narrative and constitutional erosion provoked by the Catalan crisis, a short overview of the main events occurred in the last years is offered.

Note that there are some populist elements in the Catalan crisis that have been addressed by some other scholars (Ruiz Casado 2020; Wind 2020; Queralt 2019; Barrio et al. 2018); despite being connected with what is developed here, they won't be covered in this chapter, since it focuses only on constitutional erosions. In brief, such populist elements could read as follows: (i) how in the context of a harsh economic and political crisis (austerity policies and corruption scandals) the pro-independence bid became a scape forward, (ii) how the long-term-used slogan "Spain steals from us" became the battle cry of the pro-independence campaigns with the 2008 economic downturn (the idea that the subsidised Spain lives from the productive Catalonia was a common motto those years), (iii) how the classical and Manichean populist opposition between the people and the elite has been adapted to pit the good and naïve Catalan people against the oppressive and corrupt Spanish state

[2] In the 2020 Democracy Index prepared by The Economist Intelligence Unit, Spain is considered a full democracy, whereas France, Italy or Belgium are seen as flawed democracies. Spain scores 0,73 out of 1 in the World Justice Project Rule of Law index, like France and slightly better than Italy (0,66) or Portugal (0,70).

(Barrio et al. 2018) (which is nonetheless odd, for the Catalan independence is a project designed by Catalan elites and supported by the Catalan middle and upper-middle class, a revolt of the rich, one could argue)[3].

2.1 Overview of the Events with Constitutional Relevance

Since 2012, the government of Catalonia has attempted to organise a referendum or consultation on independence. The slogans used in the campaigns urging to the organisation of the referendum have underlined the idea that this request is a democratic one ("this is about democracy") and that Catalans have the right to organise such a referendum ("the right to decide")[4]. With these approaches, the referendum supporters tried to convey the idea that the expression of the general will was the paramount value that had to be taken into account. One has to note first that although polls suggested that a majority of Catalans were in favour of being asked about independence, surveys, polls and electoral results have consistently showed that Catalonia is split into two halves when it comes to secession, for there is no majority (let alone a clear majority) in favour of independence.[5]

In Spain, the lack of political will, along with rigid constitutional impediments, has prevented holding such a referendum. As for political will, it should be noted that "the very act of staging a constitutional referendum is itself both a declaration that a people exists and a definition of

[3] Real Instituto Elcano, *El conflicto catalán*, 22 October 2017, 20. http://www.realinstitutoelcano.org/wps/wcm/connect/c0f90dae-76d1-4a8e-8f78-0058f048a44b/Catalonia-Dossier-Elcano-October-2017.pdf?MOD=AJPERES&CACHEID=c0f90dae-76d1-4a8e-8f78-0058f048a44b. last accessed 30 September 2021.

[4] In 2013, the Catalan Parliament passed the Resolution 5/X, of 23 January, proclaiming that the Catalan people is sovereign and that therefore it has the "right to decide" its own future.

[5] Note, for instance, the December 2017 elections, where the extraordinarily high turnout (79%), (in fact, the elections were considered "plebiscitarian") can give us an accurate picture of the Catalan people. Political parties supporting independence won an absolute majority (70 seats out of 127); however, the pro-independence forces were backed by around 47.60% of the electorate. The difference between the percentage of seats (55.12%) and the percentage of popular vote (47.60%) is an outcome of the Catalan electoral regime, in which rural districts where independentism is stronger are over-represented compared to the metropolitan area of Barcelona. In the 2015 and 2021 elections, results are very similar in terms of percentage of seats and votes, but the turnout in 2021 was much lower (51%), given the fatigue for the conflict.

that people" (Tierney 2009, 374–375) and that constitutional referendums in general, and independence referendums in particular, can have a "vital nation-building role" (Tierney 2009, 366). It is assumed that accepting the organisation of such a referendum would mean admitting the national and sovereign character of Catalonia. Many feel that this would threaten the national sovereignty of the Spanish people as a whole. This is one of the main reasons that underpins the Spanish main political forces' opposition to the organisation of such a referendum.

As for constitutional impediments, one must bear in mind that the current Spanish constitutional legal order does not admit that the inhabitants of an Autonomous Community decide by themselves the dismemberment of the country. The position of the Spanish Constitutional Court (SCC) (summarised in, among others, Judgments 42/2014 and most notably 259/2015) reads as follows: considering the Catalan people as sovereign (and, therefore, entitled to organise a referendum on secession) is against Articles 1.2 and 2 of the Spanish Constitution. Article 1.2 of the Spanish Constitution establishes that "[n]ational sovereignty belongs to the Spanish people, from whom all State powers emanate". Thus, national sovereignty cannot be divided. Article 2 proclaims that "[t]he Constitution is based on the indissoluble unity of the Spanish Nation, the common and indivisible homeland of all Spaniards". The Court held[6] that an Autonomous Community cannot unilaterally call a referendum of self-determination to decide on its integration in Spain, because sovereignty is only reserved to the Spanish nation. Furthermore, the central State holds exclusive competence over authorization for popular consultations through the holding of referenda (Art. 149.1 Spanish Constitution). The SCC accepts that the so-called right to decide is a legitimate political aspiration. However, this aspiration, since precluded in the current constitutional framework, should be channelled through the appropriate procedure: constitutional amendment. This position is based on the fact that Spain is a constitutional democracy, where ordinary laws have to be subject to a supreme norm, the Constitution.

Despite the clarity of the Court's position, in September 2017, the pro-independence majority in the Catalan Parliament passed two laws: 19/2017, on a referendum on self-determination, and 20/2017, on the foundation of the Republic. Both laws, ordinary Catalan laws, established

[6] The main reasoning of the Court is to be found in *Fundamentos Jurídicos* 3 and 4 of the Judgment 42/2014, of 25 March.

that they prevailed over the Spanish Constitution and the Catalan Statute of Autonomy. Needless to say, an ordinary Catalan law cannot amend the Spanish Constitution or the Catalan Statute of Autonomy, even when these laws failed to reach the qualified majority required to amend the very same Catalan Statute of Autonomy (i.e. 2/3). Besides, the extraordinary parliamentary procedure used to approve those norms reduced the period for discussion and amendment to less than a day for each bill, leaving no time for the opposition to study the norms. The Catalan Legal Advisory Council itself rejected the move, since it was also an attack to the rights of the parliamentary opposition.

Both laws were immediately challenged before the SCC, which suspended the laws and their effects, based on the preceding doctrine of the Court and later on declared both of them, by unanimity, unconstitutional (Judgments 114/2017 and 124/2017). However, the referendum took place on 1 October 2017, although without procedural guarantees. The voting led to harsh confrontation and some violent clashes with police, who were trying to prevent its occurrence, pursuant to Court orders. According to the Catalan government, 43% of the population went to the polls to vote in favour of independence.[7]

Despite a massive and unprecedented demonstration against independence that took place in Barcelona on 8 October, the former Catalan President Carles Puigdemont declared unilaterally the independence of Catalonia on 27 October. In response, the Spanish Senate enacted coercive measures in Catalonia like the imposition of the direct rule by the Spanish government (Article 155 of the Spanish Constitution): the dissolution of the Catalan Parliament and the Catalan Cabinet and the call for early elections on 21 December 2017. Surprisingly and despite initial concerns and hesitation in Madrid, direct rule was tolerated (without protests or uprisings) by Catalan society and civil servants. Probably, since independence has never been embraced by a truly large majority of the Catalan voters, the pro-independence parties lacked the internal support to further continue the game. Meanwhile, Supreme Court judges initiated criminal actions against the main Catalan authorities with the preventive imprisonment of some of them. (Such criminal consequences might also

[7] The fact that the referendum was not an official one might explain the low turnout. In an official one, one could have expected to see a much higher turnout, since "the average turnout in the 40 independence referendums held since 1980, has been 86%". Qvortrup, "Independence Referendums. History, legal status and voting behaviour", 136.

be a reason for the lack of resistance). Others, like former President Puigdemont, left Catalonia to escape from the judicial charges. All of the imprisoned politicians were finally convicted in October 2019[8], but in June 2021, all of them were pardoned and released from prison.

Now that the main events with constitutional relevance have been overviewed, let us review some of the illiberal traits of the Catalan separatist crisis: (1) the allegedly democratic character of a referendum on secession and (2) the disdain for the law and the judiciary because of the unrestricted approach to the popular will.

2.2 *The Allegedly Democratic Character of a Referendum on Secession*

Catalan pro-independence leaders have done great efforts to convince the people that organising a referendum on secession is a question of democratic quality. "Voting is normal in a normal country" was one of the most repeated slogans in the years preceding 2017. However, there are a few caveats that must be noted. In a democracy, people vote on a regular basis in competitive elections. In some democracies, there are also referendums. But only in a few of them (e.g. Canada and the UK), it has been allowed to vote on the secession of a part of the country. Many other constitutional democracies have rejected the idea that a sub-national entity can organise a referendum on secession (González Campañá 2019).

Catalan pro-independence leaders have assumed that democracy should trump any other legal principle (Vilajosana 2014, 195). They simplified the issue by stating that democracy is mainly about voting, and they misled the people by making them believe that a referendum on secession is "normal" or "ordinary". This misleading approach to a complex and emotional issue is one of the reasons why some scholars early on warned about the populist trait of the Catalan pro-independence movement (Castellà 2014, 235).

But the "democratic" flaws of the referendum do not refer only to the laws that Catalan authorities ignored. One of the grossest manipulations is the one around the allegedly democratic character of the referendum on secession itself. Such a referendum cannot be justified on the basis of democracy, if there is no agreement to hold it, because it is organised and

[8] Criminal Judgment 459/2019 of the Supreme Court, Criminal Chamber, Section one, Rec 20907/2017, of 14 October 2019.

designed by other pre-democratic elements: language, history, culture… The elements according to which Catalans apparently form a distinct nation separated from the rest of Spain. The delimitation of the demos entitled to decide is a pre-democratic choice. Margiotta explains clearly that the triggering motivation behind a referendum on secession is not democracy, but nationalism:

> Territory and voters must, in some way, be determined before deciding anything. In practice, the right to secede is granted on the basis of nationality. (Margiotta 2020, 21)

That is why she argues that "it seems impossible to justify secession entirely in terms of democracy, as it is always necessary to refer to the pre-democratic determination of criteria for belonging to the secessionist group" (Margiotta 2020, 23). Or as Closa puts it, "[i]n purely democratic terms (i.e. majority of a group), there is not prima facie criterium to assert that the democratic right to secede of a group [Catalans]must prevail over the equally democratic rejection of this right expressed by a majority of the wider demos which comprises the seceding one [Spaniards as a whole]" (Closa 2020, 55). In effect, why is it more "democratic" that only Catalans decide the destiny of Catalonia and Spain instead of all Spaniards? The democratic principle comes into the equation only after the demos entitled to secede has decided. It is only then that the democratic (procedural) question enters the equation: how the chosen demos is going to decide?

Thus, as seen, the claim about the democratic character of the referendum on secession is, at least, misleading.

2.3 The Disdain for the Law and the Judiciary Because of the Unrestricted Approach to the Popular Will

In constitutional terms, populism refers to the unrestricted popular sovereignty. People can't be wrong and therefore, leaders and parliaments should find out the way to carry out people's aspirations, regardless of the letter of the law. This is exactly what has occurred in Catalonia in the last years, notably in the fall of 2017.[9] There was an emphasis on the Catalan

[9] There was a previous discrediting task promoted by Catalan institutions. For instance, note the Catalan Parliament Resolution 1/XI, of 9 November 2015, where it is established

people as the true holders of sovereignty whose will could only be expressed through a plebiscite. In fact, it is common to populists to promote referenda as a more democratic and legitimate instrument of decision-making than the representative democracy's ordinary instruments (Wind 2020, 30).

The referendum became a moral goal, the only tool to allow for the political expression of the people's will, "to the detriment of political representation and other kind of consociational arrangements" (Barrio et al. 2018, 1001).That is why despite the preparations of the 2017 referendum had been declared null and unconstitutional by the Constitutional Court (Judgment 90/2017, of 5 July, declaring null and unconstitutional the budget allocated to conduct the referendum), pro-independence Catalan leaders insisted on their will to disobey legal requirements (Barrio et al. 2018, 1001). On 7 September 2017, the Constitutional Court suspended the referendum and warned Catalan elected politicians of their duty to comply with the law and the possible criminal responsibilities. But such warnings did not stop Catalan authorities. Oriol Junqueras, former Vice-President of the Catalan government, had insisted several times that "voting is a right that prevails over any law" and that "we [Catalan government] will disobey the Spanish laws, but we will obey the mandate that we have in the Catalan Parliament".[10]

As explained in the introduction, this opposition between legitimacy (that comes from the Catalan people, even if there is no clear majority and society is deeply divided when it comes to secession) and legality implies an illiberal version of democracy. The idea of the government of the people is taken literally and checks and balances on the popular will are rejected (Kriesi 2014, 363).

The disdain for the law is also to be found in the way the illegal referendum was implemented. Here, the standards established by the Venice Commission are noteworthy.[11] As Castellà reminds us, the Venice

that the Catalan Parliament will no longer be subject to decisions adopted by the "Spanish State", in particular those coming from the Constitutional Court, for, according to the Resolution, "it lacks legitimacy and competence".

[10] "Para blindar la consulta entraríamos en el Govern". *El Mundo*, 14 September 2014, https://www.elmundo.es/cataluna/2014/09/14/54149260268e3e6b608b457a.html last accessed 30 September 2021.

[11] Among the general studies of the Venice Commission, Code of Good Practice on Referendums CDL-AD(2007)008rev and the Revised Guidelines on the holding of referendums CDL-AD(2020)031. A summary of the criteria to be found in Venice Commission,

Commission emphasises, besides legitimacy, "the need to respect the Rule of Law, and in particular to comply with the legal system as a whole, especially with the procedural rules" (Castellà 2020, 158). The 2017 referendum failed to comply with many of the Venice Commission requirements:

- "referendums cannot be held if the Constitution or a statute in conformity with the Constitution does not provide for them".[12] Both the Spanish Constitution and the Catalan Statute of Autonomy do not provide for a referendum on secession;
- "an impartial body must be in charge of organising the referendum".[13] The electoral commission that the Catalan Parliament had appointed (without any type of qualified majority) to supervise the referendum was dissolved after the Constitutional Courts imposed its members with coercive fines (Decrees 123 and 124/2017, of 19 and 20 September 2017) and was not replaced;
- "Political parties or supporters and opponents of the proposal must be able to observe the work of the impartial body".[14] There was no provision to include opponents to overlook the work of the electoral commission;
- "the absolute minimum period between calling a referendum and polling day should be four weeks. A considerable longer period of preparation is desirable, however".[15] The Law of Referendum (Law 19/2017), an *ad-hoc* law, was passed only three weeks before the date of the referendum.

The Venice Commission had been approached by the Catalan government in their search for international legitimacy. In his letter of 2 June 2017, Mr Buquicchio, President of the Venice Commission, underlined that the Venice Commission, "the official name of which is European Commission for Democracy through the Law, has consistently emphasised the need for any referendum to be carried out in full compliance with the

Compilation of Venice Commission Opinions and Reports concerning Referendums CDL(2017)002.

[12] Venice Commission, Revised Guidelines on the holding of referendums CDL-AD(2020)031, 10.

[13] Ibid., 11.

[14] Ibid., 12.

[15] Ibid., 16.

Constitution and the applicable legislation".[16] The Catalan authorities decided to ignore the suggestions of the President of the Venice Commission and the Judgments of the Spanish Constitutional Court. This can only be explained by a populist and radical interpretation of the popular will.

In sum, in the last years, in Catalonia we have been used to a simplistic and demagogic narrative that tells us that anything can be subject to a vote, even depriving others from their rights. At the end, the secession of Catalonia is also about deciding to deprive some of our current fellow citizens, those who live in the rest of Spain, of the possibility of keeping their citizenship rights in Catalonia. Or as Stephane Dion eloquently explains, secession is about breaking the civic solidarity that unites citizens (Dion 2021, 97; See also Ovejero 2021, 41).

This populist narrative also argues that popular will is enough to trump the law, even if that popular will is not as clear as it is portrayed by the Catalan authorities. This is a risky enterprise: denying the relevance of the law and only raising it when it suits the political leadership. Such an approach is putting a great strain on the constitutional and liberal character of our democracy because it is not only undermining the Rule of Law, but the inherent pluralism to any constitutional democracy. Pluralism rejects the homogeneity of society and sees it, instead, as a heterogeneous collection of groups and individuals with often fundamentally different views and wishes (Mudde 2004, 544). On the contrary, Catalan authorities have attempted to portray the Catalan people as a homogenous community whose allegedly majoritarian will has to prevail over any law.

2.4 *Spanish Reaction to the Catalan Pro-independence Crisis*

The above section has provided an overview of the constitutional erosion provoked by Catalan leaders. We should also pay attention to the Spanish reaction thereof. Was there any type of populist behaviour that led to constitutional abuse? The section will not be covering all angles of Spanish response to the Catalan crisis (not even those with a constitutional dimension, like triggering Article 155 of the Spanish Constitution), but those elements that have arisen concerns related to populism and constitutional

[16] Document available at https://www.venice.coe.int/files/Letter%20to%20the%20President%20of%20the%20Government%20of%20Catalonia.pdf last accessed 30 September 2021.

erosion. Thus, here one has to reflect upon two different scenarios: firstly, to what extent the denial to negotiate an independence referendum can be considered an erosion of the constitutional system? Secondly, what about the judicial response to the imprisonment of Catalan leaders?

From 2012 to 2017, Spain's government rejected all calls by Catalan leaders to negotiate an independence referendum. One could argue that Spain's government did not facilitate a political solution and engaged in obstruction through silence and persistent refusal. The government did not attempt to offer any alternative to calm down the situation, but used "the Constitutional Court as a shield against the excesses of the pro-independence authorities" (Queralt 2019, 265). Spanish authorities' reaction can be considered a political error, for the response to this populist crisis should also come from politics, not only from Courts. But this poor handling of the revolt falls short of being a violation of human rights or a threat to democracy or Rule of Law (Campins 2015, 480; Qvortrup 2020, 138).[17]

As for the judicial response to the Catalan crisis, Spain's government has been criticised by the Parliamentary Assembly of the Council of Europe in a Resolution adopted in June 2021.[18] Such Resolution urged Spanish authorities, among others, to consider pardoning the Catalan politicians convicted and to enter into a dialogue with all political forces in Catalonia. The debate about pardoning the Catalan convicted politicians who had been found guilty in 2019 by the Supreme Court for sedition and misuse of public funds had been ongoing in Spain for months. On 22 June 2021, the Spanish government formally pardoned them, against the opinion of the Supreme Court and the Prosecutor and without requesting them to disown their political opinions and despite they did not show any type of regret. Besides, a dialogue table between the Spanish and Catalan governments to discuss the "political conflict" was already prompted in February 2020, and it has been reactivated in 2021 after the pardoning of the convicted politicians.

Having said that, it is fair to address the flaws of the Resolution as well, since it is based on a false presumption, namely, that "Catalan politicians

[17] In fact, the European Court of Human Rights dismissed in May 2021 the application of two Catalans injured during the 1 October referendum on the ground of lack of human rights violations.

[18] Parliamentary Assembly of the Council of Europe, Resolution 2381 (2021), *Should politicians be prosecuted for statements made in the exercise of their mandate?*.

were prosecuted and eventually convicted to long prison terms for sedition and other crimes, *inter alia* for statements made in the exercise of their political mandates". But in fact, none of the politicians were convicted for the expression of their opinions, as the Supreme Court stated in Judgment 459/2019:

> The object of the criminal charge – as we have declared proven – is the shattering of the constitutional agreement, and they are doing so through the approval of laws in open and recalcitrant disregard of the orders of the Constitutional Court. What is sanctioned, in short, is not voicing an opinion or advocating a secessionist option, but defining a parallel, constituent legality and mobilising a mass of citizens to oppose the implementation of the legitimate decisions of the judicial authority, holding a referendum declared illegal by the Constitutional Court and the High Court of Justice of Catalonia, whose result was the necessary condition for the entry into force of the law of transition, which implied a definitive break with the structure of the State.[19]

In this paragraph, the Supreme Court was, *inter alia*, reminding the position of the SCC: the pro-independence demand is a legitimate political aspiration, but since it is precluded in the current constitutional framework, it requires first a constitutional amendment. Spanish constitutional legal order, unlike Germany, does not contain eternity clauses and, therefore, such amendment would be legal, if enough majorities in the Spanish Parliament are secured.

This is why there are no strong reasons to argue that there has been a sustained constitutional erosion prompted by Spain's response to the Catalan crisis, notwithstanding the political errors that might have been committed by Spanish governments.

[19] The long judgement (almost 500 pages) along with short summaries in English can be found at: https://www.poderjudicial.es/cgpj/es/Poder-Judicial/Noticias-Judiciales/El-Tribunal-Supremo-condena-a-nueve-de-los-procesados-en-la-causa-especial-20907-2017-por-delito-de-sedicion, last accessed 30 September 2021.

3 Spain's Government (Some of Them Intended) Reforms of the Judiciary

As stated in the introduction, although the main populist erosion to the Rule of Law in Spain is taken place at the regional level, at the national level there are as well reasons for concern.

In a constitutional democracy, to protect fundamental rights and minorities, the expression of the general will has to be limited by the independence of counter-majoritarian key institutions, notably the judiciary. In effect, one of the key elements of a sound liberal democracy is the independence of the judiciary. Without independent judicial constraints on political majorities, a political system cannot properly be called a liberal democracy. If Courts are not independent and impartial, how can we be sure that they will enforce the Rule of Law for all rather than pursue a particular governing majority's interests? (Wind 2020, 87)

In the last years, within the EU, we have witnessed across several Member States, whose governments have been described as populist (namely Poland and Hungary), attempts to interfere with the judiciary by removing judges, ousting of jurisdiction, and court packings. Some of these attempts have been successful, others have been stopped by the European Court of Justice case law and by political pressure exercised by the European Commission (Magaldi 2021a; Becerril 2020; Kochenov 2019; Pech and Scheppele 2017). These judiciary reforms can erode greatly any constitutional democracy. The concerns are high, particularly also because of the difficulties to counteract these tendencies. Unfortunately, Spain is not alien to this peril, although, needless to say, the Rule of Law backsliding cannot be compared to Poland or Hungary.

3.1 The Long-standing Crisis of the General Council for the Judiciary

In the 2020 Rule of Law Report country chapter on the situation in Spain,[20] the European Commission warns, among other things, about the fact that the General Council for the Judiciary (GCJ) has been exercising its functions *ad interim* since December 2018. But it is in the 2021 edition that the Report is deeply worried about the path taken by judiciary

[20] European Commission SWD(2020) 308 final, 2020 Rule of Law Report, Country Chapter on the rule of law situation in Spain.

reforms in Spain, particularly the (attempted) reforms surrounding the GCJ.[21]

In Spain, the GCJ is the body of judicial self-governance and ensures the independence of courts and judges, yet it does not form part of the judiciary.[22] It was established to ensure the independence of the judiciary, in particular the independence regarding the executive. It exercises disciplinary action and is competent to appoint, transfer and promote judges. The GCJ consists of the President of the Supreme Court and 20 individuals, 12 judges and 8 lawyers or other jurists. The GCJ members are appointed for a non-renewable period of five years. While the Spanish Constitution requires the 8 jurists to be appointed by a three-fifths majority in each Chamber of the Spanish Parliament, it does not specify how the 12 members representing judges are to be appointed.[23] The appointment process has undergone significant changes over time and represents one of the most sensitive and contested issues. Initially, the 12 judges were elected by judges. This model was changed in 1985 by a reform prompted by the then-Socialist government. In effect, the regulation of the Judicial Council was reorganised and established by Organic Law 6/1985, of 1 July, on the Judicial Power and since then, the Parliament is also responsible for the appointment of the 12 judges with a three-fifths majority.

The 1985 reform was challenged before the Constitutional Court, that in its Judgment 108/1986, of 29 July, upheld the constitutionality of the law, but voiced some concerns regarding the shift of power to the legislature and the risk of partisan politics in the appointment procedure (Torres 2018, 1773). In effect, the Court stated (i) that the preferred model for the selection of members is direct election by judges and magistrates, (ii) that involving the Parliament entails the risk of allocation of seats depending on the parliamentary strength of political parties, and, therefore a risk of politicisation of the judiciary (iii) and finally that the appointment of members according to partisan criteria "was not admissible". Surprisingly, and despite the Court clearly understood the risks of the reform, it concluded that since there was the possibility of an interpretation in accordance with the spirit of the Constitution, there were no grounds to declare the law unconstitutional (Porras 1987, 234). The Court hoped for the

[21] European Commission SWD(2021) 710 final, 2021 Rule of Law Report, Country Chapter on the rule of law situation in Spain.

[22] Article 117 of the Spanish Constitution.

[23] Article 122 of the Spanish Constitution.

best, expecting that due to its warnings the political formations would not allocate the GCJ seats according to their parliamentary representation.[24]

In practice, the three-fifths majority requirement, rather than promoting broad political consensus, has led the Socialist Party and the Popular Party (the two main parties in Spain) to appoint the 20 candidates between them, with the inclusion of members recommended by smaller political groups, depending on whether these groups support the party in power (either the Socialist or the Popular). The risks foreseen by the Constitutional Court have become unfortunate realities. It should not surprise that as a result of this practice, the GCJ is perceived as a highly politicised body that undermines not only its own legitimacy, but also the legitimacy of the whole Spanish judiciary. Carmona refers to the situation as a "partisan colonisation" (Carmona 2020). This poses a serious problem, since Courts need to be not only independent but also perceived as independent (Torres 2018, 1779). In effect, public perception that justice is impartial is the foundation for the confidence which citizens must have in their judicial system.

As it has been shown, the Spanish model of appointing GCJ members has been, at least since 1985, contrary to the spirit of the Spanish Constitution. It is also against European standards. These standards are to be found in the 2010 Council of Europe Recommendation on judges: independence, efficiency and responsibilities. When it comes to Judiciary Councils, it provided that "at least half of members of such councils must be judges chosen by other judges from all levels of the judiciary" (para. 27).[25] The 2010 Venice Commission Report in the Independence of the Judicial System argued that "the council should have a pluralistic composition with a substantial part, if not the majority, of members being judges. Except for ex-officio members these judges should be elected or appointed by their peers".[26] The bottom line being that at least a significant number of the members of the Judiciary Councils has to be appointed by judges themselves, not by politicians.

[24] Following subsequent reforms (namely, Organic Law 4/2013, of 24 June, on the amendment of the General Council of the Judiciary), the 12 judges appointment is made upon receiving from the Council a list of candidates who have received the support of judges' associations.

[25] Council of Europe Recommendation CM/Rec(2010)12 of the Committee of Ministers to member states on judges: independence, efficiency and responsibilities.

[26] Venice Commission, Report on the independence of the Judicial System. Part I: the independence of judges CDL-AD(2010)004.

In the past, with the two mainstream parties reaching agreements quickly to renew the body, breaching European standards seemed no urgent problem. However, now, in times of polarisation and populist policies, when the Spanish Parliament is more fragmented than ever, reaching this type of agreements entails more costs for both parties. And deadlocks can occur. Secondly, with the attention that the Polish judiciary reforms have attracted, any type of government intervention in the judiciary raises suspicions and concerns in Europe, so the Spanish case cannot be overlooked.

3.2 *The Current Crisis of the General Council of the Judiciary*

Since December 2018, the GCJ has been exercising its functions *ad interim*, waiting for a renewal. Negotiations between the Socialist and the Popular Party are in a stalemate. They have been unable to reach any agreement. The acting president of the GCJ has repeatedly brought to the attention of Parliament the need to proceed with the nomination of new members and has referred to the current situation as an "institutional anomaly".[27]

It is true that the Venice Commission has stressed the importance of providing for qualified majorities to ensure that a broad agreement is found, but it has also warned against the risk of stalemates. Given that qualified majorities strengthen the position of the parliamentary opposition, the Venice Commission has also underlined the greater responsibility minorities hold not to misuse this power and the need "to conduct their opposition in a way loyal to the system and the idea of legitimate and efficient democratic majority rule".[28] The Spanish opposition, the Popular Party, with its insistence in blocking the renewal is showing a poor spirit of cooperation.

Apart from the abovementioned stalemate, something else deserves to be noted when referring to the crisis of the judiciary in Spain. In 2020, the two parliament groups that sustain the government coalition in Spain (the

[27] Press Release of the GCJ of 23 December 2019. Again, on 5 September 2021, the President of the GCJ, Carlos Lesmes, during the opening speech of the judicial course, appealed to constitutional patriotism and generosity and urged to renew the GCJ so that it can disappear from the stage of partisan struggle.

[28] Venice Commission, Opinion on the draft law on amendments to the law on the Judicial Council and judges of Montenegro CDL-AD(2018)015, para 38.

Socialist Party, PSOE and Unidas Podemos) tabled a bill[29] aimed at changing the election system of the judges of the GCJ to an absolute majority of a second vote. Thus, the 12 judges of the GCJ would continue to be elected by Parliament, but the necessary majority of three-fifth would only be required in a first vote. If such a majority cannot be reached, then the election would be made in a second vote with absolute majority. This would mean that the parliamentary majority that sustains the government will be enough to decide the composition of the GCJ putting the independence of the body at high risk. In short, the proposal was aimed to replace the three-fifth majority requirement by the less demanding absolute majority, so that there is a correlation between the composition of the GCJ and the parliamentary majority. Following criticism because of the attack to the separation of powers and the populist motivation against counter-majoritarian institutions, in May 2021, the parliamentary groups sponsoring the draft law withdrew it. In this regard, it is to be noted the Letter of the President of GRECO (Group of States against Corruption of the Council of Europe) to the Spanish Head of Delegation from 14 October 2020,[30] where Mr Marin Mrčela regretted that "[t]his legislative initiative departs from the Council of Europe standards concerning the composition of judicial councils and election of their members and may result in a violation of the Council of Europe anti-corruption standards". Also, the European Commission reacted by saying that the reform would endanger judicial independence and exacerbate the impression that the Spanish judiciary may be vulnerable to politicisation.

The withdrawal of the draft law was welcomed, but the problem is that, in fact, the current situation is already problematic. For instance, in 2021, the European Commission ranked Spain number 22 (out of 27) in the EU Justice Scoreboard[31] in terms of independence perceived by the general population, attributing this lack of autonomy mainly to political interference. The reform would have just worsened it and would have moved Spain closer to Poland. Note, for instance, the Polish GCJ equivalent body, the Krajowa Rada Sądownictwa (KRS), already famous among EU

[29] Proposal of an Organic Law to modify Organic Law 6/1985, of 23 October 2020.

[30] Document available at https://rm.coe.int/letter-to-spain-14-10-2020/1680a010c8, last accessed 30 September 2021.

[31] European Commission COM(2021) 389, The 2021 EU Justice Scoreboard. A similar problem had already been detected in the EU Justice Scoreboard of recent years, with Spain being considered one of the EU countries with the worst perception about judicial independence among its citizens (Urías 2020).

lawyers, because of the ECJ case law dealing with legislative reforms affecting it. In 2016, a Polish reform changed the way its members were appointed. While in the past, 15 of its members were elected by Judges, since then those members were going to be elected by the Parliament, with the result that 23 out of 25 members were going to be elected by either the Parliament or the Government (Magaldi 2021b). The EU questioned the level of influence of the legislative or executive authorities given that a majority of members are appointed directly by these authorities.[32]

Although this intended reform was finally not passed, the government did pass another law affecting the GCJ. On 25 March 2021, the Parliament passed a law establishing an *ad interim* regime for the GCJ that drastically reduces its functions when acting with an expired term of office.[33] Until then, the law foresaw that the GCJ remains fully functional until a new one is in place. This reform, already in force, prevents the GCJ *ad interim* from carrying out its most important function, which is to appoint senior judicial officials. Thus, the law prevents the acting Council to appoint the president of the Supreme Court, presidents of Provincial Courts and High Courts of Justice, president of the National High Court and presidents of Chambers and Supreme Court judges. It also removes other powers of the GCJ, such as the legitimacy to promote conflicts of competence between constitutional bodies. It reduces the powers of the GCJ to merely bureaucratic aspects. Such disempowerment will persist until the new GCJ is elected. The reform might cause paralysis and malfunction in Courts. The GCJ had requested the Congress to consult, during the legislative procedure, relevant stakeholders like the Venice Commission, but the Parliamentary majority supporting the government bill ignored the request and approved the reform, despite the opposition of the majority of judges' associations.

In short, the behaviour of both the government (trying to capture the GCJ with its parliamentary majority and reducing the powers of the current *ad interim* GCJ) and the opposition (rejecting any renewal of the body) erodes the legitimacy of one of the key institutions to sustain the Rule of Law in Spain.

[32] Commission Recommendation (EU) 2017/1520 of 26 July 2017 regarding the rule of law in Poland complementary to Recommendations (EU) 2016/1374 and (EU) 2017/146.

[33] Organic Law 4/2021, of 29 March, by virtue of which the Organic Law 6/1985, of 1 July, on the Judiciary, is modified in order to establish the legal regime applicable to the ad interim General Council of the Judiciary.

4 Conclusions

After the atrocities committed in WWII, there was a widespread recognition of the need to limit the power of the popular will with an emphasis on promoting rigid constitutionalism and human rights. Constitutional democracy replaced majoritarian democracies (Wind 2020, 80). But many of the tenets we took for granted are questioned these days. The recent wave of populism has been accompanied by a notion that democracy is most genuine when the will of the people is unlimited. It is argued that institutions like Courts should not interfere with the majoritarian view, since Courts, because they do not reflect (automatically, at least) the will of the people, are elitist (Wind 2020, 54). Such populist approach is eroding the legitimacy of one of the central pillars of the post-WWII legal order: counter-majoritarian institutions, particularly Courts (Wind 2020, 55).

It has been shown that, in the last years, Spain has experienced some setbacks as for the legitimacy of the Courts and the proper functioning of its judiciary. First of all, the disdain shown by Catalan authorities towards the decisions of the Constitutional Court showing a false opposition between legitimacy (i.e. will of the people) and legality (Court's judgements) is a major illiberal (or populist) trait. But one should not forget either the disloyal behaviour of both the national government and the opposition when it comes to the renewal of the GCJ or the reduction of its functions. This also undermines the quality of Spanish constitutional democracy.

Bibliography

Barrio, Astrid; Barberà, Oscar and Rodríguez Teruel, J. "'Spain steals from us!' The 'populist drift' of Catalan regionalism". *Comparative European Politics* 16, (2018): 993-1011.

Becerril, Belén. "Las instituciones europeas ante la crisis del Estado de Derecho en Hungría y Polonia." *Historia y Política* 44, (2020): 113-144.

Campins, Mar. "The European Union and the Secession of a Territory from a EU Member State." *Diritto Pubblico Comparato ed Europeo* XVII, no. 2 (2015): 479-502.

Carmona, Ana. *Renovación de los órganos constitucionales, ¿Misión Imposible?*. Agenda Pública, 21 September 2020. https://agendapublica.es/renovacion-de-los-organos-constitucionales-mision-imposible/.

Castellà, Josep M. "The Venice Commission and Referendums on Secession." In *Venice Commission Thirty-years Quest for Democracy through Law 1990-2020*, edited by Simona Granata-Menghini and Ziya Caga Tanyar, 156-167. Lund: Juristförlaget i Lund, 2020.

Castellà, Josep M. "La secesión catalana, entre la política y el derecho." *Anuario Facultad de Derecho Universidad de Alcalá* VII (2014): 227-240.

Closa, Carlos. "A critique of the theory of democratic secession." In *Between Democracy and Law*, edited by Carlos Closa, Costanza Margiotta and Giuseppe Martinico, 49-61. London: Routledge, 2020.

Closa, Carlos. "Secession from a Member State and EU Membership". *European Constitutional Law Review* 12 (2016): 240-264.

Dion, Stéphane. "Democracy against unilateral secession." In *Across Boundaries: Essays in honour of Robert A. Young*, edited by André Blais, Cristine de Clercy, Anna Lennox Esselment and Ronald Wintrobe, 83-112. Montreal: Mc-Gill-Queen's University Press, 2021.

Ginsburg, Tom and Huq, Aziz Z. *How to save a constitutional democracy.* Chicago: The University of Chicago Press, 2018.

González Campañá, Núria. "Secesión y constitucionalismo comparado." *Revista de Derecho Político* 1, no. 106 (2019): 105-135.

Kochenov, Dimitri. "Elephants in the Room: The European Commission's 2019 Communication on the Rule of Law." *Hague Journal on the Rule of Law* 11 (2019): 423-438.

Kriesi, Hanspeter. "The populist challenge." *West European Politics* 37, no. 2 (2014): 361-378.

Magaldi, Nuria. "El TJUE reafirma su competencia sobre el control de la organización judicial de los Estados Miembros." *Revista Jurídica de Catalunya* 3 (2021a): 813-820.

Magaldi, Nuria. *La politización del CGPJ y el caso de Polonia: aviso a navegantes.* Agenda Pública, 5 October 2021b. https://agendapublica.es/la-politizacion-del-cgpj-y-el-caso-de-polonia-aviso-a-navegantes/.

Margiotta, Costanza. "An update in secession as the "ultimate right": For a liminal legality." In *Between democracy and Law. The Amorality of Secession*, edited by Carlos Closa, Costanza Margiotta and Giuseppe Martinico, 9-29. London: Routledge, 2020.

Mudde, Cas. "The Populist Zeitgeist." *Government and Opposition* 39, no. 3 (2004): 541-563.

Ovejero, Felix. *Secesionismo y democracia.* Barcelona: Página Indómita, 2021.

Pech, Laurent and Scheppele, Kim L. "Illiberalism within: Rule of Law backsliding within the EU." *Cambridge Yearbook of European Legal Studies* 19 (2017): 3-47.

Porras, Antonio J. "El Consejo General del Poder Judicial según la STC 108/1986, de 29 de julio, sobre la Ley Orgánica del Poder Judicial." *Revista Española de Derecho Constitucional* 7, no. 19 (1987): 225-244.

Queralt, Argelia. "The Populist Drift of the Catalan Pro-Independence Movement." In *Integration and Desintegration in Europe*, edited by Jörn Axel Kämmerer, Markus Kotzur and Jacques Ziller, 253-280. Baden-Baden: Nomos, 2019.

Qvortrup, Matt. "Independence Referendums. History, legal status and voting behaviour." In *Between democracy and Law. The Amorality of Secession,* edited by Carlos Closa, Costanza Margiotta and Giuseppe Martinico, 133-153. London: Routledge, 2020.

Ruiz Casado, Juan Alberto. "Articulations of populism and nationalism: the case of the Catalan independence movement." *European Politics and Society* 21, no. 5 (2020): 554-569.

Tierney, Stephen. "Constitutional Referendums: A theoretical inquiry." *The Modern Law Review* 72, no. 3 (2009): 360-383.

Torres, Aida. "Judicial Self-Government and Judicial Independence: the Political Capture of the General Council of the Judiciary in Spain." *German Law Journal* 19, no. 7 (2018): 1769-1800.

Urías, Joaquín. *Spain has a Problem with its Judiciary*. Verfassungsblog, 15 January 2020. https://verfassungsblog.de/spain-has-a-problem-with-its-judiciary/.

Vilajosana, Josep M. "Principio democrático y justificación constitucional del derecho a decidir." *Revista d'Estudis Autonòmics i Federals* 19 (2014): 178-210.

Wind, Marlene. *The tribalization of Europe*. Cambridge: Polity Press, 2020.

Zakaria, Fareed. "The Rise of Illiberal Democracy." *Foreign Affairs* 76, no. 6 (1997): 22-43.

PART III

Populism and the European Union

The EU Unease About Populism

Cesare Pinelli

1 The EU as a Perfect Target of Populism

The issue of why the populist imagination meets growing favour both for what it denies and for the idea of the people's will that it encapsulates needs to be related not only to internal challenges but also, and perhaps to a greater extent, to events affecting democracies from the outside that are prone to be presented as external threats. It is here that populists are at ease in fuelling a politics of fear that implies per se the idea of a threatened people, irrespective of inner political cleavages.

Issues such as globalisation of markets and the flow of immigrants are frequently presented in such a way. However, it is the European Union's membership that gives populists their best opportunity for exploiting popular discontent towards national governments and traditional party politics. Why it is so?

Thirty years ago it had been noted that '[i]n the absence of an European government with a popular political base of its own, all possibilities of

C. Pinelli (✉)
Department of Legal and Economic Studies,
University of Roma – La Sapienza, Rome, Italy
e-mail: cesare.pinelli@uniroma1.it

J. M. Castellà Andreu, M. A. Simonelli (eds.), *Populism and Contemporary Democracy in Europe*,
https://doi.org/10.1007/978-3-030-92884-1_9

institutional transformation are entirely determined by the self-interests of national governments' (Scharpf 1998). Such prognosis has so far remained unchallenged.

It is true that, under the Lisbon Treaty, legislative decisions no longer depend on the Council acting unanimously, but on the European Parliament (EP) acting jointly with the Council, that decides on the basis of qualified majority unless the Treaties provide otherwise (Article 16 TEU). But the unanimity rule of Member States is still requested (with limited exceptions) both for the approval and for the ratification of the European treaties (Article 48 TEU). The rule that the Commission's President is appointed by the European Council 'taking into account the elections of the European Parliament', and then elected by the EP (Article 17, para 7, TEU), was indeed complemented in 2014 with the 'Spitzenkandidat system', a conventional device according to which the top candidate of the most popular party after the EU vote is nominated for the post.

However, the emergence of a true parliamentary form of government was practically impeded by the dominant role that the European Council acquired due to the fallout of the global financial crisis. Such role has not been without costs for national governments, pushing them to the centre of the EU institutional stage.

For a long time, they had preferred to remain behind it. Given the dispersal of power affecting the EU institutional arrangement, national governments were able to leave to the EU the burden of hard choices, starting with those concerning the national budget, without paying electoral costs. Rulers dislike being held accountable. It was arguably in their own interest both to maintain the EU system as it was, with no chance of identifying accountable rulers behind the blue sky and the stars, and to let people believe the media tale of 'Brussels' as a seat of inaccessible technocracy. Although clearly artificial, the divide between national politics and supranational technocratic governance permeated the popular imagination, hiding the dilemma between the adoption of long-term policies that require time to be understood by citizens and are not without risks in terms of electoral approval, and the mere administration of the present, with the related dismissal of politics. While regularly preferring the latter, the national governments' condition is to lay the blame of the European malaise on the 'obscure and unelected' officials of Brussels. While influencing the self-representation of the EU institutions, a further distance from popular imagination was put by the mainstream scholarly emphasis on a 'European post-national governance' founded on a discursive process and on contestation between interests (Shaw 1999).

The 2000 Lisbon Strategy was supported by an ambitious design of governance, the 'Open Method of Coordination', relying on coordination, peer review, networks, and heterarchy, rather than on centralised hierarchical tools of compliance. The bulk of the whole design nonetheless depended on the national governments' discretionary power in engaging in internal structural reforms of the welfare sectors (Colliat 2012). Governments soon realised that a shift of financial resources from traditional social policies to investments in technology would endanger their own electoral consent. The Commission's 2001 White Paper on European Governance echoed to an even greater extent post-national concepts, with the intention of melting together the old communitarian method and a pluralist political arrangement in which the decision-making powers of national governments are decentralised and displaced to a plethora of multilevel organisations, NGOs, civil society institutions, and public and private interests.[1]

However, it was objected, the 'governance turn' goes to the point of acting 'as an "anti-politic machine" in which accountability becomes progressively blurred, decision-making increasingly remote and obtuse, and the citizens of Europe—in whose name the EU claims to speak—evermore voiceless' (Shore 2011).

An oversimplified opposition 'pushing a "governance" approach at the expense of one honed towards a traditional notion of "government", or deliberative democracy at the expense of representative democracy' (Curtin 2005), was presupposed by the 2001 White Paper, as well as by the claim of the Commission's Green Paper that globalisation heralds the end of representative democracy as we know it.[2] Paradoxically, such an approach relied on the elitist paradigms of post-modernism with a view to get closer to citizens, in the awareness of the increasing sense of remoteness of European policies.[3]

Legal texts reveal that very anxiety, although treated with an opposite rhetoric. Think of the heroic declaration that 'while remaining proud of

[1] European Commission, *European Governance: A White Paper*, COM (2001), 428.

[2] European Commission, AS\D(2000), *The Future of Parliamentary Democracy:* Transition and Challenge in European Governance, Green Paper prepared for the Conference of the European Union Speakers of Parliament, September 2000. Available at https://ec.europa.eu/governance/docs/doc3_en.pdf. Last accessed 30 September 2021.

[3] European Commission, *European Governance: A White Paper*, 35.

their own national identities and history, the peoples of Europe are determined to transcend their former divisions and, united ever more closely, to forge a common destiny' (Preamble to the Constitutional Treaty). Furthermore, in an attempt to respond to popular discontent with 'Europe' that emerged from the 2005 French and Dutch referendums, the Lisbon Treaty solemnly states that 'The functioning of the Union shall be founded on representative democracy' (Article 10, para 1, TEU) and then adds:

> Citizens are directly represented at Union level in the European Parliament. Member States are represented in the European Council by their heads of State or Government and in the Council by their governments, themselves democratically accountable either to their national Parliaments, or their citizens

Such text presupposes that European citizens should content themselves with that version of representative democracy. The aim behind this rather thin rationale appears to be to dismiss the whole debate on the democratic deficit. At the time of the Lisbon Treaty's enactment, national governments were still attempting to hide behind the EU flag for fuelling popular distrust at home against 'Europe'. And yet, they were sawing off the branch they were sitting on. It was the Eurozone crisis that increased the dominance of intergovernmentalism (Cramme 2012) to the point of pushing national governments to the centre stage. The old game was over. The European Council's crucial role in the adoption of financial measures aimed at reducing national expenditures for the citizens' welfare could no longer be denied. It complemented for the people an image of the EU that already consisted of the fictions and the vacuity of its official language, as well as the tricks of national governments.

Being presented as a defensive move against external threats, the populist attacks on the EU have thus appeared genuine to huge sectors of the electorate, particularly to those exacerbated by the scarce governmental response to their basic needs, and forged the idea of a concrete popular will.

2 Why the EU Is So Helpless Vis-à-vis Populism

It is time to ask ourselves why does the EU appear particularly helpless vis-à-vis the populist surge. Attention needs first to be driven on the fact that, in constitutional democracies, populist parties or movements are not, nor should be, legally contrasted. Even in Germany, whose Basic Law allows the Federal Constitutional Court to declare the dissolution of any political party that seeks to undermine or abolish the free and democratic order or to endanger its existence (Article 21 BL), the Court refrained from adopting such measure against an ultranationalist party as the NPD,[4] thus declining 'to provide further fodder for the populists' familiar narrative that the establishment systematically suppresses the voice of the people'.[5] As affirmed by the FCC's President, reactions to the populist challenge should derive primarily from the political process itself (Voßkuhle 2018).

The idea that responses to populism should come from politics itself reflects a core principle such as pluralism, which constitutional democracies could not renounce without betraying themselves. It is respect for pluralism, together with the rule of law, that impedes whichever degeneration of majoritarianism into the winner-take-all rule, thus rendering, inter alia, unpredictable the electoral outcome. To the contrary, populist regimes deny in the practice the reversibility of political power, with the majority in charge willing to rest in power by all means: pluralism is there variously obstructed because it might hamper such possibility, not because it contrasts with an ideological tribute to the people's will. Respect for pluralism engenders thus a structural asymmetry in terms of power, which gives populists a competitive advantage on their adversaries.

In the light of the 'common values' enumerated in Article 2 TEU, such account can be referred to the EU as well. In particular, the EU treaty conceives pluralism against the background of a basis of beliefs and principles common to the EU and its Member States, with the implication that it cannot be superimposed on the latter. The EU treaty rests rather on the presumption that pluralism is shared by the Member States.

Nor does Article 7 TEU provide restrictions of the populist governments' conduct as such, being referred to the existence of systemic

[4] Federal Constitutional Court, January 17, 2017, *Neue Juristische Wochenschrift* 611, on which see Schuldt, *Mixed Signals of Europeanization*, 810, 817.

[5] Pirang, *Renaissance of Militant Democracy?*, www.lawfareblog.com, March 27, 2017, last accessed September 2021.

violations by a Member State of the before-mentioned values. On the other hand, its enforcement mechanisms rest ultimately in the hands of national governments as represented in the European Council. Their current inertia should be blamed vis-à-vis what has been called 'the purposeful destruction of the rule of law inside EU member states' (Müller 2016).

Here lies the specific EU's difficulty with populism. The very fact is telling that breaches of the 'common values' perpetrated by Hungary and Poland in the past decade are labelled as 'the rule of law crisis', the independence of the judiciary in particular. The populist approach challenges instead the pluralist principle no less than the rule of law. This view is shared not only among scholars, but also by independent authorities such as the Venice Commission. In a 2016 opinion regarding the Polish Constitutional Tribunal, the Commission affirmed that 'Democracy cannot be reduced to the rule of the majority; majority rule is limited by the Constitution and by law, primarily in order to safeguard the interests of minorities. Of course, the majority steers the country during a legislative period but it must not subdue the minority; it has an obligation to respect those who lost the last elections. Regarding the Constitutional Tribunal, it remarked: 'as long as the situation of constitutional crisis related to the Constitutional Tribunal remains unsettled and as long as the Constitutional Tribunal cannot carry out its work in an efficient manner, not only is the rule of law in danger, but so is democracy and human rights'.[6]

Unfortunately this is not the case of EU political institutions. The point is that in the last decade non-compliance with the common values has nonetheless become 'a principled ideological choice of several governments' (Scheppele et al. 2020), particularly of those that have dismantled the constitutional constraints with 'elegant techniques and tools' (Miljojkovich 2020). Such change should require from the EU and from the other Member States a transparent debate with the Polish and Hungarian governments. The approach of the former to the issue is instead case by case and therefore formalistic.

Since 2012, when the Commission first acknowledged the new Hungarian government's threat to the rule of law, the EU toolbox has become increasingly sophisticated: not only measures laid down in the treaties such as those of Article 7 TEU and the infringement procedures

[6] CDL-AD(2016)001, *Opinion no. 833/2015 on Amendments to the Act of 25 June 2015 on the Constitutional Tribunal of Poland*, adopted by the Venice Commission at its 106th Plenary Session (Venice, 11–12 March 2016).

provided in Articles 258 and 259 TFEU, but also the ECJ caselaw with rule of law implications, and mechanisms for compliance via dialogue and engagement (the Framework for the Rule of Law, the new Commission Rule of Law reporting cycle, the Council Dialogue on the Rule of Law). And yet, none of these tools has proved to guarantee the common values and the rule of law in particular.

The Regulation on the rule of law conditionality approved on 16 December 2020 is likely to confirm the case-by-case approach. After having stated that 'the following may be indicative of breaches of the principles of the rule of law: (a) endangering the independence of the judiciary; (b) failing to prevent, correct or sanction arbitrary or unlawful decisions by public authorities, including by law-enforcement authorities, withholding financial and human resources affecting their proper functioning or failing to ensure the absence of conflicts of interest; (c) limiting the availability and effectiveness of legal remedies, including through restrictive procedural rules and lack of implementation of judgments, or limiting the effective investigation, prosecution or sanctioning of breaches of law' (Article 3), the Regulation refers to 'appropriate measures' to be taken whenever 'breaches of the principles of the rule of law in a Member State affect or seriously risk affecting the sound financial management of the Union budget or the protection of the financial interests of the Union in a sufficiently direct way' (Article 4).

Being referred to breaches of the rule of law that undermine the Union's financial interest, the scope of the mechanism is indeed far stricter than that required for the rule of law's maintenance. A Member State, it has been argued, could decide to attack civil society groups or discriminate against LGBT people or persecute individual independent judges, without being held responsible of violating the conditionality mechanism (Pech 2020).

As for the formulation, reference to breaches of the rule of law that 'affect or seriously risk affecting the sound financial management of the Union budget or the protection of the financial interests of the Union in a sufficiently direct way' (Article 4 Reg.) runs counter to premises of the rule of law such as clarity, foreseeability, and anti-arbitrariness, and might even have proved Hungary's and Poland's capacity 'to drive EU institutions so far into mocking the rule of law in the spirit of defending it. Then again, this is exactly what illiberal constitutional engineering is about: using familiar constitutional and legal techniques for ends that subvert constitutionalism and the rule of law' (Uitz 2020).

The legal drafting's vagueness, to tell the truth, fairly corresponds to EU law standards and cannot be therefore attributed to the manoeuvres of

Hungary and Poland. But the objection goes far beyond the drafting. It demonstrates that, while dealing with the illiberal ideology championed by those countries, the EU appears affected from bureaucratic legalism, whose affinities with autocratic legalism are closer than with constitutional democracy's principles, namely of 'common values'. This is a sad conclusion indeed. But EU's friends should not hide it: *Amicus Plato, sed magis amica veritas.*

Bibliography

Colliat, Rémi. "A Critical Genealogy of European Macroeconomic Governance." *European Law Journal* 18, no. 6 (2012): 6–23.

Cramme, Olaf. "The Worrying Inevitability of EU Intergovernmentalism." *Policy Network*, 2012. https://www.ucl.ac.uk/european-institute/news/2012/dec/worrying-inevitability-eu-intergovernmentalism.

Curtin, Deirdre. "Tailoring Legitimacy to the Shape of the EU." *European Constitutional Law Review* 1, no. 3 (2005): 421–426.

Miljojkovich, Teodora. "Shilly Shallying and the EU's Dichotomous Response to the Rule of Law Crisis." *Democracy 2020. Assessing Constitutional Decay, Breakdown, and Renewal Worldwide*, edited by Tom Gerald Daly and Wojiech Sadursky, 222-226. IACL-AIDC (e-book),2020. https://www.iacl-democracy-2020.org/ebook.

Müller, Jan-Werner. "Reflections on Europe's 'Rule of Law Crises." In Kjaer-Olson (eds.), *Critical Theories of Crisis in Europe. From Weimar to the Euro*, 161-176. London: Rowman and Littlefield, 2016.

Pech, Laurent. "The Rule of Law Compromise: The EU's Gift to Autocrats." *Green European Journal*, (2020). https://www.greeneuropeanjournal.eu/the-rule-of-law-compromise-the-eus-gift-to-autocrats/.

Scharpf, Fritz W. "The Joint-Decision Trap: Lessons from German Federalism and European Integration." *Public Administration* 66, no. 3 (1998): 239–265.

Scheppele, Kim Lane; Kochenov, Dimitry Kochenov and Grawoska-Moroz, Barbara. "EU values are Law after All. Enforcing EU Values through Systemic Infringement Actions by the European Commission and the Member States of the European Union." *Yearbook of European Law* 39, (2020): 3–121.

Shaw, Jo. "Postnational Constitutionalism in the European Union." *Journal of European Public Policy* 6, no. 4 (1999): 579–597.

Shore, Cris. "European Governance or Govermentality? The European Commission and the Future of Democratic Government." *European Law Journal* 17, no. 3 (2011): 287–303.

Uitz, Renáta. "Towards an EU Cast in the Hungarian and Polish Mould. Why the December 2020 Compromise Matters." *VerfBlog*, (2020). https://verfassungsblog.de/towards-an-eu-cast-in-the-hungarian-and-polish-mold/.

Voßkuhle, Andreas. "Demokratie und Populismus." *Der Staat* 57, no. 1 (2018):120–134.

The Authoritarian Conjuncture in Europe and Liberals' Crocodile Tears

Giovanni Guerra

1 Introduction. The Authoritarian Drift in Europe … a Liberals' Fault

According to a broad number of studies, in the last decade Europe seems to have embarked to a large extent on an authoritarian course (Kreuder-Sonnen 2018). Authoritarian traits emerge from the domestic developments of some Member States, namely Hungary and Poland, where in recent years nationalist and populist right-wing parties have come to power, threatening several core values of European constitutional liberal tradition, such as rule of law, political pluralism and minority rights (Kelemen 2017; Halmai 2019). At the same time, there are many elements that lean towards authoritarianism rather than constitutionalism at supranational level too, as a consequence of the reforms carried out during the Euro-crisis in the field of EU economic governance (Somek 2015). These features can be traced in the increasing rigour and pervasiveness of the system of intergovernmental coordination and supranational

G. Guerra (✉)
Department of Legal Sciences, University of Siena, Siena, Italy

J. M. Castellà Andreu, M. A. Simonelli (eds.), *Populism and Contemporary Democracy in Europe*,
https://doi.org/10.1007/978-3-030-92884-1_10

surveillance to which national economies and budgets have been subjected. Moreover, the existence of an authoritarian pattern becomes particularly evident if we take into account the "occupation regime" (Scharpf 2011, 185) orchestrated by the *Troika* in some of the countries which have received financial assistance through the bailout mechanisms.

The chapter argues that populism, which liberals constantly criticise, is not an accident of history, appeared out of nowhere. It represents a direct consequence of the way through which liberal elites have shaped the European integration process by resolutely insulating macroeconomic policymaking from the control of their societies. For this reason, liberals should blame primarily themselves. As admitted by a long-standing liberal as Zielonka, little doubts exist about the fact that "liberals cannot act as innocent victims of a malicious populist assault", because the "EU was an institution totally controlled by liberals and they are partly responsible for making the anti-European campaign relatively easy if not legitimate to some degree" (Zielonka 2018, 122). Following the argumentative path proposed by Bugarič, the chapter aims to demonstrate that the populist backlash against EU traces its roots back primarily to the lack of meaningful economic and social alternatives to neoliberal policies (Bugarič 2020), which have been progressively codified by liberal elites into EU Treaties and the economic governance to the point of resulting over-constitutionalised.

So, in order to demonstrate this, Sect. 2 offers an overview of the evolution of European economic integration process, delineating the main steps that have led to the transformation of the embedded liberalism paradigm epitomised by the Treaty of Rome into the authoritarian economic liberalism paradigm informing the new EU economic governance. Section 3 examines why there are very few margins left to the European citizens to organise a legitimate political opposition within the EU system, whose impermeability to social demands facilitates the rise of populist parties articulating their claims against the European project itself. Then, Sect. 4 explores the reasons for which it does not seem possible to break free from the grasp of austerity and structural reforms under the current EU Treaties and EU economic governance framework. Finally, after taking stock of existing relation between the populist surge in the EU and what it has been called liberal "extreme centrism", the responses provided by the EU to cope with the COVID-19 pandemic crisis are briefly analysed, trying to elucidate whether they have really marked a discontinuity with the solutions experienced until now.

2 From Embedded Liberalism to Authoritarian Liberalism: Prioritising Market Imperatives over Social Emancipation

It is necessary to analyse the ways trough which liberal elites have shaped the European economic integration in order to understand the populist surge against EU.

During the first decades after World War II, known as "thirty glorious years" (Fourastié 1979), Western European societies experienced an unprecedent period of economic growth and prosperity. At national level the main efforts were devoted to the set-up of democratic constitutions, grounded on the proclamation of collective self-determination, the protection of human dignity and fundamental rights (with the important inclusion of social rights), the institutionalisation of social conflict and the promotion of social emancipation against the economic oppression exercised by unregulated markets (Dani 2012; Somek 2014). The achievement of these goals was guaranteed by the edification of a robust welfare state along with a large use of the Keynesian toolbox: expansionary fiscal policies supporting internal demand, progressive taxation and full employment strategies (Judt 2005).

At supranational level the picture is more complex and controversial. The Treaty of Rome, signed in 1957, marked the enactment of the European Economic Community (EEC), aimed to create a common market based on the famous "four fundamental freedom", namely goods, people, services and capital. Furthermore, taking into account the Treaty provisions, it is easy to notice that "social policy did not play much of a role" (Streeck 2019, 120). According to Maestro Buelga, there would be an ontological irreconcilability between the fundamental decision to establish an open market with free competition and the democratic-social constitutionalism (Maestro Buelga 2007). If not an incompatibility, it is undeniable that EEC arose under the sign of what Mancini have called "founding fathers' social frigidity". Indeed, while national "capitalist law-makers have not actuated, but have started the undertaking for which they have been called by the workers' protests or by the bourgeois' guilty conscience, to foster the slow progress of the equality", the "european founders" were not interested into "reforming the man's condition who has to sell his workforce". So, we have to admit that the labour and social law "traced *in apicibus* in Rome, [...] and later developed by Bruxelles, does not stem from the critic of the unequal relationship which leads to the major conflicts at the heart of the capitalist system" (Mancini 1988).

On the contrary, many commentators argue that this contraposition does not exist. The limited competences assigned to the supranational level in the social policy sphere, rather than being considered as a sort of "original sin" of EEC settlement, "reflected the explicit objective of a division of labor between national and EEC rulers that was seen as virtuous for both the market and the welfare state" (Ferrera 2005, 92). In this perspective, the framework of the Treaty of Rome, decoupling the social protection issues and economic realm (Scharpf 2002, 646), may reveal a "social empathy" (Giubboni 2006, 30); in the sense, the choice to leave the social, fiscal and monetary spheres in Member States' hands, opening the economic sphere to the intervention of the EEC, was intended to protect the Member States' capacity to exercise their social prerogatives according to their peculiarities (Giubboni 2006). Therefore, it could be argued that, although the demarcation between economic and social domains may look rather artificial (Dani 2018, 34), the European economic integration process, in its early years, was meant to "rescue the nation state" (Milward 2000, 216) (and its welfare model) through the combination of supranational free trade and domestic state interventionism. This mix can be captured by the felicitous expression of "embedded liberalism" (Ruggie 1982, 379).

The caution surrounding the EEC Treaty normative dedicated to capital freedom of movement seems to corroborate the hypothesis according to which the process of European integration was conceived as a way of pursuing the original commitments of national democratic constitutional self-government. Compared to the legal provisions concerning services, goods and people, which were supposed to flow almost freely, the art. 3 of the EEC Treaty collocated the free movement of capital down the list, reserving to it the *status* of "second-class citizen" (Abdelal 2007, 48), since it was supposed to be achieved "progressively" and "to the extent necessary to ensure the proper functioning of the common market" (art. 67 EEC Treaty). This was a conscious decision. The complete suppression of all restrictions on capital flows would have surely implied the repudiation of a fundamental instrument of domestic economic policy to preserve national fiscal systems.

The end of embedded Liberalism era coincided with the worldwide call for the "neoliberal counter-revolution", which took place in the late 1970s (Mitchell and Fazi 2017, 71). It has reversed the subservient role of the market, emancipating it from politics and society. As shown by Moravcsik, the neoliberal drift in the European continent has been sponsored by a "centrist coalition"—headed by the conservative Thatcher, the Socialist moderate Mitterrand and the Christian-Democrat Kohl—grounded on a general consensus around the necessity to complete supranational market liberalisation (Moravcsik 1991, 52). In 1986 this convergence brought to the adoption of the Single European Act (SEA), which represented a crucial step in the opening of the European markets. From that moment Member States lost their autonomy in managing welfare issues.

During this period, it should not be underestimated the key role played by the Court of Justice in pushing towards supranational market liberalisation. It is true that CJEU initially seemed inclined to elaborate an interpretation of the economic freedoms as a manifestation of the principle of non-discrimination on the basis of nationality (Maduro 1999, 143). However, starting from the *Cassis De Dijon* judgement in 1979, the CJEU chose to embrace an obstacle-based interpretation of the free movement of goods, later extended to the other factors of production, boosting at full strength the competitive market paradigm (Dani 2018, 34).

The birth of the European Economic and Monetary Union (EMU) in 1992 revealed the permanent European commitment to neoliberal ideology. As it is well known, the ratification of the Maastricht Treaty has entailed the creation of a single currency—with the devolution of the monetary competence to a new independent supranational institution, the European Central Bank—and the submission of the Member States' economies and budgets under a strict process of intergovernmental coordination and supranational surveillance. The design of this settlement was inspired by the will to guarantee: the development of an open market economy with free competition (artt. 4, 98, 105 EC Treaty), in which all restrictions on the movement of capital, not only between Member States, but also among them and third countries, are prohibited (art. 56 EC Treaty); the maintenance of price stability (artt. 4, 105 EC Treaty) and the avoidance of excessive deficits (art. 104 EC Treaty). Given that picture, it is evident that the main goal was to make compulsory the assumption of a vast structural reform programme around Europe. To quote Carli's words, the Italian Treasury Minister during the negotiation of the Maastricht Treaty, this turning point would have involved a radical rethink of the legislation through which has been erected the Social State: "the rejection of the mixed economy model, the abandonment of the economic planning", and "the redefinition of the public expenditure composition method" (Carli 1993, 436). In short, the EMU would have entailed the dismissal of the Keynesian *paraphernalia*.

Moreover, there is further evidence in favour of the EMU characterisation as a neoliberal construction. The creation of an economic and monetary union like the one that has been erected with the Maastricht Treaty appears as the concretisation of an obscure prophecy made by Hayek in an essay written in 1939 (Streeck 2014; Chessa 2016). According to the famous spiritual father of the Austrian-American neoliberalism, the best way to neutralise the scope of the economic policies of the individual States is to allow the free movement of goods, men and capital over national frontiers (Hayek 1958, 258). Since they are beyond the domestic control, covered by the protection of an Interstate Federation, the Member States will no longer be able to affect the spontaneous price determination process. Therefore, the "Union [would have inexorably] becom[e] one single market" (Hayek 1958, 258). But the thing that catches the eye more is the Hayek's insistence on the incapacity of the States belonging to an Interstate Federation to pursue an autonomous monetary policy: national central banks would have been replaced by a federal system of central banks (Hayek 1958, 259), exactly like the European System of Central Banks. In addition, Hayek has argued that, even if the domestic economic capacity had been thus limited, it is not to say that the federal government should have taken over the functions which the States can no longer perform and should have done all the planning and regulating which the States cannot do anymore (Hayek 1958, 261). So, at this point, it seems hard to deny that the European economic and monetary, but non-fiscal Union built upon the Maastricht Treaty closely resembles the neoliberal Intestate Federation imagined by Hayek.

The Treaty of Lisbon has simply consolidated the above-mentioned framework. It is only in the late 2000s that European integration made another crucial step. Precisely, the European response to the financial and economic crisis has precipitated the EU in an era of authoritarian liberalism (Wilkinson 2013). This term, as reminded by Menéndez, was coined by Heller in the early 1930s to polemically describe the authoritarian mode of carrying out policies by the Brüning and Von Papen conservative cabinets to cope with the violent economic crisis of that time (Menéndez 2015, 287). Well, the use of this expression in relation to the reforms enacted at the time of the Euro-crisis seems to be adequate on the grounds that it captures various symptoms of EU recent developments: first, the start of a process of "de-democratisation", referring to the bypassing of parliamentary authority and debate, both at national and supranational levels, during the launch of most of the legal innovations concerning the EU economic governance; second, the capitulation to the "TINA" narrative, that is the refrain according to which "There Is No Alternative" to neoliberal structural reforms (privatisations, liberalisations, welfare cuts, labour market reforms) imposed through the euro-regime by the European Council and the Council—and their euro-version, that is the Eurosummit and the Eurogroup—as well as by the *Troika* (ECB, Commission and IMF) (Wilkinson 2018).

This depiction seems to hit the mark. For sure, it is undeniable that the role played by the Council and Eurogroup in the negotiations surrounding bailouts resembled to a sort of "harsh dictatorship" which rules according to a form of "deliberative authoritarianism" (Schmidt 2020, 117) imposing fiscal consolidation measures in return for financial assistance. The same can be said for the role of the Commission, described as an "unaccountable ayatollah of austerity" (Schmidt 2020, 176). Elements of authoritarianism can be also found in the top-down process incapsulated in the TSCG, which have led to the transposition of the balance budget rule provided for therein into national legal system "preferably at constitutional level" (art. 3 TSCG). A disturbing authoritarian connotation embraces the new design of the European economic governance system too. Indeed, the European Semester, the Macro Imbalance Procedure and the Excessive Deficit Procedure have transformed the annual cycle of coordination and surveillance of the Eurozone states' economic policies and budgets into a system based on "discipline and punish" in order to oblige the more insubordinate Member States to adopt structural reforms compliant with the *diktats* of the markets (Oberndorfer 2014).

Well, since during the Euro-crisis some authority structures of the European legal order have been imbued with aspects of authoritarianism in an attempt to fortify economic liberalism, it is completely understandable the progressive European citizens' disaffection to European projection. How it is intended to explain in the subsequent pages, it is properly the absence of alternative economic and social policies and the lack of appropriate legal and political accountable structures for their implementation to enhance popular discontent against the European Union, facilitating the rise of populism around the continent.

3 Technocratic Ethos, Depoliticised Decision-Making, and Unaccountable Executive-Dominated Supranational Governance. Little Room for Legitimate Political Opposition

In 2007 Mair published a brilliant essay under the title "Political Opposition and the European Union", which even today can be considered one of the best sources to explain the proliferation of populist parties across Europe and the diffusion of a sense of diffidence, not to say hostility, towards the EU itself. The main conclusions of this work about the possibility to integrate into the European polity an organised political opposition within the European political and legal system are quite bitter. According to Mair, even if "we enjoy the right to participate in EU decisions by casting a vote, whether for our putative national representatives who go to the various Councils or for our European representatives who go to the European Parliament in Strasbourg, we emphatically lack the right to organise opposition within the system, in the sense that 'we lack the capacity to do so'". Furthermore, EU is a "depoliticized" entity which in turn produces "depoliticization" (Mair 2007, 7). So, "once we cannot organise opposition *in* the EU, we are then almost forced to organise opposition *to* the EU. To be critical of the policies promulgated by Brussels is therefore to be critical of the polity; to object to the process is therefore to object to the product" (Mair 2007, 8).

Unfortunately, we have to admit that nothing has changed. Perhaps the situation has even worsened, considering that the room to exercise legitimate political opposition has been consistently curtailed at the time of the Euro-crisis. Sure, there is no doubt the European Union has put in field a restyling of its institutional setting, trying to open it to politicisation and to improve its democratic pedigree. The obvious reference here is the *Spitzenkadidaten* process launched in the occasion of the European Parliamentary (EP) election of 2014. According to its supporters, the agreement reached among main European political parties by proposing a candidate to be designated as the President of the European Commission was aimed to provide a stronger democratic legitimation to the President of that organ which retains the monopoly of EU legislative initiative. In this way, the competitive selection of the Commission's head office would have been able to inoculate a higher level of political representativeness in the EU law-making. Above all—always according to its defenders' opinion—*Spitzenkadidaten* experiment would have involved a real parliamentarisation of the EU, reinforcing the link between Commission and the EP.

Well, the hopes that *Spitzenkadidaten* formula would have been able to entail more parliamentarisation and more politicisation were misplaced (Fabbrini 2015, 578; Goldoni 2016, 284). Starting with the question of whether or not this process has equipped the EU with a fully parliamentary government, the answer cannot be affirmative for many reasons linked to the presence of certain elements that sound very unfamiliar to the parliamentary government model. First, a true relationship of confidence between Commission and EP does not subsist: even if EP holds the power to vote down the Commission in its entirety, the EP can exercise it exclusively on the basis of moral (not political) reasons. In addition, the EP's statutory mandate has a five-year fixed term, and any one institution can dissolve the EP. Second, the provision according to which the Commissioners "may not, during their term of office, engage in any other occupation, whether gainful or not" (art. 245 TFEU) represents an evident contradiction with another tenet of parliamentary government model, that is the parliamentary *status* of executive members.

As regards the question whether or not the *Spitzenkadidaten* process has enhanced the political credential of the Commission, also this time the response cannot be positive. How is it possible to consider Commission as a genuine political institution, since this organ in ensuring "the application of the Treaties", in superintending "the application of Union law under the control of the Court of Justice" or "in carrying out its responsibilities" "shall be completely independent" and "shall neither seek nor take instructions from any Government or other institution, body, office or entity" (TEU Art. 17 TEU)? Furthermore, the political potential of the Commission is extensively narrowed down by the role which it plays within the European economic governance framework: not acting as a government in strict sense, but as an all-seeing economic police, tasked with guarding Member States' economic performances and sanctioning the more undisciplined of them, like a technocratic institution.

Anyway, at a closer look, the roots of angry times which the EU is experiencing are much deeper, and they concern the problematic relation that has been developed across time between European public law and national constitutional democracy. Following the efficacious tripartition proposed by Dani, we can distinguish three different paradigms operating during the European integration process, *grosso modo* corresponding to the three phases described in the first chapter of this work: the "complementary paradigm" in the embedded liberalism era, the "competitive paradigm" during the neoliberal drift era, and the "encroachment paradigm" in the authoritarian liberalism era (Dani 2016a).

Until SEA, as we have seen, a symbiotic relationship was built up between national constitutional democracy and European public law. A clear technocratic ethos undoubtedly characterised supranational institutions, since they performed through a mostly technical and refractory to politicisation law-making process, the s.c. "Community Method", which at that time involved exclusively executive institutions. The Strasbourg's Assembly exercised only a consultive function during its first thirty years of life. However, the narrow scope of supranational institutions' action has prevented in this period the manifestation of the corrosive effects over national constitutional democracies potentially stemming from the supranational regulatory state.

After 1986 the above-mentioned equilibrium has deteriorated. Supranational institutions have started to acquire more and more competences in areas with pronounced redistributive consequences, previously reserved to national democratic intervention. Certainly, this enlargement of functions has been accompanied by an attempt to emulate some elements belonging to the imaginary of national constitutional democracies: for example, the Maastricht Treaty in 1992 introduced the European Citizenship and the Nice European Council of 2000 proclaimed the adoption of the European Charter of Fundamental Rights. Nevertheless, the supranational actors have ceased to be instrumental in enhancing the principles inspiring national constitutional democracies.

It is in this phase that European integration process commenced to manifest almost fully its transformative potential (Bickerton 2012). Taking into account the EMU, it has worked like a *vincolo esterno*—that is an "external constraint"—aimed to promote a deep-rooted transformation of Member States' economies and welfare systems through the enactment of a broad set of reforms (Dyson and Featherstone 1999). The strategy that has been traced is very refined: national elites congregated in the intergovernmental *fora* at supranational level seemed to be inclined to invoke more external constraints that governments can commit themselves to (Radaelli 2002, 233), so as to be able to justify to their domestic public opinions the necessity to carry out structural reforms by presenting them in terms of "European obligation" (Bickerton 2015, 55). From this perspective, it is noticed an evident tendency in the EU context according to which governments prefer to seek their legitimacy in their relations with each other, with the consequence that the horizontal ties between them have taken precedence over the links between government and their own societies (Bickerton 2016, 73). In this way, it became easier for national governments to avoid the citizens' potential objections against the already embarked pro-fiscal discipline programme. So, it can be asserted that EMU with its constraints has provided national governments with the opportunity to elude domestic popular will or, at least, the complex pluralist bargain process related to a matter of such importance (Della Sala 1997).

When the financial and economic crisis deflagrated around 2008, the original equilibrium characterising the foundational years definitively collapsed. It is true that thanks to the Lisbon Treaty EP evolved into a legislative organ enjoying the same degree of the Council, as well as national parliaments became an integral part of the supranational law-making process. However, from 2010 EU has shown "its crudest intergovernmental and technocratic profile by extending its regulatory style to even more salient policy fields to promote the degree of convergence of national economies required by a single currency" (Dani 2016b, 80). It is necessary to consider in more detail the new EU economic governance framework to become aware of this.

Apropos of how the EU economic governance has been reformed, the wide recourse to international law (TSCG, EFSF and ESM) obviously has determined the exclusion of the EP. However, the EP's position has turned out to be marginal even when it was decided to intervene according to the "Community Method", like in the case of Six-Pack and Two-Pack regulations (Bressanelli and Chelotti 2018). The choice to go outside the EU legal framework has not helped NPs either, since national governments have resorted to stratagems of all kinds to avoid any interruption of the approval and ratification processes, such as fast-track procedures and legislative mergers (Maatsch 2017). In general, this crisis resolution method by intergovernmental summits behind closed doors has led to problems of poor transparency too (Dawson and de Witte 2013, 834).

Then, with respect to how the EU economic governance is articulated and works, its new design looks to be incompatible with the rituals of national parliamentary democracy. The entire system is heavily executive dominated (Curtin 2014): the European Council—by setting general economic priorities—and the Commission in liaison with the Council—by delivering country-specific recommendations (CSRs)—call the shots, while parliamentary institutions, both at national and supranational levels, have been placed on the sidelines of the system. In particular, the EP's role seems to be very weak, since it has to be informed and consulted only in specific occasions, but it has no decision making-making power (Fasone 2014, 174). At best, it has been entitled to organise impalpable and vanish "economic dialogues" with the executive European branch.

At the same time, the NPs' prerogatives on their budgetary cycles have been strongly diminished, because of the rigid timetable established with the European Semester, which does not fit with the time normally required to take healthy parliamentary debates. Moreover, in the case that Draft Budgetary Plans sent by euro area Member States to the Commission and the Eurogroup seem not to be in line with the country specific medium-term objective, as defined in the reformed Stability and Growth Pact (SGP), and the CSRs the Commission has gained the power to ask them to revise their DBPs until 30 November (art. 7 Reg. EU No. 473/2013). Well, in such cases, it is self-evident that since the DBPs have to be presented from Member States to the Commission no later than 15 October, the national parliamentary activity put in place after this date faces the risk to be suspended (Capuano and Griglio 2014, 244).

In addition, even if, according to Recital 16 Reg. EU No. 1175/2011, NPs should be duly included along the preparation of National Reform Programmes and Stability Programmes we have to admit that this Regulation "does not stipulate an obligation for NPs to be involved in formulating these programmes" (Jancic 2016, 186). The same can be said about what contemplated by art. 3 Regulation EU No. 472/2013: when the Commission takes the decision to subject a Member State to enhanced surveillance, the latter shall adopt measures aimed to address the sources or potential sources of difficulties, and the Commission shall, where relevant and in accordance with national practice, inform the NP of this Member State about the above-mentioned measures. It is evident that this provision implies that NPs might not be informed of these measures by their governments. It also suggests that these measures may be agreed between the Commission and the national governments without the guarantee of a prior parliamentary participation. *Rebus sic stantibus*, "the alienation of NPs becomes tangible" (Jancic 2016, 188).

What is worst, the EU economic governance framework reveals a wide accountability deficit. None of EU executive institutions can be held accountable along this process: the Commission lacks of its own political mandate, and "no one Np can sanction or change more than one government or executive body that contributes to it" (Lord 2017, 680). As pointed out by Crum, in the context of the new economic governance, NPs, but also EP, find themselves at "the losing side of a reinforced two-level of game" (Crum 2018, 269) involving primarily the Member State governments, the intergovernmental institutions assembled in Bruxelles and the Commission.

Finally, as regards the substance of EU economic governance, the EU domains have been overly enlarged. The *spectrum* of supranational surveillance has been extended to pensions, employment rate, productivity, wages and more, so much that "there is no more nucleus of sovereignty left to Member States" (Somek 2015, 342). But what is most upsetting is the exacerbation of the post-political and technocratic character of the EU as well as of its policymaking process, as proved by "the proliferation of macroeconomic indicators" which have given rise to "a form of public power informed by expertise and insulated from the vagaries of politics" (Dani 2016a, 421). Already at the time of the Maastricht Treaty, with its famous convergence criteria, and the SGP, enacted in 1997 and later reformed in 2005, numerical constraints occupied an important role. However, the EU crisis measures have put an absolute emphasis on these instruments, as we can notice in relation to the more stringent national budgetary constraints as reformulated by TSCG and Two-Pack. Now NPs are embroiled in an increasingly close grid of targets and quantitative measurements which bring them to succumb to the technocratic logic inspiring the euro-national budgetary cycle.

In sum, in the light of the progressive emersion of an unaccountable and technocratic executive-dominated supranational governance tasked with driving even more deeply its neoliberal regulatory machine at the social core of national constitutional democracies, it is really hard to argue that there are margins to exercise a legitimate political opposition within the EU system. The choice to manage Euro-crisis by "shielding macroeconomic policymaking from the intrusion of mobilise and angry societies" (Bickerton 2012, 150) has proved to be a failure, facilitating the increase of diffidence towards EU among the most fragile sections of European citizens hit by the economic crisis. As we will see in the next section, since every attempt to contest this framework and its imperatives has been brutally thwarted, it is quite astonishing that there is still someone surprised by the diffusion of Eurosceptic attitudes and populist parties around Europe.

4 Over-constitutionalisation of Neoliberal Policies: There Is No Legal Alternative but to Follow Structural Reforms

Considering the picture portrayed, it could be affirmed that in the occasion of the Euro-crisis the codification process of a specific economic theory—that is, the neoliberal one—into the European public law has been accomplished. Indeed, all the set of regulations of different sizes that has been enacted at supranational level to cope with the crisis has led to a "petrification" (Closa 2015) of political options favouring fiscal discipline and austerity.

Certainly, secondary legislation and soft law have always played a significant role in delivering neoliberal structural reforms. Just to give an example, one can think of the ECB's coercive letter, jointly written by Trichet and Draghi, sent to Italian government in August 2011 (Scicluna and Aurer 2019, 1433). In this missive, the former and the incumbent ECB governors suggested—to put it mildly—the adoption of a long list of structural reforms, such as the liberalisation of local public service, a large-scale privatisation, the revision of collective wage barging system, public expenditures cuts and a constitutional reform tightening fiscal rules. Moreover, the letter even fixed the legislative instrument to enact the above-mentioned reforms (decree-law) and the deadline within which these reforms should have been ratified by Parliament (sic!).

However, the main role in dictating neoliberal policies has always been reserved to primary legislation, that is the EU Treaties. On close examination, the EU Treaties are full of minute and detailed prescriptions which reveal a clear commitment to neoliberal ideology: since policy directives emanating from EU Treaties in areas like market, employment and industrial policy come with a pre-determined direction, relevant alternatives in favour of Keynesian interventionism are practically banned. Following a famous concept developed by Grimm, it might be said that EMU system and its neoliberal policies are "over-constitutionalized" (Grimm 2016, 307). In this context, also the indications coming from the CJEU should not be underestimated, notably the "constitutionalisation of austerity" (de Witte 2018, 487) into EMU framework put into effect with the *Pringle* judgement.

The reverberations of over-constitutionalisation do not remain confined to supranational law but radiate into national public law too. The last example along this line is represented by the choice made in 2018 by the

Italian President of Republic, Mattarella, to not appoint Savona as a Minister of Economy and Finance. Mattarella, in the declaration issued to justify his veto, asserted that his refusal has been motived by two reasons: first, it would be precluded to Italian MEF to be a supporter of a line that could have provoked, even inevitably, the Italy's exit from the Eurozone; second, the appointment as an MEF of an economist that expressed serious misgivings about the irreversibility of single currency would have triggered an increase in the cost of "spread", jeopardising the savings of Italian citizens. Well, it is highly questionable that an economist which almost thirty years ago served as Minister of Industry under the Ciampi's euro-friendly cabinet shall not be considered as an appropriate candidate only because he has changed his opinion about eurocurrency and the policies on which it has been built. And if that is the case, from the "Savona affaire" one could draw the impression that in the context of EU economic governance it is forbidden to express scepticism about the EMU ties, let alone try to legally change EMU in order to revitalise the prescriptions of removing the obstacles to the realisation of substantive equality included in the Italian and other European Constitutions, almost as if a "*pactum ad excludendum*" has taken shape against who criticize the current EU economic governance system (Dani and Menéndez 2020).

The over-constitutionalisation of neoliberal policies in the framework of EU economic governance goes hand-in-hand with a parallel process of "de-constitutionalisation" concerning democratic-social principles incorporated into national public law. The Greek case is certainly the most emblematic one (Katsaroumpas 2018). During the Euro-crisis Greece received financial assistance three times, coming to find itself under a sword of Damocles, at the mercy of Member State creditors and the infamous *Troika*. Considering that the content of the various conditionality measures adopted in the context of bailouts has been *de facto* unilaterally imposed by the creditor States as well as by the *Troika*, it should not be inappropriate to assert that in this situation Greece has retained its sovereignty "only on paper" (Streeck 2012, 67).

The sensation that, under conditionality regime, there is no legal alternative but to follow austerity is well represented by the third Greek bailout. With the victory of SYRIZA at the elections of January 2015, the Greek government tried to free the country from the grip of conditionality. For some months the situation seemed to ameliorate, since the *Troika* supervisory expeditions were stopped. The SYRIZA government decided to adopt policies without prior consulting creditors too, many times even against the *Troika*'s will. The call for a consultive referendum on the conditions of a new financial assistance package proposed by Commission, BCE and FMI in the summer of 2015 and the large prevalence of OXI votes were the last straw. As it is well known, "the Greek Government had to pay a high price for its defiance of the *Troika*'s technocratic advice" (Marketou 2017, 186). At the end of the Eurosummit held from 12 to 13 July 2015, the Greek government was forced to agree the implementation "without delay" of a set of priority reforms. Specifically, for some of these reforms a strict three-day deadline was established (sic!). But there is more. Reading the Statement of the aforesaid Eurosummit we see that it was also imposed to Greek authorities to re-examine with a view to amending legislations that were introduced in the last months by backtracking on previous programme commitments or identify clear compensatory equivalents for the vested rights that were subsequently created.

The challenge launched by Tsipras against *Troika*'s austerity ***diktats*** could have been the occasion to question the neoliberal policies stemming from EU economic governance in order to lay the basis for rebuilding a more social and democratic EU. Unfortunately, European liberal elites have done everything to prevent that from happening. In a certain sense, as shareably argued by Guazzarotti (2017, 12), following the reconstruction of some '900s memories made by Judt (2008, 191), the situation which EU currently faces because of liberal elites' preferences is very reminiscent of French military forces' condition at the time of German Nazis' invasion. The debacle of the French Army cannot be explained exclusively in military terms. Behind it there are also crucial political reasons. Specifically, in Vichy's first national defence minister opinion, the general Weygand, who led the troops in the last days of the conflict, the main source of apprehension was not represented by the German Nazis Army, but by a potential communist uprising in Paris upon the heels of a defeat. Well, since there are no plans to commence communist insurrections in Europe, when actually xenophobic, nationalist and populist parties of extreme right are now asserting themselves more and more easily taking advantage of the social malaise generated by the economic crisis and the austerity measures recommended by EU in response to it, it is questionable whether the project to promote neoliberal structural reforms through the European economic governance has been really a forward-looking one.

5 Conclusion. Populism, Liberal "Extreme Centrism" and COVID-19 Crisis

Liberal elites' insistence on neoliberal policies, and austerity have generated an increment of the most vulnerable European citizens' malaise. Hence, populist and nationalist parties had easy game into exploiting the precarious conditions of their angry societies triggered by the economic and financial crisis and the austerity measures enacted to cope with it, redirecting people's discontent against the EU and the European project itself. The rise of Orban's Fidesz party *docet*. In 2008 Hungary was one of the first European countries that received financial assistance from IMF-EU, and the population suffered huge losses because of austerity measures introduced in order to fix financial stability (Bugarič 2020, 483). Well, it would be an error to neglect this close link between the rise of nationalism and Euroscepticism in Hungary and the enactment of anti-crisis measures imposed through macroeconomic conditionality.

The cause of the current authoritarian conjuncture in which EU have fallen into lies primarily in the progressive consensus on neoliberal policies built by centre-right and centre-left parties. Liberal ""extreme centrism" (Wilkinson 2019) has failed to secure democracy and the social state in the EU, putting itself against them. And in doing so it has paved the way to the rise of populism. In this sense, the current populist surge can be considered as a response of a period of "undemocratic liberal policies" (Mudde 2016, 30).

The COVID-19 pandemic crisis would be an opportunity to revise the commitment of the EU economic governance to neoliberal ideology. Few steps forward have been taken. For example, the quantitative constraints on national budgets established in the SGP have been suspended, giving to national communities a little breath. Moreover, the *Next Generation EU* can be considered the more significant investment and recovery plan that is ever been developed by EU in its history. However, it must be underlined that the technocratic strategy "governing by rules and ruling by numbers" (Schmidt 2015) has not been definitively abandoned, but only temporarily set aside. What is most worrying is the missed rejection of the macroeconomic conditionality arrangements which have been included into European public law with the Two-Pack. The spectre of enhanced surveillance looms large over the *Pandemic Crisis Support Credit Line* (PCSCL) of the ESM, as well as the eventuality that the recipient countries may be forced to prepare a macroeconomic adjustment programme (Dani and Menéndez 2020).

European commissioners Gentiloni and Dombrovskis have sent to Eurogroup a letter in which they have excluded that these mechanisms will operate for the future in case a Member State resorts to the PCSCL. Unfortunately, because of the nature of this instrument, which is not truly a source of law, the missive represents only a mere auspice. If the EU wants to change, opening itself to the values of democratic-social constitutionalism, it has to put much more effort than it has done until now.

References

Abdelal, Rowi. *Capital Rules. The Construction of Global Finance*. Cambridge: Harvard University Press, 2007.

Bickerton, Chris. *European Integration: From Nation-States to Member States*. Oxford: Oxford University Press, 2012.

Bickerton, Chris. "A Union of Member States." In *The New Intergovernmentalism: States and Supranational Actors in the Post-Maastricht Era*, edited by Chris Bickerton, Dermot Hodson, and Uwe Puetter, 51–72. Oxford: Oxford University Press, 2015.

Bickerton, Chris. *The European Union. A Citizens Guide*. London: Penguin, 2016.

Bressanelli, Edoardo and Nicola Chelotti. "The European Parliament and Economic Governance: Explaining a Case of Limited Influence." *The Journal of Legislative Studies* 24, no. 1 (2018): 72–89.

Bugarič, Bojan. "The Populist Backlash against Europe. Why Only Alternative Economic and Social Policies Can Stop the Rise of Populism in Europe." In *EU Law in Populist Time. Crisis and Prospects*, edited by Francesca Bignami, 477–504. Cambridge: Cambridge University Press, 2020.

Capuano, Davide Alberto and Elena Griglio. "La nuova governance economica europea. I risvolti sulle procedure parlamentari italiane." In *Il sistema parlamentare euro-nazionale. Lezioni*, edited by Andra Manzella and Nicola Lupo, 227–265. Torino: Giappichelli, 2014.

Carli, Guido. *Cinquant'anni di vita italiana*. Roma-Bari: Laterza, 1993.

Chessa, Omar. *La Costituzione della moneta. Concorrenza, indipendenza della banca centrale e pareggio di bilancio*. Napoli: Jovene, 2016.

Closa, Carlos. "The Transformation of Macroeconomic and Fiscal Governance in the EU." In *The Future of Europe: Democracy, Legitimacy and Justice after the Euro Crisis*, edited by Serge Champeau, Daniel Innerarity, and Miguel Poiares Maduro, 37–56. Lanham: Rowman and Littlefield, 2015.

Crum, Ben. "Parliamentary Accountability in Multilevel Governance: What Role for Parliaments in Post-Crisis EU Economic Governance?" *Journal of European Public Policy* 25, no. 2 (2018): 268–286.

Curtin, Deirdre. "Challenging Executive Dominance in European Democracy." *The Modern Law Review* 77, no. 1 (2014): 1–32.

Dani, Marco. "Rehabilitating Social Conflicts in the European Public Law." *European Law Journal* 18, no. 5 (2012): 621–643.

Dani, Marco. "The Rise of the Supranational Executive and the Post-Political Drift of European Public Law." *Indiana Journal of Global Legal Studies* 24, no. 2 (2016a): 399–428.

Dani, Marco. "The Subjectification of the Citizen in European Public Law." In *Constructing the Person in EU Law: Rights, Roles, Identities*, edited by Loïc Azoulai, Ségolène Barbou des Places, and Etienne Pataut, 55–88. Oxford: Hart, 2016b.

Dani, Marco. "The EU Transformation of the Social State." In *The EU Social Market Economy and the Law: Theoretical Perspectives and Practical Challenges for the EU*, edited by Delia Ferri and Fulvio Cortese, 31–50. New York: Routledge, 2018.

Dani, Marco and Augustín José Menéndez. "Soft-conditionality Through Soft-law: le insidie nascoste del Pandemic Crisis Support," in *LaCostituzione.info*, May 10, 2020, http://www.lacostituzione.info/index.php/2020/05/10/soft-conditionality-through-soft-law-le-insidie-nascoste-del-pandemic-crisis-support/.

Dawson, Mark and Floris de Witte. "Constitutional Balance in the EU after the Euro-Crisis?" *The Modern Law Review* 76, no. 5 (2013): 817–844.

de Witte, Floris. "Interdependence and Contestation in European Integration." *European Papers* 3, no. 2 (2018): 475–510.

Della Sala, Vincent. "Hollowing Out and Hardening the State: European Integration and the Italian Economy." *West European Politics* 20, no. 1 (1997): 14–33.

Dyson, Kenneth and Kevin Featherstone. *The Road to Maastricht: Negotiating Economic and Monetary Union*. Oxford: Oxford University Press, 1999.

Fabbrini, Sergio. "The European Union and the Puzzle of Parliamentary Government." *Journal of European Integration* 37, no. 5 (2015): 571–586.

Fasone, Cristina. "European Economic Governance and Parliamentary Representation. What Place for European Parliament?" *European Law Journal* 20, no. 2 (2014): 164–185.

Ferrera, Maurizio. *The Boundaries of Welfare. European Integration and the New Spatial Politics of Social Protection*. Oxford: Oxford University Press, 2005.

Fourastié, Jean. *Les trente glorieuses: ou, la révolution invisible de 1946 à 1975*. Paris: Fayard, 1979.

Giubboni, Stefano. *Social Rights and Market Freedom in the European Constitution. A Labor Law Perspective*. Cambridge: CUP, 2006.
Goldoni, Marco. "Politicising EU Lawmaking? The Spitzenkandidaten Experiment as a Cautionary Tale." *European Law Journal* 22, no. 3 (2016): 279–295.
Grimm, Dieter. *Constitutionalism. Past, Present, and Future*. Oxford: Oxford University Press, 2016.
Guazzarotti, Andrea. "Sovranità e integrazione europea." *Rivista AIC*, no. 3 (2017): 1–12.
Halmai, Gábor. "Populism, Authoritarianism and Constitutionalism." *German Law Journal* 20, no. 3 (2019): 296–313.
Hayek, Friedrich August. "The Economic Conditions of Inter-state Federalism." In *Individualism and Economic Order*, 255–272. Chicago: University of Chicago Press, 1958.
Jancic, Davor. "Parliamentary Involvement in the Economic and Monetary Union after the Euro Crisis". In *Interparliamentary Cooperation in the Composite European Constitution*, edited by Nicola Lupo and Cristina Fasone, 183–206. Oxford: Hart, 2016.
Judt, Tony. *Postwar. A History of Europe since 1945*. New York: Penguin, 2005.
Judt, Tony. *Reappraisals. Reflection on the Forgotten Twentieth Century*. New York: Penguin, 2008.
Katsaroumpas, Ioannidis. "De-Constitutionalising Collective Labour Rights: The Case of Greece." *Industrial Law Journal* 47, no. 2 (2018): 465–503.
Kelemen, Roger Daniel. "Europe's Other Democratic Deficit: National Authoritarianism in Europe's Democratic Union." *Government and Opposition* 52, no. 2 (2017): 211–238.
Kreuder-Sonnen, Christian. "An Authoritarian Turn in Europe and in European Studies?" *Journal of European Public Policy* 25, no. 3 (2018): 452–464.
Lord, Cristopher. "How Can Parliaments Contribute to the Legitimacy of the European Semester?" *Parliamentary Affairs* 70, no. 4 (2017): 673–690.
Maatsch, Aleksandra. *Parliaments and the Economic Governance of the European Union: Talking Shops or Deliberative Bodies?* London: Routledge, 2017.
Maduro, Miguel Poiares. *We, the Court: The European Court of Justice and the European Economic Constitution*. Oxford: Hart, 1999.
Maestro Buelga, Gonzalo. "Estado de mercado y Constitución económica: algunas reflexiones sobre la crisis constitucional europea." *Revista de Derecho Constitucional Europeo* 8 (2007): 43–73.
Mair, Peter. "Political Opposition and the European Union." *Government and Opposition* 42, no. 1 (2007): 1–17.
Mancini, Giuseppe Federico. "Principi fondamentali di diritto del lavoro nell'ordinamento delle Comunità europee." In *Il lavoro nel diritto comunitario e l'ordinamento italiano*. Padova: Cedam, 1988.

Marketou, Afroditi. "Greece: Constitutional Deconstruction and the Loss of National Sovereignty." In *Constitutional Change through Euro-Crisis Law*, edited by Thomas Beukers, Bruno de Witte, and Claire Kilpatrick, 179–198. Cambridge: CUP, 2017.

Menéndez, Augustín José. "Herman Heller NOW." *European Law Journal* 21, no. 3 (2015): 285–294.

Milward, Alan. *The European Rescue of the Nation State*. 2nd ed. New York: Routledge, 2000.

Mitchell, William and Thomas Fazi. *Reclaiming the State. A Progressive Vision of Sovereignty for a Post-Neoliberal Word*. London: Pluto Press, 2017.

Moravcsik, Andrew. "Negotiating the Single European Act: National Interests and Conventional Statecraft in the European Community." *International Organization* 45, no. 1 (1991): 19–56.

Mudde, Cas. "Europe's Populist Surge: A Long Time in the Making." *Foreign Affairs* 95, no. 6 (2016): 25–30.

Oberndorfer, Lukas. "A New Economic Governance through Secondary Legislation? Analysis and Constitutional Assessment: From New Constitutionalism via Authoritarian Constitutionalism to Progressive Constitutionalism." In *The Economic and Financial Crisis and Collective Labour Law in Europe*, edited by Niklas Bruun, Klaus Lörcher, and Isabelle Schömann, 25–54. Oxford: Hart, 2014.

Radaelli, Claudio. *The Italian State and the Euro: Institutions, Discourse and Political Regime*. In *European States and the Euro: Europeanization, Variation and Convergence*, edited by Kenneth Dyson, 212–237, Oxford: Oxford University Press, 2002.

Ruggie, John Gerard. "International Regimes, Transactions and Change: Embedded Liberalism in the Postwar Economic Order." *International Organization* 36, no. 2 (1982): 379–415.

Scharpf, Fritz Wilhelm. "The European Social Model: Coping with the Challenges of Diversity." *Journal of Common Market Studies* 40, no. 4 (2002): 645–670.

Scharpf, Fritz Wilhelm. "Monetary Union, Fiscal Crisis and the Preemption of Democracy." *Journal for Comparative Government and European Policy* 9, no. 2 (2011): 163–198.

Schmidt, Anne Vivian. "The Forgotten Problem of Democratic Legitimacy: Governing by the Rules and Ruling by the Numbers." In *The Future of the Euro*, edited by Mathhias Matthijs and Mark Blyth, 90–116. Oxford: Oxford University Press, 2015.

Schmidt, Anne Vivian. *Europe's Crisis of Legitimacy. Governing by the Rules and Ruling by Numbers in the Eurozone*. Oxford: Oxford University Press, 2020.

Scicluna, Nicole and Stefan Aurer. "From the Rule of Law to the Rule of Rules: Technocracy and the Crisis of EU Governance." *West European Politics* 42, no. 7 (2019): 1420–1442.

Somek, Alexander. *The Cosmopolitan Constitution*. Oxford: OUP, 2014.
Somek, Alexander. "Delegation and Authority: Authoritarian Liberalism Today." *European Law Journal* 21, no. 3 (2015): 340–360.
Streeck, Wolfgang. "Markets and People. Democratic Capitalism and European Integration." *New Left Review* 73, no. 1 (2012): 63–71.
Streeck, Wolfgang. *Buying Time. The Delayed Crisis of Democratic Capitalism*. London and New York: Verso, 2014.
Streeck, Wolfgang. "Progressive Regression: Metamorphoses of European Social Policy." *New Left Review* 118 (2019): 117–139.
Wilkinson, Michael. "The Specter of Authoritarian Liberalism: Reflections on the Constitutional Crisis of the European Union." *German Law Journal* 14, no. 5 (2013): 527–560.
Wilkinson, Michael. "Authoritarian Liberalism. The Conjuncture Behind the Crisis." In *The Crisis Behind the Crisis: The European Crisis as Multi-Dimensional Systemic Failure of the EU*, edited by Eva Nanopoulos and Fotis Vergis, 101–121, Cambridge: Cambridge University Press, 2018.
Wilkinson, Michael. "Authoritarian Liberalism in Europe: A Common Critique of Neoliberalism and Ordoliberalism." *Critical Sociology* 45, no. 7–8 (2019): 1023–1034.
Zielonka, Jan. *Counter-Revolution. Liberal Europe in Retreat*. Oxford: Oxford University Press, 2018.

The "EU Populist Crisis": The Effect of Populism on the EU Legal Order and Vice Versa: Populism, EU Responses and EU Constitutional Identity

Helle Krunke, William Alexander Tornøe, and Caroline Egestad Wegener

1 Introduction, Concepts and Methods

The EU has experienced many crises during the past 15 years including the "populist crisis" or the "rule of law crisis", as it is often referred to. However, no matter what the crisis is called, it seems to go beyond the

The authors wish to thank project student Djellza Fetahi for assistance with finding sources for parts of the article and for adapting the article to the correct house style.

H. Krunke (✉)
Centre for European and Comparative Legal Studies, University of Copenhagen, Copenhagen, Denmark
e-mail: helle.krunke@jur.ku.dk

W. A. Tornøe • C. E. Wegener
University of Copenhagen, Copenhagen, Denmark
e-mail: caew@danskerhverv.dk

J. M. Castellà Andreu, M. A. Simonelli (eds.), *Populism and Contemporary Democracy in Europe*,
https://doi.org/10.1007/978-3-030-92884-1_11

scope of the EU legal principle of rule of law. In this chapter, we explore the interaction between populism and the EU legal order both ways. We ask how populism has affected the general features of the EU legal system, and how the EU responses to populism have affected populism using Poland as a case study. To answer these questions, we study empirics in the form of EU's responses to populism in Member States and in particular in Poland, general changes in the EU legal system linked to these responses, and actions taken by Poland as a response to the actions of the EU. In particular, the chapter focuses on the possible impact on EU constitutional identity, as this aspect has not been emphasised in legal literature. As a last point, the chapter uses the Polish constitutional crisis as a case study, as it offers a complete overview of all the instruments employed by the EU to fight populism.[1] In order to achieve these goals, the chapter will proceed along the following lines. The first section presents the EU toolbox of responses to populism. The second section analyses the general effects that populism has had on the EU legal order. The third section discusses whether populism has contributed to a crystallisation of EU constitutional identity. In the fourth section, we turn the picture around and ask which effect the EU responses have had on populism using Poland as a case study. The fifth section among others discusses the presumed effect of the rule of law Mechanism introduced by Regulation 2020/2092. Section 6 concludes.

Before embarking on this task, it is necessary to stipulate our working definition of populism. Defining populism is indeed an unforgiving task as it is an elusive concept. Unlike the major ideologies of socialism or liberalism, there is no "main work" defining the framework of populism as opposed to "The Capital" by Marx or the works of Locke or Smith. Instead, populism should be defined by the actions and functions of regimes being characterised as populist. When observing populism, several characteristics emerge.

Initially, populism is characterised by claiming to represent one true and homogenous "people" (the people or real people) often embodied in one charismatic leader. The goal is to implement the people's will and in doing so not being limited or governed by anything but this same will.

[1] On the Polish case of "democratic backsliding", see for instance Koncewicz, *The Politics of Resentment and First Principles in the European Court of Justice*, 457-476.

The people are positioned against the elite. Thus, populism seeks to implement what can be described as a rule of the majority, where the people's will is the only true point of orientation and limitation. Thus, politics and political power have no other limitation, for example, protecting minorities. This is of course a moral indicator and not a legal one. Populism is also inherently opposed to systems or institutions, for instance, checks and balances and constitutional guarantees that can slow or hinder the implementation of the people's will (Tornøe and Wegener 2020, 20).

Less commonly, but still frequent, populism is characterised by a general aversion to "outsiders". Populism latches on to pre-existing ideologies, for example, nationalism, as populism does not in itself entail a left- or right-wing policy. Populism may also, due to its "impatience" and antipathy towards hindrances to the implementation of the people's will, pose a danger to democracy and the rule of law. Finally, populism seeks direct forms of government and strives to remove layers between the government and the people.[2]

"EU constitutional identity" is still a contested term. In this article, we will rely on Gerhard van der Schyff's definition, which builds on the individuality of a constitutional order whether national or supranational:

As an analytical device, constitutional identity can aid the study of a particular constitutional order and the comparison of orders by focussing on the individuality of each order. In this way, the constitutional essence of an order is emphasised based on its own experience and account of that experience. Viewed from this angle, every constitutional order possesses an identity that can be protected in various ways, even though an order might not use the term "identity" as such. This applies to all constitutional orders irrespective of whether an order has a codified constitution or not, as constitutional identity is not a synonym for, or limited to, codified constitutions. On this characterisation not only national orders but also a supranational order such as the EU possesses constitutional identity (van der Schyff 2015, 18).

According to Schyff, EU constitutional identity emphasises the EU as a distinct supranational actor in the field of constitutional law (van der Schyff 2015, 16).

[2] Ibid.

2 The EU Toolbox of Responses to Populism EU Toolbox

2.1 The EU Framework to Strengthen the Rule of Law

The EU Framework to Strengthen the Rule of Law (the Framework) was introduced in 2014 by a communication from the Commission.[3] The Framework was revised in 2019.[4] The aim of the Framework is to quickly react to systemic threats against the Rule of Law and maybe even prevent the activation of the Article 7 procedure. Furthermore, the aim of the Framework is to support other tools such as the preliminary rulings and the infringement procedure (Tornøe and Wegener 2020, 35).

The Framework works in three phases of dialogue to create fast suggestions from the Commission to the Member State in order to "fix the problem". In phase one, the Commission identifies the threat and starts the dialogue with the Member State in question. In phase two, the Commission issues one or more recommendations to solve/eliminate the threat of the Rule of Law. The recommendations have deadlines for the Member State to make changes accordingly. Finally, in phase three, the Commission follows up on the situation in the Member State to check if the threat actually has been eliminated.[5] The Framework has only been initiated with one Member State: Poland.[6]

2.2 Article 7 TEU: Procedure

Article 7 introduces the possibility to suspend a Member State's rights as a consequence of breaching the values of the EU as listed in Article 2 TEU. Its Sect. 1 allows the Commission, the Parliament or one-third of the Member States to determine if there is a clear risk of a Member State breaching the values, and by a majority of four-fifths of the Council. The Parliament must consent before the Council can take a vote. Section 2 empowers the Council to suspend Member State's rights, that is, voting rights, on a proposal by the Commission or one-third Member States and with the Parliament consenting. A decision by Sect. 2 must be approved unanimously in the Council. The procedure can be activated in instances of breaches of the Member State that do not involve EU law. This

[3] COM (2014) 158 final.
[4] COM (2019) 163 final.
[5] COM (2014) 158 final, 7–8.
[6] COM (2019) 163 final, 3.

underlines the importance of the procedure and the protection of the values (Tornøe and Wegener 2020, 42).

2.3 *Preliminary Rulings*

According to article 267, the ECJ has the competence to interpret the treaties and to determine the meaning and validity of EU law when so requested by national courts. National courts can have the ECJ rule on preliminary questions when it is necessary for the national case. The aim of the preliminary rulings is to ensure that EU law is interpreted and applied uniformly in all Member States.

2.4 *The Infringement Procedure: Article 258-260 TFEU*

Article 258 TFEU stipulates that if the Commission considers that a Member State has failed to fulfil one of its obligations deriving from the Treaties the Commission may bring the case before the ECJ. Beforehand the Commission must deliver a reasoned opinion, allowing the Member State to submit its observations. The Commission sets out a deadline for the Member State to comply with the Commission's reasoned opinion. In case of non-compliance, the Commission can submit the case to the Court of Justice. Finally, it is implied by Article 260, paragraph 1, that if the Court of Justice finds that the Member State has failed to fulfil its obligation under the Treaties, it must take the necessary steps to comply with the judgement. In extension paragraph 2 to states that in case of non-compliance with a judgement the Commission can bring the case before the court after having heard the Member State. The Court of Justice can impose on the Member State a lump sum as well as periodic penalty payments.

2.5 *Interim Measures: Article 279 TFEU*

Article 279 TFEU simply prescribes that the Court of Justice in any case where it deems it necessary may prescribe interim measures. This is further specified in the Rules of Procedure of the Court of Justice.[7] Some formal

[7] Rules of Procedure of the Court of Justice of 25 September 2012 (OJ L 265, 29.9.2012), as amended on 18 June 2013 (OJ L 173, 26.6.2013, p. 65), on 19 July 2016 (OJ L 217, 12.8.2016, p. 69), on 9 April 2019 (OJ L 111, 25.4.2019, p. 73) and on 26 November 2019 (OJ L 316, 6.12.2019, p. 103).

criteria must be adhered to, but essentially three material criteria must be met to prescribe interim measures: *fumus boni juris* (the application must not be unfounded), urgency, and balancing of interests. It is also possible to apply for interim measures without hearing the opposing party due to the urgency of the case.

Lastly, a comment is due concerning the enforcement of the interim measures. Neither TFEU nor the procedural rules directly prescribe how interim measures can be enforced. However, in the order of 20 November 2017 in case C-441/17 *Białowieża* the Court of Justice found that Article 279 TFEU allows for the Court of justice to impose any interim measure to enforce other interim measures, even if the applicant has only applied for "ordinary measures" the Court of Justice can prescribe such measures "ex officio".

2.6 Rule of Law Mechanism/Conditionality

Following a substantial amount of controversy in the Council, The European Parliament passed Regulation 2020/2092 in December 2020, prescribing the so-called Rule of Law Mechanism. The mechanism envisages compliance with the principle of rule of law as a condition to benefiting from the Union budget (MFF). So far, the Mechanism has not been applied.

The Mechanism allows for the Commission to propose measures to be adopted by the Council implementing economic sanctions until the Member State complies with the principle of rule of law. However, some conditions must be met before measures can be adopted. The quintessential prerequisite that must be met is that the infringement of the principle of rule of law is connected to the Union budget or the financial interests of the Union and that the infringement concerns the actions of any of the Member States' public authorities at any governmental level.

3 Observations on the Effects of Populism on the EU Legal System in General

Based on the discussion of different EU responses to populism in Sect. 3, we may make a number of general observations on the reactions chosen by the EU. First, the EU has responded to populism through a value-based approach with an outset in Article 2, TEU, on fundamental values of the

EU focusing on the principle of rule of law. Second, the EU responses to populism combine political/soft law instruments initiated by the political EU institutions as well as judicial instruments applied by the CJEU. Third, existing instruments (Article 7 (TEU), Articles 278 and 279 TFEU)) as well as new instruments such as the new EU Framework to Strengthen the Rule of Law introduced in 2014, amended in 2019, and the new budgetary sanctions introduced in 2020, have been applied/introduced. Fourth, and in relation to the previous points, the EU responses draw on preventive measures as well as responses with sanctions. Fifth, the EU's strategy consists of a combination of the different instruments. The different instruments can be used in combination, and application of one instrument may even strengthen the impact of another.

From these observations on the reactions of the EU to populism, we naturally move on to make some general observations on the impact of populism on the EU legal system. Populism seems to have had a more lasting impact on the EU legal system, which goes beyond the specific and concrete recommendations, opinions and judgements. The populist crisis has created a general awareness in the EU of fundamental EU values. One might say that the crisis has pushed the EU towards an even more value-based legal system but also a transformation of values to legally enforceable principles. In particular, the reactions to populism have caused a more precise and detailed interpretation and implementation of the EU principle of rule of law. The EU principle of rule of law has become an "umbrella" principle for many other legal principles, which are interpreted as sub-principles of the rule of law principle. We also see a recent move towards a focus on new EU principles as a reaction to populism. Both of these trends reflect that many EU legal principles are challenged by populist actions. We shall return to the two mentioned trends in Sect. 5 where we in connection with these observations ask whether populism has contributed to a crystallisation of EU constitutional identity. Another interesting impact of populism on the EU legal system is that the effectiveness of existing available EU tools and their interplay in cases of violations of EU Law have been tested. This way, the flaws of the EU legal sanction system have been highlighted. Though, some of these flaws were already anticipated ex. the difficulties of applying Article 7, part 2, it has now become clear at a very concrete level how serious the impact is and that calls for possible reforms of the EU legal system in order to more effectively handle violations of general EU legal principles.[8] One reaction triggered by the populist crisis has been for the EU to develop new preventive and sanctioned responses to violations of the EU principle of rule of law. Finally, populism has driven a closer cooperation between the EU legal system and the European Convention of Human Rights system including the Venice Commission. This is among others reflected when the EU institutions refer to the recognition of legal principles at the European Court of Human Rights and standards, opinions, and recommendations by the Council of Europe. They *"provide well-established guidance to promote and uphold the rule of law"*.[9]

4 Crystallising EU Constitutional Identity Through the Challenge of Populism?

While national constitutional identity has its legal basis and a definition in the TEU, Article 4, Part 2, and in the case law of the CJEU, EU constitutional identity is according to some authors still a contested concept. In 2020, Martins for instance wrote that "[c]ontrary to the Member State constitutional identity, which under various denominations has pre-occupied doctrine and jurisprudence since the sixties, and has deepened within the last two decades, the notion of a EU constitutional identity has emerged and developed over the last decade as a novel concept still in progress of crystallisation" (Martins 2020, 36). Other authors such as Van der Schyff embraces the concept of EU Constitutional identity and we rely on his definition. The current populist crisis in the EU seems to be a driver of a more well-defined EU constitutional identity. EU's fundamental values and principles are by some scholars viewed as common constitutional principles (Kadelbach 2020, 14, 18) and the crisis has forced the EU to reflect on and refine the interpretation and scope of its values and principles. Some scholars even characterise the fundamental values in Article 2, TEU, as a shared constitutional profile of the EU and its Member States, and as constitutive to the European identity (von Bogdandy and Ioannidis

[8] Scheppele and Kelemen have put forward a series of more promising legal alternatives for enforcing liberal democratic values (within the existing legal framework) than applying Article 7. See Scheppele and Kelemen, *Defending Democracy in EU Member States*, 413–456.

[9] COM(2020) 580 final. Wigand, Christian, Katarzyna Kolanko and Alice Hobbs. "2020 Rule of Law Report – Questions and Answers." *European Commission*. Accessed April 6, 2020. https://ec.europa.eu/commission/presscorner/detail/en/qanda_20_1757.

2014, 59; Kaczorowska 2013, 28; van der Schyff 2015, 18). In light of this, the current development may lead to a crystallisation of EU's constitutional identity.

Looking back at the history of the EU, we find a number of events, which are linked directly or indirectly to a crystallisation of EU values. One might call them "constituting moments" in defining an EU identity and maybe even an EU constitutional identity. The Coal and Steel Community was a reaction to the Second World War and the Cold War, and this way the background of the EU was a wish to avoid war and violations of human dignity in Europe in the future (Martins 2020, 36–37). The Declaration on European Identity based on the Copenhagen Conference in 1973, following Denmark's, the UK's, and Ireland's accession to the EC, emphasised human rights as part of European identity. The Maastricht Treaty extended EU powers and parts of literature have stated that this called for a need for legitimating the new EU powers. This was handled among others by the formulation of common EU values in the Treaty (Belov 2017; Faraguna 2017, 1619). With the Nice Treaty, Article 7, TEU, is revised. The context is the East enlargement, and Austria's right-wing government (1999), which caused sanctions from 14 MS's (Halmai 2018, 11; Sadurski 2010, 394). EU fundamental values were emphasised in the following Treaty on a Constitution for Europe. The Kadi judgement[10] on fundamental rights is said to be the CJEU's first contribution to establishing an EU constitutional identity (Martins 2020, 36). This takes place one year after the Lisbon Treaty was signed (after the failed Treaty on a Constitution for Europe) and one year before the Lisbon Treaty stepped into force, which also meant that the EU Charter on Fundamental Rights changed its status from political to legal. Finally, the "Rule of law crisis" has triggered a crystallisation of EU's values and principles both at the political institutions and at the CJEU, especially as regards the EU principle of rule of law but not only.

We shall emphasise two observations as regards the process of crystallisation of EU values through the "rule of law crisis". First, the rule of law principle in Article 2, TEU, is being defined as an "umbrella principle", which covers many sub-principles. This development is summarised very well in the Commission's description of Article 2, TEU, when the "Rule of Law Report Mechanism" was launched

[10] Joined cases C-402/05 P and C-415/05 P.

> **The rule of law includes principles such as legality, implying a transparent, accountable, democratic and pluralistic process for enacting laws; legal certainty; prohibiting the arbitrary exercise of executive power; effective judicial protection by independent and impartial courts, effective judicial review including respect for fundamental rights; separation of powers; and equality before the law**. These principles have been **recognised by the European Court of Justice—with recent case law of particular importance**—and the European Court of Human Rights. In addition, the Council of Europe has developed standards and issued opinions and recommendations that provide well-established guidance to promote and uphold the rule of law. (bold inserted by authors).[11]

As part of this process, values are transformed into enforceable principles.

A second important observation is that the EU starts to crystallise other values in Article 2, TEU. The Commission has expressed and summarised it the following way

> "**The European Rule of Law Mechanism is one element of a broader endeavour at the EU level to strengthen the values of democracy, equality, and respect for human rights**. It will be **complemented by a set of upcoming initiatives [...]** to **promote a society in which pluralism, non-discrimination, justice, solidarity and equality prevail**."[12] (Bold inserted by authors)

This way, the challenge of populism has already contributed to a crystallisation of EU's fundamental values and principles—by some scholars viewed as common constitutional principles, a shared constitutional profile of the EU and its Member States, and as constitutive to the European identity (von Bogdandy and Ioannidis 2014, 59; Kaczorowska 2013, 28; Lavelle 2019, 35; van der Schyff 2015, 13)—especially in the field of rule of law, and there seems to be a potential for a continuation of this process bringing in other fundamental EU values including democracy and fundamental rights. The latter has already been included as part of EU constitutional identity by the CJEU in 2008.

[11] COM(2020) 580 final. Wigand, Christian, Katarzyna Kolanko and Alice Hobbs. "2020 Rule of Law Report – Questions and Answers." *European Commission*. Accessed April 6, 2020. https://ec.europa.eu/commission/presscorner/detail/en/qanda_20_1757.

[12] Ibid.

In light of this, it seems plausible to claim that the "EU rule of law crisis" has emphasised the EU as a distinct supranational actor in the field of constitutional law. It has driven a crystallisation of and a more well-defined EU constitutional identity based on the EU's experiences during the crisis—which can probably also be viewed as a strengthening of the EU (at least from a legal perspective) bearing in mind that this is not a zero-sum game.

5 The Effects of the EU Tools on Populism: The Polish Case

5.1 *Methodology Applied: General and Specific Effect*

For the sake of evaluating the effects of the application of EU tools on populism in the context of the Polish case, a distinction is made between specific effect and general effect.

Specific effect is understood as whether the applied tool, in a narrow sense, reached its goal. In other words, did the application of the tool force the Member State to bring the infringement to a halt?

General effect is understood as whether the applied tool, in a wider sense, has compelled the Member State to cease its general populist steps harming the rule of law principle

5.2 *The Rule of Law Framework and the Activation of Article 7 TEU*

The Framework was activated towards Poland by a dialogue in January 2016 and the second phase was concluded with a recommendation on 27 July 2016. The Framework was initiated in lieu of the judicial reforms initiated after the change of government in 2015. Phase two was initiated as the dialogue of phase one seemed ineffectual. The phases of the Framework were finished in the fall of 2017, after a total of three written recommendations from the Commission and answers from the Polish government.

The three recommendations from the Commission were mainly centred around the changes to the Polish Constitutional Court. The Polish government had changed the rules of process of the court, the majority rules and appointed a new president of the court. The government had also appointed five new judges to the court, three of which conflicted with the constitution. The efficiency of the court and the access to correct constitutional review of new laws were restricted by the changes. Even though Poland made some minor changes to the laws after the recommendations, the big picture was pretty much the same at the end of the process: the Constitutional Court was weakened, and the effectiveness of judicial review of legislation was thus questionable (Tornøe and Wegener 2020).

As the Polish government did not comply with the recommendations of the Commission, the Framework had limited, if any specific effect. As a general effect, the Framework should be capable to trigger a process based on dialogue and cooperation. This does not seem to have been successful either as the Polish government continued their judicial reforms after 2017 as well.

As a consequence, the Commission activated the Article 7 TEU procedure. In its proposal, the Commission repeated its concerns and recommendations from the Framework dialogue and suggested that the Council should determine a clear risk of breach of Article 2 TEU in accordance with Article 7 (1) TEU. The risks regarding the Constitutional Court were now affecting the entire judicial system of Poland. As of today, the Council still has not made a final decision regarding the matter.

As the Council has not made a decision, the activation of Article 7 has had no specific effect on the Rule of Law in Poland. Article 7 (1) only opens the possibility to determine a clear risk of breach of the values of the EU. It is therefore questionable if a final decision from the Council will trigger a specific effect. A decision might be able to create a general effect because of a possible political pressure on Poland but have not occurred yet (Tornøe and Wegener 2020, 44–45).

The Framework and Article 7 procedure present many similarities. Both reactions are quickly initiated which is a pro—but at the same time, the reactions do not have a time limit, which is a con. Finally, it is a positive element that these instruments were successful at least in creating a dialogue with the Member State, and they should theoretically be able to create the best general effect on the Rule of Law as this is one of their aims (Tornøe and Wegener 2020, 86).

5.3 *Preliminary Rulings Regarding Poland*

There have been a number of preliminary rulings regarding Polish law either from Polish courts or from other Member States' courts in the period of the Polish judicial reforms (2015 until today). This Article has examined two cases: C-216/18 Minister of Justice and Equality and C-585/18 A.K.

(a) C-216/18—Minister of Justice and Equality

This case originated in the Irish High Court. The High Court was asking the ECJ for an interpretation of the rules on the European arrest warrant and if the rules implied an obligation for the Irish court to examine the independence of the courts in Poland and the security of the defendant's rights to a fair trial. The ECJ answered that the Irish court could not assume there was a clear risk of breach when a proposal for decision regarding Article 7 (1) was only proposed but not passed by the Council. The Irish court therefore had to assess the risk for an infringement of the defendant's rights in the specific case. In this specific case, the Irish court found that the risk of the defendant's rights being breached was not strong enough to prevent the Irish court from effectuating the arrest warrant.

(b) 5.3.2. C-585/18—A.K.

The A.K. case at the ECJ was a ruling on the combined cases C-585/18, C-624/18 and C-625/18. All the national cases originated in two chambers of the Polish Supreme Court. All cases concerned the early retirement of Supreme Court judges and the denial to prolong one judge's term in office. The Polish court was asking the ECJ if the new disciplinary chamber of the Polish Supreme Court was in accordance with Article 2 and 19 (1) TEU, Article 267 (3) TFEU and Article 47 of the EU Charter of Fundamental Rights and if not, if the other chambers of the Supreme Court should set aside rules of competence of the disciplinary chamber. The ECJ defined the principle of independent courts and judges and left the actual evaluation of the disciplinary chamber to the Polish court. If the Polish court found that the disciplinary chamber did not work in accordance with the principle of independence, then the precedence of EU law would allow the Supreme Court to set the competence of the disciplinary chamber aside and rule in the cases itself.

In both national cases, different chambers of the Polish Supreme Court found that the disciplinary chamber was not an independent court in accordance with EU law. The Polish government and the judges of the disciplinary chamber did not agree and no changes in the organisation of the courts have therefore been made.

The preliminary rulings did not have a specific effect on the Rule of Law in Poland but did have a specific effect in the national cases as the rulings affect the outcome of the national courts' rulings. C-216/18 has had a specific effect in other cases about a European Arrest warrant issued by Poland and C-585/18 has been referenced by the ECJ in infringement rulings regarding the independence of the courts.

On the one hand, it is a pro that the rulings give the ECJ an opportunity to create such binding precedent for interpretation across the EU. On the other hand, it is a con that the EU cannot itself commence the preliminary rulings—they take their origin in cases in the Member States—and the EU or ECJ cannot introduce sanctions if the Member States do not comply with the rulings without commencing an infringement procedure.

5.4 *Infringement Proceedings Against Poland*

Two infringement proceedings have been concluded and resulted in the Court of Justice ruling that Poland infringed Article 19(1), second subparagraph, by not having insured the independence of the Polish judiciary.[13] Other proceedings concerning the independence of the judiciary are still in progress and therefore cannot form part of this analysis. However, in one of these cases, the court of Justice ordered interim measures to avoid irreparable damage.[14]

In both the settled cases, the retirement age of the judges was lowered, also affecting judges already in office, while simultaneously granting the Polish government the power to extend a judge's term in office two times for up to six years, which otherwise resulted in the retirement of the judges. The Polish authorities were not bound by any specific criteria, and there was no time limit for the processing of application for extension. As judges remained in office until a decision had been made, the Court of Justice found that the judges were not safe from political pressure emanating from their career's dependence on the extension. However, as interim

[13] Judgement of 5 November 2019 in Case C-192/18 concerning the independence of the judges in the ordinary courts in Poland, and judgement of 24 June 2019 in case C-619/18 concerning the independence of the judges of the Polish supreme court.

[14] Order of 8 April 2020 in Case C-791/19 R concerning the National Council of the Judiciary's lack of independence affecting the disciplinary chamber in the Supreme Court further affecting the general independence of the Polish Judiciary.

measures were not prescribed in one case, they will be examined individually.

In the third case, which has not yet been concluded, the Court of Justice has prescribed interim measures. The Commission claimed that the new disciplinary system endangers the independence of the judiciary as the content of judgements following the amendments could constitute a disciplinary offence. The fact that the new disciplinary chamber in the Supreme Court could not be considered independent also contributed to this. Finally, the Commission argued that Poland had infringed its obligation under Article 267 TFEU as a motion for a preliminary ruling could constitute a disciplinary offence.

(a) Case C-619/18—The Supreme Court

The Court of Justice ruled the specific provisions in the Polish legislation as contrary to EU law. This resulted in the legislator changing these provisions and reinstating the judges who had been retired against their will. Subsequently, no similar provisions were implemented. This is equally supported by the fact that no proceedings concerning the infringement of the judgement were initiated. However, it should not be forgotten that in this case the Court of Justice prescribed interim measures. It is clear from the facts of the case, that the illegal provisions were abolished after the order of the Court of Justice and before the judgement. The interim measures also prevented Poland to continue acting in line with the provisions in question and forced Poland to reinstate the judges of the Supreme Court.

This implies that the infringement proceedings combined with the interim measures had a very concrete or specific effect and that the interim measures allowed to quickly counter the effects of the provisions in question. However, it can be questioned if it had a general effect as no other legislative acts which were challenged in the Article 7-proceedings were abolished.

As a side note, in this case the expedited procedure was granted by the Court of Justice resulting in the case been processed in 14 months.

(b) Case C-192/18—The Ordinary Courts

In this case, the Court of Justice similarly found that the provisions lowering the retirement age and granting the minister of justice the power to extend the term in office of the judges were illegal. Consequently, this meant that the provisions had to be abolished. No subsequent proceedings have been initiated.

The action was brought before the court on 15 March 2018 and the Court of Justice made its ruling on 5 November 2019. Notably, the Commission had not applied for interim measures.

During the proceedings, Poland explained that the provisions were modified from 12 April 2018. At first, this seems to imply that Poland complied with the Commission's grievances towards the provisions. However, some sources indicate that the Minister of Justice had retired several judges and since the judgement did not prescribe them to reinstate, it is unclear whether this was the case. Furthermore, even though the provision was amended the changes still allowed for judges' terms of office. It shifted the authority to the National Council of the Judiciary (which has been the subject of several cases)[15] and only changed the considerations to consider when deciding slightly. Lastly, even though it was stated in the judgement that the lack of obligation to provide the motivation for the decision was part of the illegality of the provisions, the new provisions did not change this.

The previous show that the infringement proceeding had a specific effect as it resulted in the illegal provisions' amendment. However, it can be called into question if the goal of the proceedings was achieved to full extent as it is implied that not all judges were reinstated. The proceedings have had a limited general effect as it did not result in any other (positive) changes apart from what the judgement itself prescribed.

(c) 5.4.3 Case C-791/19—The National Council of the Judiciary

The proceedings in the current case have not yet been concluded, why it is only applicable when examining the effect of interim measures.

The Court of justice prescribed interim measures stating that the application of the provisions was to cease, essentially entailing that the disciplinary chamber should abstain from handling cases. However, contrary to case C-619/18, in this case Poland did not comply with the order of interim measures. This undermines the previous assessment of Interim measures and implies that in this case the response had neither a specific nor general effect.

[15] E.g. C-487/19, C-791/19, and C-204/21.

As a side note, consideration should be given to the fact that in the order of 20 November 2017 in C-441/17 the Court of Justice found that within the frame of interim measures it was allowed to prescribe penalty payments. In that case, this seemed to have ensured the compliance.

5.5 *The Effect of Infringement Proceedings Before the Court of Justice and Interim Measures*

When comparing the different preceding findings, it becomes clear that the infringement procedure has an effect. It has a specific effect resulting in the abolishment of the illegal provisions. However, applying a broader perspective the only limited or no general effect is achieved as the proceedings did not result in Poland amending other provisions damaging the Rule of Law; however, the ruling forms a part of the jurisprudence of the Court of Justice and therefore has some general effect.

Following the examination of case C-619/18, it is implied that there is a higher degree of efficiency when applying interim measures as opposed to when not applied. However, following the examination of C-791/19, it becomes clear that it is not absolute efficiency as Poland did not comply with the order.

A final comment can be made concerning the time scope of the infringement proceedings. Concerning C-619/18, the case was initiated 14 August 2018 and concluded on 24 June 2019. C-192/18 commenced on 29 July 2017 and concluded on 15 November 2019, amounting to more than two years. Case C-791/19 was initiated on 3 April 2019 and has not yet been concluded. All three cases were previously subject to the Article 7-proceedings against Poland, why they in reality have had an even longer life span. Notably only in C-619/18 the expedited procedure was applied. Comparing this to the previous findings, it implies that this tool improves the efficiency further.

Ultimately, it can be concluded, that the greatest effect is achieved by applying both the expedited procedure and interim measures. Contrarily, the adequateness of the procedure without these additional measures can be questioned as the damage may already have been inflicted when the judgement is pronounced.

The advantages of the infringement proceeding are that it entails a specific legal effect. However, the downside to this very specific effect is the lack of general effectiveness concerning the compliance with the Rule of Law as a general principle. It is also a disadvantage that the sanctioning of an infringement of a judgement requires new proceedings. If a case is subject to the expedited procedure, it can be an advantage to use the infringement proceeding as the temporal aspect is very short. The opposite is the case if the procedure is not granted.

Concerning the interim measures, they have a specific legal effect and can be used swiftly, which is a big advantage when defending the Rule of Law. However, it is disadvantageous that interim measures depend on the existence of an independent case. The tool also has some of the same problems and advantages as the infringement proceeding itself, as it has a narrow scope of application and there is no automatic sanction in case of non-compliance, unless the Court ordered otherwise initially. The effectiveness can also be called into question as Poland did not comply with one order.

5.6 *The Presumed Effect of the Rule of Law Mechanism*

As the Rule of Law Mechanism (the Mechanism) has not yet been applied, it is difficult to conduct a case study. However, as strengths and weaknesses appear from the preceding analyses of the applied tools, a "preliminary" assessment can be attempted, by theoretically applying the preceding conclusions to the Mechanism.

The competent authority to pass measures is the Council. A qualified majority (15 out of 27 Member States) may pass the measures proposed by the Commission. Thus, the number of positive votes is required compared to the Article 7-procedure. This seems to be an improvement.

The Mechanism prescribes that from the date when the Commission has notified the Member State that it intends to propose measures the maximal processing time is seven months, exceptionally nine months. This is equally an improvement as this is a recurring disadvantage. However, it may also result in the measures not being passed as the Council may not be able to pass a decision within the time frame due to political disputes.

The Mechanism also has an elaborate definition of the Rule of Law. This may also prove to be an advantage as the obligations of a Member State become clearer than otherwise. Prima facie, the clearer definition will most likely enable the Mechanism to be applied to more cases than previous.

Also, for the sake of the application of the Mechanism, it sets out that the Member State is attributable of all breaches, as these are defined in the regulation, for example, endangering the independence of the judiciary, by public authorities at all governmental levels. The Mechanism sets out specific criteria concerning which type of actions that can constitute a breach of the Rule of Law. The overall criteria are that the actions breaching the rule of law of a public authority affect or seriously risk affecting the sound management of Union funds or the financial interests of the Union. However, there is a presumption that a breach of the Rule of Law concerning the functioning of Public authorities or the legal system affects the sound management of the Union Funds, that is, if a body deciding who will be awarded the contract in a public procurement does not function and EU funds are involved this would be the case. This system entails that the majority, if not all, of the populist measures from the Polish cases can be addressed through the Mechanism.

Finally, the Mechanism prescribes certain measures. These measures essentially constitute economic sanctions by disrupting payments or recollection of previous instalments or refusal to approve programmes. Unless otherwise specified in the Council decision, the Member State still has the same obligations towards the citizens in its country, for example, if regional aid is revoked, the planned construction works would still need to be carried out. It should be noted that the measures are directly applicable to the Member State and do not require a previous procedure to be completed, that is, unlike the infringement proceedings. This system may prove to be effective as it aims to ensure that the citizens do not suffer directly due to the actions of the Member State. This is further supported by the fact that Poland is one of the largest beneficiaries of EU funds, which implies a large economic incitement. It is also important to note that it is also possible to pass the measures before the damage has an impact, which can be an important factor, that is, this played a large role in C-619/18.

The Mechanism can be used to counter both specific and general dangers to the rule of law, which most likely will prove to be a strength as the lack of either has shown to be a weakness of the previous tools. The fact that the Commission must hear the Member State is also a positive aspect as it preserves the dialogue from other legal tools which may mediate before hard sanctions are passed. It can be contemplated whether an outright penal fine would strengthen the effect even further. If the Mechanism has a weakness, per the preceding analysis, it is that the decision-making body is the Council. This has previously proven to inhibit the effectiveness. However, all in all, the Mechanism appears appropriate to solve most of the problems raised throughout the Polish cases.

6 Conclusions

We have shown that populism has impacted the EU legal system at a general level in a number of ways. These are changes, which seem to have a more permanent character. Importantly, populism seems to have an effect on general values and principles of the EU, which has led to a transformation of values to legally enforceable principles and a more precise and detailed interpretation and implementation of the EU principle of rule of law. Two interesting trends are that (1) the EU principle of rule of law has become an "umbrella" principle for many other legal principles, which are interpreted as sub-principles of the rule of law principle, and (2) we also see a recent move towards a focus on new EU principles as a reaction to populism. We have shown how different events in the history of the EU are linked to moments of defining values, identity and constitutional identity of the EU, and in light of this that populism seems to be a contemporary driver in crystallising EU constitutional identity.

Through the study of Poland as a case, we have shown that the EU has several reactions in their toolbox, which might be able to counter populism within the Union. The choice of tool depends on the national case and whether the EU wishes for a specific or general effect.

The Rule of Law Framework and Article 7 TEU should primarily be used to create a dialogue with the Member State in question and aim at changing the mindset towards the Rule of Law. However, the tools cannot ensure a general or political effect.

The Member States themselves can also contribute to defend the Rule of Law against populism, by applying preliminary rulings to the ECJ in order to have the ECJ interpret EU law regarding national cases related to the Rule of Law in either their own or other Member States. This allows for a general effect due to the binding nature of ruling from the ECJ and the possible precedent of the case. It also creates a specific effect in the national cases.

Concerning the infringement procedure, it is clear that the procedure can be an adequate tool to counter specific populist challenges to the rule of law, if it is utilised in the proper manner. The best practice case is the application of the procedure accompanied by the expedited procedure and interim measures. In the present case this ensured compliance with the ruling at a preceding stage. This thesis is further underlined as in the case where interim measures and the expedited procedure were not applied, the subsequent compliance with the judgement can be disputed. Lastly, it should be noted that the effectiveness of interim measures to some extent depends on either the Member State's will to comply or that the Court of Justice decides to describe penalty payments in case of non-compliance.

When it comes to the Rule of Law Mechanism, we have shown through a comparison with the adequateness of other tools what the adequateness of the Mechanism can be presumed to be. Following this, it appears that the Mechanism is quite adequate to deal with populist threats towards the rule of law in both a specific and general sense. Notably, the lower majority rule, the immediate economic sanctions and the time limit for the process are features, which contribute in a positive manner.

In conclusion, an interaction between populism and the EU legal order has taken place both ways. Populism has had an effect on the general features of the EU legal system, and the EU responses to populism have had some effect on populism (based on the Polish case study). The crises of the EU contribute to defining the Union; its legal system, values and identity. This way, crises may even end up strengthening the EU in a longer-term perspective.

Bibliography

Belov, Martin. "The Functions of Constitutional Identity Performed in the Context of the Constitutionalization of the EU Order and Europeanization of the Legal Orders of the EU Member States." *Perspectives on Federalism* 9, no. 2 (2017): 72–96.

Faraguna, Pietro. "Constitutional Identity in the EU – A Shield or a Sword?" *German Law Journal* 18, no. 7 (special issue) (2017): 1617–1640.

Halmai, Gábor. "The Application of European Constitutional Values in EU Member States." *European Journal of Law Reform* 20, no. 2–3 (2018): 10–34.

Kaczorowska, Alina. *European Union Law*. 3rd edition. Abingdon: Routledge, 2013.

Kadelbach, Stefan. "Are Equality and Non-Discrimination Part of the EU's Constitutional Identity?" In *The European Union as Protector and Promoter of Equality. European Union and its Neighbours in a Globalized World*, vol 1, edited by Thomas Giegerich, 13–24. Cham: Springer, 2020. https://doi.org/10.1007/978-3-030-43764-0_3.

Koncewicz, Tomasz Tadeusz. "The Politics of Resentment and First Principles in the European Court of Justice", 457–476. In *EU Law in populist Times*, edited by Francesca Bignami 413–456. Cambridge: Cambridge University Press, 2020.

Lavelle, Patrick. "Europe's Rule of Law Crisis: An Assessment of the EU's Capacity to Address Systemic Breaches of Its Foundational Values in Member States." *Trinity College Law Review 22*, (2019): 35–50.

Martins, Ana Maria Guerra. "Equality and Non-Discrimination as an Integral Part of the EU Constitutional Identity." In *The European Union as Protector and Promoter of Equality. European Union and its Neighbours in a Globalized World*, vol 1, edited by Thomas Giegerich, 25–44. Cham: Springer, 2020. https://doi.org/10.1007/978-3-030-43764-0_3.

Sadurski, Wojciech. "Adding a Bite to the Bark? A Story of Article 7, EU enlargement and Jörg Haider." *Columbia Journal of European Law* 16, no. 3 (2010): 385–426.

Scheppele, Kim Lane and Kelemann, Daniel R. "Defending Democracy in EU Member States. Beyond Article 7 TEU". In *EU Law in populist Times*, edited by Francesca Bignami, 413–456. Cambridge: Cambridge University Press, 2020.

Tornøe, William A. and Caroline E. Wegener. *What should the EU do about Poland's populist* PiS, Master's thesis, University of Copenhagen, 2020.

van der Schyff, Gerhard. "Characterizing the Identity of Constitutional Orders: A Comparative National and EU Perspective." *Berliner Online-Beiträge zum Europarecht*, no. 105 (2015).

von Bogdandy, Armin and Ioannidis, Michael. "Systemic Deficiency in the Rule of Law: What it is, what has been done, what can be done." *Common Market Law Review* 51, no. 1 (2014): 59–96.

Wigand, Christian, Katarzyna Kolanko and Alice Hobbs. "2020 Rule of Law Report – Questions and Answers." *European Commission*. Accessed April 6, 2020. https://ec.europa.eu/commission/presscorner/detail/en/qanda_20_1757.

Judicialising the Rule of Law Through the Preliminary Ruling

Cristina Saenz Perez

1 Introduction

The rule of law crises experimented by some EU Member States have exposed gaps in the definition of the rule of law and inadequacies in its enforcement within the EU (Kelemen and Blauberger 2016; Müller 2015; Kochenov and Pech 2015). This chapter analyses these controversial issues and evaluates how the preliminary reference is contributing to settling these contradictions. Relying on vertical judicial dialogue, the preliminary ruling regulated in Article 267 of the Treaty on the Functioning of the European Union (TFEU) is becoming instrumental to flagging systemic deficiencies of the rule of law at Member State level. This process has been favoured by the ineffectiveness of the political enforcement instrument of the rule of law in Article 7 of the Treaty of the European Union (TEU). The high majorities required by this provision (unanimity in the European Council to determine "the existence of a serious and persistent breach by

C. Saenz Perez (✉)
University of Leeds, School of Law, Leeds, UK
e-mail: C.SaenzPerez@leeds.ac.uk

J. M. Castellà Andreu, M. A. Simonelli (eds.), *Populism and Contemporary Democracy in Europe*,
https://doi.org/10.1007/978-3-030-92884-1_12

a Member State of the values referred to in Article 2 (TEU)" and qualified majority in the Council to adopt sanctions) have limited the effectiveness of this political instrument. Instead, the preliminary reference mechanism is emerging as an alternative to analyse the compatibility of systemic violations of the rule of law at Member State level with EU law.

Although there have been examples of rule of law violations at EU level throughout its history, the systemic breaches analysed in this chapter exceed isolated reforms which may challenge specific safeguards of this founding value of the EU. This analysis is focused on articulated programmes of legislative or constitutional reforms aimed at weakening internal checks and balances that shape the separation of powers at Member State level (Pech and Scheppele 2017). Examples of these reforms can be found in the constitutional amendments introduced by Hungary or the legislative reforms completed in Poland.[1] These comprehensive processes pose a threat to founding values of the EU, such as democracy or the rule of law, which EU political institutions (primarily the European Commission and the Council) struggle to contain. It is for this reason that examining the vertical judicial dialogue facilitated by Article 267 TFEU as a rule of law enforcement tool is more pertinent than ever. This analysis starts by defining the rule of law as a founding value and constitutional principle of the EU in Sect. 2 to, then, examine its relevance to the functioning of the preliminary reference mechanism in Sect. 3. Building on this analysis, Sect. 4 outlines how the preliminary reference is emerging as a rule of law enforcement tool, whereas Sect. 5 considers its limitations beyond the areas in which primary legislation is being implemented, such as the Area of Freedom, Security and Justice (AFSJ).

2 Defining the Rule of Law

The rule of law constitutes a founding value of liberal democracies and, as such, one of the constitutional principles shared by EU Member States. However, defining its scope and meaning is far more complex. On the one hand, the rule of law encompasses multiple legal principles that define the

[1] On the rule of law backsliding in Poland: The Venice Commission for Democracy through Law, Opinion on amendments to the Act of 25 June 2015 on the Constitutional Tribunal of Poland, CDL-AD(2016)001 of 11 March 2016; Sadurski, *How Democracy Dies (in Poland)*.

ideal of a democratic state (Waldron 2008). It is for this reason that the rule of law is conceived as an umbrella concept that includes different sub-principles, such as legality, judicial review, or fundamental rights (Pech 2010, 369). On the other hand, choosing the values or principles that are contained within this definition determines the conception and priorities that are pursued through the rule of law. Widely speaking, this decision is determined by the adscription to 'thick' or 'thin' conceptions of the rule of law (Williams 2010, 73).

Thin conceptions of the rule of law are also conceived as formalistic definitions that equate it with the principle of legality. This notion is in line with Raz's definition of the rule of law that conceived it as an obstacle to the exercise of arbitrary power (Raz 1979). For this goal to be achieved, laws should comprise the following characteristics: these should be prospective, adequately publicised, clear, and relatively stable, whilst law-making should be guided by open, stable, clear, and general rules (Raz 1979). Thick definitions of the rule of law, instead, define a more substantive notion of the rule of law that encompasses guarantees, such as the principles of equality, human dignity, or the protection of human rights (Raz 1979). For instance, Allan states that the separation of powers, the principles of legality, judicial review, or judicial independence should be accompanied by substantive safeguards, such as the protection of civil and political rights (Raz 1979). Other authors go beyond this definition and incorporate social, cultural, and economic rights as essential safeguards of the rule of law (Weeramantry 2000, 53). These discrepancies regarding the scope and meaning of the rule of law also exist within EU law, complicating any analysis of its enforceability and nature.

Under Article 2 TEU, the rule of law has now been enshrined to the status of a founding value of the EU, together with "respect for human dignity, freedom, democracy, equality and respect for human rights, including the rights of persons belonging to minorities". This provision does not provide a definition of the rule of law and requires, instead, a wider analysis of the CJEU's case law to clarify what is the understanding of this value within the EU to, then, examine its possible enforcement. Traditionally, the definition of the rule of law has been influenced by the primary objective of the EU (the creation of an internal market) and its development after the Cold War in which the EU and its liberal conception of Western democracies seemed uncontested. In this context, the CJEU developed an interpretation of the rule of law that was essentially linked to a formalistic or thin definition. According to this view, the rule of law constituted, primarily, an instrument to ensure the coherence of the EU project, according to which the guarantees of uniformity, primacy, and effectiveness of EU law required that Member States were constrained not by the use of force but by the primacy of the law (Bertea 2005).[2]

The CJEU examined this thin notion of the rule of law in its early rulings in *Van Gend en Loos*[3] or *Costa v Enel*.[4] These judgements established the creation of a new legal order of international law that binds Member States and individuals.[5] This "new legal order" followed a formalistic view of the rule of law, according to which EEC institutions and Member States were subject to EEC law. This definition was linked to guaranteeing the integrity of the internal market, as "there can be no unified market without a common law, no common law without a uniform interpretation, no uniform interpretation unless the common law takes precedence".[6] These initial definitions of the rule of law guaranteed the consistency of EEC law but did not consider substantive safeguards of this value, such as the protection of fundamental rights. The priority was to guarantee the functioning of the internal market.

The Court's first attempt at providing a comprehensive definition of the rule of law as a principle of EEC law appears in *Les Verts*.[7] According to this judgement, "the European Economic Community is a community based on the rule of law, inasmuch as neither its member states nor its institutions can avoid a review of the question whether the measures adopted by them are in conformity with the basic constitutional charter, the treaty".[8] In other words, the Court concluded that the EEC had set up a system based on the rule of law, whereby all decisions adopted by Member States and its own institutions were subject to judicial review. Ultimately, the existence of a system of effective remedies had the aim of guaranteeing the consistency and uniform interpretation of EEC law. The Court followed here a formalistic conception that considers that "the key

[2] See also President Commission lecture,"Uniting in peace: the role of law in the European Union". Available online at https://cadmus.eui.eu/bitstream/handle/1814/22135/JMLecture25_BarrosoEUI.pdf?sequence=1 last accessed 30 September 2021.

[3] Case 26/62 *Van Gend en Loos v Nederlandse Administratie der Belastingen* [1963] ECR 1.

[4] Case 6/64 *Flaminio Costa v E.N.E.L.* [1984] ECR 585.

[5] *Costa v Enel* (n 17).

[6] President of the ECJ Robert Lecourt, "Speech on the X anniversary of the ECJ" (1968) EC Bulletin 12-1986, 23.

[7] Case 294/83 *Parti écologiste "Les Verts" v European Parliament* [1986] ECR 1339.

[8] Ibid., para 23.

to the notion of the rule of law is the reviewability of decisions of public authorities by independent courts" (Jacobs 2007, 35). Its priority was to maintain the supremacy and uniformity of EU law.

The EU's compliance with this thin conception of the rule of law has been questioned within the field of Justice and Home Affairs (JHA) in which the option of review through the preliminary reference mechanism was limited before the Lisbon Treaty (Peers 2001). Such limitations were removed by this Treaty, but these still remain within the Common and Foreign Security Policy (CFSP) despite the CJEU's emphasis on the status of the rule of law in the *Kadi* saga.[9] Within these areas, nonetheless, the Court prioritises a formalistic interpretation of the rule of law that is tied to Article 19(1) TEU. According to this provision, "Member States shall provide remedies sufficient to ensure effective legal protection in the fields covered by Union law". This interpretation of Article 19(1) TEU seeks to guarantee that EU law is uniformly and effectively applied across the EU, which is achieved through a system of effective remedies at Member State and EU levels.

Despite the prevalence of this thin or formalistic view of the rule of law, recent case law and institution documents show an evolution towards a substantive definition consistent with the status of fundamental rights within the EU constitutional framework. A systematic interpretation of Article 2 TEU, for instance, would require that the rule of law is interpreted together with other values, such as human rights, human dignity, freedom, democracy, or equality. The CJEU has analysed this connection,[10] acknowledging that "the review by the Court of the validity of any Community measure in the light of fundamental rights must be considered to be the expression, in a Community based on the rule of law, of a constitutional guarantee stemming from the EC Treaty as an autonomous legal system".[11] This demonstrates that judicial review as a safeguard of the rule of law may also be instrumental to protecting fundamental rights when EU law is being implemented. This CJEU's case law in these areas ties a formal interpretation of the rule of law that prioritises the uniformity

[9] Joined cases C-402/05 and C-415/05 *Yassin Abdullah Kadi and Al Barakaat International Foundation v Council of the European Union and Commission of the European Communities* [2008] ECR I-06351 (*Kadi I*); Joined Cases C-584/10, C-593/10 and C-595/10 *European Commission and Others v Yassin Abdullah Kadi* ECLI:EU:C:2013:518 (*Kadi II*).

[10] Lenaerts, *The Kadi Saga*, 707-715.

[11] *Kadi I*, para 316.

and effectiveness of EU law to the protection of fundamental rights when EU law is being implemented, reflecting a thicker or substantive conception of the rule of law. This is consistent with definitions developed by the Commission, according to which the "[the rule of law] makes sure that all public powers act within the constraints set out by law, in accordance with the values of democracy and fundamental rights, and under the control of independent and impartial courts".[12] Nevertheless, the actionable nature of the rule of law remains essentially connected with Article 19(1) TEU and the right to an effective remedy.

3 The Preliminary Reference Mechanism and the Definition of Judicial Independence

The preliminary reference mechanism has played an essential role in defining the meaning and limits of the rule of law within the EU. This mechanism sets in motion a process of judicial dialogue between the CJEU and national courts that has contributed to defining the fundamental principles of EU law, for example supremacy or the right to an effective remedy (Tridimas 2003, 11). At the same time, the preliminary reference as an instrument that guarantees the uniform and effective implementation of EU law is essential to the guarantee of the formal or thin conception of the rule of law. One of the essential components of this thin notion of the rule of law, namely the judicial independence of courts, constitutes a precondition to the operation of the preliminary reference mechanism.[13]

The preliminary reference mechanism relies on the sincere cooperation and mutual trust that must exist between EU courts provided that two requisites are met. First, the Member State court must identify a relevant question of EU law that needs clarification.[14] Second, the referring court must be an 'EU court' within the meaning of the CJEU.[15] The notion of what constitutes an EU court was first examined in *Broekmeulen*.[16] According to this decision, an EU court must fulfil the following

[12] European Commission, *A new EU Framework to strengthen the Rule of Law* (Communication) COM/2014/0158 final, 4.

[13] Case C-54/96 *Dorsch Consult Ingenieurgesellschaft mbH v Bundesbaugesellschaft Berlin mbH* [1997] ECR I-04961, para 23.

[14] TFEU, art 267; Case C-224/01 *Gerhard Köbler v Republik Österreich* [2003] ECR I-10239, para 118.

[15] *Dorsch Consult Ingenieurgesellschaft mbH v Bundesbaugesellschaft Berlin mbH* (n 29).

[16] Case C-246/80 *C. Broekmeulen v Huisarts Registratie Commissie* [1981] ECR 2311.

requirements: decide in proceedings that could affect the exercise of Community rights, operate with the consent of public authorities and with their cooperation, and deliver decisions which are final in matters concerning Community law after a proceeding *inter partes*.[17] The Court's case law delimiting what constitutes an EU court under Article 267 TFEU has been developed in subsequent cases. According to it, a court or tribunal can refer questions to the CJEU if it is established by law and permanent, has compulsory jurisdiction, rules in proceedings *inter partes*, applies rules of law, and is independent.[18] This last requirement constitutes one of the essential safeguards of formal notions of the rule of law which may be questioned by national reforms that seek to undermine its protection at Member State level.

Judicial independence under Article 267 TFEU must be interpreted in accordance with the guidelines provided in the context of Articles 19(1) TEU and 47 CFR, which include internal and external safeguards against interference. If these requirements are not fulfilled, a court cannot be considered an EU court for the purposes of the preliminary reference, and thus, it cannot engage in a vertical dialogue with the CJEU.[19] The Court has an abundant case law that examines the relevance of external protections of judicial independence that, if removed, limit the capacity of a judicial body to act as an EU court.[20] These guarantees include the protection against arbitrary removal from office[21] and the provision of a level of remuneration commensurate to the tasks undertaken.[22] For instance, the Court has ruled that the elimination of safeguards against arbitral removal from office undermines the capacity of national courts to submit preliminary references under Article 267 TFEU.[23] In contrast, the elimination of these safeguards would challenge the coherence of EU law, as it would increase the risk of fragmentation when national courts lose access to the

[17] Ibid., para 17.

[18] Case C-394/11 *Valeri Hariev Belov v CHEZ Elektro Balgaria AD and Others* of 31 January 2013, ECLI:EU:C:2013:48, para 38.

[19] Ibid..

[20] Case C-503/15 *Ramón Margarit Panicello v Pilar Hernández Martínez* of 16 February 2017 ECLI:EU:C:2017:126, paras 36-43.

[21] Case C-619/18 *European Commission v Republic of Poland* of 24 June 2019 ECLI:EU:C:2019:531, para 45.

[22] Case C-64/16 *Associação Sindical dos Juízes Portugueses* of 27 February 2018 ECLI:EU:C:2018:117, para 43.

[23] Joined Cases C-558/18 and C-563/18 *Miasto Łowicz v Skarb Państwa — Wojewoda Łódzki and others*, Opinion of Advocate General Tanchev, ECLI:EU:C:2019:775, para 92.

CJEU through the preliminary reference mechanism.[24] It is an instrumental interpretation of the rule of law as a formal value of the EU which confers jurisdiction to the CJEU to examine the independence of the referring court.

At the same time, the preliminary reference can examine whether a national reform guarantees the independence of the judiciary, as this also constitutes a prerequisite of the right to an effective remedy under Article 19(1) TEU. In *Associação Sindical dos Juízes Portugueses*,[25] the CJEU held that EU courts must fulfil EU standards of independence and impartiality to be able to provide effective remedies and guarantee the enforcement of EU law. In this case, the CJEU had to examine whether the measures adopted by the Portuguese legislature to reduce the remuneration of Court of Auditors' judges were compatible with Article 19(1) TEU. These measures, adopted in the context of the austerity measures implemented by Portugal during the financial crisis, were challenged by an association of judges who brought an annulment action in front of the Portuguese Supreme Court. This association alleged that national measures reducing the salary of the judges of the Court of Auditors challenged the principle of judicial independence. Following these allegations, the Supreme Court of Portugal referred a question to the CJEU asking about the compatibility of these national measures with Article 19(1) TEU.

In its decision, the Court did not deem these measures incompatible with EU law, but it held that Article 19(1) TEU imposes obligations on national courts adjudicating in fields covered by EU law.[26] According to the CJEU's case law, Article 19(1) TEU guarantees the independence and impartiality of the national judiciary in the fields covered by EU law. This provision "gives concrete expression to the value of the rule of law stated in Article 2 TEU",[27] insofar as it guarantees the judicial review of national decisions in areas covered by EU law. Conversely to Article 47 CFR, which permits the review of the independence of national courts when substantive EU provisions are being implemented, Article 19(1) TEU widens this possibility to situations of national courts that may eventually interpret EU law (Krajewski 2018, 404). In any case, both provisions have

[24] *European Commission v Republic of Poland* (n 37) para 45.

[25] *Associação Sindical dos Juízes Portugueses* (n 38) paras 32-34.

[26] *Associação Sindical dos Juízes Portugueses* (n 38) paras 34-38.

[27] Ibid., para 32.

developed equivalent notions of judicial independence,[28] according to which the judiciary must be protected against internal and external pressures.[29] Externally, the judiciary must be safeguarded against any intervention or pressure, particularly from the executive, liable to jeopardise the independent judgement of its members[30] (including salary reductions).[31] Internally, the independence of the judiciary requires impartiality that is equated to objectivity and absence of conflict of interest with the case adjudicated.[32] These requirements guarantee that EU courts can participate in the vertical dialogue with the CJEU under Article 267 TFEU and provide effective remedies under Article 19(1) TEU.

4 The CJEU as an Enforcer of the Rule of Law

The preliminary reference has emerged as a powerful instrument to enforce the rule of law in the context of the populist regimes of Poland and Hungary, where it has filled the gap left by the ineffectiveness of political enforcement tools. An example of its implementation as a rule of law enforcement mechanism is found in *Minister of Justice and Equality v LM*,[33] in which the Court limited the enforceability of the European arrest warrant system (EAW) due to the existence of systemic violations of the rule of law in the issuing state (Poland). In this decision, the CJEU analysed the effects of judicial reforms that impair the capacity of the issuing court to guarantee the accused's right to a fair trial under Article 47 CFR on the execution of EAWs. In such cases, the Court refused a suspension of the system of horizontal judicial cooperation which characterises the AFSJ.[34] Instead, it established that the executing court should examine the effect that such systemic violations of the rule of law may have on the individual surrendered before refusing the execution of the EAW. This analysis built on the CJEU's judgement in the joined cases

[28] Case C-506/04 *Wilson v Ordre des Avocats du Barreau de Luxembourg* [2007] ECR I-08613.

[29] Ibid. paras 51-53.

[30] Ibid. para 51; Case C-103/97 *Köllensperger and Atzwanger* [1999] ECR I-551, para 21; Case C-407/98 *Abrahamsson and Anderson* [2000] ECR I-5539, para 36.

[31] *Associação Sindical dos Juízes Portugueses* (n 38) para 45.

[32] *Wilson* (46) para 52; *Abrahamsson and Anderson* (n 48) para 32.

[33] Case C-216/18 *Minister for Justice and Equality v LM* of 25 July 2018, ECLI:EU:C:2018:586.

[34] Ibid. para 34.

of *Caldararu and Aranyosi*,[35] which articulated as a two-stage test to evaluate situations in which the fundamental rights of the individual surrendered may be at risk.

In the first stage, the executing court has to examine whether there are "systemic or generalised deficiencies concerning the judiciary of that Member State, such as to compromise the independence of that State's courts".[36] During this first stage, the executing court could examine the Commission's reasoned proposal adopted against Poland under Article 7(1) TEU as an evidence of these systemic violations.[37] Once this first stage has been completed, the executing court has to analyse "whether, in the particular circumstances of the case, there are substantial grounds for believing that, following his surrender to the issuing Member State, the requested person will run that risk".[38] During this second stage, the CJEU empowers the executing court to examine the independence of another national court, turning the executing court into an enforcer of the rule of law. In these judgements, the conception of the rule of law is substantive and linked to the right to a fair trial: if the issuing court is not independent, then the individual's right to a fair trial in the Member State of surrender may be at risk.[39]

However, in recent preliminary references, the CJEU has gone a step further and characterised the independence of the judiciary as a requirement that defines the status of the issuing judicial authority under Article 6(1) of the Framework Decision on the European Arrest Warrant (FDEAW).[40] According to this case law, the independence of the issuing authority constitutes a prerequisite so that a Member State authority can issue EAWs.[41] In this case law, the CJEU reproduces the standards set under Articles 267 TFEU and 19(1) TEU, according to which a Member State court has to be independent and impartial in order to be considered an EU court capable of establishing a judicial dialogue with the CJEU or provide effective remedies.

[35] Joined Cases C-404/15 and C-659/15 *Pál Aranyosi and Robert Căldăraru v Generalstaatsanwaltschaft Bremen* of 5 April 2016, ECLI:EU:C:2016:198.

[36] *Minister for Justice and Equality v LM*, para 68.

[37] Ibid. para 69.

[38] Ibid. para 68.

[39] Ibid. para 79.

[40] Council Framework Decision 2002/584/JHA of 13 June 2002 on the European arrest warrant and the surrender procedures between Member States [2002] OJ L 190/1.

[41] Joined cases C-354/20 and C-412/20 *L and P* of 5 February 2021, ECLI:EU:C:2020:1033 (*Openbaar Ministerie*).

The CJEU analysed the status of the issuing court in the context of a preliminary reference issued by the Amsterdam District Court when executing an EAW in the so-called *Openbaar Ministerie* decision.[42] In this case, the CJEU had to decide whether the issuing Polish court was affected by national reforms that might compromise its judicial independence and whether such events questioned its capacity to issue EAWs. In this decision, it held that an 'issuing court' within the meaning of Article 6(1) FDEAW must conform to EU standards of independence and impartiality in the execution of its responsibilities.[43] In other words, the concept of 'issuing judicial authority' under the FDEAW is linked to a formal notion of the rule of law that requires that the independence of national authorities is safeguarded.[44] This analysis had already been developed in previous cases in which the CJEU had to establish whether public prosecutors or police authorities fulfilled EU independence and impartiality standards to be deemed issuing judicial authorities.[45] In these analyses, the Court considered whether the functional dependence of public prosecutors from the executive could affect their ability to guarantee the fundamental rights of the accused in cross-border proceedings. These standards set by the CJEU are, then, implemented by executing courts in a decentralised manner, with national courts examining the judicial independence of equivalent courts in other Member States.

Beyond the AFSJ, the preliminary reference mechanism has become essential to analyse judicial reforms adopted by Member States. *A.K. and Others*[46] is a clear example of how this mechanism may be used to examine such reforms in areas in which Member State courts are not implementing EU law (Zelazna 2019).[47] In this case, the analysis concerned the compatibility of Disciplinary Chamber created within the Polish Supreme Court with EU requirements of independence and impartiality. In this

[42] Ibid.

[43] Ibid. para 38.

[44] On the notion of judicial independence as a prerequisite of mutual trust within the AFSJ: Mitsilegas, *Autonomous Concepts*, 67-70.

[45] See Joined Cases C-566/19 and C-626/19 *Parquet général du Grand-Duché de Luxembourg v JR and Openbaar Ministerie v YC* of 12 December 2019, ECLI:EU:C:2019:1077; Joined Cases C-508/18 and C-82/19 *Minister for Justice and Equality v OG and PI* of 27 May 2019, ECLI:EU:C:2019:45; Case C-453/16 *Criminal proceedings against Özçelik* of 10 December 2016, ECLI:EU:C:2016:860.

[46] Case C-585/18 *A.K. and Others v Sąd Najwyższy* of 19 November 2019, ECLI:EU:C:2019:982.

[47] Zelazna, *The Rule of Law Crisis Deepens in Poland*, 907-912.

decision, the CJEU relied on ECtHR's case law to examine the judicial standards that must be guaranteed by EU courts under Article 19(1) TEU.[48] Although it ultimately left the application of these requirements in the Polish context to the referring court, the CJEU included the features of the Disciplinary Chamber that it deemed problematic under Article 19(1) TEU: the exclusive jurisdiction granted to the Disciplinary Chamber on the retirement of Supreme Court judges,[49] the limited jurisdiction of the Disciplinary Chamber outside this area,[50] and its high degree of autonomy from the Polish Supreme Court.[51]

In the context of the domestic implementation of *A.K. and Others*, nonetheless, some of the limitations of the preliminary ruling mechanism became evident. In this case, the Polish Supreme Court held that having regard to the circumstances and the criteria set by the CJEU, the Disciplinary Chamber was not an EU court within the meaning of EU law.[52] This analysis prevented any examination of the independence of the new Disciplinary Chamber, as the requirements set by the CJEU were only applicable to those courts that fulfil the standards set in *Broekmeulen*. As a consequence, even if the Court expressed its own doubts about the compatibility of this Chamber with EU law, it has continued performing its judicial tasks. The CJEU will have another opportunity to decide on the compliance of this Disciplinary Chamber with EU law in the proceedings lodged by the Commission following the decision of the Supreme Court of Poland in the domestic interpretation of *A.K. and Others*.[53]

The proceedings initiated by the Commission show some of the weaknesses of the preliminary ruling mechanism, particularly when the cooperation of national courts is questionable. These limitations are explored further in the CJEU's decision in *Miasto Lowicz and Others*.[54] These joined cases originated in preliminary references issued by two Polish judges who

[48] Ibid., para. 132.
[49] Ibid., para. 148.
[50] Ibid., para. 150.
[51] Ibid., para. 151.
[52] See Supreme Court of Poland, Judgment of 5 December 2019, III PO 7/18; Supreme Court of Poland, Judgment of 15 January 2020, III PO 8/18 and III PO 9/18.
[53] Case C-791/19 *European Commission v Republic of Poland,* Action brought on 25 October 2019.
[54] Joined Cases C-558/18 and C-563/18 *Miasto Łowicz v Skarb Państwa — Wojewoda Łódzki* of 26 March 2020, ECLI:EU:C:2020:234.

had to rule on cases in which the Polish state was a party.[55] In the light of the recent judicial reforms in Poland and the setting up of the Disciplinary Chamber, they raised concerns that their independence may be compromised, as disciplinary proceedings may be initiated against them if they ruled against the State. The Court, nonetheless, deemed these references inadmissible, as the main disputes in the proceedings had no connection with EU law.[56] At the same time, the Court held that despite these limitations, "provisions of national law which expose national judges to disciplinary proceedings as a result of the fact that they submitted a reference to the Court for a preliminary ruling cannot therefore be permitted".[57] Although these claims were obiter dicta, they show the Court's concerns over processes of rule of law backsliding and the lack of adequate instruments to redress them.

Although the CJEU exposed some of the limitations of the preliminary reference in this area, its interpretation of Article 19(1) TEU was quite restrictive and contrary to previous decisions, such as *Associação Sindical dos Juízes Portugueses* or *Vindel*.[58] A more coherent approach to the interpretation of Article 19(1) TEU may be found in the Opinion of Advocate General (AG) Tanchev in *Miasto Lowicz*.[59] A.G. Tanchev considered that the inadmissibility of this preliminary reference was not connected to the nature of the main proceedings but rather to the hypothetical nature of the concerns expressed by the referring judges.[60] The lack of ongoing disciplinary actions at Member State level when the preliminary references were submitted determined their inadmissibility, not the nature of the main proceedings in which the Polish judges were adjudicating. In other words, the questions referred were merely hypothetical, and this determined their inadmissibility. This interpretation of Article 19(1) TEU would widen the scope of the preliminary ruling as an enforcement instru-

[55] Cases C-563/18 and C-558/18 *Miasto Łowicz v Skarb Państwa*, Request for a preliminary ruling from the Sąd Okręgowy w Łodzi (Poland) lodged on 3 September 2018 [2019] OJ C 44/8.

[56] *Miasto Łowicz and others*, para 49.

[57] Ibid., para 58.

[58] Case C-49/18 *Carlos Escribano Vindel v Ministerio de Justicia* of 7 February 2019, ECLI:EU:C:2019:106.

[59] Joined Cases C-558/18 and C-563/18 *Miasto Łowicz v Skarb Państwa — Wojewoda Łódzki*, Opinion of Advocate General Tanchev delivered on 24 September 2019, ECLI:EU:C:2019:775.

[60] Ibid., para 118.

ment, as a similar reference would be admissible if the referring judges had been sanctioned by the Disciplinary Chamber, as they effectively were later in the proceedings.

5 The Preliminary Reference Mechanism and the Risk of Politicisation

The preliminary reference has been particularly successful in enforcing a substantive interpretation of the rule of law linked to fundamental rights such as the right to fair trial under Article 47 CFR, when EU secondary legislation is being implemented. Evidence of this development can be seen in recent judgements, such as *Minister of Justice and Equality v LM* or *Openbaar Ministerie*. But these judgements have also raised concerns about the role that the CJEU is playing in this process.

On the one hand, the CJEU has limited its judgements to providing guidelines on EU standards of judicial independence, but it has been rejected a blanket halt to judicial cooperation with Member States affected by these judicial reforms. The Court reasoned that halting judicial cooperation "would mean that no court of that Member State could any longer be regarded as a 'court or tribunal' for the purposes of the application of other provisions of EU law, in particular Article 267 TFEU".[61] In other words, the Court has shown its concerns that a blanket halt of judicial cooperation with Polish courts would also affect the preliminary reference mechanism, as it would challenge the status of these organs as 'EU courts' within the meaning of Articles 19(1) TEU and 267 TFEU.[62] Such a decision would increase the risk of fragmentation and would put the coherence of EU law at risk, as Polish courts (whether affected by these national reforms or not) would lose access to the CJEU when relevant questions of EU law arise.

On the other hand, the preliminary ruling mechanism entails that Member States' courts have to interpret and apply EU requirements of judicial independence in connection with Articles 19(1) TEU and 47 CFR. This has a clear drawback when the referring court is affected by these national judicial reforms, as the *A.K. and Others* case demonstrates. In these cases, the domestic application of these standards may be

[61] *Openbaar Ministerie* (n 59), para 44.

[62] *Dorsch Consult Ingenieurgesellschaft mbH v Bundesbaugesellschaft Berlin mbH* (n 29), para 23.

hampered, and the intervention of the European Commission through infringement actions will be necessary. This limits the effectiveness of the preliminary reference as an alternative to political enforcement mechanisms or infringement proceedings.

In the AFSJ, nonetheless, the implementation of the standards set by the CJEU rests in the executing courts, which have to evaluate whether the issuing courts fulfil EU standards of judicial independence and impartiality. This, in turn, constitutes another challenge to the principle of mutual trust, according to which Member State courts should accept that courts in other Member States share equivalent independence and impartiality standards (Wendel 2018; Lenaerts 2020). The Court enables Member State courts to examine the independence of equivalent courts in other Member States under exceptional circumstances, an exception that questions the status of mutual trust as the underpinning of judicial cooperation in criminal matters.

When executing judicial cooperation instruments, this mechanism permits the creation of a decentralised system of checks and balances through which national courts can enforce the rule of law in connection with EU secondary legislation. Nevertheless, the generalisation of this mechanism as a rule of law enforcement mechanism also poses some risks. First, the legitimacy of the judiciary of another Member State in the process of deciding whether a foreign court fulfils EU standards of independence is dubious. Within the EU's constitutional framework, this task has, primarily, a political nature under Article 7 TEU. It is questionable whether, outside the CJEU, other EU courts have the legitimacy to intervene and decide on the organisation of the judiciary in another Member State. Furthermore, normalising this mechanism as a tool to counter rule of law violations entails attributing political decisions, such as the organisation of the judiciary or the definition of the rule of law, to the judiciary of 27 Member States which are not democratically accountable (Guild 2006, 272).

6 Conclusions

The preliminary ruling mechanism provides an instrument whereby the CJEU can interpret EU law and establish a dialogue with national courts. In the case of national rule of law crises, this instrument enables the Court to strike a balance between the rights to a fair trial under Article 47 CFR and to an effective remedy under Article 19(1) TEU and the principles of sincere cooperation that should guide the judicial dialogue between courts. It is through this balancing exercise that the vertical dialogue established between Member State courts and the CJEU becomes an indirect instrument to set EU standards of judicial independence and redress situations in which these minimum standards are not fulfilled.

Despite its relevance as a tool to redress systemic violations of the rule of law, the preliminary reference mechanism has numerous limitations. On the one hand, it is not designed to tackle breaches of the rule of law emerging as a result of a democratic crisis occurring at Member State level. On the other hand, generalising the implementation of the preliminary reference mechanism as a rule of law enforcement tool would entail attributing political decisions, such as the organisation of the judiciary or the definition of the rule of law, to the CJEU alone. It is for these reasons that the preliminary reference mechanism cannot replace Article 7 TEU as a rule of law enforcement instrument without raising new challenges to the values of democracy and the rule of law within the EU.

Bibliography

Bertea, Stefano. "Looking for Coherence within the European Community." *European Law Journal* 11, no. 1 (2005): 154-172.

Guild, Elspeth. *Constitutional challenges to the European Arrest Warrant*. Amsterdam: Wolf Legal Publishers, 2006.

Jacobs, Francis. *The sovereignty of law: The European way*, Cambridge: Cambridge University Press, 2007.

Kelemen, Daniel R. and Blauberger, Michael. "Introducing the debate: European Union safeguards against member states' democratic backsliding." *Journal of European Public Policy* 24, no. 3 (2016): 317-320.

Kochenov, Dimitry and Pech, Laurent. "Monitoring and Enforcement of the Rule of Law in the EU: Rhetoric and Reality." *European Constitutional Law Review* 11, no. 3 (2015): 512-540.

Krajewski, Michał. "*Associação Sindical dos Juízes Portugueses*: The Court of Justice and Athena's Dilemma." *European Papers* 3, no. 1 (2018): 395-407.

Lenaerts, Koen. "New Horizons for the Rule of Law Within the EU." *German Law Review* 20, no. 1 (2020): 29-34.

Mitsilegas, Valsamis. "Autonomous Concepts, Diversity Management and Mutual Trust in Europe's Area of Criminal Justice." *Common Market Law Review* 45, no. 1 (2020): 45-78.

Müller, Jan Werner. 2015. "Should the EU Protect Democracy and the Rule of Law inside Member States?" *European Law Journal* 21, no. 2: 141-160.

Pech, Laurent. "A Union Founded on the Rule of Law': Meaning and Reality of the Rule of Law as a Constitutional Principle of EU Law." *European Constitutional Law Review* 6, no.3 (2010): 359-396.

Pech, Laurent and Scheppele, Kim Lane. "Illiberalism Within: Rule of Law Backsliding in the EU." *Cambridge Yearbook of European Legal Studies* 3, no. 8 (2017): 3-47.

Peers, Steve. "Mission accomplished? EU Justice and Home Affairs law after the Treaty of Lisbon." *Common Market Law Review* 48, no. 3 (2001): 661-693.

Raz, Joseph. "The rule of law and its virtue". In *Liberty and the rule of law*, edited by Cunningham, Robert L., 3-21. Texas: A&M University Press, 1979.

Sadurski, Wojciech. "How Democracy Dies (in Poland): A Case Study of Anti-Constitutional Populist Backsliding." *Sydney Law School Research Paper*, no.18 (2018).

Tridimas, Takis. "Knocking on heaven's door: Fragmentation, efficiency and defiance in the preliminary reference procedure." *Common Market Law Review* 40, no. 1 (2003): 9-50.

Waldron, Jeremy. "The Concept and the Rule of Law." *Georgia Law Review* 42, no. 1 (2008): 1-61.

Weeramantry, Lucian G. *The International Commission of Jurists: The Pioneering Years*, Amsterdam: Kluwer Law International, 2000.

Wendel, Mattias. "Mutual Trust, Essence and Federalism – Between Consolidating and Fragmenting the Area of Freedom, Security and Justice after *LM.*" *European Constitutional Law Review* 15, no. 1 (2018): 17-47.

Williams, Andrew. *The ethos of Europe: values, law and justice in the EU.* Cambridge: Cambridge University Press, 2010.

Zelazna, Ewa. "The Rule of Law Crisis Deepens in Poland after *A.K. v. Krajowa Rada Sadownictwa and CP, DO v. Sad Najwyzszy.*" *European Papers* 4, no. 2 (2019): 907-912.

PART IV

Populism, the Pandemic and the Future of Democracy

Preserving Democracy and the Rule of Law in a Pandemic. Some Lessons from the Venice Commission

Josep Maria Castellà Andreu

1 Introduction

The health crisis provoked by the COVID-19 is a global emergency, yet the legal responses to it have been eminently national. The pandemic has raised legal-constitutional reflections in the affected countries on the reaction of public authorities, on the problems of the application to the current crisis of the states of exception foreseen by national legal systems and on the impact the adopted measures have on fundamental rights and the

An extended version of this text has been published in Spanish in Paloma Biglino y Juan F. Durán (eds), *Los efectos horizontales de la covid-19 sobre el sistema constitucional: estudios sobre la primera oleada*, Fundación M. Giménez Abad, Zaragoza, 2021.

J. M. Castellà Andreu (✉)
University of Barcelona, Barcelona, Spain
e-mail: castella@ub.edu

J. M. Castellà Andreu, M. A. Simonelli (eds.), *Populism and Contemporary Democracy in Europe*,
https://doi.org/10.1007/978-3-030-92884-1_13

separation of powers. In all countries, there is indeed a tension between the need for effective and rapid responses to the pandemic and the necessity to preserve the rule of law and constitutional democracy, in particular the system of checks and balances and the guarantee of fundamental rights. Although the legal responses to the crisis varied significantly in each country, there are, nonetheless, certain common features: the protagonism of central executives, the use of emergency legislation, and the restriction of fundamental rights in the name of the safety. At the same time, the use of exceptional powers by some European governments to confront the health crisis and its social and economic consequences has been seen with some concern in public opinion and in broad legal sector.

The COVID-19 crisis can be analysed from different legal perspectives. In this work we will adopt the approach employed by the European Commission for Democracy through Law of the Council of Europe, known as the Venice Commission, one of the international organisations that have intervened in the present global health crisis.[1] Specifically, we will focus on the impact the pandemic has on constitutional democracy and the separation of powers, taking the Spanish case as an outstanding example of the problems mentioned.

Insofar, the Venice Commission has published three documents related to the COVID-19 pandemic. These documents explicitly recognise the relevance of the current health crisis in our societies and its impact on the founding objectives of the Council of Europe and the Venice Commission itself since its inception in 1990: the safeguarding of democracy, human rights and the rule of law. This justifies from the outset the attention reserved by the Venice Commission to the emergency derived from COVID-19. Besides, there may be another implicit reason for the attention paid to the current crisis by the Venice Commission. The guidelines that it had previously elaborated for the management of emergency situations were designed, just like that on the states of exception, to face serious problems of public order and national security crisis, or natural or health catastrophes of lesser magnitude. The first novelty of the current

[1] The Venice Commission has been included in the so-called Transnational Legal Orders (TLOs) and plays an important role in global constitutionalism, in terms of its function, membership and values, as it operates on legal norms relating to democracy, human rights and the rule of law. See Craig, *Constitucionalismo transnacional: la contribución de la Comisión de Venecia*, 90 ss. The author draws on the definitions of Halliday and Shaffer and apply them to the Venice Commission.

health crisis, and its effects on the economy, lies in its severity, duration and effects. Even though many of the general principles of emergency law are applicable to the new situation, updation and adaptation was necessary. The Reflections[2] and the Interim Report[3] contribute to this. Both documents take into account only the first wave of the pandemic, until the summer of 2020, without taking into account subsequent waves, which present characteristics partly different, both as regards the incidence of the pandemic, and the legal and political responses to it. The Interim Report focuses on actions carried out by EU Member States (and the United Kingdom) to address the pandemic and its effects on democracy, the rule of law and human rights. Earlier the Venice Commission had published a Compilation,[4] which contains the reiterated doctrine of the Venice Commission on emergency law.

These contributions of the Venice Commission include parameters that can help to assess the use of the exceptional powers by States during the COVID-19 pandemic and, in particular, in the case of Spain. The First Section refers to the types of states of emergency and the principles that should guide their regulation and application by States. The Second Section analyses the criteria of the Venice Commission in relation to the redistribution of powers during states of emergency and the parliamentary control of governmental decisions, affecting the parliamentary, constitutional and pluralist nature of democracy, in addition to judicial control, affecting the rule of law. To conclude, the responses of the public powers to the emergency caused by the pandemic will be related to the populism that threatens our democratic and constitutional systems.

[2] Respect for democracy, human rights and the rule of law during states of emergency—Reflections (CDL-PI(2020)005rev). Published on 26 May 2020, by N. Alivizatos, U. Bilkova, I. Cameron, O. Kask, and K. Tuori. The document was "taken into account" by the Plenary session of the Venice Commission of June 2020. Available at: https://www.venice.coe.int/webforms/documents/?pdf=CDL-PI(2020)005rev-e.

[3] Interim report on the measures taken in the EU Member States as a result of the COVID-19 crisis and their impact on democracy, the rule of law and fundamental rights, adopted by the Plenary session on 8 October 2020 (CDL-AD(2020)018). Available at: https://www.venice.coe.int/webforms/documents/default.aspx?pdffile=CDL-AD(2020)018-e.

[4] Compilation of Venice Commission opinions and reports on states of emergency, CDL-PI(2020)003. Published on 16 April 2020. Available at: https://www.venice.coe.int/webforms/documents/default.aspx?pdffile=CDL-AD(2020)018-e

2 The Venice Commission and States of Emergency. Types of Exceptional States and the Principles Governing Them

2.1 *Opting for the Rule of Law Model*

As the Reflections recall, there are two theoretical approaches to situations of abnormality or exception on the part of States. First, the so-called sovereign approach, which corresponds to the decisionist approach and evokes Carl Schmitt's way of dealing with them, based on the possibility for the State to adopt all the measures necessary to guarantee public health without the limit of what is provided for by the constitutional legal system or by forcing its interpretation in that direction. And second, an approach based on the rule of law, in which the law, and the Constitution in particular, regulates and, therefore, rationalises and limits the exercise of power in exceptional states, even if it does so in a different way to normal situations. The Venice Commission opts for the second approach, as it is appropriate for constitutional democracies.[5] However, in our constitutional states, the real danger is not so much to opt for one model or the other, but to avoid decisionist leakages in the responses given by governments or the parliamentary majorities that support them. In the next paragraph the effects of the legal system's provision on states of emergency are analysed.

2.2 *Types of States of Emergency and Their Regulation*

It should be noted at the outset that "state of emergency" is the generic term usually employed by the Venice Commission to encompass all the different exceptional states, which are given different names in each legal system, as well as other emergency regulations. Therefore, the Commission seems to adopt a broad and material concept of emergency, as opposed to the stricter concept of exceptional state, formally identified in national Constitutions—as is the case in Spain.

The Venice Commission distinguishes between the different types of states of emergency that are usually provided for by national legal systems, when more than one is envisaged, normally following an objective criterion—based on the type of emergency in question—and/or another

[5] Reflections (CDL-PI(2020)005), para. 8; Interim Report CDL-AD(2020)018, paras 18–19.

criterion referring to the gravity of the extraordinary situation.[6] Accordingly, the distinction must take into account the "nature, severity and duration of the extraordinary situation". These aspects will determine the "type, extent and duration of the emergency measures".[7] By introducing this plurality of criteria for identifying each type of state of emergency, a flexible approach is chosen which takes into account the plurality of approaches in comparative law and which, furthermore, allows for a certain degree of modulation in the application of the state of emergency, depending on the seriousness and duration of the specific event. But, at the same time, the relative vagueness of the criteria for the delimitation of the different states of emergency can prompt the authority declaring such a state, to use the type of state that allows for the greatest governmental intervention with the lesser checks. Hence the need, as will be seen, to specify by national law, as precisely as possible, the causes that may trigger the application of a state of emergency or another.

In this light, the choice of an objective criterion by the Organic Law regulating exceptional states, that is, of alarm, exception and siege (LO 4/1981), based on Article 116 of the Spanish Constitution, led Spain to declare a state of alarm in March 2020, and not a state of exception, because the factual situation was in line with what envisaged in art. 4.b) of the Organic Law ("health crises, such as epidemics and serious pollution situations"). Yet, the intensity of the restrictions to fundamental rights that it entailed generated a doctrinal debate on the compatibility of the measures adopted with the state of alarm, in which some authors strongly argued for the necessity of declaring a state of exception instead, entailing different powers and guarantees (Aragón Reyes 2020; Fernández de Casadevante 2021, 150).[8]

The Spanish Constitutional Tribunal in judgment 148/2021, of 14 July 2021, concerning Royal Decree 463/2020 declaring the first state of alarm, found that the restriction on the right to free movement of citizens actually amounted to a suspension of that right, not permissible during a state of alarm, but in a state of exception. The decision of the Tribunal reflects the difficulties in reconducing the pandemic crisis to one of the

[6] Emergency Powers CDL-STD(1995)012; Compilation CDL-PI(2020)003, 6.

[7] Interim Report CDL-AD(2020)018 para. 20.

[8] In various blogs and interventions on public media intervened in the debate, amongst many others, J. Díaz Revorio, C. Flores Juverías y C. Vidal. Against E. Vírgala, J. Tajadura, J. De Miguel y J.M. Castellà.

three existing exceptional states, and evidences the need for a legislative reform clarifying the circumstances corresponding to each exceptional state. The Venice Commission's Interim Report provides an overview of the situation in the EU Member States and the United Kingdom, in which it classifies the legal responses of these States according to whether or not they have declared a state of emergency and according to the legal basis of the emergency measures adopted. As a first point, the Report adopts a broad criterion of state of emergency, including both the exceptional states provided for in national Constitutions and other sectorial emergency regulations, especial health ones, regulated by specific legislation. When a state of emergency has been declared, some States have chosen to use one of the constitutionally envisaged exceptional states (nine countries, seven of them by governmental decision, including Spain, and two by Parliament, including Portugal), whilst others have preferred not to apply these exceptional states—even envisaged in their respective constitutions—and to make use of the legislation envisaged for health emergencies, with the adoption of specific measures either by Parliament or by the government (five countries, including Germany, France, and Italy). In contrast, 14 other countries have preferred to use ordinary legislation, with adaptations to the circumstances dictated by the pandemic situation, without declaring exceptional states or using emergency legislation (e.g. Austria, Belgium, Greece and the United Kingdom).[9] Thus, in the Interim Report, the Commission carries out an analysis according to a material or substantive criterion, without limiting itself to examining only the cases of those countries that have made a legal declaration of a state of emergency. In doing so, it takes into account and assesses the legal response to the pandemic of all EU states and the UK, irrespective of the route chosen to deal with the health emergency.

It should be also added that the responses given by the different states have not been static, rather they have remarkably varied during the pandemic. The Spanish case is a good case in point. We can distinguish at least four distinct and successive phases to date (March 2020–January 2022). First, after an initial period of uncoordinated and largely improvised measures taken by the various national and territorial public authorities, the national government decreed a state of alarm, which was extended by Congress on up to six occasions for periods of 15 days (Royal Decree 463/2020, in force from 14 March to 21 June 2020). Second, after the

[9] Interim Report CDL-AD (2020)018, paras 35–38 and 41–43.

cessation of the state of alarm, the model known as "co-governance", which had already been tried and tested in the last extensions of the state of alarm, was chosen, consisting of the recovery of political management powers by the Autonomous Communities and some coordination by the central government and inter-territorial cooperation through the Inter-territorial Health Council. This second phase saw the approval of a wide variety of regional regulations adopted pursuant to Organic Law 3/1986, of 14 April 1986, on public health (Article 3), and Law 29/1998, on contentious-administrative jurisdiction (recently modified in relation to the courts responsible for authorising or ratifying administrative measures adopted by the different health authorities in relation to urgent and necessary measures for public health entailing non-individualised limitation of fundamental rights, Law 3/2020, of 18 September, Articles 8, 10 and 11). The third phase, coinciding with the upturn of the pandemic in what is known as the second wave and the legal problems caused by the application of the aforementioned ordinary regulations, with a new recourse to the state of alarm, first for some municipalities in the Community of Madrid (Royal Decree 900/2020, of 9 October) and then for the whole of Spain (Royal Decree 926/2020, of 25 October). This decree, with a single extension approved by Congress for six months (Decree 956/2020, of 3 November), empowers the regional authorities to adopt measures restricting mobility and social gatherings, without having to request judicial authorisation. Finally, after the conclusion of the second national state of alarm, ended on 9 May 2021, the situation went back to that of the second phase, i.e. the situation was managed with ordinary instruments. During all these phases, no reform of Organic Law 3/1986 on public health has been discussed by the Parliament, notwithstanding the requests coming from the opposition parties and the academia.

The Venice Commission introduces a prescriptive criterion in relation to states' use of emergency powers. On this point, it explicitly declares its preference for the "de jure state of emergency" or "de jure constitutional emergency powers" model, because it offers greater guarantees for fundamental rights, the rule of law and democracy compared to the "extra-constitutional system" or "de facto state of emergency".[10] However, the Commission, as we have already mentioned, leaves it to the free choice of states to opt for emergency legislation based on constitutionalised exceptional states or other sectorial legislative provisions on health emergencies.

[10] Ibid., paras 29–31; Reflections CDL-PI(2020)005, paras 22–24.

This broad consideration of the so-called constitutional model may lead to confusion due to the name that designates it, since it allows justifying the option for states of emergency derived from unwritten constitutional principles or included in an "(organic) law" (sic) based on the Constitution. In reality, the model that offers the greatest guarantees is the one derived from the Constitution itself in the strict sense. The broad interpretation of the constitutional or legal criterion does not prevent the Commission from identifying the Constitution as the most appropriate norm for establishing the "basic provisions" on the identification of such states and their delimitation, given that emergency powers "usually restrict basic constitutional principles".[11] Another thing is that the development corresponds to the legislator, and here the Commission shows a preference for a qualified legislator, such as the organic legislator. The Reflections also stress that such regulation must be general and approved prior to the declaration, during times of normality.[12]

2.3 Principles on the States of Emergency

Exceptional states in the broad sense, or states of emergency, as addressed by the Venice Commission, must be governed by different principles that operate, with due adaptations, in three different moments and situations: their regulation, activation and application.[13] These principles guide the fundamental areas of public and private life on which emergency law is projected: not only fundamental rights but also the separation of powers. The principles to be taken into account are listed in the various documents, but not all of them are systematically cited in a single closed and exhaustive list. For this reason, the following list is an attempt to organise them as comprehensively as possible, although possible reiterations may be admitted.

First, we can highlight the principles of legality or rule of law, necessity and proportionality in the strict sense.[14] To these must be added others such as the formal nature of their proclamation, and that of exceptionality,[15]

[11] Reflections CDL-PI(2020)005, para. 26.

[12] Reflections CDL-PI(2020)005, paras 29–30.

[13] On the difference between the last two see: Interim Report CDL-AD(2020)018, para. 28.

[14] Emergency Powers, CDL-STD(1995)012, 30; Compilation CDL-PI(2020)003, 5.

[15] France—Opinion on the Draft Constitutional Law on "Protection of the Nation" CDL-AD(2016)006, para. 28; Compilation CDL-PI(2020)003, 7.

as well as the principle of differentiation between the various exceptional states, according to which all emergencies cannot be confused or treated in the same way (we have referred to this in the previous section).[16] The Reflections, to recapitulate, mention, in addition to the aforementioned principles of the rule of law, necessity and proportionality, the principle of temporariness, the principle of effective parliamentary and judicial scrutiny, the principle of predictability of emergency legislation and the principle of loyal cooperation between institutions.[17]

Before referring in greater detail to the application of these principles to the organisation of powers in the next section, it is worth mentioning, in general terms and beforehand, the content and consequences derived from some of the aforementioned principles.

For the Venice Commission, observance of the rule of law and the principle of legality, and specifically that of legal certainty, entails, among other consequences, that the rules governing the state of emergency should be a) adopted prior to the declaration of the state of emergency; b) clear and avoid open clauses ("the regulation of these powers should be as detailed as possible")[18]; c) when Parliament delegates powers to the Executive "the objectives, content and scope of this delegation of powers should be explicitly defined in a legislative act",[19] as this avoids leaving broad areas of action in the hands of executive powers without clear and determined empowerment.

With regard to the principle of temporariness, the Venice Commission notes, on the one hand, that the exceptional measures with which most European states have dealt with the pandemic are issued for a limited period, subject to extension. Only in a few states were they adopted without setting a time limit, but using clauses relating to the permanence of the situation (Croatia and Hungary). In such cases, the Commission recommends that, in order for such declarations to be considered lawful, there should be a regular review of the situation.[20] On the other hand, as a prescriptive criterion, it is indicated that, whatever the mode of

[16] Turkey—Opinion on the amendments to the Constitution adopted by the Grand National Assembly on 21 January 2017 and to be submitted to a National Referendum on 16 April 2017 CDL-AD(2017)005, para. 73; Compilation CDL-PI(2020)003, 8.

[17] Reflections CDL-PI(2020)005, paras 6–16.

[18] Interim Report CDL-AD(2020)018, para. 58.

[19] Ibid., para. 58. With a reference to Rule of Law Chechlist CDL-AD(2016)007, para. 1.4.iii.

[20] Interim Report CDL-AD(2020)018, paras 46–49.

regulation used, in addition to parliamentary and judicial control, the measures should cease to be in force as soon as the circumstances that led to their approval are over.[21] On this last point, however, the Commission accepts that, first, the emergency measures may be made more flexible as the situation evolves and, second, given the prolongation in time of certain effects of the situation giving rise to the emergency, a special legal regime may be maintained after the end of the state of emergency. In such a case, however, the principles of checks and balances between powers and acquired rights should apply.[22]

The Spanish case offers a good example of what has just been pointed out. At first the situation that prevailed between June and October 2020 has been called "new normality", without it being a return to the previous situation, given the health, social and economic circumstances. Subsequently the long duration of the extension of the last state of emergency—six months—without effective control by the Congress of Deputies, raised problems of compatibility with the Venice Commission standards. The Venice Commission has indeed stated that "the longer the emergency regime lasts, the further the state is likely to move away from the objective criteria that may have validated the use of emergency powers in the first place. The longer the situation persists, the lesser justification there is for treating a situation as exceptional in nature with the consequence that it cannot be addressed by application of normal legal tools".[23] The Spanish Constitutional Tribunal in its judgement 183/2021 declared the unconstitutionality of this six months period for being excessive and unjustified. The principle of necessity concerns the type of rules to be adopted during the state of emergency. These rules must be linked to the emergency situation.[24] Thus, it is not possible to take advantage of the rules enacted to deal with the emergency to include structural rules intended to be permanent, such as those that introduce changes in the organisation and functioning of the institutions.[25] This is precisely what has happened in Spain in relation to certain changes in the composition of

[21] Ibid., para. 25.

[22] Ibid., paras 26–27.

[23] Ibid., para. 51. The paragraph cites an excerpt taken from: Turkey—Opinion on Emergency Decree Laws nn 667–676 adopted following the failed coup of 15 July 2016 CDL-AD(2016)037, para. 41; Compilation CDL-PI(2020)003, 22.

[24] Interim Report CDL-AD(2020)018, paras 23–24.

[25] Turkey—Opinion on Emergency Decree Laws nn 667–676 adopted following the failed coup of 15 July 2016, CDL-AD(2016)037, para. 80; Compilation CDL-PI(2020)003, 22.

the Commission of the National Intelligence Centre (CNI), approved during the first state of alarm in 2020, declared unconstitutional in judgment 110/2021 of 13 May.

Finally, and as a consequence of the principle of exceptionality, the Compilation recalls that constitutional reform cannot be carried out during an exceptional state.[26] This principle is enshrined in many constitutions. In the Spanish case, with respect to the beginning of the reform (Article 169 SC). It is one thing for constitutions to be drafted or reformed substantively as a consequence of major crises or social or political changes (constitutional moments), and another for such constitutional changes to take place in the midst of an exceptional state.

3 The Venice Commission's Views on the Separation of Powers During States of Emergency

3.1 Redistribution of Powers During Emergencies

With regard to the redistribution and exercise of powers during states of emergency, the Venice Commission takes as its starting point the effect on the distribution of powers in comparative law.[27] Thus, it notes that the health crisis has affected the normal functioning of parliamentary life (difficulty in holding face-to-face meetings with the attendance of all parliamentarians). In such circumstances, the position of central governments has been strengthened, while parliaments have been "relegated to a secondary role".[28]

As mentioned above, the Venice Commission advocates the application of the principles of control and loyal cooperation between institutions. Both principles constitute the two sides of the relationship between national and local institutions, and between majority and opposition in the declaration and implementation of the state of emergency. Thus, the broadest possible political consensus must be sought in the parliamentary

[26] Turkey—Opinion on the amendments to the Constitution adopted by the Grand National Assembly on 21 January 2017 and to be submitted to a National Referendum on 16 April 2017, CDL-AD(2017)005, para. 29; Compilation CDL-PI(2020)003, 25, with a specific reference to the Spanish case.

[27] Interim Report CDL-AD(2020)018, para. 52.

[28] Ibid., paras 61, 64.

assembly in the adoption of the state of emergency and, at the same time, parliamentary control in its execution in addition to inter-territorial cooperation in politically composite states should be ensured. The meaning of the "principle of the normal functioning of the public powers" must be interpreted in this light; it cannot mean functioning in the same way as in normal times, which is precisely what the emergency leaves aside. The Compilation makes a reference to Spain, specifically to Art. 116.5 SC, as an example of a guarantee of the principle of the normal functioning of public powers:

> Emergency rule may or may not involve changes in the distribution of powers among organs of the State or shifts in the competences of such organs. In some cases (eg in Spain and Portugal) the normal functioning of the constitutional organs is not affected by the emergency rule. [...] Normally, the declaration of a state of emergency involves the transfer of additional powers to the executive.[29]

With this background, the Commission recommends enhancing parliamentary scrutiny over the executive and the provision of qualified majorities in parliaments to declare and/or extend the state of emergency so to involve the opposition in the decision. Indeed,

> Many constitutions provide for the possibility of the executive to legislate in emergency situations. Parliament should be involved in this process through the approval of the declaration of the state of emergency, and/or through ex post scrutiny of the emergency decrees or any extension of the period of emergency. Participation of the opposition in those matters may be ensured by requiring a qualified majority for the prolongation of the state of emergency beyond the original period (CDL-AD(2016)006, para.63). It may also be useful to limit the legislative powers of the executive in emergency situations to certain specific matters, so that the executive cannot use its legislative functions to suppress opposition rights. The Venice Commission has emphasised that parliamentary life should continue throughout a state of emergency, and indicated that Parliament should not be dissolved during the exercise of emergency powers (CDL-AD(2016)006, para 62). It is recommended not to undertake constitutional amendments during situations of emergency (CDL-AD(2017)005, para 29). These limitations prevent the

[29] Emergency Powers CDL-STD(1995)012, 16; Compilation CDL-PI(2020)003, 14.

executive from using an emergency as a pretext for curtailing the rights of the opposition.[30]

As indicated in the Reflections, Parliament is responsible for approving the state of emergency, or at least extending it. The latter is the provision in Spain with respect to the state of alarm (Article 116 CE). The Commission offers a criterion to the legislator: a qualified majority "may" be required to approve the extension of the exceptional state.[31] It also refers to the possible creation of commissions of inquiry to facilitate control over the government's use of emergency powers. In this way, the principle of protection of the opposition is given concrete form, either with requirements of parliamentary consensus for the declaration or at least for the maintenance of emergency powers, so that they are not used to bypass Parliament or to limit the powers of parliamentary minorities, or in the control of the exercise of exceptional powers by the government.[32] In the Spanish case, the provision for a six-month extension means that Parliament's role in monitoring the application of the state of emergency is reduced during this period. The decree extending the state of emergency (Decree 956/2020 of 3 November) refers to "accountability" (Article 14), but in reality it limits itself to establish an obligation for the President of the government to appear every two months before the plenary of Congress, and for the Minister of health to appear every month before the congressional health Committee. Yet information is not accountability in the strict sense. However, the Constitutional Tribunal, in judgment 183/2021, only declared unconstitutional such periods of one and two months for the appearance of the members of government before the Congress. Besides, the Tribunal found a violation of the participatory rights of MPs (Article 23 of the Spanish Constitution) caused by the Resolution of the Congress of Deputies Bureau suspending some parliamentary activities (STC 168/2021).

The Venice Commission refers to the frequent use in such exceptional circumstances of government regulations having force of law, such as decree laws, and the intervention of Parliament in their validation (in

[30] Parameters on the Relationship between the Parliamentary Majority and the Opposition in a Democracy: a Checklist CDL-AD(2019)015, para. 121; Compilation CDL-PI (2020)003, 16.

[31] Reflections CDL-PI(2020)005, para. 84

[32] Ibid., para. 82.

Spain more than 30 since March 2020, in addition to the many approved by the Autonomous Communities). The Reflections consider legitimate use of these types of rules during exceptional states, but with strict limits on their validity and purpose.[33]

The particular circumstances caused by the health crisis—reduced mobility and public meetings—require changes in the way Parliament functions. The Venice Commission's latest document, the Interim Report, devotes some considerations on how EU Member States have dealt with the situation: remote working, reinforcement of digital tools and so on. The Commission's main warning in this regard focuses on the need to maintain plenary sessions and not to temporarily replace parliamentarians or reduce attendance at sessions, as face-to-face discussion is crucial to the debate.[34]

All in all, the Venice Commission applies to this issue its long-standing doctrine on the centrality of Parliament in the public life of a country. A secondary role of the Parliament during a state of emergency can affect the functioning of democracy, hence the Commission's emphasis on the functions that the Parliament must exercise in relation to such a state of emergency. The Venice Commission therefore concludes:

> the Covid-19 crisis should not be used as an opportunity to render governments more powerful at the expense of parliaments and at any rate not permanently. In order to prepare for the future, serious consideration should be given to identifying the best scenario and ensure that the necessary regulatory framework is in place to fulfil it as well as identify to what extent some of these measures could be maintained over time, regardless of whether or not there is an emergency. Parliament should be the centre of a country's political life, and in order to maintain this status, the necessary tools and mechanisms must be in place to ensure this. Continuation of the work of parliament should be considered an essential requirement during a crisis, and steps—for instance, in allowing and improving digital meetings of parliament when physical meetings are impossible—must be taken to maintain parliamentary work without difficulty in such situations in the future.[35]

[33] Ibid., paras 63–64. With a reference to: Parameters on the Relationship Between the Parliamentary Majority and the Opposition CDL-AD(2019)019, paras 119–212. For a review of the factual situation: Interim Report CDL-AD(2020)018, para. 64.

[34] Interim Report CDL-AD(2020)018, para. 75.

[35] Ibid., para. 72.

The Reflections also mention the role of experts[36] and of the military.[37] With regard to the armed forces, the Compilation takes the example of Spain to attest the existence in some countries of special military units to carry out tasks during emergencies (the UME). The contribution of experts or technicians and consultative bodies is barely developed, except to indicate that it contributes to strengthening the government and weakening Parliament. In any case, the so-called technocratic approach brings us to the relevant question of the relationship between science and public decision-making in crisis situations and how risk management and accountability take place (Esteve Pardo 2020).

Finally, the territorial organisation of the state in decentralised systems is also affected by states of emergency. Thus, as far as the relationship between central and territorial governments is concerned, the Venice Commission admits, despite the scant attention devoted to the issue, as a general rule, that the powers of the central government may limit those of sub-national authorities: "In some federal States, the declaration of emergency rule may involve the shift of competences from the State and local authorities to the central government".[38] Other documents constrain the scope of such a limitation, which could not go as far as the suspension of autonomy,[39] or a recentralisation beyond the requirements of the exceptional state.[40] The Reflections are more cautious and stress the application of the principles of loyal cooperation and mutual respect.[41] Also at the local level, there is a greater protagonism of the executive over the legislature, whether through the approval of decree laws, decrees or other infra-legal norms to deal with the emergency. The Spanish case is illustrative of two extreme positions: in the first state of alarm (in its first phases: March–May 2020), national government centralisation was total, leaving the Autonomous Communities to implement the measures and giving the

[36] Reflections CDL-PI(2020)005, para. 69.

[37] Report on the Democratic Control of the Armed Forces CDL-AD(2008)004, para.125; Compilation CDL-PI(2020)003, 27.

[38] Emergency Powers CDL-STD(1995)012, 16; Compilation CDL-PI(2020)003, 26; Interim Report CDL-AD(2020)018, para. 54.

[39] Opinion on the draft law on the legal regime of the state of emergency of Armenia CDL-AD(2011)049, para. 34; Compilation CDL-PI(2020)003, 26.

[40] Turkey—Opinion on the Provisions of the Emergency Decree Law N° 674 of 1 September 2016 which concern the exercise of Local Democracy CDL-AD(2017)021, para. 92; Compilation CDL-PI(2020)003, 26.

[41] Reflections CDL-PI(2020)005, para. 61.

meetings of the Conference of Presidents a merely informative character; in the next state of alarm decree, the regional governments are empowered to adopt decisions relating to it, with hardly any coordination and cooperation from the central government. The central government has the power to declare a state of alarm, but the autonomous communities maintain their ordinary powers, although their exercise may be affected by the measures adopted by the government. According to Art. 7 of Organic Law 4/1981, the government can delegate these powers to the president of an autonomous community when the declaration affects "exclusively" its territory. Conversely, as the pandemic has a national outreach, the government has inadequately decided to delegate its powers to all presidents. (De la Quadra-Salcedo, 2021, 82–83).

3.2 *Judicial Control and Maintenance of the Rule of Law*

The Venice Commission reiterates the need for judicial scrutiny, in addition to parliamentary one, over the declaration of a state of emergency and over the measures taken by the executive "against the risks of abuse". This is linked to the principle of upholding the rule of law. The greater margin of discretion granted to the government should not make it difficult for the judicial system to provide individuals with an "effective remedy" in the event of a violation of individual rights.[42] Such control can be exercised both by the ordinary and constitutional jurisdiction of each state, as well as by international judicial or quasi-judicial bodies, in particular the European Court of Human Rights. In order to comply with this principle, the guarantee of the independence of the courts and the maintenance of their functioning is emphasised, except in cases of absolute necessity or material impossibility.[43]

In the Commission's documents a preference for constitutional justice is visible. They even affirm that it should have the power to order "interim measures".[44] Yet, this will ultimately depend on the legislation of each state as to respective boundaries between ordinary and constitutional jurisdiction. The preference for constitutional justice makes sense at least

[42] Interim Report CDL-AD(2020)018, paras 77, 79.

[43] Reflections CDL-PI(2020)005, paras 87, 89.

[44] Ibid., para. 88. The preference for constitutional justice is nuanced, but not for the adoption of interim measure, in the Interim Report. See: Interim Report CDL-AD(2020)018, para. 88.

for the declaration of a state of emergency, although such an option may negatively affect the very possibility of claiming control. In the Spanish case, it is well known that standing for constitutional review is restricted. This question is at the basis of the consideration, in Spain, of the Decree declaring the state of alarm and those extending it as acts with the force of law (STC 83/2016, in relation to the first state of alarm of 2010). This means that it is impossible for the rules declaring or extending the state of alarm to be challenged by affected or interested individuals. A different matter is the acts or decrees implementing the state of alarm, whose a posteriori control corresponds, in the first place, to the contentious-administrative jurisdiction, and, subsidiarily, to the review of the Constitutional Tribunal through an appeal for protection (recurso de amparo) for infringement of a fundamental right. Apart from the above, there is the provision for judicial authorisation or ratification of the administrative measures that fall outside the scope of the alarm decree, as we have previously seen (Law on Contentious-Administrative Jurisdiction).

The Venice Commission admits that jurisdictional control is often limited in practice due to "judicial self restraint", as has already occurred in certain decisions on the declaration of the state of emergency due to the pandemic or on the measures adopted in its application (Constitutional Court of the Czech Republic or Serbia; different has been the case in Portugal or France). This is particularly true in relation to derogations provided for in international human rights instruments, where the European Court of Human Rights has recognised a wide margin of appreciation for each State.[45] This does not mean, however, that judicial control is waived in such cases or in general. The principles of necessity and proportionality still apply in assessing the restriction and derogation of rights.

In the Spanish case, it can be observed that such judicial deference to the government has been habitual—although certainly not unanimous—in the different tribunals in relation to the application of measures restricting fundamental rights. This adds to the habitual deference of the Constitutional Tribunal towards the executive in the recourse to Law Decrees (even more pronounced during the previous financial crisis). The Constitutional Tribunal has already delivered four judgments: two on the Royal Decrees declaring both states of alarm, a third on some provisions

[45] Ibid., paras 21, and 83–84. With a reference to the doctrine of the European Court of Human Rights. See: Canosa Usera, *El marco internacional y supranacional de la reacción estatal europea,* 38.

of a Law Decree, and the fourth on an individual direct appeal against a resolution of the Bureau of the Congress. All these decisions were rendered in proceedings initiated by Vox MPs. A divided Constitutional Tribunal partially upheld these appeals, with separate opinions criticising the majority for not being deferential towards the government (for instance, the dissenting opinion of Maria Luisa Balaguer to judgment 183/2021).

4 Conclusions

Prior the COVID-19 the logic that predominated when rationalising the use of exceptional powers in constitutional states governed by the rule of law had been that of exceptional states arising from serious political crises of public order or natural or health crises with circumscribed effects. Hence the difficulties posed by the inclusion of emergencies such as the one now besetting us, which partly—though only partly—explain the varied options followed in European states. This same logic has been the constant orientation in legal studies on exceptional states to date in different—European states, including Spain. Yet, this does not mean that many of the criteria legally or judicially established are not applicable to the current pandemic, although there are certain regulatory gaps and certain adaptations are required. This will undoubtedly oblige legislators to contemplate specific regulations that provide adequate coverage for situations of this kind.

What has just been said in general terms also applies to the documents related to the states of emergency adopted by the Venice Commission in previous years. This explains the rapid and agile reaction of the Venice Commission since the beginning of the pandemic. The documents analysed in these pages, particularly the Reflections and the Interim Report, adapt the general standards for states of emergency (collected in the Compilation) to the particularities of the current pandemic and fill this gap. These contributions, based on international, comparative and constitutional law and good practices in states, derive criteria that can be used to guide legislative reforms that appear necessary in the light of the pandemic or to assess and interpret existing norms.

The Venice Commission noted that the state of emergency entails changes in the relationship between the different state organs, in favour of the central government. Hence, as we have seen, it stressed the temporarily limited or provisional and "truly" exceptional nature of the measures adopted, preferably by applying constitutional emergency rules, and their subjection to the principles of necessity and proportionality. However, this does not prevent the rule of law from remaining fully in force and the provision of safeguards against possible misuse in the adoption and application of such measures by governments.[46] Nevertheless, to face the COVID-19 crisis some states have made recourse to regulatory instruments other than states of emergency. And, even in those that have declared a state of emergency, this has been done simultaneously with the approval of decree laws, and after the cessation of such states, there has been no return to the previous constitutional normality, but rather special rules have been issued or applied under the umbrella of a "new normality", as the health crisis has dragged on and the economic and social crisis has gained momentum. Thus, either because of the long duration of states of emergency, or because of the use of emergency legislation outside these states, we are faced with a long-term application of special rules, in principle of a transitory nature, generally of a sub-legal rank (ministerial orders and resolutions), which extend the scope of emergency law beyond its traditional boundaries. All this results in the blurring of the special guarantees related to emergency law, in particular as regards parliamentary scrutiny of executive acts.

The concentration of powers in the executive hands and the loss of parliament's centrality, as well as the government's habitual use of legislative powers, are not new situations that have arisen in the current emergency situation. What has happened is an acceleration of known and studied trends in most constitutional systems. This coincides in time with the presence of populist parties in the governments of several European and non-European states. Thus, in some countries, political polarisation and the difficulty of reaching agreements with the opposition in Parliament have been exposed, as well as the questioning of judicial control over governmental measures. In this way, the various populisms in power have found in the current pandemic an optimal context to accelerate their divisive and confrontational political agenda and a pretext to justify the approval of rules that grant governments broad regulatory and decision-making powers while limiting their political and judicial control. The erosion of constitutional democracies is thus accentuated.

[46] Opinion on the Draft Constitutional Law on "Protection of the Nation" of France CDL-AD(2016)006, para. 51; Compilation CDL-PI(2020)003, 12.

In emergency situations, the Venice Commission makes clear the option for the constitutional model of the exceptional state and what this entails: the guarantee of state security and public safety in a democracy with full respect for the rule of law and fundamental rights, which are the founding objectives of the Council of Europe and of the Venice Commission itself:

> The security of the State and of its democratic institutions, and the safety of its officials and population, are vital public and private interests that deserve protection and may lead to a temporary derogation from certain human rights and to an extraordinary division of powers. However, emergency powers have been abused by authoritarian governments to stay in power, to silence the opposition and to restrict human rights in general. Strict limits on the duration, circumstances, and scope of such powers are therefore essential. State security and public safety can only be effectively secured in a democracy which fully respects the Rule of Law. This requires parliamentary control and judicial review of the existence and duration of a declared emergency situation in order to avoid abuse.[47]

Bibliography

Aragón Reyes, Manuel. "Editorial. Covid-19: aproximación constitucional a una crisis." *Revista General de Derecho Constitucional*, no. 32 (2020).

Canosa Usera, Raúl. "El marco internacional y supranacional de la reacción estatal europea ante la emergencia sanitaria." In *El derecho constitucional ante la COVID-19*, edited by Enrique Arnaldo Alcubilla and Raúl Canosa, 25–47. Madrid: Wolters Kluwer, 2020.

Craig, Paul. "Constitucionalismo Transnacional: la contribución de la Comisión de Venecia." *Teoría y Realidad Constitucional*, no. 40 (2017), 79–109.

De la Quadra-Salcedo Janini, Tomás. "Estado de alarma y lucha contra la pandemia." In *Los efectos horizontales de la covid-19 sobre el sistema constitucional: estudios sobre la primera ola*, edited by Paloma Biglino Campos and Juan Fernando Durán Alba, 59-85. Zaragoza: Fundación M. Giménez Abad, 2021.

Esteve Pardo, José. "La apelación a la ciencia en el gobierno y gestión de la crisis de la Covid-19." *Revista de Derecho Público: teoría y método* 2, (2020), 35–50. DOI: https://doi.org/10.37417/RPD/vol_2_2020_272

Fernández de Casadevante Mayordomo, Pablo. "Normalidad y emergencia constitucional en la Unión Europea." In *La protección del orden constitucional en Europa*, edited by Josep Maria Castellà, 125–156. Madrid: PPE, 2021.

[47] Rule of Law Checklist (CDL-AD(2016)007), para. 51; Compilation CDL-PI(2020)003, 4.

The Duration of the State of Alarm in Spain and the Problems Posed for Democracy

Andrés Iván Dueñas Castrillo

1 Introduction

During the COVID-19 pandemic in Spain, two states of alarm have been decreed that have affected the entire national territory.[1] One factor that differentiates the two states of alarm has been the exercise of control related to their duration by the Legislative. The duration of the first was

[1] The text of the first state of alarm, which underwent some modifications after successive extensions, can be consulted at https://www.boe.es/buscar/doc.php?id=BOE-A-2020-3692 last accessed 30 September 2021; while the second can be found at the following site: https://www.boe.es/boe/dias/2020/10/25/pdfs/BOE-A-2020-12898.pdf last accessed 30 September 2021. It should be noted that there has been another state of alarm, decreed on 9 October 2020, but which only affected some municipalities in the Autonomous

This work is part of the research project entitled "Human Rights in a multilevel scenario. Two examples: participation and privacy" (VA023G19), funded by the *Junta de Castilla y León* (Regional Government of Castilla and Leon).

A. I. D. Castrillo (✉)
Department of Constitutional Law, University of Valladolid, Valladolid, Spain
e-mail: andresivan.duenas@uva.es

J. M. Castellà Andreu, M. A. Simonelli (eds.), *Populism and Contemporary Democracy in Europe*,
https://doi.org/10.1007/978-3-030-92884-1_14

made possible by successive 15-day extensions (there were six in total), approved by the Congress of Deputies, or Lower House,[2] while the second state of alarm has a duration of six months thanks to a single extension, also ratified by the Congress of Deputies.[3] This chapter attempts to analyse parliamentary control over the duration of the state of alarm in Spain, specifically regarding the potentially excessive six-month extension during the second state.

The measures taken during both states of alarm that have restricted fundamental rights have highlighted the importance of legislative control over the executive branch even more. For this reason, Article 116 of the Spanish Constitution (hereafter, SC) establishes the key role of the Congress of Deputies in these situations, in addition to the impossibility of dissolving this Chamber during any of the states of alarm regulated in this precept, as well as the impossibility of modifying the principle of government accountability during such states.

In Spain, the Congress of Deputies is responsible for controlling both the substance and form of states, or situations, that are classified under the Law of Exception. The Constitution establishes predetermined time limits for a state of alarm and exception, and Congress itself is responsible for determining the duration of the most damaging of all, which is the state of siege. However, the second state of alarm, as indicated at the beginning, has been extended for six months by the Parliament[4] without the possibility of revoking this situation. Due to political negotiation, the parliamentary groups managed to at least introduce into the extension of the state of alarm greater scrutiny of the government's action to mitigate the pandemic during this time through the bi-monthly appearance of the President of the Government before the Plenary of Congress, together with another monthly appearance by the Minister of Health before the Health and Consumer Affairs Commission. However, in spite of such appearances, the six-month period might seem excessively long when it

Region of Madrid, and was only in force for 15 days: https://www.boe.es/buscar/doc.php?id=BOE-A-2020-12109 last accessed 30 September 2021.

[2] All of these, along with other regulations related to the pandemic, can be consulted in compilation of the following Official State Gazette: https://boe.es/biblioteca_juridica/codigos/codigo.php?id=355_COVID-19_Derecho_Europeo_y_Estatal__andtipo=Candmodo=1 last accessed 30 September 2021.

[3] The text of the extension is available at the following website: https://www.boe.es/diario_boe/txt.php?id=BOE-A-2020-13494 last accessed 30 September 2021.

[4] Throughout the entire text, Parliament is used as a synonym for the Congress of Deputies.

comes to measures that affect the foundation of various fundamental rights. Moreover, both national and regional governments are being granted much greater power to carry out such measures than would occur in a normal situation.

In short, the pandemic is fomenting many legal problems, which are being studied by the constitutional doctrine.[5] It would be impossible to explore each legal difficulty in a work of this nature. For this reason, in the following section an attempt will be made to look at one specific problem: the reaction of the various Parliaments during this time and, more specifically, whether the six-month extension of the second state of alarm in Spain due to COVID-19 might be unconstitutional.

2 Brief Notes Regarding the State of Alarm in Spain

The legal systems of most nations regulate the way in which they manage emergency situations through what is known as the Law of Exception. Article 116 of the Spanish Constitution addresses this issue, which provides for three different exceptional situations: alarm, exception, and siege. The historical antecedents of these regulations can be found in texts such as the English Riot Act, or in those referring to the French Revolution of 1789 (Fernández de Gatta Sánchez 2020, 5). In this way, constitutional systems aim to "react efficiently to the needs posed by a crisis without temporarily abrogating democracy or the rule of law", and as such, "neither the social, political, nor jurisdictional control of public authority should dissipate" (Aragón Reyes 2020a, 1).

Until the enactment of the 1978 Constitution, Spain had not established a procedure for this type of situation. In other countries, such as Italy, it was preferred that the Constitution should not expressly regulate these states of alarm, precisely because of the fear that power would be concentrated in the government in emergency situations, which had caused so much damage in the era of the Fascist dictatorship (Camoni Rodríguez 2021, 231).

The Venice Commission refers to states of emergency in three documents: the Compilation of Venice Commission Opinions and Reports on

[5] For all of the authors who have approached this topic, see the works of Biglino and Durán (eds.), *Los Efectos Horizontales de la COVID-19.*

States of Emergency (CDL-PI(2020)003)[6]; the Reflections about Respect for Democracy, Human Rights, and the Rule of Law during States of Emergency (CDL-PI(2020)005rev)[7]; and the Interim Report on the Measures Taken in EU Member States as a Result of the COVID-19 Crisis and their Impact on Democracy, the Rule of Law, and Fundamental Rights (CDL-AD(2020)018).[8] In these documents, the Commission mentions and reiterates the principles that should govern this type of state or situation: legality, necessity, and proportion in the strictest sense; the explicit nature of its proclamation and its exceptional aspect; and the Rule of Law principle, the provisional nature, as well as effective parliamentary control and scrutiny, among others (Castellà Andreu 2020, 13). In addition to these principles, it must not be forgotten that another inseparable feature of these types of rules is their provisional nature, or in other words, they are only valid as long as the circumstances that led to them continue to exist (Balaguer Callejón 2020, 132).

The response of the countries in the different Nations of the European Union has not been uniform. Some have opted to make use of these exceptional states regulated in their Constitutions. Others have chosen to make use of the legislation established for health care precautions. Still, others have opted to use ordinary legislation (Castellà Andreu 2020, 9).

Spain is in the first category. It has used its constitutionally mandated right of exception, as mentioned above, by declaring a state of alarm, which was intended for situations involving health crises, among others (Article 2 of Organic Law 4/1981, of 1 June, on states of alarm, exception, and siege—hereinafter, *LOAES*). Although not dealt with in this chapter, it bears mentioning that even though there has been scarce disagreement as to the appropriateness of declaring this particular state, given that there was no doubt that its *de facto* assumption had been fulfilled, there has been discussion as to whether the measures imposed during the

[6] https://www.venice.coe.int/webforms/documents/?pdf=CDL-PI(2020)003-e last accessed 30 September 2021.

[7] https://www.venice.coe.int/webforms/documents/?pdf=CDL-PI(2020)005rev-e last accessed 30 September 2021.

[8] https://www.venice.coe.int/webforms/documents/?pdf=CDL-AD(2020)018-e last accessed 30 September 2021.

first state of alarm entailed a limitation or suspension of fundamental rights, in which case a state of exception should have been declared.[9]

According to Biglino Campos,[10] it could be said that there have been three phases in Spain: the first phase of centralisation, with the initial state of alarm in which the government had sole command of the pandemic and centralised some of the powers of the Autonomous Regions between 14 March and 21 June, at which point the sixth extension of the state of alarm ceased to be in force; the second, which the author refers to as "coordination", is the phase in which the State continued to exercise its powers, but through the coordination function set out in Article 149.1.16 SC; finally, the third phase of "co-governance" has been in force since the second state of alarm was declared on 25 October due to the COVID-19 pandemic, with a six-month extension that has empowered regional governments to take measures restricting fundamental rights.

The state of alarm, according to the Constitutional Court itself, is the least intense (Solozábal Echavarría 2020, 2) state of crisis and has affirmed that the Royal Decree and its extensions have the force of law (STC 83/2016), which has led to other problems, such as the place occupied in the sources of law by regional governmental rules of a regulatory nature that impose measures restricting fundamental rights. In any case, the essence of the state of emergency in particular, and emergency law in general, is "to safeguard a minimum but irrefutable level of freedom and security which, despite the circumstances, is imposed on public authorities, so that in such a situation those in power have guidelines that go beyond being subjected to the dictates of saving the Nation at all costs" (Solozábal Echavarría 2020, 3). Nevertheless, what happens when there is improper use of these instruments and their appropriate parliamentary control is not guaranteed?

[9] See the doctrinal discussions that took place during the weeks in which the first state of emergency was in force. For all of the authors who have approached this topic, see Arroyo, *"Estado de alarma o estado de excepción"* (https://www.fundacionmgimenezabad.es/es/estado-de-alarma-o-estado-de-excepcion); or Aragón, "Hay que tomarse la Constitución en serio" (https://elpais.com/elpais/2020/04/09/opinion/1586420090_736317.html).

[10] Biglino, *El impacto de la COVID*, 7-10. Copy on loan from the author pending publication.

3 A Brief Overview of the Control Function of Parliament

Before fully delving into legislative control of the duration of the state of alarm, it is necessary to make several briefs, general comments on the current condition of Parliament's control function in the parliamentary form of government in general, and in Spain in particular.

Nowadays, citizens are the ones who are the focus of discussions in Parliament. They are the ones who must be persuaded and convinced, not the Congressional Members, as the latter have previously made their decision within their parliamentary groups. However, the most serious problem we currently find in the control function of Parliament is the way in which the parliamentary majority tends to act as a *steamroller*, to such an extent that on some occasions it could be said that the executive branch controls the opposition.[11] Although the current parliamentary structure in Spain has allowed the legislative branch to play a greater role due to the need to reach agreements in order to govern, the fact that the President of the Government is a figure above any other in our system has led some authors to describe the Spanish form of government as "presidential parliamentarianism" (Aragón Reyes 2002, 49).

Currently, a large part of this doctrine argues that inter-branch conflict has become obsolete, and it is better to speak of the relationship between the government and the opposition (Pegorario 2011, 549). Furthermore, authors such as Rubio Llorente have argued that the legislature exercises its control function in all of its activities beyond the instruments of control in the strictest sense of the word. For this reason, one must differentiate between control in Parliament and control by Parliament (Rubio Llorente 2012, 687).

In reality, the feeling at the present time is that parliamentary control is not efficient. Minority groups do not have real access to the instruments of governmental control, and it would be necessary to readjust such instruments to the new social realities of the Institution of Parliament (López Guerra 2002, 32). Moreover, the COVID-19 pandemic has not

[11] An example of this can be seen in the creation of the Parliamentary Commission of Inquiry into what is known as "*Operación Kitchen*". See also: Dueñas, *¿Comisiones de Investigación para controlar al Gobierno o a la oposición*?. Available at https://www.fundacionmgimenezabad.es/es/comisiones-de-investigacion-para-controlar-al-gobierno-o-la-oposicion last accessed 30 September 2021.

helped to improve this situation and has made it even more difficult for the opposition to scrutinise the government (Dueñas Castrillo 2019, 129).

4 Control of the Duration of the State of Alarm Extension in Spain

4.1 *The Reaction of the Various Parliaments and Control of the Duration During the First State of Alarm*

As noted in the introductory paragraphs, the first state of alarm was extended six times, always on a fortnightly (15-day) basis. The initial weeks of home confinement had important practical consequences for some Parliaments that did not have the tools to adapt to the new circumstances, with "their lack of foresight being compensated by a capability for resilience and transformation in the face of uncertainty" (Fernández Gutiérrez 2021, 63). In the beginning, the truth is that all of the Parliaments of Spain, both regional and national, decided to essentially stop their activity, because they understood that their functioning was directly affected by the health decisions that had been adopted (Tudela Aranda 2020, 7). In other words, the crisis caused by COVID-19 resulted in "a disruption of the normal functioning of Parliament, together with a possibly notorious limitation of Article 23 of the Constitution", which could have affected our form of government· Thereafter, they gradually resumed their activity through various measures that bear mentioning at this point.

There were two main groups among the various Parliaments during the first state of alarm, as García-Escudero has pointed out: those who decided to suspend the session or resort to Permanent Deputation, and those who decided to maintain their activity in a reduced way, sometimes using telematic instruments (García-Escudero Márquez 2020, 277). Starting with the former, Permanent Deputation, this solution is arguably the one most open to criticism.[12] The Spanish legal system established this

[12] In some Parliaments, such as that of Andalusia, the Permanent Deputation approved decree-laws that modified more than 20 existing laws. Recently, the Constitutional Court has admitted an appeal on the grounds of unconstitutionality denouncing this practice: https://www.elconfidencial.com/espana/andalucia/2021-01-27/tc-admite-recurso-psoe-diputacion-permanente_2925315/?utm_source=twitterandutm_medium=socialandutm_campaign=ECDiarioManual last accessed 30 September 2021.

institution in order to maintain the continuity of the Legislative Assembly in times of parliamentary inactivity. Its main function is to safeguard the powers of the Chamber, or in other words, it has "the function of safeguarding the integrity of the Constitution and of managing those situations which endanger the powers of Parliament" (Mellado Prado 1988, 71). This body replaces the plenary only when it is unable to meet, which is why it has minimal functions, and this can occur in two cases: during periods when Parliament is not in its usual session and when its mandate has expired (Seseña Santos 2016, 224). Therefore, the controversy revolves around the question of "whether the Permanent Deputation can be summoned in a situation such as the one that has currently been unfolding, in the absence of a specific rule, and by applying a dubious analogy" (García-Escudero Márquez 2020, 288.). There is no provision for the Permanent Deputation to meet in the event of a pandemic such as the one currently taking place, although it is true that this could guarantee a minimum involvement of the parliamentary institution "in those situations in which withdrawal, even temporary, places excessive power in the hands of the Executive branch, and in those situations in which without the exercise of such power the functioning of the system as a whole would be disrupted" (Mellado Prado 1988, 49).

Another of the solutions adopted by regional Parliaments has been the delegation of votes, which is equally controversial as, if not more so than, the use of Permanent Deputation. Some authors have supported the possibility of introducing it at the regional level, given the fact that among other reasons, the personal nature and non-delegable feature of the vote is only intended for Congressional Deputies and Senators in Article 79.3 SC (Presno Linera and Ortega Santiago 2009). However, it has also been stated that this does not prevent the solution from being applied to regional members of Parliament as well, as this is one characteristic of our model of representative democracy that also affects the regional Parliaments (De Miguel Bárcena 2010, 150). The same criticism can be applied to another measure adopted in some assemblies: weighted voting (Fernández de Simón Bermejo 2020, 152).[13]

[13] This measure was adopted in the Murcia Regional Parliament and has been defended by some authors, given that with this solution, "in no case would there be an alteration in the results of the votes, and these would always be in accordance with the composition of the Chamber and the majorities formed on each occasion".

Voting that is not in-person, or telematic voting, has been one of the least damaging options for guaranteeing the *ius in officium* of Members of Parliament. This is the solution that was adopted by the Congress of Deputies and the Senate, as well as by some regional assemblies after the first weeks of confinement. Earlier, the Bureau of the Congress of Deputies had stopped counting parliamentary deadlines, and its activity was reduced to a minimum for one month after the first state of alarm extension had expired. Precisely as a result of the need to authorise extensions, the activity of the Plenary was reactivated, always in a limited format, but maintaining the parliamentary presence and immediacy that the Constitutional Court has emphasised in recent decisions (SSTC 19/2019 and 45/2019) (García-Escudero Márquez 2020, 299). The Plenary Sittings also validated numerous decrees/laws, and the ordinary control sessions resumed on 15 April, allowing the government to give an account of its activity during the first state of alarm. It could be said that successive authorised extensions (even though support for such extensions diminished during the last few) represented an endorsement by Parliament of the government's measures against the pandemic.

In any case, two distinct moments can be discerned in the control function of the government during the first state of alarm caused by COVID-19. The first moment occurred when the Congressional Bureau decided to suspend plenary sessions, although they continued to be held for the exclusive purpose of authorising extensions of the state of alarm (the first two) and for the validation of decrees-laws involving specific measures against the pandemic. The second moment was the lifting of the suspension of time limits (approximately from mid-April 2020 onwards), which, as mentioned above, led to the return to ordinary control sessions. In any case, the capability of the Spanish Parliament to control the government was affected, especially at the most critical moments of the pandemic (Dueñas Castrillo 2020). In other words, there was "a paradox in the sense that when faced with greater executive power, there was a kind of parliamentary vacuum, at least initially, as the function of guidance and control partly disappeared".

The most significant problem in terms of controlling the duration of the state of alarm at this early stage was when the government announced in mid-May of 2020 that it was seeking authorisation for a final extension of the state of alarm for 30 days instead of 15, as had been the case up to that point. The aim was precisely to avoid the stumbling block of coming to Congress every 15 days at the very moment when the government's parliamentary support was at its lowest. The fear that no further extensions would be authorised led to this announcement, yet in the end it was not carried out. In other words, the executive branch was tempted to bypass Parliament, which was an attempt to evade the compulsory control that had to be carried out, and has become effective with the six-month extension of the second state of alarm.

4.2 *The Excessive Six-Month Extension of the Second State of Alarm*

In preceding sections, it has been clearly pointed out that activation of the Law of Exception has significantly strengthened the position of the government, "because the purpose is undoubtedly to give it the power to be the body that makes the decisions demanded by the circumstances promptly and in the most decisive manner possible" (Solozábal Echavarría 2020, 4). However, this "change in the institutional functioning of the State does not imply the absence of political responsibility of the authorities, nor their legal exemption, and in a constitutional State there is no bill of indemnity that ensures immunity of public authorities for their actions during exceptional periods" (Solozábal Echavarría 2020, 4). As previously pointed out, this is expressly stated in Article 116, sections five and six, of the Spanish Constitution. However, it has been observed in the analysis herein that the position of Parliament was affected during the first state of alarm and, as discussed below, during the second as well. Moreover, this has also been the case in other European countries where the legislative branch has played a very minor role. Some examples include Italy (Mastromarino 2020, 8), the United Kingdom (Sánchez Ferro 2020), and France (Alcaraz 2020, 13), or the highly controversial case of Hungary, where the government has taken advantage of the pandemic to introduce measures restricting fundamental rights without respecting the sources of law and restricting the powers of Parliament (Barroso Márquez 2021, 266-267).

In the specific case of the second state of alarm, the Council of Ministers of 27 October 2020 agreed to request a six-month extension from the Congress of Deputies, which the latter authorised on 29 October 2020 with the support of 194 deputies in favour, 99 abstentions, and 53 votes against the extension. Therefore, the executive branch gained broad support in the Congress of Deputies and achieved its objective. However, the duration of this extension has created numerous constitutional problems.

First of all, it should be noted that this time limit raises problems of admissibility in the light of the Venice Commission's approach, which states the following:

The longer the emergency regime lasts, the further the state is likely to move away from the objective criteria that may have validated the use of emergency powers in the first place. The longer the situation persists, the lesser justification there is for treating a situation as exceptional in nature with the consequence that it cannot be addressed by application of normal legal tools.[14]

Article 116, section two, of the Spanish Constitution simply establishes that a state of alarm shall be decreed by the government for a maximum period of 15 days, and the government must inform the Congress of Deputies of this act. Moreover, "this period may not be extended without the authorisation of the Congress of Deputies". With the approval of the extension, there is an "*ad extra* formalisation of the prior authorisation of the Congress of Deputies, either (...) by endorsing government proposals in the request for an extension, or by establishing them directly" (Solozábal Echavarría 2020, 15). Just like the decree declaring the state of alarm, the parliamentary authorisation also has the value, or rank, of a law (ATC 7/2012, FJ 4).

As some authors have pointed out, it is true that neither the Constitution nor the *LOAES* (Organic Law of Alarm, Exception and Siege) contains a provision preventing the extension of the state of alarm for more than 15 days (Arroyo 2020b). However, it is no less true that if a literal, systematic, and teleological interpretation of the Constitution is carried out and, furthermore, if it is taken into account that the activation of the state of alarm is capable of granting "immense, uncontrolled power to the National Government, which can assume the powers of any authority" (Álvarez 2002, 34), the six-month extension of the state of alarm might be an infringement of the constitutional mandate.

It should also be noted that in the parliamentary form of government, Parliament must be the central institution of the system, which must oversee the actions taken by the executive branch. It has already been mentioned above that Article 116.6 of the Spanish Constitution stipulates that

[14] CDL-AD(2020)018-e, *Interim report on the measures taken in the EU member States as a result of the COVID-19 crisis and their impact on democracy, the Rule of Law and Fundamental Rights*, adopted by the Venice Commission at its 124th online Plenary Session (8-9 October 2020), para. 51.

the declaration of any of the exceptional states regulated in this precept shall not modify the principle of government responsibility. Therefore, as Arroyo Gil contends, such a long extension might seem to be outside the spirit of our constitution, insofar as the Law of Exception must be interpreted restrictively, and this implies a significant alteration of the normal functioning of public powers, even if the state of alarm ends up lasting the entire period, but with successive authorisations for extensions approved by the Congress of Deputies, as happened between March and June.[15]

There are other arguments for concluding that the six-month extension is unconstitutional. According to Aragón Reyes, the maximum period for authorisation of an extension is 15 days for several reasons. First, because the provision is literal. Article 116.2 of the Spanish Constitution stipulates that a state of alarm decreed by the government for a period of 15 days may be extended for the same period of time, which "can only refer to the period already set by the decree, insofar as extending it means, in essence, repeating it, as opposed to extending it". Second, an authorised extension is set at 15 days due to the aim of the provision, or in other words, "to ensure the periodic intervention of Congress by authorising the extension, so as to ensure that Congress exercises its own control over the extension (and possible future extensions)". For this reason, the Constitution establishes a guarantee that the Congress must intervene every 15 days so that the decision regarding the extension is not left in the hands of the majority in the Lower House, because "the minority would then be prevented from exercising its right to parliamentary control, and the public would be denied knowledge of the debate" on the extension. Moreover, this author points out that such parliamentary intervention is not only intended to hold the government accountable for its actions during this period, but for the Lower House "to be periodically involved in the co-decision on the prolongation of the state of alarm", thereby exercising a control/sanction function regarding whether or not to authorise an extension.[16]

In addition to the above, Parliament's own control would make it possible to examine whether the factual assumption that led to the declaration of the state of alarm still exists, or whether the situation in the specific case of the pandemic has changed, and therefore whether the same measures should continue, or if other measures should be taken, either more or less

[15] Arroyo, *¿Estado de alarma sin control?*.

[16] All citations are taken from: Aragón Reyes, *La prórroga del estado de alarma*.

restrictive,[17] or even whether the state of alarm should only apply to part of the national territory. The six-month extension of the second state of alarm prevents these debates from taking place and does not allow Parliament to make such decisions. However, the State of Alarm Decree itself, in its first final provision, has established that the government "may issue successive decrees modifying the provisions of this decree, of which it will have to report to the Congress of Deputies in accordance with the provisions of Article 8.2 of Organic Law 4/1981, of the 1st of June". What the architects of this regulation have forgotten is that Article 6, section two, of the *LOAES* stipulates that the Congress of Deputies is the only body empowered to "establish the scope and conditions in force during the extension" and that under no circumstances can the government unilaterally modify the extension decree without the authorisation of Parliament. In short, according to Álvarez García, with the decree of the second state of alarm, the national government might be able to modify the measures established therein without Congress having retained for itself any capacity for political control, so the government does not need the authorisation of Congress to adopt measures that are even more restrictive, such as total home confinement (Álvarez García 2020).

Regarding the extension period, it has also been argued that its maximum limit could be 30 days instead of 15 if a systematic interpretation of Article 116, Sections two and three, of the Spanish Constitution was conducted, whereby the state of alarm could not be extended beyond the 30 days established as the maximum (Arroyo 2020). Furthermore, it has been argued that the extension of the only state of alarm that had been declared prior to the pandemic (Royal Decree 1717/2010 of 17 December) was for 30 days, yet it is no less true that "past unconstitutionality can never serve to remedy future unconstitutionality" (Aragón Reyes 2020b).

Although the following comments are outside the scope of this study, it is important to mention briefly another serious problem with regard to parliamentary control that the second state of alarm has generated, which is the control of the measures restricting fundamental rights that is being carried out. As mentioned above, the State of Alarm Decree and its successive extensions have the status of law and can be appealed before the Constitutional Court. This is consistent with our sources of law if we take into account that it may affect fundamental rights, which can only be

[17] This problem has been seen when several Autonomous Regions have requested to set the curfew earlier or called for confinement of their citizens.

regulated by law. However, the second State of Alarm Decree, which designates the Presidents of the Autonomous Regions (and Autonomous Cities) as the "delegated authority" (Article 2), allows them to take measures restricting fundamental rights through regulatory rules, which cannot be controlled by the Congress of Deputies and which cannot be overturned by the regional Parliaments, as they are provisions without the status of law, which constitutes a possible alteration of our sources of law and an avoidance of the parliamentary control that these types of provisions must have.[18]

5 Conclusions

The Spanish legal system is among those that chosen to have their Constitution regulate the cases in which the Law of Exception should be declared. Article 116 of the Spanish Constitution regulates states of alarm, exception, and siege. The first of these is implemented during health crises, which is why it has been established twice so far during the pandemic and has been in force throughout the country. Its proclamation can initially be made unilaterally by the government, but within a maximum period of 15 days the Congress of Deputies must authorise its extension for it to remain in force. This ensures Parliament's control over an act, which has actually occurred, that can give great power to governments and allow them to establish measures restricting fundamental rights.

The first state of alarm involved house confinement in the first weeks of the pandemic, which disrupted the normal functioning of the institutions. The various Spanish Parliaments reacted in different ways to this situation. In fact, in the beginning they were not even able to continue their activity. The Congress of Deputies managed to meet and adopt exceptional measures during the first month of confinement, due to the mandatory action to authorise 15-day extensions of the state of alarm. From mid-April of 2020 onwards, it managed to resume its usual control sessions, and a total of six extensions were finally authorised, all for a period of 15 days.

[18] One example is the unilateral curfew in the Autonomous Region of *Castilla y León*, which was set to an earlier time of 8 p.m. and remained in force for about one month without the regional parliament being able to avoid it, until the Order of the High Court of Justice of *Castilla y León* overturned this measure on 16 February 2021 for infringing on the provisions of the State of Alarm Decree, which stipulates that the curfew cannot be imposed earlier than 10 p.m.

The situation in the second state of alarm was different. Only a single six-month extension has been authorised, raising doubts about its constitutionality. A possible interpretation that is literal, teleological, and systematic regarding the Constitution suggests that this period of time is excessive and contrary to the Supreme Constitutional Rule, even more so when a changing scenario is being regulated and when the executive branch (both state and regional) exercises much greater power than in a normal situation and is taking measures that affect fundamental rights through infra-legal norms.

All of the above makes it possible to speak of a headlong rush forward by governments away from the political controls inherent in any democratic state governed by the Rule of Law. This parliamentary control, which had already been weakened, has now become even weaker at the precise moment it is most needed.

Now more than ever, the need for a Parliament must be defended, for it is nothing less than a demonstration of our commitment to constitutional democracy and political pluralism. In terms of democracy, the actions of today may be mirrors that are dangerous to gaze at in the future when new crises require the adoption of exceptional measures.

Bibliography

Alcaraz, Hubert. "El estado de emergencia sanitaria en Francia". In *Los Efectos Horizontales de la COVID-19 sobre el sistema constitucional: estudios sobre la primera oleada*, edited by Paloma Biglino Campos and Juan Fernando Durán Alba, 523-543. Zaragoza: Fundación Manuel Giménez Abad, 2020.

Álvarez García, Vicente J. "El comportamiento del Derecho de crisis durante la segundo ola de la pandemia." *El Cronista del Estado Social y Democrático de Derecho*, no. 90-91 (2020): 26-41.

Aragón Reyes, Manuel. "¿Un parlamentarismo presidencialista?" *Claves de Razón Práctica*, no. 123 (2002): 42-49.

Aragón Reyes, Manuel. "COVID-19: aproximación constitucional a una crisis". *Revista General de Derecho Constitucional*, no. 32 (2020a): 1-5.

Aragón Reyes, Manuel. "Hay que tomarse la Constitución en serio." *El País*, 10 April, (2020b). https://elpais.com/elpais/2020/04/09/opinion/1586420090_736317.html.

Aragón Reyes, Manuel. "La prórroga del estado de alarma." *El País*, 28 October (2020c), https://elpais.com/opinion/2020-10-28/la-prorroga-del-estado-de-alarma.html.

Arroyo Gil, Antonio. "¿Estado de alarma o estado de excepción?". *Fundación Manuel Giménez Abad*, 1 May, (2020a), https://www.fundacionmgimenez-abad.es/es/estado-de-alarma-o-estado-de-excepcion.

Arroyo Gil, Antonio. "¿Estado de alarma sin control?" *Agenda Pública,* October 28, 2020b, https://agendapublica.es/estado-de-alarma-sin-control/.

Balaguer Callejón, Francisco. "Crisis sanitaria y Derecho Constitucional." *Teoría y Realidad Constitucional*, no. 46 (2020): 121-140.

Barroso Márquez, Juan Francisco. "Estado de Derecho, iliberalismo y poderes de emergencia: oportunismo político en Hungría". In *La Constitución en tiempos de pandemia*, edited by Andrés Iván Dueñas Castrillo, Daniek Fernández Cañueto, Pablo Guerrero Vázquez and Gabriel Moreno Gonzalez, 257-278. Madrid: Dykinson-Universidad de Valladolid, 2021.

Camoni Rodríguez, Daniel. "COVID-19 y fuentes del Derecho en Italia: una complicada perspectiva de Derecho Constitucional." In *La Constitución en tiempos de pandemia*, edited by Andrés Iván Dueñas Castrillo, Daniek Fernández Cañueto, Pablo Guerrero Vázquez and Gabriel Moreno Gonzalez, 33-256. Madrid: Dykinson-Universidad de Valladolid, 2021.

Castellà Andreu, Josep María. "La Comisión de Venecia y los estados de emergencia: la necesaria preservación del Estado de Derecho y la democracia constitucional durante la crisis de la COVID-19". In *Los Efectos Horizontales de la COVID-19 sobre el sistema constitucional: estudios sobre la primera oleada*, edited by Paloma Biglino Campos and Juan Fernando Durán Alba, 437-464. Zaragoza: Fundación Manuel Giménez Abad, 2020.

De Miguel Bárcena, Josu. "La personalidad e indelegabilidad del voto y las reformas de los reglamentos de los Parlamentos autonómicos." *Revista Española de Derecho Constitucional*, no. 90 (2010): 149-169.

Dueñas Castrillo, Andrés Iván. "El necesario control al Gobierno. Un análisis en el nuevo escenario autonómico tras las elecciones de mayo de 2015." *Revista de Derecho Político,* no. 104 (2019): 117-155. https://doi.org/10.5944/rdp.104.2019.24311

Dueñas Castrillo, Andrés Iván. "Las relaciones Parlamento-Gobierno durante el estado de alarma por COVID-19". In *Los Efectos Horizontales de la COVID-19 sobre el sistema constitucional: estudios sobre la primera oleada*, edited by Paloma Biglino Campos and Juan Fernando Durán Alba,43-57. Zaragoza: Fundación Manuel Giménez Abad, 2020.

Fernández de Gatta Sánchez, Dionisio. "El Estado de alarma en España por la pandemia del coronavirus y sus problemas constitucionales legales." *Ars Iuris Salmanticensis*, no. 33 (2020): 27-40.

Fernández de Simón Bermejo, Encarnación. "La actuación de la Asamblea Regional de Murcia desde la declaración del estado de alarma por la crisis sanitaria provocada por el COVID-19." *Cuadernos Manuel Giménez Abad,* no. 8 (2020): 147-154.

Fernández Gutiérrez, Marco. "El Parlamento ante la COVID-19." In *La Constitución en tiempos de pandemia*, edited by Andrés Iván Dueñas Castrillo, Daniek Fernández Cañueto, Pablo Guerrero Vázquez and Gabriel Moreno Gonzalez, 63-82. Madrid: Dykinson-Universidad de Valladolid, 2021.

García-Escudero Márquez, Piedad. "La ductilidad del Derecho Parlamentario en tiempos de crisis: actividad y funcionamiento de los Parlamentos durante el estado de alarma por COVID-19." *Teoría y Realidad Constitucional*, no. 46 (2020): 271-308.

López Guerra, Luis. "Organización y funcionamiento del Parlamento del futuro". In *El Parlamento del Siglo XXI. VIII Jornadas de la Asociación Española de Letrados de Parlamentos*, edited by Francesc Pau i Vall, 29-43. Valencia: Tecnos, 2002.

Mastromarino, Anna. "La respuesta a la emergencia COVID-19: el caso italiano". In *Los Efectos Horizontales de la COVID-19 sobre el sistema constitucional: estudios sobre la primera oleada*, edited by Paloma Biglino Campos and Juan Fernando Durán Alba, 545-566. Zaragoza: Fundación Manuel Giménez Abad, 2020.

Mellado Prado, Pilar. "El problema de la continuidad del Parlamento: la Diputación Permanente." *Revista de Derecho Político*, no. 27-28 (1988): 45-75.

Pegorario, Lucio. *Derecho constitucional comparado*. Bogotá: Universidad Libre de Colombia, 2011.

Presno Linera, Miguel y Ortega Santiago, Carlos. *La sustitución temporal de los representantes políticos*. Madrid: Centro de Estudios Políticos y Constitucionales, 2009.

Rubio Llorente, Francisco. *La forma del poder. Estudios sobre la Constitución*. Madrid: Centro de Estudios Políticos y Constitucionales, 2012.

Sánchez Ferro, Susana. "La respuesta británica frente a la crisis desatada por la COVID-19." In *Los Efectos Horizontales de la COVID-19 sobre el sistema constitucional: estudios sobre la primera oleada*, edited by Paloma Biglino Campos and Juan Fernando Durán Alba,487-522. Zaragoza: Fundación Manuel Giménez Abad, 2020.

Seseña Santos, Laura. "El Pleno y la Diputación Permanente." In *Manual AELPA del Parlamentario*, edited by Xosé Anton Sarmiento Méndez, 145-186. Madrid: AELPA-Wolters Kluwer, 2016.

Solozábal Echavarría, Juan José. "Algunas consideraciones generales sobre el estado de alarma." In *Los Efectos Horizontales de la COVID-19 sobre el sistema constitucional: estudios sobre la primera oleada*, edited by Paloma Biglino Campos and Juan Fernando Durán Alba, 19-43. Zaragoza: Fundación Manuel Giménez Abad, 2020.

Tudela Aranda, José. "Parlamento y crisis sanitaria." In *Cuadernos Manuel Giménez Abad*, no. 8 (2020): 6-17.

“To Watch and Control the Government”. ‘Rediscovering’ Parliaments’ Oversight Function

Marco Antonio Simonelli

1 Introduction

The COVID-19 triggered a wide academic and political debate about its impact on constitutional democracy, and in particular on how parliaments have been marginalised during the crisis.[1] As a matter of fact, the management of the pandemic and of its economic and social consequences has been dominated by national governments (Bar-Siman Tov 2020, 12). In principle this situation is nor new—emergency situations have always been

[1] In the academic literature see amongst many: Griglio, *Parliamentary oversight under the Covid-19 emergency*, 52; Windholz, *Governing in a pandemic*, 93-113. Concerning political reactions see: European Parliament, *Resolution of 13 November 2020 on the impact of COVID-19 measures on democracy, the rule of law and fundamental rights* (2020/2790(RSP)), P9_TA(2020)0307.

M. A. Simonelli (✉)
University of Barcelona, Barcelona, Spain
e-mail: m.a.simonelli@ub.edu

J. M. Castellà Andreu, M. A. Simonelli (eds.), *Populism and Contemporary Democracy in Europe*,
https://doi.org/10.1007/978-3-030-92884-1_15

dealt with by governments—neither worrying, as "[t]he concept of emergency rule is founded on the assumption that in certain situations of political, military and economic emergency, the system of limitations of constitutional government has to give way before the increased power of the executive".[2] Far from being an isolated and temporally limited phenomenon, the marginalisation of parliaments during the pandemic has to be seen as the last episode of a long-standing evolutionary trend of constitutional democracy, which sees parliaments sidelined in their traditional role of legislators.

Besides, in the last two decades, two intertwined threats have accelerated and exacerbated this trend, menacing the role and the legitimacy of legislatures. First, the expansion of executives functions beyond the boundaries fixed by the constitution, which is reducing parliaments to mere validators of governmental actions. Second, of course, populism. In its quest for a direct relationship with the 'true people', populist parties disregard any form of intermediation between the leader and his people, above all parliaments. Consequently, when they are in power, parliaments are gradually hollowed out of any meaningful powers *vis-à-vis* a strong unaccountable executive.

Against this backdrop, the present chapter tries to identify, by analysing the parliaments' reactions to executives' dominance during the COVID-19 emergency, possible solutions to reinstate parliaments at the centre of the political system. In particular, it argues that the loss of law-making functions may be at least partially compensated by an alternative—but not less important—function: overseeing executive's actions. After all, as John Stuart Mill famously affirmed in 1861 "the proper office of a representative assembly is to watch and control the government" (Stuart Mill, 1861).

In order to reach this stated aim, the chapter will proceed in the following order. Section 2 sets the background of the chapter, explaining why legislatures are not going to regain a prominent role in the production of norms. Section 3 illustrates how executives' aggrandisement and populism have contributed to opening a crisis in the mechanisms of constitutional democracy and explains why strengthening the oversight function of parliament can represent a remedy. In Section 4 the reaction of parliaments to

[2] CDL-AD(2020)018 *Interim Report on the measures taken in the EU Member States as a result of the COVID-19 crisis and their impact on democracy, the rule of law, and fundamental rights,* adopted by the Venice Commission at its 124th online Plenary Session (8-9 October 2020), para. 19.

executive dominance during the pandemic will be analysed, with a special focus on the Italian and Spanish parliaments. Section 5 identifies which of these reactions may provide some solutions to the challenges posed by populism to contemporary democracy and concludes.

Before embarking on this task, a few brief methodological premises are necessary. First, in the context of this chapter when we refer to the crisis of representative democracy, we are pointing to a set of concurring factors that reduced parliamentary policy-making power, defined as the formal ability of parliaments to legislate and to constraint executive rule making (Mezey 1979, 23). To put it otherwise, in the following pages the crisis of representative democracy will be considered only through the prism of the parliament-government relationship. Second, the solutions that will be presented at the end of this chapter only refer to parliamentary systems, that is, for systems in which exists a relationship of confidence between the parliament and the executive.

2 The Role of the Parliament in Contemporary Constitutional Democracy

In the traditional notion of separation of powers the government's essential function is 'executing' the laws approved by the parliament. The parliament is to be the sole bearer of legislative powers, and any involvement of the government in the legislative process is considered unnecessary (Montesquieu, 1748, 405). Yet, this notion has long lost its validity.

All democratic constitutions of the twentieth century indeed recognise a prominent role for the government in law-making. Governments in situations of extraordinary urgency and necessity are empowered to adopt law decrees;[3] they can receive a delegation from the parliament to adopt norms having force of law to regulate highly technical and complex matters;[4] and government legislative initiative receives a preferential treatment in the rules of procedure of many European parliaments.[5] Actually, a rapid comparative overview of executives' legislative powers in European

[3] See: Article 77(1) Italian Constitution; Article 86 Spanish Constitution. A relevant exception is France, as the 1958 Constitution, contrary to the two preceding constitutions (those of 1870 and 1946), does not empower the government to adopt law decrees.

[4] See: Article 76 Italian Constitution; Article 82 Spanish Constitution.

[5] For a comparative overview: Vintzel, *Les armes du gouvernement dans la procédure législative. Etude comparée: Allemagne, France, Italie, Royaume-Uni.*

constitutions allows to safely conclude that in contemporary constitutional democracy the government is not intended to be a mere executer of parliamentary laws, as it was in the nineteenth-century liberal state (Fabbrini and Vassallo 1999).

Having said that, it would be misleading to explain the sidelining of legislatures with exclusive reference to the increased role of executives in the production of norms, as also the judiciary invaded the space once reserved to parliamentary law. Immediately after WWII, many European States reacted to the failure of parliamentary regimes in preventing descent into totalitarianism by introducing a more sophisticated version of the rule of law (Pinelli 2011, 13), characterised by the introduction of a strong counter-majoritarian power: a constitutional court empowered to carry out judicial review of legislation. This model, referred to as democratic constitutional state, was so successful that, during the second half of the twentieth century, European constitutional judges started to shape legal systems on an equal footing with the legislative and executive powers, assuming a role of negative legislators.[6] Nevertheless, some authors, especially from north-American scholarship, maintained a critical stance towards this shift of power from democratically elected parliaments to unelected, unaccountable, judges, fearing that an excessive judicial activism may end up eroding the democratic component of constitutional democracy (Hirschl 2007). To some extent, the declining role of parliaments as legislator goes hand in hand with the empowering of constitutional courts as negative legislators.

A third element concurring to determine the declining role of legislatives is the rise of the s.c. 'technocratic governance' (Vibert 2007). Lacking electoral incentives to pursuing long-term policies, political majorities preferred to delegate to experts and technicians regulatory competences in a vast array of field (Pinelli 2011, 13), from media law to the regulation of financial markets. These bodies, albeit being created within the executive, enjoy a certain degree of autonomy from both the government and the parliament, and allow for an expertise-based regulation.[7] Yet, this solution ended up negatively affecting the representative dimension of democracy,

[6] To a point that the twentieth century has also been dubbed the 'century of constitutional justice', in contrast with the nineteenth century usually considered the parliaments' century. See: Groppi, *Riformare la giustizia costituzionale*, 37.

[7] Extensively on the European model of independent authority see: De Somer, *Autonomous Public Bodies and the Law. A European Perspective,* in particular, 1-22.

as it has further reduced the scope for parliamentary law-making, letting unelected experts rule.

Finally, also the opening of contemporary democracies towards international law has multiplied the number of actors involved in law-making processes at different levels governance, probably ending once for all the centrality of statute law (Corkin 2013). To this regard, it should not be obliterated that also EU Membership contributes to marginalise the role of parliaments in the constitutional system. First and foremost because many legislative competences have been transferred to the EU, so that national legislation is pre-empted in these fields, and second because executives are government's ministers who represent national interests in the EU institutions, whereas national parliaments have little or no say at all (Ragone 2020, 150).

Ultimately, it seems evident that the diminishing role of parliaments in the production of norms is not a transitory phenomenon; rather it constitutes a long-lasting evolutionary trend of contemporary democracy, according to which legislatures have been conceding more and more powers to governments, judges, and experts (Loughlin 2019, 443). Nevertheless, it is not possible to overlook that the legislature's position in the political system has weakened up to a point that the very functioning of representative democracy is called into question.[8] It is therefore necessary to investigate the factors that have opened up the crisis of parliaments.

3 Are Parliaments in Crisis?

At this point, it is necessary to go back to the beginning of this chapter and illustrate the two factors that are altering the delicate equilibrium of contemporary constitutional democracy.

First, the relegation of parliaments to a subordinate position to executives aggrandising well beyond the boundaries fixed by the constitution. A common feature of all European democracies—emerged in all its evidence during the pandemic (Ginsburg and Versteeg 2021, 4-5)—is in the executive dominance within national legal systems (Loughlin 2019, 435). The increased technical complexity of societal problems and the necessity of

[8] For a comparative overview of legislatives' decline in Europe see: Khmelko, Stapenhurst, and Mezey (eds) *Legislative Decline in the 21st Century. A Comparative Perspective*. The decline of parliament as the main norm-producer is also considered a part of a more general crisis of representative democracy as a whole. For a wide-ranging analysis of the crisis of representative democracy see: Dahrendorf, *Después de la democracia*; Tudela Aranda, Castellà, Exposito, Kölling (eds), *Libro blanco sobre la calidad democrática en España*.

providing rapid answers to issues arising ever more rapidly appear to have rendered statute law radically unfit as an instrument to regulate public life. As a matter of fact, since at least 9/11, Europeans have been living in what has been called a permanent state of emergency (Agamben 2003, 12-13), characterised by a reduction of parliamentary activity to a mere endorsement of governments' actions to deal with collective threats; first terrorism, then the economic crisis, and now the pandemic.

This phenomenon has manifested itself with particular evidence in Italy and Spain where, in the last two decades—and especially after the economic crisis of 2010 (Longo 2017; De La Iglesia Chamarro 2013)—the governments have frequently used their power to adopt law decrees in absence of a real urgency,[9] creating a situation of an apparently 'endless emergency' (Simoncini 2006; Agamben 2003). Looking at the bigger picture, however, also this tendency is part of a global trend, according to which decision-making powers are transferred to executives (Curtin 2014, 3). Nevertheless, this transferral blurs electoral accountability and democratic control, opening up a creep that threatens to hollow out the parliament of any meaningful power (Mair 2013).

Second, in this already troublesome setting, during the last decade populism made its appearance on the scene as a major factor of disruption in European democracies.[10] In its most commonly accepted notion, populism is an ideology that considers society to be ultimately separated into two homogeneous and antagonistic groups, 'the pure people' and 'the corrupt elite' (Mudde 2004, 543). The supposed aim of populist movement is to enhance the representativeness of the constitutional system as a whole and reaffirm the centrality of popular will, which they claim to embody (Castellà 2020, 4). Once on power populists usually claim that the parliament is the sole legitimate authority to be obeyed in a democracy, an authority which is conceived fundamentally as free from any legal constraint. Therefore, the natural target of populist parties are counter-majoritarian institutions, above all judges.

Hence, at least from a theoretical point of view, one should expect a strengthening of the parliament's position once a populist majority reaches

[9] For Italy see amongst many: Piergigli, *Le Regole della produzione normativa*; For Spain: Carmona Contreras, *Articulo 86*, 1277-1287.

[10] For a critical comparative overview of the impact of populism see: C. Mudde C. and C. Rovira Kaltwasser C. (eds), *Populism in Europe and the America. Threat or Corrective for Democracy*?, (Cambridge, CUP, 2012).

the power, and many authors have actually tried to consider populism as a corrective for representative democracy (Mudde and Cristóbal 2012). Against the above-mentioned tendency, according to which parliaments have been conceding more and more powers to unelected bodies, populism could indeed function as a corrector, by reaffirming the principle of representation and thus the centrality of the parliament.

At a closer analysis, however, things are not all like this.[11] In its quest for a direct relationship with the 'true people', populist parties disregard any form of intermediation between the leader and the people, above all parliaments. This implies that, at least in a first phase,[12] populist parties tend to advocate for an extensive use of referenda and other instruments of direct democracy, thus contributing to the marginalisation of parliaments in decision-making processes. Also, thanks to the opportunities offered by social media, the populist leader can communicate directly with his/her people, making parliaments superfluous as a forum for debate.[13] Finally, empirical evidences suggest that all forms of populism have in common a reluctancy to accept any constraint on executive actions, thereby including those imposed by the legislature (Mudde 2007).

In practice, this attitude has been translated into legal reforms aimed either at downsizing parliaments, like it happened in Italy,[14] where the

[11] It has also been suggested that the emergence of populist parties may function as a corrective to democracy, but when those parties reach the power, they become a threat. See: Ruth, "Populism and the Erosion of Horizontal Accountability in Latin America," 358.

[12] As Isaiah Berlin has observed, after a first phase in which the people are continuously interrogated with referenda about his will, a second phase follows in which the populist leader affirms to know the will of his people without the need of consulting him. See: Berlin, *To define populism*, 143.

[13] It is interesting to note that already in 1935 Walter Benjamin saw this trend coming: '[s]ince the innovations of camera and recording equipment make it possible for the orator to become audible and visible to an unlimited number of persons, the presentation of the man of politics before camera and recording equipment becomes paramount. Parliaments, as much as theaters, are deserted'. See: Benjamin, *The Work of Art in the Age of Mechanical Reproduction*, 23-24. Available at: https://web.mit.edu/allanmc/www/benjamin.pdf.

[14] Similar proposals have been presented both in France and in Spain. In the political programme of the right-wing populist *Rassemblement National*, the downsizing of both the lower and upper houses of the French parliament is one of the 144 commitments that Marine Le Pen assumed for the 2022 presidential elections. See: https://rassemblementnational.fr/pdf/144-engagements.pdf. In Spain, the right-wing populist party Vox together with the Popular Party has agreed to cut down the size of the Madrid Autonomous Community parliament, where they support a coalition government. See: https://www.rtve.es/noticias/20210609/pp-vox-acuerdan-reducir-101-diputados-asamblea-madrid/2101081.shtml.

populist Five Star Movement pushed a constitutional reform that reduced the number of MPs by roughly one-third,[15] or at placing the parliament under the governmental supervision, thus completely reversing the normal relationship between the legislative and the executive in a parliamentary system.[16] All in all, in the populist perspective, the parliament is an unnecessary intermediary institution, which represents and defends only the interests of the elites, and populism, rather than as a corrective for representative democracy, is a major factor of its crisis.

Against this backdrop, parliaments find themselves stripped away of substantial law-making powers and helpless *vis-à-vis* ever-stronger executives. Yet, if contemporary democracy is built upon the assumption that parliaments, as the primary vehicle of electoral representation, must have a leading role in the constitutional system (Issacharoff 2018, 450), the removal of parliaments from the centre of the political system is not sustainable in the long run. It is thus mandatory to reflect upon possible alternatives through which parliaments can inject democratic legitimacy into the political system.

Being precluded, for the reasons above stated, the path of re-legitimising the political system through outputs, i.e. legislation, the most promising alternative seems to focus on one of the traditional functions of parliaments, that is the oversight of government's actions.[17]

Parliamentary oversight is intended here as a multipurpose function embracing both the limiting and the sharing of executive powers (Griglio 2020, 69), which guarantees that the government's decisions are provided

[15] The lower house size was reduced from 630 to 400 members, whilst the upper house from 315 to 200. On the significance of this reform for the role of the Italian Parliament see: Di Majo, *Riduzione del numero di parlamentari e centralità del parlamento*, 40-77.

[16] The most prominent example is Hungary. More in details about the reforms implemented by the Orban's government concerning the role of parliament see: Szente, *How Populism Destroys Political Representation*, 1609-1618.

[17] In the same sense, an official document of the Inter-Parliamentary Union—an international organisation comprising 189 national parliaments—defines parliamentary oversight as "a key marker of parliament's relevance in the 21st century". See: Inter-Parliamentary Union and United Nations Development Programme, *Global Parliamentary Report 2017: Parliament's Power to Hold Government to Account: Realities and Perspectives on Oversight*, 11. Available at: https://www.ipu.org/resources/publications/reports/2017-10/global-parliamentary-report-2017-parliamentary-oversight-parliaments-power-hold-government-account last accessed 30 September 2021.

with the necessary democratic legitimacy.[18] In this sense, parliamentary oversight has a twofold purpose: on the one hand it safeguards the principle of representation, and on the other it serves to trigger executive's accountability. Its scope includes not only the review and monitoring of executive's actions, but also acts adopted by the parliaments aimed at orientating the actions of the executive, in particular as regards the implementation of policies, legislation, and budget.

The necessary counterpart of the parliamentary oversight power is the executive's accountability towards the legislature,[19] which can be ensured by various means. There are formal mechanisms—interpellations, questions, motions of confidence—and informal ones, for example the screening by political parties of potential cabinet members (Strøm et al. 2006, 70); soft mechanisms, like reporting duties towards the parliament, or hard ones, above all the possibility to force one minister, or the whole government, to resign.[20] Also, since the transparency and the openness of the decision-making procedures are fundamental conditions to enhance public trust in decision-making procedures, also fact-finding missions and *ad hoc* inquiry committees can be considered as *ex ante* accountability instruments. Lastly, there are those parliamentary acts—like resolutions, recommendations, the institution of non-permanent committees for the elaboration of legislative proposals—aiming at orientating executive's policies.[21] Albeit those acts are outside the framework of accountability instruments, they can facilitate parliamentary oversight by providing a clear backdrop against which evaluating the government's actions whilst allowing the parliament to directly influence executive's norm-making.

From this standpoint, strengthening the oversight powers of parliaments appears particularly promising to face the challenges posed by

[18] In political scholarship this form of legitimisation is known as 'throughput legitimacy', a concept that has been employed especially with reference to multilevel governance as an alternative way to elections to provide the legal system with the necessary legitimacy. See: Schmidt and Wood, *Conceptualizing throughput legitimacy*, 727-740.

[19] Actually, the least common denominator of all parliamentary democracies is that the executive is accountable to the parliament and can be voted out of office by the latter. See: Strøm, Müller, and Bergman (eds.), *Delegation and Accountability in Parliamentary Democracies*, 12-13.

[20] For a more detailed categorisation of the various types of accountability mechanisms see: Griglio, *Parliamentary oversight under the Covid-19 emergency*, 62-65.

[21] Those kinds of acts are known in the Italian constitutional tradition as "atti di indirizzo" and constitute an exercise of the corresponding parliamentary function—the '*funzione di indirizzo*'.

populism and ever-more dominant executives. On the one hand, in fact, by ensuring the accountability, transparency, and openness of executive's actions, parliaments provide decision-making procedures with a source democratic legitimacy that enhances the representativeness of the legal systems, thus filling in the legitimacy gap that populism supposedly aims to correct. On the other, expanding the accountability toolkit of parliaments means putting more constraints on government's actions and obliging it to share its powers with the parliament.

Having clarified that populism and executive's aggrandisement are the real challenges for the equilibrium of constitutional democracy and identified the strengthening of parliamentary oversight as a possible answer to these threats,[22] the next step is to illustrate the solutions adopted by national parliaments for holding the executive to account during the COVID-19 emergency.

4 Parliaments During the Pandemic. The Italian and Spanish Cases

The health, social, and economic crises provoked by the COVID-19 constituted an unprecedented challenge for parliaments and more in general for constitutional democracy (Murphy 2020, 13-14). During the pandemic, the scope for legislative interventions was extremely narrow, as the rapid evolution of the disease required a real-time decision-making radically incompatible with the unavoidable delays and uncertainties of a legislative procedure.[23] Besides, especially during the s.c. first wave, the normal functioning of parliaments was significantly affected, with plenary sessions reduced to a minimum.[24] Unsurprisingly, then, the pandemic

[22] Many studies have already evidenced that parliaments have played a decisive role in constraining and checking the executives' actions during the pandemic. See in particular: Ginsburg and Versteeg, *The Bound Executive*.

[23] Actually, from an institutional point of view one of the most visible effect of the pandemic has been the predominance of executives as law-makers. Also on this point see: Ginsburg and Versteeg, *The Bound Executive*.

[24] The Venice Commission Observatory on emergency situations prepared a comparative report on how the activity of national parliaments were affected during the s.c. first wave. It results that albeit only a minority of parliaments suspended their activities, many convened only when provided for the constitution, in most of the cases for the validation of law decrees. Thereportisavailableat:https://www.venice.coe.int/files/EmergencyPowersObservatory//T13-E.htm.

represented an opportunity for populist rulers to tighten their grip on power, by further loosening constraints coming from the parliament and the judiciary (Fourmont and Ridard 2020, 1).[25] At the same time, the exceptional powers exercised by executives and the heavy restrictions on fundamental rights imposed by emergency measures made the necessity for a close parliamentary oversight over executive's actions all the more compelling, as the Venice Commission emphasised "[l]egislative control over the acts and actions of emergency rule authorities and special procedures for such control are important for the realisation of the rule of law and democracy".[26]

Parliaments actually resorted with much more frequency than in normal times to oversight instruments, and given the circumstances, they had to be creative as to the arrangement concretely put in place to ensure the government's accountability. For these reasons, assessing the activity of European national parliaments during the COVID-19 can help to identify new practices and procedures which may guarantee the smooth functioning of constitutional democracy well after the end of the emergency. As anticipated in the introduction, the scope of the analysis is limited to two case studies, Italy and Spain.[27]

The Italian constitutional system was not prepared for the challenge posed by the COVID-19 pandemic. The Italian Constitution does not contain any provision regulating exceptional states,[28] and ordinary legislation related to crisis management did not confer any extraordinary powers on the government.[29] Also, Italy has been the first European country to be hit by the virus. It is therefore unsurprising that, especially during the first

[25] Fourmont and Ridard, *Parliamentary oversight in the health crisis*, 1.

[26] CDL-PI(2020)005rev, *Respect for democracy, human rights and the rule of law during states of emergency—Reflections*, paras 79-80. Available at: https://www.venice.coe.int/webforms/documents/?pdf=CDL-PI(2020)005rev-e last accessed 30 September 2021.

[27] In addition to the reasons exposed along the text (see: above, fn 26) the choice of the Italian and Spanish cases is due to the fact that they are the only two Western democracies with a populist party in the ruling majority.

[28] The only provision which foresees the possibility for the government to wield *extra-ordinem* powers is Article 78, which only affirms that the parliament declares the war and confer to the government all the necessary powers. In any case, the applicability of this provision was not considered as the provision refers only to war *stricto sensu*. On the point see: Lupo, "L'attività parlamentare in tempi di coronavirus," 139-140.

[29] The most relevant provisions in the ambit of crisis management are the Code of the Civil Protection (Legislative Decree 2/2018), on the basis of which the state of emergency was declared by the Italian government on 31 January 2020 and Law 833/1978 establishing the

phase of the emergency—from February to April 2020—the government reaction has been to 'flood' the legal order with law decrees and secondary acts (Massa-Pinto 2020), with the Italian Parliament that essentially gave a blank cheque to the government (Clementi 2020, 44).

A turning point in the parliament-executive relationship during the pandemic has been the validation process of Law Decree 19/2020. During the debate, the MPs decided to step into the management of the crisis and approved various amendments aimed at enhancing the oversight power of the assembly. In particular, the original text provided that Decrees of the President of the Council of Ministers (*Decreti del Presidente del Consiglio dei ministri*, most often abbreviated 'DPCM') would be sent to parliament within the day following their publication in the Official Journal. During validation, an amendment reversed the order, strengthening the role of parliament. In its approved version, the law obliges the government to illustrate in advance to the parliament the content of the measures to be adopted and to take into account the parliament's position. Besides, the President of the Council, or a minister delegated by it, has to appear every two weeks before the parliament to report about the implementation of these measures.[30] The combined effect of these two amendments allowed the parliament to influence the content of the DPCMs and to follow closely their implementation, as the President of the Council appeared regularly before both chambers to inform them.

The parliament also managed to guarantee itself a role in the decisions relative to the extension of the state of emergency, which according to Article 24 of Legislative Decree 2/2018 are taken by a decision of the Council of Ministers without consulting the parliament. On 28 and 29 July 2020, the President of the Council announced to the Chamber of Deputies and the Senate the government's intention to extend the state of emergency. In the debates, two identical majority resolutions were approved, committing the government to set 15 October as the deadline for the extension. The executive, which initially intended to fix the deadline on 31 December, complied with the parliament's recommendation. The same procedure was followed for the second and third extensions of

national health service. Extensively on the law of the emergency in the Italian legal order: Tresca, "Le fonti dell'emergenza L'immunità dell'ordinamento al Covid-19", 200-214.

[30] Only where this is not possible for reasons of urgency related to the nature of the measures to be adopted, the government shall provide for information after the adoption of the measure (Article 2, paragraph 1). Such circumstance only occurred twice. See: Lippolis, *Il rapporto parlamento-governo nel tempo della pandemia*, 270.

the state of emergency, to 30 April and 31 July respectively. With the majority resolutions approved by both chambers, the parliament committed the government to extend the state of the emergency to the deadline indicated in the resolution. The fourth and fifth extensions, until 31 December 2021 and 31 March 2022 respectively, were instead contained in a Law Decree, thus placing parliamentary oversight *ex post facto*. In any case, what is relevant is that a procedure that was at the outset carried out exclusively within the executive has been to some extent 'parliamentarised'.[31] It is also noteworthy that the Chamber of Deputies never suspended its weekly sessions dedicated to MPs' questions, the s.c. question time, and to urgent interpellation addressed to government members (Griglio 2020, 60).

Contrary to the Italian Constitution, the Spanish one does regulate exceptional states. Further, Organic Law 4/1981 provides a detailed discipline of the governmental powers during an exceptional state.[32] Yet, in Spain the crisis management has hardly been less controversial than in Italy, the main issue being the choice of, exceptional state amongst the three listed in Article 116 of the Spanish Constitution. The choice fell on the state of alarm that,[33] according to Article 4 of Organic Law 4/1981 is declared by the government alone, with any subsequent extension authorised by the Chamber of Deputies, which shall also detail the conditions and the scope of governmental powers during the extension.[34] The state of alarm has been extended for a total of six times[35] and expired on 21 June 2021.

[31] Thus aligning the procedure with the recommendations of the Venice Commission, which require parliamentary involvement, either *ex ante* or *ex post*, on the extensions of the emergency state. Most recently see: CDL-PI(2020)005rev, *Reflections*, paras 63-64.

[32] Organic Law 4/1981 of 1 June 1981 (*de los estados de alarma, excepción y sitio*).

[33] Many authors have criticised this decision, arguing that the government should have asked the parliament to declare a state of exception, which, unlike the state of alarm, allow for the suspension of some fundamental rights. See: Aragón Reyes, *Editorial. Covid-19*, 1-5. This opinion has been substantially confirmed by the Spanish Constitutional Tribunal in its judgement on the constitutionality of the Royal Decree declaring the state of alarm. See: STC 148/2018 of 14 July 2021.

[34] Article 6, Organic Law 4/1981. Thus the predominant role of the Chamber of Deputies over the Senate is self-evident in the crisis management. On the point see: García-Escudero Márquez, *Actividad y funcionamento de las Cortes Generales durante el estado de alarma*, 20.

[35] For a chronological review of the various declarations and the measures adopted with each of them see: https://www.lamoncloa.gob.es/covid-19/Paginas/estado-de-alarma.aspx.

During the first phase of the emergency, the parliament remained essentially passive leaving up to the government to deal with the emergency: all new sessions were postponed and most of parliamentary activity was suspended for two weeks. The plenary of the Chamber of Deputies was convened only for authorising the state of alarm, and once per week the Minister of Health appeared before the Health Committee of the Chamber of Deputies (Tudela Aranda 2020, 7). After this initial phase of inactivity, the parliament progressively increased its involvement in the crisis management. On 15 April 2020, for the first time, MPs were allowed to ask questions and interpellate government members during a plenary session (García de Enterría Ramos and Navarro Mejía 2020, 264).[36] The following 7 May, the Chamber of Deputies approved the creation of a non-permanent committee to elaborate proposals for the social and economic reconstruction (*Comisión para la reconstrucción Social y Económica*).[37] In its two months of activity, the committee has held twelve sessions, in which it has hosted more than twenty-five appearances of government's members and representatives of other public bodies.[38] Its conclusions, endorsed by the plenary in two separate sessions on 22 and 29 July, contain the guidelines and objectives to be pursued in the aftermath of the crisis.

On the following 29 October, the Chamber of Deputies authorised the extension of the state of alarm disposed by Royal Decree 926/2020 and introduced some amendments to the text proposed by the government.[39] In particular, Article 14 was amended to impose an obligation for the President of the Council to appear every two months before the Chamber of Deputies "to give an account of the data and actions of the Spanish Government in relation to the application of the state of alarm", whilst the original text only contained an obligation for the Minister of Health to

[36] Garcia de Enterría Ramos and Navarro Mejía, *La actuación de las Cortes Generales durante el estado de alarma*, 264.

[37] Diario de Sesiones del Congreso de los Diputados, XIV Legislatura, n.72. The legal basis for the creation of this committee has been Article 53 of the Rules of Procedure of the Chamber of Deputies, which allows the plenary to create non-permanent committee without investigative powers.

[38] A brief overview of the composition, functioning and activities of the committee can be found at: https://www.congreso.es/web/guest/notas-de-prensa?p_p_id=notasprensaandp_p_lifecycle=0andp_p_state=normalandp_p_mode=viewand_notasprensa_mvcPath=detalleand_notasprensa_notaId=37009, last accessed 30 September 2021.

[39] Chamber of Deputies, Resolution of 29 October 2020 (BOE n. 291 of 4 November 2020).

appear once per week before the Health Committee of the Chamber of Deputies.[40]

In conclusion, this brief comparative overview has evidenced some analogies between the reactions of the two parliaments. First, both legislatures maintained in place the sessions dedicated to questions and interpellations to government's member and even introduced some new obligation for them to appear before the parliament to inform it on the decisions to be made in the context of the crisis. Second, both parliaments adopted innovative instruments to enhance their participation in the management of the crisis. Whether those instruments can represent long-term solution for reinstating the parliament at the core of constitutional democracy will be discussed in the conclusions.

5 Conclusions

Before illustrating the arrangements that may help strengthening the parliaments against the challenges posed by populism and aggrandising executives, it is necessary to make a premise. In the exceptional context of the pandemic, parliamentary oversight has been essentially majority-driven, with the opposition relegated to a subordinate role (Griglio 2020, 68). This raises some concerns as to the effectiveness of the oversight, because too often the parliamentary majority is reluctant to trigger the executive's accountability (Duenas Castrillo 2020, 45). Yet, parliamentary oversight cannot be reduced to the ability of the parliament to scrutiny and sanction the government. Resolutions, motions, and non-legislative decisions of the parliament also constitute a form of parliamentary oversight, as long as they politically commit the government to follow the indications of the legislature. Admittedly, also from this standpoint, it is evident that only the majority is able to constraint the government, with the opposition only capable to increase the transparency of executive's activities with questions and interpellations. In any case, this concern is more nuanced concerning the Italian and Spanish cases, as the fragmentation of the government coalition makes the two governments more responsive to the instructions of the supporting parliamentary majority. With this *caveat* in

[40] The original text only contained an obligation for the Minister of Health to appear once per week before the Health Committee of the Chamber of Deputies. See: Article 14, Royal Decree 926/2020, of 25 October, (*por el que se declara el estado de alarma para contener la propagación de infecciones causadas por el SARS-CoV-2*), BOE n. 282 of 25 October 2020.

mind, it is time to put forward the possible lessons that can be learnt from the two case studies.

Even though Italian scholars are divided on the evaluation of the parliament's behaviour during the pandemic,[41] it cannot be disputed that the Italian parliament managed to increase its involvement in crisis management by establishing new oversight practices. In particular, the possibility for the parliament to monitor the adoption and implementation by the government of acts having force of law. In Italy, concerning law decrees, parliamentary control only takes place at the moment of its validation. As regards legislative decrees, Article 14(4) of Law 400/88 only obliges the government to ask the position of the parliament when the duration of the delegation exceeds two years,[42] but in parliamentary practice the government asks the opinion of the competent legislative committee on the scheme of the delegated act also for delegation of less than two years (Tarli Barbieri 2009, 151). In Spain, notwithstanding Article 82(6) of the Constitution explicitly foresees the possibility of introducing in the delegating law 'additional forms of control' over the government's exercise of normative powers, the Spanish constitutional doctrine is wary about the possibility of introducing further parliamentary checks, as this would transform the legislative decree into a complex act prohibited by the Constitution (Dominguez Vila 2018, 33). Be that as it may, considering a more generalised use of the obligation for the government to inform the parliament and take into account its position before the entry into force of the delegated act would enhance the government's accountability towards the parliament and enhance the latter participation in governmental law-making procedures. A similar arrangement could be envisaged when a law decree empowers the government to adopt implementing acts, as it is the case for all the law decrees adopted by the Italian parliament during the pandemic.

In general, the opinions of Spanish constitutional scholarship have been rather critic towards the attitude of the parliament during the pandemic. Nevertheless, a lesson can be learnt also from the Spanish experience. Specifically, the oversight tool that deserves more attention is the creation

[41] For a positive assessment of parliamentary activity during the pandemic see: Lippolis, *Il rapporto parlamento-governo nel tempo della pandemia*, 274-275. For the opposite position instead see: Clementi, *Il lascito della gestione normativa dell'emergenza*, 43-46.

[42] Article 14(4), Law 23 August 1988 n. 400, (*Disciplina dell'attività di Governo e ordinamento della Presidenza del Consiglio dei Ministri*).

of the Committee for the social and economic reconstruction. The creation of non-permanent committees for elaborating proposals and guidelines for future actions of both the parliament and the government may in fact allow the parliament to focus on specific issues and opening up a path for a more equilibrated sharing of norm-making powers between the executive and the parliaments.

On a more critical note, it has to be remarked that neither the Italian Parliament nor the Spanish one created inquiry committees to investigate government's responsibility in the management of the pandemic. In Italy, the creation of such a committee was proposed already in May 2020. However, in July 2021, two amendments proposed by the parties supporting the government limited the scope of the investigation to what happened in China before 30 January 2020,[43] raising serious doubts on the usefulness of such a committee. In Spain, instead, the ruling majority repeatedly blocked the creation of investigating committees proposed by the opposition.

Overall, it seems that even though the two parliaments refrained from employing accountability instruments *stricto sensu*, they were proactive in implementing new practices to guarantee their participation in governments' decisions. Such an approach is undoubtedly useful to contain the first threat identified in this chapter, that is executives' aggrandisement, as it allows parliaments to orient governmental norm-making, creating a sort of co-decision procedure between the two institutions (Griglio 2020, 65).

Conversely, the populist challenge requires in first place a parliament willing and capable of holding the executive to account, and this brings us back to the problem of the lack of incentives for parliamentary majorities to trigger the executive's accountability. Faced with this apparently unsolvable problem, a first solution is to enhance the transparency and openness of government's activities, as this is a fundamental requisite for ensuring the executive's accountability. To this regard, the informative duties imposed by both the Italian and Spanish parliaments on government's members during the pandemic are going in the right direction. A second solution could be to increase the instruments the opposition has to scrutiny the government's action, for example by allowing the opposition to

[43] DOC XXII-A, n. 42, 15 July 2021, *Istituzione di una Commissione parlamentare di inchiesta sulle cause dello scoppio della pandemia di SARS-CoV-2 e sulla congruità delle misure adottate dagli Stati e dall'Organizzazione mondiale della sanità per evitarne la propagazione nel mondo.*

create investigative committees.[44] On this aspect, however, the Spanish and Italian parliaments do not constitute good examples.

The future equilibrium of constitutional democracy will be determined by the capacity of parliaments to establish themselves as the primary fora for elaborating proposals capable of steering government's law-making in fundamental matters, whilst at the same time holding the government to account for its failures in taking into account the parliament's instructions. Only if they will manage to do so, the loss of parliaments' centrality in law-making will be properly compensated by an effective parliamentary oversight.

Bibliography

Agamben, Giorgio. *Lo stato di eccezione*. Torino: Bollati Boringhieri, 2003.

Aragón Reyes, Manuel. "Editorial. Covid-19: aproximación constitucional a una crisis." *Revista General de Derecho Constitucional*, no. 32 (2020): 1–5.

Bar-Siman Tov, Ittai. "Covid-19 meets politics: the novel coronavirus as a novel challenge for legislatures." *The Theory and Practice of Legislation* 8, no. 1–2 (2020): 11–48.

Berlin, Isaiah. "To Define Populism." *Government and Opposition* 3, no. 2 (1968): 137–179.

Carmona Contreras, Ana M. "Articulo 86." In *Comentario a la Constitución Española: 40 aniversario 1978-2018 (Vol. 1)*, edited by Carmen Montesinos Padilla, Pablo Perez Tremps and Alejandro Saíz Arnaiz, 1277–1287. Valencia: Tirant lo Blanch, 2018.

Castellà, Josep Maria, Marco Antonio Simonelli, Mátyás Bencze; Fruzsina Gárdos Orosz, Zoltán Szente, Helle Krunke, and Sune Klinge. "Populist constitutionalism. Its impact on the constitution, the judiciary and the role of the EU", *DEMOS Working Paper* (2020). https://openarchive.tk.mta.hu/433/1/Populist_Constitutionalism_Final%20.pdf

Clementi, Francesco. "Il lascito della gestione normativa dell'emergenza: tre riforme ormai ineludibili." *Osservatorio Costituzionale*, no. 3 (2020): 33–47.

Corkin, Joseph. "Constitutionalism in 3D: Mapping and Legitimating Our Lawmaking Underworld." *European Law Journal* 19, no. 5 (2013): 636-661. DOI:10.1111/eulj.12019

Curtin, Deirdre. "Challenging Executive Dominance in European Democracy." *The Modern Law Review* 77, no. 1 (2014): 1–32.

[44] A good case is in point is the European Parliament where, pursuant to Article 226 of the Treaty on the Functioning of the European Union, an investigating committee can be created at the request of a quarter of its component Members.

Dahrendorf, Ralf. *Después de la democracia*. Madrid: Crítica, 2002.

De La Iglesia Chamarro, Asunción. "Crisis económica y expansión del ejercicio normativo del Gobierno. En particular, los decretos-leyes nacionales y autonómicos." *Estudios de Deusto* 61, no. 2 (2013): 69–80.

De Somer, Stéphanie. *Autonomous Public Bodies and the Law. A European Perspective*. London: Edward Elgar, 2017.

Di Majo, Luca. "Riduzione del numero di parlamentari e centralità del parlamento." *Rivista del Gruppo di Pisa*, no. 3 (2020): 40–77.

Dominguez Vila, Antonio. "El control parlamentario de la legislación delegada en los ordenamientos autonómicos." *Revista General de Derecho Constitucional* 27, no. 33 (2018): 1–35.

Duenas Castrillo, Andrés. "Las relaciones Parlamento-Gobierno durante el estado de alarma por COVID-19." In *Los Efectos Horizontales de la COVID sobre el sistema constitucional*, edited by Paloma Biglino Campos and Juan Fernando Durán Alba, 43-58. Zaragoza: Fundación Manuel Giménez Abad, 2020.

Fabbrini, Sergio and Vassallo, Salvatore. *Il governo. Gli esecutivi nelle democrazie contemporanee*. Roma-Bari: Laterza, 1999.

Fourmont, Alexis and Ridard, Basile. "Parliamentary oversight in the health crisis." *European Issues*, no. 558 (2020): 1–11.

García de Enterría Ramos, Andrea and Navarro Mejía, Ignacio. "La actuación de las Cortes Generales durante el estado de alarma para la gestión de la crisis del COVID-19." *Revista de las Cortes Generales* 108, (2020): 245–288. DOI: https://doi.org/10.33426/rcg/2020/108/1487

García-Escudero Márquez, Piedad. "Actividad y funcionamento de las Cortes Generales durante el estado de alarma por COVID-19." *Cuadernos Manuel Giménez Abad. El Parlamento ante la COVID-19*, no. 8 (2020): 18-27.

Ginsburg, Tom and Versteeg, Mila. "The Bound Executive. Emergency Powers during the Pandemic." *International Journal of Constitutional Law*, (2021): 1–38. DOI: doi:10.1093/icon/moab059

Griglio, Elena. "Parliamentary oversight under the Covid-19 emergency: striving against executive dominance." *The Theory and Practice of Legislation* 8, no. 1–2 (2020): 49–70.

Groppi, Tania. "Riformare la giustizia costituzionale: dal caso francese indicazioni per l'Italia." *Rassegna Parlamentare* 52, no. 1 (2010): 37–56.

Hirschl, Ran. *Towards Juristocracy. The Origins and Consequences of the New Constitutionalism*. Boston: Harvard University Press, 2007.

Issacharoff, Samuel. "Populism versus Democratic Governance." In *Constitutional Democracy in Crisis?*, edited by Mark A. Graber, Sanford Levinson and Mark Tushnet, 445-458. Oxford: Oxford University Press, 2018.

Khmelko, Irina, Rick Stapenhurst, and Michael L. Mezey (eds.). *Legislative Decline in the 21st Century. A Comparative Perspective*. London: Routledge, 2020.

Lippolis, Vincenzo. "Il rapporto parlamento-governo nel tempo della pandemia." *Rivista AIC*, no. 1 (2017): 268–277.

Longo, Erik. *La legge precaria. Le trasformazioni della funzione legislative nell'età dell'accelerazione*. Torino: Giappichelli, 2017.

Loughlin, Martin. "The Contemporary Crisis of Constitutional Democracy." *Oxford Journal of Legal Studies* 39, no. 2 (2019): 434–454.

Lupo, Nicola. "L'attività parlamentare in tempi di coronavirus." *Forum di Quaderni Costituzionali*, no. 2 (2020): 121–142.

Mair, Peter. *Ruling the Void: The Hollowing of Western Democracy*. London-New York: Verso, 2013.

Massa-Pinto, Ilenia. "Il diritto costituzionale di fronte all'emergenza CoVID-19: la costituzione in senso funzionale e la (in)consapevolezza delle tendenze auto-distruttive del sistema." *Lo Stato*, no. 14 (2020): 315–330.

Mezey, Michael L. *Comparative Legislatures*. Durham: Duke University Press, 1979.

Mudde, Cas. "The Populist Zeitgeist." *Government and Opposition* 39, no. 3 (2004): 541-563. https://doi.org/10.1111/j.1477-7053.2004.00135.x

Mudde, Cas. *Populist Radical Right Parties in Europe*. Cambridge: Cambridge University Press, 2007.

Mudde, Cas and Rovira Kaltwasser Cristóbal (eds.). *Populism in Europe and the America. Threat or Corrective for Democracy?*. Cambridge: Cambridge University Press, 2012.

Murphy, Jonathan. *Parliaments and Crisis: Challenges and Innovations*. Stockholm: International Idea, 2020. https://doi.org/10.31752/idea.2020.22

Piergigli, Valeria. *Le Regole della produzione normativa*. Torino: Giappichelli, 2009.

Pinelli, Cesare. "The Populist Challenge to Constitutional Democracy." *European Constitutional Law Review* 7, no. 1 (2011): 5–16.

Ragone, Sabrina. *Parlamentarismos y crisis económica: afectación de los encajes constitucionales en Italia y España*. Barcelona: Bosch, 2020.

Ruth, Saskia Pauline. "Populism and the Erosion of Horizontal Accountability in Latin America." *Political Studies* 66, no. 2 (2018): 356–375. DOI: https://doi.org/10.1177/0032321717723511

Schmidt, Vivienand and Wood, Matthew. "Conceptualizing throughput legitimacy: Procedural mechanisms of accountability, transparency, inclusiveness and openness in EU governance." *Public Administration* 97, no. 4 (2019): 727–740.

Simoncini, Andrea. *L'emergenza infinita: la decretazione d'urgenza in Italia*. Macerata: EUM, 2006.

Strøm, Kaare; Müller, Wolfang C. and Bergman, Torbjörn (eds.). *Delegation and Accountability in Parliamentary Democracies*. Oxford: Oxford University Press, 2006.

Stuart Mill, John. *Considerations on Representative Government* (1861). Cambridge: Cambridge University Press, 2010.

Szente, Zoltán. "How Populism Destroys Political Representation(Anti-) Parliamentary Reforms in Hungary after 2010." *DPCE Online*, no. 2 (2019): 1609–1618.

Tarli Barbieri, Giovanni "La delega legislativa nei più recenti sviluppi.", in *La delega legislativa. Atti del seminario svoltosi in Roma Palazzo della Consulta, 24 ottobre 2008*, 93-206. Milano: Giuffrè, 2009.

Tresca, Michela. "Le fonti dell'emergenza. L'immunità dell'ordinamento al Covid-19." *Osservatorio Costituzionale*, no. 3 (2020): 200–214.

Tudela Aranda, Jose. "Parlamento y crisis sanitaria—Reflexiones preliminares." *Cuadernos Manuel Giménez Abad. El Parlamento ante la COVID-19*, no. 8 (2020): 6–17.

Tudela Aranda, Jose; Josep Maria Castellà Andreu, Enriqueta Exposito, and Mario Kölling. *Libro blanco sobre la calidad democrática en España*. Madrid: Marcial Pons, 2019.

Vibert, Frank. *The Rise of the Unelected: Democracy and the New Separation of Powers*. Cambridge: Cambridge University Press, 2007.

Vintzel, Céline. *Les armes du gouvernement dans la procédure législative. Etude comparée: Allemagne, France, Italie, Royaume-Uni*. Paris: Dalloz, 2011.

Windholz, Erik L. "Governing in a pandemic: from parliamentary sovereignty to autocratic technocracy." *The Theory and Practice of Legislation* 8, no. 1–2 (2020): 93–113.

Pandemic, Populism, and Polarisation

Rafael Rubio Nuñez

1 Disinformation and Fear: A Complex Balance Between Efficient Responses and Legal Shortcuts

Following the outbreak of the COVID-19 pandemic, the political context has suffered an earthquake that, moving between paralysis and emergency, has brought to light some of the substantive debates about the role of democracy in today's Europe. It has also fuelled the crisis facing democracy around the world. In the context of this debate, there are three major domains in which populism was able to spread during the pandemic: the efficacy vs. legitimacy debate, the freedom vs. security debate, and the debate over institutional guarantees vs. the need to respond. All three concern the key elements of democracy such as separation of powers, respect for human rights, or holding of elections. Disinformation has generated a climate in which different political actors have further contributed to the erosion of democracy.

It is a common practice to start any reflection related to the crises by highlighting its threats and opportunities. De facto, the crises operate as a

R. Rubio Nuñez (✉)
Department of Constitutional Law, Complutense University, Madrid, Spain
e-mail: rafita@ucm.es

J. M. Castellà Andreu, M. A. Simonelli (eds.), *Populism and Contemporary Democracy in Europe*,
https://doi.org/10.1007/978-3-030-92884-1_16

stress test that assesses the credibility and robustness of some policies and institutions, and effectiveness of the political leadership in crisis management, and oftentimes it tends to accelerate the social and economic processes that were already well underway.

For the matter at hand, the unprecedented public health crisis that generated economic and sociopolitical disruptions has brought forward some potential debates about the state of democracy in Europe. Due to the pandemic, governments are facing challenges of balancing fundamental freedoms and the principles of the democratic decision-making, on the one hand, and risk aversion to protect health rights as well as the urgent call to end the crisis, on the other. The collision of rights and principles imposed on decision makers a duty to provide a balance between the two, and to prioritise certain rights over others.

When the World Health Organization (WHO) declared, on 11 March 2020, that the COVID-19 outbreak had reached the level of a global pandemic and called for countries to take urgent and drastic measures to contain the spread of the virus,[1] governments around the world took different actions. In these responses, which varied greatly across the countries, several options can be highlighted.[2]

Constitutional exceptionalism is a favourite term of the international bodies. In their perspective, its formal nature and the constitutional guarantee provide a sufficient legal instrument. However, in strictly social and political terms resorting to constitutional mechanisms is perceived as something exceptional, not necessarily negative, and it fuels the political debate over the efficiency of the response as well as its broader effects on individual rights and separation of powers. Therefore, the responses varied across the EU. Some countries took advantage of this constitutional provision, while others adopted only the specific provisions dedicated to the state of emergency despite the enabling constitutional framework that allows adoption of the exceptionality. At the same time, the preference of most of the countries has been for ordinary legislative measures avoiding declaration of the state of emergency or invoking emergency laws.[3] Regardless of their nature, all measures adopted to address the

[1] "WHO Director-General's opening remarks at the media briefing on COVID-19 - 11 March 2020".

[2] Council of Europe Venice Commission, "Interim Report on the measures taken in the EU member states as a result of COVID-19 crisis and their impact on democracy, the rule of law and fundamental rights".

[3] Ibid., para. 35-38 and 41-43.

coronavirus pandemic have had a wide spectrum of effects on governance, democracy, rule of law, and human rights.

Given the globality of the issue at stake and the tendency of the responses to be of a national nature, some common elements with respect to legal and political structure and, regardless of the differences in which states have reacted, can be emphasised. The diverse responses that spanned the globe suffered from deeply rooted pressure caused by the political, social, and economic abnormality, which impelled searching for an equilibrium between the need for effective and rapid responses to crisis and preservation of the rule of law and constitutional democracy, and in particular, checks and balances and the validity of fundamental rights. Henceforth, we can highlight responses that share some populist features. The COVID-19 outbreak has led to an increase of uncertainty and fear, that constitutes the breeding ground for populism to thrive. This situation has triggered quick responses, "no matter the cost", in terms of individuals' rights and freedoms.

Some of the classic elements of populism flourished among the public. One of them is the corporate and mystical conceptualisation of the state that defines the state as an entity that exercises the popular sovereignty over the conscience of the individuals and which response to crises remains unquestioned. In this sense, the state determines the best for each person while an individual, that, being part of this machinery, doesn't obey the order becomes a threat to the system. Along the same lines, the kind of an official "truth" is stretched, in an informal but largely effective way, which, in the name of science, suppresses any dissident voice. Cases including disqualification of laboratory leak theory, which was later proven to have been at least abrupt, provide a good example of this. Confronted with the passions, illusions, and ideals of the people, superficial and risky answers are proposed, promising the impossible and neglecting rational approaches to decision-making, and triggering social frustration with the government. This expansion of the executive power, vested with the capacity to meet the needs, places the rest of the institutions on a secondary level, while checks and balances are undermined by the will of people to accommodate their interests. There are also those who call for safeguarding the rights of people against the elites who ignore public concerns and interests. In this light, elites are accused of moral decay, corruption, and injustice, which is at odds with the Rousseau's natural goodness of man, generally attributed to society.

Hitherto more populist trends are on a rise. Some authoritarian states have either denied the problem or cast it adrift. Others, mainly those in opposition, by taking advantage of the situation, claimed that some restrictions are an attempt by the governments to grant themselves more power and even to provoke a regime change. The third type can be referred to as techno-populist that opts mainly for technocratic solutions, thereby putting the politics to the background. The moment was ideal: breakdown of the basic consensus, polarisation, questioning the truth to renounce its democratic aspiration, the geopolitical opportunity in the attribution of responsibilities and searching for solutions such as vaccines. Another trend, which rests mainly in the battlefield of values, attributes the crisis to pre-existing problems such as environmental ones, and introduces the defense of other pre-existing agendas into the Covid agenda. "The presidential mutations, the sovereign retreat and, ultimately, that volitional-popular decisionism and populist expansion, which marked the electoral cycle in the West, (and which) have found their perfect storm" can be added to this list (Sanz Moreno 2020).

2 Populist Features

In this context, three ways in which populist trends have been developing can be highlighted:

a) An authoritarian response: Contrary to the effective model of democracy, citizens tend to seek certainty and assurance at the expense of their liberties. Having embraced this vision of democracy, citizens seek certainty and assurance at the expense of their freedoms. A longing for sovereignty mixed with fear and anger replaces the illusion which in the wake of the panic also recurs to authoritarian drifts in the name of security, "longing for a political power capable of putting order there where disorder reigns", which Maldonado correctly noted prior to the outbreak of the coronavirus. This fear provokes "a reinforcement of the sovereign will of the people that goes hand in hand with the weakening of the liberal counterweights of the democratic system" (Maldonado 2020). A positive vision of the future is replaced by the fear of it and therefore a popular demand for protection. Desire for protection might imply closure of borders and push for denomination of virus not only to shed light on its origins but also to reduce panic, as if recognising its external origin would immunise from its effects.

b) An effective response: The temptation to bypass institutional checks and oversight mechanisms to seek more rapid and efficient solutions by some governments. In this respect, Schmitt's words about Weimar Republic become relevant: "liberal democracies will be consumed in the effort to shape the general will" (Schmitt 2008). In this sense, democracy is perceived as a system unable to offer answers in real time, today and now. This perception is accented towards procedures including the parliamentary ones which rely on their own time frame to guarantee the fulfilment of their functions. A cyclical temptation to embrace sovereignty without limitations of liberty.
c) A popular reaction: An uprising against the "impositions", fuelled by what has come to be called infodemic. By promoting simple solutions and answers that define populism, it reinforced a radical discourse characterised by the detachment from institutions of authority and proliferation of conspiracy theories. The uprising which coexists with a spiral of silence like Hobbes's Leviathan extends its power over opinions, imposing an official truth to end the cacophony prevalent in any human society. According to Maldonado, this represents "a paradox of an increasingly complex world with increasingly simple interpretations" (Maldonado 2020).

2.1 An Authoritarian Response: A Sovereign Nostalgia

The worldwide spread of the coronavirus gave rise to a wave of praise for the "virtues" of authoritarian governments or dictatorships. During the health crisis, a bunch of countries championed mainly by Singapore, Russia, and China are believed to have performed better, both in their efforts to contain the virus and in the process of vaccination. These responses have been treated as a model for governance and have to some extent shaped the global geopolitical map (vaccine diplomacy of China and Russia in Latin America, later caught up with the European Union). The renunciation of institutional consensus and the denunciation of the "old party system" have led to the rapid expansion of the executive power, with some evident populist features.

The institutional approach of the European Union, on the other hand, has been portrayed as slow, hesitant, and somewhat ineffective. Erratic decisions regarding closure of borders, the vicissitudes of vaccines and vaccination process, and disagreements over so-called vaccination passport are just some examples of it. In addition, the responses of the member states lacked consistency and tended to change depending on the circumstances and altering governmental decisions. The President of the European Commission herself has admitted vaccine rollout failure and its negative consequences. The consensus trap, mentioned by Darnstädt (Darnstädt 2005), is observed in the institutions including the European Commission.

The pandemic has presented a strain on existing legal systems, and therefore, it raised a concern to develop a clear legal framework that should be adopted in the emergency situations. In this respect, "the constitutional system" is seen as a main guarantor of fundamental rights, the rule of law, and democratic principles. This has also been noted by the Venice Commission, the Council of Europe's advisory body. In accordance with this constitutional basis, regulations must be general, preferably organic, and approved amid normal times.[4]

As is well known, the state of emergency is a special legal regime of powers and rules that is adopted by the public institutions to address a serious public threat. Current international law and practically all national legal systems adhere to this approach. Albeit more flexible legal regime,[5] the state of emergency is regulated by law, always based on the primacy of the rule of law comprising five essential elements: legality, legal security, prevention of abuse (or misuse) of powers, equality before the law and non-discrimination, and access to justice. As pointed out by Castellà (Castellà Andreu 2020), countries that don't have constitutional provisions to enact emergency measures should comply with the principles of the rule of law as well as with the principles of necessity and proportionality, temporality, parliamentary scrutiny or oversight, judicial review, preparedness of emergency legislation, and loyal cooperation between institutions (Castellà Andreu 2020).

Pertaining to the risks of authoritarian behaviour that dispenses with basic checks and balances, respect for fundamental rights and freedoms gains more importance. Although there is room for limitations and restrictions, fundamental rights and freedoms can be suspended "only in very exceptional circumstances" during the validity of the state of emergency. It is also possible to derogate from the obligations under international human rights treaties. This provision is envisaged by the European

[4] Council of Europe Venice Commission, "Interim Report", para. 29-30.

[5] Council of Europe Venice Commission, "Respect for Democracy, Human Rights and the Rule of Law during States of Emergency: Reflections", para 8.

Convention on Human Rights (art. 15) or the UN International Covenant on Civil and Political Rights (art. 4) and has been invoked by several member states during the coronavirus outbreak.[6] However, the use of this provision is dictated by certain procedural and substantive conditions including following the key principles of necessity, proportionality, exercised on a temporary basis, and keeping the international organisation fully informed.[7] Furthermore, there is a list of rights that cannot be a subject to any derogation but can be restricted or limited following the above noted principles and legitimate purpose.[8]

In addition, the procedure to extend the suspension of rights is not well defined, which must also be subject to the principles of exceptionality and legality. Experience shows that there is a regulatory deficit for such situations as they are inconsistent with the anticipated state of emergency or legislation on sanitary emergencies (material and the contentious guarantee of the same). This has allowed government to go beyond the law, given the need to provide immediate response. The ruling of the Spanish Constitutional Court represents a good example of this shortcoming.

Among the rights impaired by the pandemic, the right to vote deserves special attention due to its role in the exercise of the rest. During the pandemic, around 150 countries confronted with the challenge to hold elections. It wasn't an easy task as the indispensable nature of voting rights might conflict with the electoral process. The initial delay and rescheduling of elections to ensure sufficient guarantees (in terms of making the postponement decision, the required majorities, the intervention of the parliament, etc.) was followed by decisions made by some countries to hold the elections under special voting arrangements and extreme sanitary measures.

Current legislation has proved to be deficient to adapt to this precarious time. States lacked foresight or agility which in turn led to controversial approaches that put the legal security and electoral integrity at stake, albeit for the most part it was settled amicably. Regardless of the solution, legal certainty, equality of the parties, and respect for voting rights must

[6] Ten countries of the European Union suspended the application of international and regional human rights instruments during this crisis: Albania, Armenia, Estonia, Georgia, Latvia, Macedonia, Moldova, Romania, San Marino and Serbia.

[7] Council of Europe Venice Commission, "Interim Report", para. 15-16.

[8] Council of Europe Venice Commission, "Respect for Democracy, Human Rights and the Rule of Law during States of Emergency: Reflections", para. 40. Also in Council of Europe Venice Commission, "Interim Report", para. 14.

be observed. Elections are a process comprising the rules and regulations that are essential. Changing the rules around voting amid elections or disregard for potential flow-on effects can be detrimental. It is also emphasised in the Code of Good Practices in Electoral Matters adopted by the Venice Commission where it states that "the stability of the law is crucial for the credibility of the electoral process".[9] Legal changes are advised to take place over a year prior to decision to postpone or suspend elections. Unfortunately, given the unprecedented character of the situation, changes in electoral playbook spanned the globe. In this regard, governments are required to ensure that these changes are limited, clearly communicated, and implemented with a simultaneous improvement of training and establishment of effective procedures. Even so, it is inevitable that these decisions tend to be politicised, and in some cases, they come down to the courts.

Ultimately, as for the rights, the global crisis demonstrated the relevance of reconsidering the protection of the social rights and the need to develop universal public health services, where the figure of "ombudsman" is of vital importance both for the protection of rights during the crisis and for the assistance provided to citizens affected by the emergency measures.[10]

2.2 An Effective Response: Institudemia

Rule of law is considered as a cornerstone of democracy, and one of the ways to weaken democracy is to turn democratic processes into a dead letter. This doesn't occur instantly, but it is the final stage of the crumbling process that develops in a progressive manner. The powers of the state, whether individually or in a coordinated way, begin to create exceptions, driven by the gravity of the threat and the need for rapid and efficient response. This leads to the erosion of the normative and institutional architecture on which the principle of the rule of law rests upon. In this manner, which is also quite paradoxical, and as masterfully portrayed in the 1966 Oscar-winning movie *A Man for All Seasons* directed by Fred Zinneman about Tomas Moro, moving forward by circumventing controls causes an inverse effect. When institutions call for the protection of the rule of law, they realise that its key functions decayed and they turn out

[9] Council of Europe Venice Commission, "Code of Good practice in Electoral matters".
[10] Council of Europe Venice Commission, "Interim Report", para. 99.

to be the ones who contributed to its dismantling, impelled by their tendency to make exceptions in the established legislation.

As discussed in relation to fundamental rights, exceptionality doesn't imply the suspension of the rule of law. Rather, some restrictions and limitations can be adopted, and in some serious cases, certain rights can be a subject to derogation or suspension. As previously noted, it is allowed only if these restrictions meet the requirements of legality, necessity, and proportionality, and they ought to be time bound. Despite these parameters, restrictions of the individual rights result in the centralisation of power, strengthening of the executive, and weakening of the system of the checks and balances. Hence, it is essential to have a prior and adequate legal framework and a broad consensus that would ensure clear limits and periodic review of the measures. In case of the need to extend the measures currently in place, they must follow regulatory compliance with the principle of vested powers and the principle of checks and balances. Moreover, these principles must be secured against consequences of any shift in the distribution of powers. Under these circumstances, powers of the parliamentary and judicial oversight (internal and external) must be strengthened since it was recognised to have exhibited a significant self-restraint. A complementary role of the institutions such as the Ombudsman or independent mass media must be acknowledged as well.

However, the emergency brought by the pandemic led to the shift in governance. Central governments gained more power while the role of other institutions has been marginalised.[11] Among these institutions, Parliament was perhaps the one to have been adversely affected the most. Performing its control functions while the executive was assuming special powers contributed to the progressive recovery of its legislative functions and maintaining its symbolic role as an "essential service", sending a message of public example by continuing its activities and its presence in the setting of national sovereignty. These goals have been forced to coexist along with safeguarding the health of its members and staff, and the requirement of agile and effective solutions encountered by novel and unexpected developments. These objectives have had to coexist with the preservation of the safety of its members and staff and urgency to accommodate public needs produced by the pandemic. Parliaments around the world have been challenged by the COVID-19 crisis (Rubio and Gonzalo Rozas 2020). Although a false dilemma over the preservation of the

[11] Ibid, para. 61 and 64.

system of checks and balances and suspension of this mechanism on the grounds of management efficiency was raised, it is inaccurate to underestimate the role of parliaments during times of uncommon social tension. Parliamentary participation in crisis management is crucial to distinguish between democratic mechanism and strategies employed by the autocratic counterparts, and to guarantee legitimacy, justice, and efficiency. Therefore, where it was legally possible parliaments continued to assume their role in the debate and scrutiny of emergency legislation (with a qualified majority in some specific cases), oversight of the government action (entirely or through specific committees), or the approval of the extraordinary budgets.[12]

We must be prudent to prevent inclination towards adoption of merely technocratic forms of governance, which could disrupt the logic behind separation of powers. The importance of the territorial division of powers is another element that should be considered as it constitutes another complementary system of separation of powers in the decentralised forms of governance during the state of emergency. Central governments can limit the powers of the subnational authorities by transferring the competences neither without declaring suspension of autonomy,[13] nor without re-centralisation beyond the requirements of the state of emergency.[14] Instead, adoption of the principle of loyal collaboration and mutual respect should be encouraged.[15]

These centralising tendencies should be addressed by an increased parliamentary control and judicial review, over both the declaration of the state of emergency and the measures adopted. These oversight mechanisms may correspond to both ordinary and constitutional jurisdiction of the state, and those exercised by international bodies (both judicial and quasi-judicial entities), most notably the European Court of Human

[12] The Parliamentary Assembly of the Council of Europe, in its Recommendation 1713 (2005), has pointed out: "*Exceptional measures in any field must be supervised by parliaments and must not seriously hamper the exercise of fundamental constitutional rights*".

[13] CDL-AD(2011)049, *Opinion on the draft law on the legal regime of the state of emergency of Armenia*, Adopted by the Venice Commission at its 89th Plenary Session (Venice, 16-17 December 2011), para. 34.

[14] CDL-AD(2017)021, *Opinion on the Provisions of the Emergency Decree-Law N° 674 of 1 September 2016 which concern the exercise of Local Democracy in Turkey*, adopted by the Venice Commission at its 112th Plenary Session (Venice, 6-7 October 2017) para. 92.

[15] CDL-PI(2020)005rev, *Respect for democracy, human rights, and the rule of law during states of emergency-reflections*, para. 61.

Rights. To comply with the principles of oversight and accountability, courts must be guaranteed an impartiality and independence, except for an overriding need or practical infeasibility.[16]

Although it depends on the political system, given the significance and risks associated with this option, Venice Commission emphasises the role of the constitutional justice which has capacity to grant "provisional measures".[17] While Venice Commission admits that jurisdictional control is usually limited in practice due to a "judicial self-restrain", it doesn't imply complete concession of control, as it was observed in Portugal, France, or Spain.

2.3 Public Reaction: An Infodemic

The third populist risk is associated with the public reaction. Populist narratives, which provide simple answers to complex questions, were largely antagonistic in the beginning of the crisis as they oscillated between downplaying the threat or suddenly declaring its end, while the virus itself has been positioned as an instrument of the global conspiracy for geopolitical battles or even as a mechanism that elites employed to deprive us of our freedoms. The mainstream media has significantly contributed to the spread and further consolidation of these discourses. However, these media outlets were driven primarily by defamation, pseudo-media sites, by the embrace of populist political options, and in some cases by reckless complicity of the individuals with the influence in media.

On some occasions, political leaders like Trump, Bolsonaro, or Lopez Obrador dismissed or downplayed the coronavirus threat. Others have gone further by embracing denial and conspiracy including Ortega and his infamous "Love in the times of Covid" march and Turkmenistan, which claims to have had suffered zero COVID-19 cases. Nor will there be any as Gurbanguly Berdimuhamedov vetoed the word "coronavirus" in official documents and the media. However, the most common reaction has been seeking the union that would produce an identity feeling. In this way, aggravated by rivals' external signs, any critical judgement is hindered

[16] Ibid., para. 87 and 89.

[17] Ibid, para. 88. (*The preference for constitutional justice is qualified, but not its adoption of provisional measures,* in the Council of Europe Venice Commission, "Interim report", para. 78).

by severe errors committed in while dealing with the sudden and explosive nature of the pandemic.

As Sanz states: “The pandemic spread the virus; the populists, the anger in their towns” (Sanz Moreno 2020). To achieve it, disinformation has proved to be a main part of the populist toolkit. The information gap was exacerbated by ignorance and communication strategies that sought to reduce panic, in some cases by manipulating information for distraction that did not address the informational demand, inherent to people of the contemporary information society, especially when faced with uncertainty and fear. This plethora of misinformation has gained a new meaning as it became known as “infodemic” or epidemic of “information”. These attempts to disseminate wrong information in order to win the battle of the story are argued to hamper public health response and quality of democracy.

Social media networks and personal communication platforms like Telegram and WhatsApp became a global battlefield, prominence of which was amplified by changing circumstances, widespread boredom, and anxiety. They also transformed into an area for the construction and fixation of truths and beliefs, predominant or imagined, stirring and yet indisputable. Ignorance created a void space in which communication is frequently filled with rumours and polarised attitudes. Information search process, characterised by a possibility to select the news “A La carte”, representative of today’s informational ecosystem of the internet, allows accessing answers that are consistent with the personal views. This, more than ever, led to reinforcement of one’s prejudices and reaffirmed an infernal or beatific vision, which at the same remains the “reality” of the one encountering the information.

This infinite offer of information, which is just put at our fingertips, is further reinforced by the algorithmic gatekeeping that predicts individual preferences and reinforces them in a way that is unlikely to be noticed by the user. When exposed to algorithmically curated information, users tend to assume that the information reflects the reality, albeit differences are increasingly noticeable. Arguments and information selected by individuals transform into their own in a way that eventually is perceived as “truth” that are later defended with an authentic conviction, although it is a result of biased perception of reality rather than critical thinking. Reality is therefore what confirms our viewpoint and the flawed perspective of others. One’s truth neglects the “truth” of others and considers them as misleading and deceptive. Where there is no “truth” there is no rivalry. Once becoming part of a team, the single purpose is, thereafter, to defend the colours and to triumph no matter the consequence. This way of simplifying skews the perception of reality. In addition, political actors remain outside in the parallel universe which makes any possibility of dialogue practically impossible.

Henceforth, a combination of these two effects leads first to an increased fragmentation and further to polarisation. There is a tendency to target those who produce more interactions and who incidentally tend to be more radical. This is common not only in politics but also in social platforms as algorithms find more extreme content to optimise user interaction without considering its character. As a result of this process, more polarisation occurs. Instead of decline, the echo that emerged in the social networks extends far beyond.

These developments have taken place in an environment that has already been experiencing democratic backsliding and struggle to communicate and transmit knowledge. While at first glance, the transmission of information, in this context, is horizontal, the priority is given to more resourceful entities that are equipped to influence the public exchange of information. In this political climate, polarisation is enhanced and exacerbated by technology which not only offers broader and faster forms of distribution, but also seriously compromises its content, as well as our perception of contrasting views and those behind them.

Under the given scenario, the polarisation was fuelled by the exaltation of own identity, which exploits the community feeling, belonging to the outside, the virus, its creators, or the governments in charge of health management. A collective feeling that, instead of carving out breaches, it exploited and intensified the existing ones. By taking advantage of this fragmentation, tribal groups arise and become more homogenised by acquiring a sense of belonging that leads them to take sides and act collectively, and only accepts the actions of his group while rejecting others. This is achieved by exploiting networks' autonomous dynamics and accelerating with misinformation or distortions which affect the perception of the rest. It goes on to exalt affiliates, by amplifying the content of the one that grabs more attention and generating an imitation effect in which it competes for acceptance and popularity. Meanwhile, anyone who is bold to disagree or provide alternative points of view is rejected with the same enthusiasm, incorporating attacks coordinated from reference accounts. One can always go further in the level of exaggeration, without examining the credibility of arguments, as defeating a rival becomes more important than changing the rules.

The battle for attention also generates polarisation (Peirano 2019). Individuals seek to stand out over the average by inducing originality, heterodoxy, intensity, or volume. It was observed that once the rumour reached these groups, the dramatism of the promoted ideas surged (a look at the way any topic related to pandemic was treated on twitter helps to grasp this idea). In this way, the tension wasn't circular but linear and continuous and to a certain extent expansive. It starts from "well, what about you" to "and you more" (which is a qualitative leap). Furthermore, as it makes difficult to access content that does not follow that line, it reinforces internal prejudices, which in turn makes rectification almost impossible. Personal ideas and beliefs are underpinned by turning to the most irrational and ridiculous of others as if polarisation was just a game, a plot trick without social consequences.

Thereby, "zero tolerance" is embraced against anything that goes contrary to one's way of thinking. Policy framed in this manner is presented as an eternal chess game, a zero-sum game, where moves always depend on the opponent and the victory as a final goal. This process, typical of the infodemic, becomes contagious as it forces others to take sides in the information warfare. The one, who embraces the true faith, with a religious conception of politics, despises the dissident, incapable of capturing the reality. This becomes a source of hatred towards one who is equidistant, independent, and who eventually is perceived as traitor and enemy.

This prompts the movements that deny the existence of the virus, discredit the efficacy and safety of vaccines, and suspect hidden intentions. This has had an impact on the provision of healthcare as some false sanitary recommendations emerged as a result of these narratives, strengthening populist discourses. Another implication is the reaction of the platforms that, in response to health threats, acted on by eliminating accounts, content, or redirecting to official information on any content related to the pandemic, to allow users to compare the information. Nevertheless, these efforts have produced side effects. The most striking one is the one related to the claim that the virus originated from the Chinese laboratory. This theory emerged early on in a crisis due to the lack of information and was quickly dismissed as a conspiracy theory, receiving implicit censorship from social media users and mass media as well as explicit censorship by social media platforms that did not hesitate to label or even remove it. However, more than a year later, following exhaustive investigations, we see how this lab leak theory has gained traction, receiving widespread attention, and turning into caveat about the responsibility for the hasty decisions that opt for erasing information (without any criteria or procedure other than a will of the digital platforms) and its profound undemocratic effects.

3 Concluding Remarks

This populist boom, illustrated in the discussion above, and looking back at the European Union, suggests that pandemic sparked by the novel coronavirus doesn't imply the acceleration of the processes entailing the construction of Europe, the deepening of democracy of the EU, and bringing citizens closer to their institutional structures in shaping the future of Europe. Instead, it demonstrated the opposite. Strengthening the European project is not necessarily a consequence of the pandemic; rather it is an ideal that today is more difficult to achieve than prior to the crisis and therefore it requires greater effort.

As illustrated, exceptional situations require exceptional actions such as temporary suspension of certain rights or an extraordinary separation of powers. However, these developments should proceed on a temporary basis and under the conditions dictated by the circumstances and scope of the necessity. The supremacy of the rule of law shall remain by ensuring parliamentary control and judicial review of the essence and duration of a declared state of emergency to avoid any abuse of power.

Similarly, risks that misinformation poses to public health require a response, but it must be ensured against potential secondary effects on fundamental rights such as freedom of expression. Sanz warns about rising trends that pose a threat to democracy (Sanz Moreno 2020):

- Anti-elitist. Upswinging mistrust towards science and, what is even worse, the aristocratic pride of scientific community in an uncertain and rapidly transforming field.
- Anti-pluralist. Reinforcing the role of the people as an omnipotent power not subject to any restrain, beyond its electoral revalidation and its foreseeable authoritarian mutation.
- Anti-dialogic/anti-rational, which turns public management into a game of identities and feelings.

All of these can be reduced to identity politics, or bloc politics, where institutions are diffused at the service of each other. As stated in an alarmingly accepted interpretation: "as they are willing to do anything, we cannot give up playing by their own rules, even if they wear democracy down". In this vein, faith in democracy is replaced by democracy as an act of faith. From the democracy of ideas there is a transition towards the democracy of beliefs, as "we have ideas, but we live on beliefs" (Ortega y Gasset 1997).

When institutional paths are curtailed, the recourse to dialogue and justice ceases to function and thus heavily relies on the extent of power. The legitimacy of the other to govern is questioned, and any action of ours, even if it exceeds the legal framework, is justified, paving the way for dangerous anti-politics. Consequently, polarisation is a step that precedes confrontation marked by strong emotions that are difficult to suppress.

Clearly, simple solutions that have been boasted by populist leaders have fallen short of mitigating the unprecedented public health crisis. Despite the lack of a uniform approach to coronavirus pandemic, the end of the crisis is not yet in sight and will largely depend on future policy responses. What is more, there is no doubt that an ongoing health crisis will turn into a long-term economic crisis and further reinforce the populist discourse against the establishment and bloc politics. Both crises are also likely to trigger an institutional stagnation. What remains is to lower the expectations, improve the efficiency of crisis management, not yield to providing explanations, resist the perverse dynamics of confrontation, and above all recognise the primacy of the democratic rules. This is essential for defending these principles and seeking legitimacy beyond bare efficiency.

Bibliography

Castellà Andreu, Josep Maria. "La Comisión de Venecia y los estados de emergencia: la necesaria preservación del Estado de Derecho y la democracia constitucional durante la crisis de la covid-19." In *Los Efectos Horizontales de la COVID sobre el sistema constitucional*, edited by Paloma Biglino Campos and Duran Alba, Juan Fernandez. Zaragoza: Fundación Manuel Giménez Abad, 2020.

Darnstädt, Thomas. *La trampa del consenso*. Madrid: Trotta, 2005.

Maldonado, Arias Manuel. *Nostalgia del soberano*. Madrid: La Catarata, 2020.

Ortega y Gasset, José. *Ideas y Creencias* (Ideas and Beliefs). Madrid: Alianza Editorial, 1997.

Peirano, Marta. *El enemigo conoce el sistema: manipulación de ideas, personas e influencias después de la economía de la atención*. Madrid: Debate, 2019.

Rubio, Rafael and Gonzalo Rozas, Miguel Angel. "Presencialidad y excepcionalidad en el parlamento en tiempos de pandemia global." In *¿Política confinada? Nuevas tecnologías y toma de decisiones en un contexto de pandemia*, edited by Josep María Reniu and Víctor Sanchez Meseguer, 73-94. Madrid: Aranzadi Thomson Reuters, 2020.

Sanz Moreno, Jose A. "Democracia en pandemia: comunicación, redes y populismo." In *¿Política confinada? Nuevas tecnologías y toma de decisiones en un contexto de pandemia*, edited by Josep María Reniu and Víctor Sanchez Meseguer, 305-340. Madrid: Aranzadi Thomson Reuters, 2020.

Schmitt, Carl. *Constitutional Theory*. Durham: Duke University Press, 2008.

Might COVID-19 Help Strengthening European Democracies?

Tania Groppi

1 Pre-pandemic Democratic Regression

The COVID-19 pandemic, which ravaged the world in 2020 and continued in 2021, occupies a prominent place among the "new challenges" for contemporary democracy. This unexpected and most undesirable event hit Europe at a very delicate moment, when many of the fragilities of its democracies and of the European construction itself have been apparent for at least the last 15 years. Perhaps, we can consider as a turning point the French and Dutch referendums of 2005, which rejected the proposal for a European Constitution. After this date—which followed shortly after the EU enlargement to the East, with the entry, in 2004, of ten new Member States—a crisis began that affected both the Member States and the European Union (EU), and which is not only specific to the European regional area. On the contrary, we can say that it is a global crisis, in the double sense that it affects democracies all over the world and that it is a

T. Groppi (✉)
Department of Business and Law (DISAG), University of Siena, Siena, Italy
e-mail: tania.groppi@unisi.it

J. M. Castellà Andreu, M. A. Simonelli (eds.), *Populism and Contemporary Democracy in Europe*,
https://doi.org/10.1007/978-3-030-92884-1_17

consequence of global phenomena, such as economic globalisation and new communication technologies.

Many indicators confirm that, since 2005, a "democratic regression" has begun in the world (Repucci and Slipowitz 2021). The V-Democracy report shows that, in 2020 (based on data of 2019), "[f]or the first time since 2001, autocracies are in the majority: 92 countries—home to 54% of the global population" (Lührmann et al. 2020).

In Europe, we find specific aspects, such as the economic-financial crisis of the Eurozone and the waves of migration, especially in 2015, which have brought more than 1 million migrants and refugees to the European continent in one year. Faced with these phenomena, we have witnessed, in many countries, the growing electoral success of anti-European or xenophobic movements that have called into question the founding values of the European states and of the Union itself, in one country, the United Kingdom, even leading to its exit, with Brexit.

It is in this already weakened political, economic and social situation that COVID-19 arrives. Indicators examining the "state of health" of democracies have shown that COVID-19, or, to be more precise, the measures taken by the public authorities to react to it, have generally had a negative impact on democracies.

For example, almost 70% of the countries covered by the Democracy Index developed by the Economist Intelligence Unit registered a decline in their overall score, "as country after country blocked to protect lives from the new coronavirus. The global average score fell to its lowest level since the index began in 2006." The new EIU Democracy Index report, the latest in a series of assessments from a variety of democracy assessment organisations, paints a rather bleak picture as well.[1]

Also on the European continent, though less than in other parts of the world, there are reports showing a backsliding of democracies, as noted by Idea International. According to this report,[2] the four non-democratic regimes in the region (the authoritarian regimes of Azerbaijan and Belarus and the hybrid regimes of Russia and Turkey) implemented measures to curb the pandemic that raise concerns from a democracy and human rights perspective, as did 8 out of 40 democracies (or 20% of them). Democracies

[1] Available at: https://www.eiu.com/n/campaigns/democracy-index-2020/, last accessed 30 September 2021.

[2] Avaialble at: https://www.idea.int/publications/catalogue/regional-democratic-trends-europe-and-during-covid19, last accessed January 2022.

with worrying developments were mainly those that were regressing or eroding also before the pandemic. Bulgaria, Hungary and Serbia stand out in this respect, but also, to a lesser extent, Poland, Slovenia and Ukraine. The remaining two countries—Israel (which this chapter takes into account, although geographically not in Europe) and Slovakia—were the only democracies that had not registered democratic declines in the five years before the pandemic, but have still implemented measures to curb the pandemic that present concerns from a democracy and human rights perspective.

In the following pages, I will try to reflect on the challenges that COVID-19 poses for European democracies, in the sense of the elements of negativity, in order to identify, in line with the tile of this chapter, whether there are some positive aspects that are emerging in some national experiences and in the European Union itself.

2 The Challenges of Emergency Situations for Constitutional Democracy

The starting point here is the notion of constitutional democracy. In a nutshell it is a system, or a form of state, in which the sovereign popular will is combined with the rule of law to guarantee pluralism and fundamental rights. All this with the aim of maintaining peace, social cohesion, stability and unity in pluralist societies, without denying complexity and differences. And, therefore, by rejecting the identity belonging on the basis of ethnicity, the small, close and barbaric homelands, through the option in favour of a "great solidarity," based on the "daily plebiscite" and on the nation-demos. The European model, sometimes also called the "post-war paradigm," unlike the US model, provides also for the constitutionalisation of social policies and is characterised by its openness towards international law. It is an open constitutional state: in the sense that accepted a weak external sovereignty, integrated in a multilevel system of decision-making.

At the level of institutional mechanisms, this form of state is based on the separation between two decision-making circuits: the one where popular sovereignty operates (and the representative principle) and the one where the institutions of guarantee operate, first and foremost, constitutional justice, which is a necessary institution in this form of state.

The emergency always implies—regardless of the events that generate it, and of the specific legal regulation—an increase in the power of governments, due to the timeliness of the necessary measures and the need for intervention by the public authorities through public administration. The emergency also implies a limitation of rights that does not follow the rules foreseen for "normal times," implying the prevalence of some of them. All this for a limited period of time, related to the permanence of the factual elements that justify it.

Here we find the first challenge: how to strengthen the powers of governments without undermining the rule of law, in the sense of the separation and balance of powers. In other words, how to involve parliament, allowing it to develop its oversight over decisions taken by the majority, and how to ensure judicial review of measures. This has been further complicated by the characteristics of this emergency, where "social distancing" has implied a reduction in the activities of parliaments and the judiciary.

Without wishing to further elaborate on this point, we can say that the key here is the principle of "loyal cooperation between institutions,"[3] which does not mean the abandonment of, but the complement to the separation of powers, and which is particularly important, especially in the face of the emergency, as the Italian Constitutional Court has emphasised.[4]

The second challenge is more directly related to the guarantee of fundamental rights. Rights in "normal conditions" can be limited, in order to protect other rights and public interests, but according to a balance in which neither becomes a "tyrant," as, for example, the Italian Constitutional

[3] See: Italian Constitutional Court judgement no. 379/1992. Also the principle is affirmed in Article 13(2) of the Treaty on the European Union concerning EU Institutions and in Article 4(3) of the same Treaty concerning Member States.

[4] As the former president of the Italian Constitutional Court, Marta Cartabia, held: "The full implementation of the Constitution requires a choral commitment, with the active, loyal cooperation of all institutions, including Parliament, Government, Regions, Judges. This cooperation is also the key to dealing with the emergency. The Constitution, in fact, does not contemplate a special right for exceptional times, and this for a conscious choice, but it also offers the compass to 'navigate the high seas' in times of crisis, starting from the loyal cooperation between institutions, which is the institutional projection of solidarity among citizens." See: Constitutional Court, press release of 28 April 2020, presenting the report of President Marta Cartabia on the activities of the Constitutional Court in 2019. Available at: https://www.cortecostituzionale.it/documenti/comunicatistampa/CC_CS_20200428_Relazione_Annuale_2019_Cartabia.pdf, last accessed 30 September 2021.

Court has shown in a decision on the balance between the right to a healthy environment and the right to work.[5]

Here again, in general, the emergency may require, for some time, that one right or public interest must prevail, overriding the others. In the case of COVID-19, it was the right to health and, finally, the right to life, at least for some, since the pandemic implies a concrete risk to life, which was brought to the fore. The measures to prevent and contain the spread of the disease—involving the so-called lockdown of economic and social activities, with the few exceptions in the food sector—have led to a major restriction, a near-hollowing out, of many rights, such as freedom of movement, freedom of assembly, freedom of worship, the right to education, family life, freedom of enterprise and political rights.

The key here is the principle of proportionality, between the actual situation and restrictive measures, although if it is not easy to clarify the factual circumstances, due to a lack of scientific knowledge and homogeneous statistical data, it is also very difficult to assess the proportionality of the measures.

It should be noted that authoritarian regimes do not encounter such challenges. In authoritarian states there is no difference between normality and emergency: we can say that emergency is their natural situation (Groppi 2020a). This is why the solutions adopted in countries like China or Iran are of no interest to us.

3 Lessons for the Future

A year and a half into the pandemic, we can begin by assessing what has happened. It is perhaps too early to speak of lessons, but something can already be said.

The first analyses of the indicators focus on the word “resilience,” underlining that in established democracies institutions have adapted quite well and that the limitation of rights has been reasonable. Different is the discourse for democracies that were already in crisis: in Europe, for example, Hungary’s further regression seems of particular concern.

Looking more specifically at the situation in Italy, it seems to me that the strong point has been the very orderly response of the population especially in the first phase and the rapid reorganisation of the parliament and the judiciary, albeit with different decisions (the parliament in

[5] See Constitutional Court judgement no. 85/2013.

presence with distancing, the judiciary with remote hearings). In general, we cannot speak of real democratic problems in the management of the emergency, although there were dysfunctionalities and there is room for improvement, especially in the relationship between the government and the regions, as evidenced by the Constitutional Court's decision recognising the state's competence for anti-pandemic measures, taking into account "international prophylaxis" as a competence title.[6]

If we rely on these initial data, we can agree with those who emphasises that the emergency does not radically change things, but acts as an accelerate of already ongoing trends. This corresponds to the etymology of the word in all romance languages, from the Latin *emergere*, composed of *e* (out) + *mergere* (to sink, to submerge), and shows us that emergence is something that not only comes to the surface, but also brings something to the surface (Groppi 2020b). Of course, it is a subject that would need a lot of research, not only legal, but also political, and there are already many projects underway.[7]

In any case, it seems to me that we can put forward at least three elements that may help to have a more positive outlook for the future. The emergency has brought to the surface some elements of the institutional system that were somewhat forgotten, and which can, if developed with appropriate policies, strengthen constitutional democracy:

(a) Public health systems are an important part of the European identity and the guarantee of a high level of public health is enshrined also in Article 35 of the EU Charter of Fundamental Rights. The reforms implemented during the sovereign debt crisis with the objective of reducing public spending on health, have reduced their effectiveness. The pandemic made clear that a functioning and well-financed public health system is of vital importance. In Italy, for instance, Lombardy was not able to stop the contagion also because of its health care model, which was largely privatised and lacked a network of territorial proximity.

[6] Constitutional Court judgement no. 37/2021. The Court held that the regional legislature, even if endowed with special autonomy, may not encroach by its own rules upon a matter concerning the COVID-19 pandemic, a globally spread disease, and whose management therefore lies entirely within the exclusive legislative competence of the state, by way of international prophylaxis.

[7] See, for instance: https://www.democratic-decay.org/research, last accessed 30 September 2021.

(b) The emergency has highlighted the need for competent politicians and a close relationship between them and technicians, in our case scientists. This has determined a pause in the tendencies towards the devaluation of knowledge that have characterised populist governments and seems to have an impact on the populist parties themselves, which are evolving towards a different attitude towards the institutions, which they want to be a part of.

(c) Within this framework, a central role is being played by the European Union, with its new policies, which can be synthesised in the Next-Generation EU. The EU seems to have abandoned the failed neoliberal approach of the last decade, in favour of one aimed at regaining credibility by delivering tangible benefits to its citizens, investing on the health system, maintaining high-quality social services and high environmental standards.

Finally, we cannot fail to underline an important element of weakness of the entire post-war democratic system that the pandemic has highlighted: we live in what Ulrich Beck called "the global risk society," but we do not have institutions that can provide global responses. Financial and economic risks related to migratory flows, global terrorism, global warming and epidemics. It is emblematic that a small event involving bats and pangolins in a remote Chinese province becomes the biggest catastrophe since the post-war period. While these phenomena, these events, happen, the law has difficulty providing answers. Even more than in other fields, such as environmental protection, the impact of globalisation on health has been underestimated at the legal level. However, scientists, virologists, who have now suddenly become stars, after having worked for years in the obscurity of their laboratories, have been saying this for some time: to the extent that "Global Health" studies are widespread. Instead, despite the dizzying developments in the free movement of people and goods over the last thirty years, the legal response is entrusted to "old" or, if we want to be more benevolent, ancient instruments, that is, to the international organisations built in the aftermath of World War II, in particular the World Health Organisation, its constitution dates 22 July 1946, which moves with all the limits inherent in such institutions. That is to say, its acts are not binding on states; they are generally located in that grey area that jurists call "soft law". The same limits apply to other types of more recent interventions, such as the United Nations Sustainable Development

Goals, political objectives set by the United Nations, that have to be achieved by 2030.

In particular, Goal 3, ensuring healthy lives and promoting well-being for all at all ages, includes among its targets, that of "[s]trengthening the capacity of all countries, in particular developing countries, for early warning, risk reduction and risk management for global health," to be assessed on the basis of "International Health Regulations (IHR) capacity and preparedness for health emergencies." A fine objective, but at this stage it remains only an aspiration that clashes with the unwillingness of states to begin more intensive collaboration, leading to the transfer of some of their powers to a global level of decision-making.

In short, although globalisation has emphasised the "territorial" nature of viruses, the geography of power, which is still based on borders, is totally inadequate to guarantee the right to health in the face of a pandemic, if not through emergency containment measures, which essentially consist of limiting other fundamental rights. In this field too, we are called upon to make a leap, that is, to move away from the territorial scale of responses. This is a perspective to work on. At the moment, the huge vacuum in which the old states continue to move is striking, being the only points of reference, albeit limited and almost impotent, in the face of the very small and very agile virus.

Bibliography

Groppi, Tania. "Le sfide del coronavirus alla democrazia costituzionale." *Consultaonline*, no. 1 (2020a): 192–196. https://www.sipotra.it/wp-content/uploads/2020/03/Le-sfide-del-coronavirus-alla-democrazia-costituzionale.pdf.

Groppi, Tania. "Emergenza vs. normalità: una dicotomia inevitabile?" *La rivista Il Mulino*, June 4, 2020b, https://www.rivistailmulino.it/news/newsitem/index/Item/News:NEWS_ITEM:5253.

Repucci, Sara and Slipowitz, Amy. "Democracy Under Siege. Freedom in the World 2021." *Freedom House* https://freedomhouse.org/sites/default/files/2021-02/FIW2021_World_02252021_FINAL-web-upload.pdf.

Lührmann, Anna, Seraphine F. Maerz, Sandra Grahn, Nazifa Alizada, Lisa Gastaldi, Sebastian Hellmeier, Garry Hindle and Staffan I. Lindberg. 2020. "Autocratization Surges – Resistance Grows. Democracy Report 2020". *Varieties of Democracy Institute (V-Dem)* https://www.v-dem.net/media/filer_public/de/39/de39af54-0bc5-4421-89ae-fb20dcc53dba/democracy_report.pdf.

The manufacturer's authorised representative in the EU is Springer Nature Customer Service Centre GmbH, Europaplatz 3, 69115 Heidelberg, Germany. If you have any concerns regarding our products, please contact ProductSafety@springernature.com

Printed and bound by CPI Group (UK) Ltd, Croydon, CR0 4YY
30/09/2026
02225502-0011